IMPORTANT! READ CAREFULLY: This End User License Agreement ("Agreement") sets forth the conditions by which Cengage Learning will make electronic access to the Cengage Learning-owned licensed content and associated media, software, documentation, printed materials, and electronic documentation contained in this package and/or made available to you via this product (the "Licensed Content"), available to you (the "End User"). BY CLICKING THE "I ACCEPT" BUTTON AND/OR OPENING THIS PACKAGE, YOU ACKNOWLEDGE THAT YOU HAVE READ ALL OF THE TERMS AND CONDITIONS, AND THAT YOU AGREE TO BE BOUND BY ITS TERMS, CONDITIONS, AND ALL APPLICABLE LAWS AND REGULATIONS GOVERNING THE USE OF THE LICENSED CONTENT.

1.0   SCOPE OF LICENSE

1.1   <u>Licensed Content.</u> The Licensed Content may contain portions of modifiable content ("Modifiable Content") and content which may not be modified or otherwise altered by the End User ("Non-Modifiable Content"). For purposes of this Agreement, Modifiable Content and Non-Modifiable Content may be collectively referred to herein as the "Licensed Content." All Licensed Content shall be considered Non-Modifiable Content, unless such Licensed Content is presented to the End User in a modifiable format and it is clearly indicated that modification of the Licensed Content is permitted.

1.2   Subject to the End User's compliance with the terms and conditions of this Agreement, Cengage Learning hereby grants the End User, a nontransferable, nonexclusive, limited right to access and view a single copy of the Licensed Content on a single personal computer system for noncommercial, internal, personal use only. The End User shall not (i) reproduce, copy, modify (except in the case of Modifiable Content), distribute, display, transfer, sublicense, prepare derivative work(s) based on, sell, exchange, barter or transfer, rent, lease, loan, resell, or in any other manner exploit the Licensed Content; (ii) remove, obscure, or alter any notice of Cengage Learning's intellectual property rights present on or in the Licensed Content, including, but not limited to, copyright, trademark, and/or patent notices; or (iii) disassemble, decompile, translate, reverse engineer, or otherwise reduce the Licensed Content.

2.0   TERMINATION

2.1   Cengage Learning may at any time (without prejudice to its other rights or remedies) immediately terminate this Agreement and/or suspend access to some or all of the Licensed Content, in the event that the End User does not comply with any of the terms and conditions of this Agreement. In the event of such termination by Cengage Learning, the End User shall immediately return any and all copies of the Licensed Content to Cengage Learning.

3.0   PROPRIETARY RIGHTS

3.1   The End User acknowledges that Cengage Learning owns all rights, title and interest, including, but not limited to all copyright rights therein, in and to the Licensed Content, and that the End User shall not take any action inconsistent with such ownership. The Licensed Content is protected by U.S., Canadian and other applicable copyright laws and by international treaties, including the Berne Convention and the Universal Copyright Convention. Nothing contained in this Agreement shall be construed as granting the End User any ownership rights in or to the Licensed Content.

3.2   Cengage Learning reserves the right at any time to withdraw from the Licensed Content any item or part of an item for which it no longer retains the right to publish, or which it has reasonable grounds to believe infringes copyright or is defamatory, unlawful, or otherwise objectionable.

4.0   PROTECTION AND SECURITY

4.1   The End User shall use its best efforts and take all reasonable steps to safeguard its copy of the Licensed Content to ensure that no unauthorized reproduction, publication, disclosure, modification, or distribution of the Licensed Content, in whole or in part, is made. To the extent that the End User becomes aware of any such unauthorized use of the Licensed Content, the End User shall immediately notify Cengage Learning. Notification of such violations may be made by sending an e-mail to infringement@cengage.com.

5.0   MISUSE OF THE LICENSED PRODUCT

5.1   In the event that the End User uses the Licensed Content in violation of this Agreement, Cengage Learning shall have the option of electing liquidated damages, which shall include all profits generated by the End User's use of the Licensed Content plus interest computed at the maximum rate permitted by law and all legal fees and other expenses incurred by Cengage Learning in enforcing its rights, plus penalties.

6.0 FEDERAL GOVERNMENT CLIENTS

6.1   Except as expressly authorized by Cengage Learning, Federal Government clients obtain only the rights specified in this Agreement and no other rights. The Government acknowledges that (i) all software and related documentation incorporated in the Licensed Content is existing commercial computer software within the meaning of FAR 27.405(b)(2); and (2) all other data delivered in whatever form, is limited rights data within the meaning of FAR 27.401. The restrictions in this section are acceptable as consistent with the Government's need for software and other data under this Agreement.

7.0 DISCLAIMER OF WARRANTIES AND LIABILITIES

7.1   Although Cengage Learning believes the Licensed Content to be reliable, Cengage Learning does not guarantee or warrant (i) any information or materials contained in or produced by the Licensed Content, (ii) the accuracy, completeness or reliability of the Licensed Content, or (iii) that the Licensed Content is free from errors or other material defects. THE LICENSED PRODUCT IS PROVIDED "AS IS," WITHOUT ANY WARRANTY OF ANY KIND AND CENGAGE LEARNING DISCLAIMS ANY AND ALL WARRANTIES, EXPRESSED OR IMPLIED, INCLUDING, WITHOUT LIMITATION, WARRANTIES OF MERCHANTABILITY OR FITNESS FOR A PARTICULAR PURPOSE. IN NO EVENT SHALL CENGAGE LEARNING BE LIABLE FOR: INDIRECT, SPECIAL, PUNITIVE OR CONSEQUENTIAL DAMAGES INCLUDING FOR LOST PROFITS, LOST DATA, OR OTHERWISE. IN NO EVENT SHALL CENGAGE LEARNING'S AGGREGATE LIABILITY HEREUNDER, WHETHER ARISING IN CONTRACT, TORT, STRICT LIABILITY OR OTHERWISE, EXCEED THE AMOUNT OF FEES PAID BY THE END USER HEREUNDER FOR THE LICENSE OF THE LICENSED CONTENT.

8.0 GENERAL

8.1   <u>Entire Agreement</u>. This Agreement shall constitute the entire Agreement between the Parties and supercedes all prior Agreements and understandings oral or written relating to the subject matter hereof.

8.2   <u>Enhancements/Modifications of Licensed Content</u>. From time to time, and in Cengage Learning's sole discretion, Cengage Learning may advise the End User of updates, upgrades, enhancements and/or improvements to the Licensed Content, and may permit the End User to access and use, subject to the terms and conditions of this Agreement, such modifications, upon payment of prices as may be established by Cengage Learning.

8.3   <u>No Export</u>. The End User shall use the Licensed Content solely in the United States and shall not transfer or export, directly or indirectly, the Licensed Content outside the United States.

8.4   <u>Severability</u>. If any provision of this Agreement is invalid, illegal, or unenforceable under any applicable statute or rule of law, the provision shall be deemed omitted to the extent that it is invalid, illegal, or unenforceable. In such a case, the remainder of the Agreement shall be construed in a manner as to give greatest effect to the original intention of the parties hereto.

8.5   <u>Waiver</u>. The waiver of any right or failure of either party to exercise in any respect any right provided in this Agreement in any instance shall not be deemed to be a waiver of such right in the future or a waiver of any other right under this Agreement.

8.6   <u>Choice of Law/Venue</u>. This Agreement shall be interpreted, construed, and governed by and in accordance with the laws of the State of New York, applicable to contracts executed and to be wholly preformed therein, without regard to its principles governing conflicts of law. Each party agrees that any proceeding arising out of or relating to this Agreement or the breach or threatened breach of this Agreement may be commenced and prosecuted in a court in the State and County of New York. Each party consents and submits to the nonexclusive personal jurisdiction of any court in the State and County of New York in respect of any such proceeding.

8.7   <u>Acknowledgment</u>. By opening this package and/or by accessing the Licensed Content on this Web site, THE END USER ACKNOWLEDGES THAT IT HAS READ THIS AGREEMENT, UNDERSTANDS IT, AND AGREES TO BE BOUND BY ITS TERMS AND CONDITIONS. IF YOU DO NOT ACCEPT THESE TERMS AND CONDITIONS, YOU MUST NOT ACCESS THE LICENSED CONTENT AND RETURN THE LICENSED PRODUCT TO CENGAGE LEARNING (WITHIN 30 CALENDAR DAYS OF THE END USER'S PURCHASE) WITH PROOF OF PAYMENT ACCEPTABLE TO CENGAGE LEARNING, FOR A CREDIT OR A REFUND. Should the End User have any questions/comments regarding this Agreement, please contact Cengage Learning at Delmar.help@cengage.com.

Legal Terminology

*for Transcription
and Court Reporting*

DELMAR CENGAGE Learning

Options.

Over 300 products in every area of the law: textbooks, online courses, CD-ROMs, reference books, companion websites, and more – helping you succeed in the classroom and on the job.

Support.

We offer unparalleled, practical support: robust instructor and student supplements to ensure the best learning experience, custom publishing to meet your unique needs, and other benefits such as Delmar Cengage Learning's Student Achievement Award. And our sales representatives are always ready to provide you with dependable service.

Feedback.

As always, we want to hear from you! Your feedback is our best resource for improving the quality of our products. Contact your sales representative or write us at the address below if you have any comments about our materials or if you have a product proposal.

Accounting and Financials for the Law Office • Administrative Law • Alternative Dispute Resolution • Bankruptcy Business Organizations/Corporations • Careers and Employment • Civil Litigation and Procedure • CLA Exam Preparation • Computer Applications in the Law Office • Constitutional Law • Contract Law • Court Reporting Criminal Law and Procedure • Document Preparation • Elder Law • Employment Law • Environmental Law • Ethics Evidence Law • Family Law • Health Care Law • Immigration Law • Intellectual Property • Internships Interviewing and Investigation • Introduction to Law • Introduction to Paralegalism • Juvenile Law • Law Office Management • Law Office Procedures • Legal Nurse Consulting • Legal Research, Writing, and Analysis • Legal Terminology • Legal Transcription • Media and Entertainment Law • Medical Malpractice Law Product Liability • Real Estate Law • Reference Materials • Social Security • Sports Law • Torts and Personal Injury Law • Wills, Trusts, and Estate Administration • Workers' Compensation Law

---

DELMAR CENGAGE Learning
5 Maxwell Drive
Clifton Park, New York 12065-2919

For additional information, find us online at:
www.delmar.cengage.com

Legal Terminology

for Transcription and Court Reporting

Cathy J. Okrent, J.D.

Admitted to Practice: United States Supreme Court,
Federal and State Courts of New York
Member: New York State Bar Association

Foreword by
Margie Wakeman Wells, CRI
College of Court Reporting

DELMAR
CENGAGE Learning

Australia • Canada • Mexico • Singapore • Spain • United Kingdom • United States

Title: Legal Terminology for Transcription and Court Reporting
Author: Cathy J. Okrent

Vice President, Career and Professional Editorial: Dave Garza

Director of Learning Solutions: Sandy Clark

Acquisitions Editor: Shelley Esposito

Managing Editor: Larry Main

Product Manager: Melissa Riveglia

Editorial Assistant: Lyss Zaza

Vice President, Career and Professional Marketing: Jennifer McAvey

Marketing Director: Debbie Yarnell

Marketing Manager: Erin Brennan

Marketing Coordinator: Jonathan Sheehan

Production Director: Wendy Troeger

Production Manager: Mark Bernard

Content Project Manager: Glenn Castle

Art Director: Joy Kocsis

Technology Project Manager: Tom Smith

Production Technology Analyst: Thomas Stover

Library of Congress Control Number: 2008927647

ISBN-13: 978-1-4180-6085-5

ISBN-10: 1-4180-6085-2

Delmar
5 Maxwell Drive
Clifton Park, NY 12065-2919
USA

Cengage Learning products are represented in Canada by Nelson Education, Ltd.
For your lifelong learning solutions, visit **delmar.cengage.com**
Visit our corporate website at **cengage.com.**

Notice to the Reader

Publisher does not warrant or guarantee any of the products described herein or perform any independent analysis in connection with any of the product information contained herein. Publisher does not assume, and expressly disclaims, any obligation to obtain and include information other than that provided to it by the manufacturer. The reader is expressly warned to consider and adopt all safety precautions that might be indicated by the activities described herein and to avoid all potential hazards. By following the instructions contained herein, the reader willingly assumes all risks in connection with such instructions. The publisher makes no representations or warranties of any kind, including but not limited to, the warranties of fitness for particular purpose or merchantability, nor are any such representations implied with respect to the material set forth herein, and the publisher takes no responsibility with respect to such material. The publisher shall not be liable for any special, consequential, or exemplary damages resulting, in whole or part, from the readers' use of, or reliance upon, this material.

Printed in Canada

3 4 5 6 7 8   18 17 16 15

Dedication

To my contributor Margie Wakeman Wells for all of her hard work on this book. Decades of experience working with reporters and teaching students of court reporting are evident throughout these pages. My sincere thanks are extended far more than you possibly imagine.

Contents

Foreword

Congratulations on choosing a book that will launch you on a path toward your goals in the legal field. This text is a unique combination of legal terminology and English concepts—both essential to your future in court reporting or legal transcription. The wealth of information here, presented in a straightforward and easy-to-understand manner, along with practice exercises to help reinforce the principles learned, will move you quickly toward your goals.

As a teacher of 30-plus years of court reporter training, a proofreader for a court reporting firm, and a national lecturer on court reporting punctuation, I know that an understanding of legal terms and of English grammar, punctuation, word pairs, and proofreading is essential to success in the legal field. Production of a transcript encompasses every aspect of a person's knowledge of legal terminology and English. The information in this text provides a firm foundation in these areas.

This text is designed so that students who are learning legal terminology can also work on related English principles. It is the intent that the English skills sections of this book combine with the legal terminology to form a complete package. As students learn legal terminology, they are developing a corresponding skill level in English. This combination gives students the ability to put together the final product—a transcript.

The content of the English sections is tied directly to the content of the legal sections. The material for the punctuation/capitalization section in each chapter relates to the case in that chapter. Similarly, the word pairs and the one word/two word/hyphenated selections relate to the legal terminology and the case in the chapter. When, at the end of the unit, the students are asked to transcribe the case, they will be bringing into play all the knowledge they have gained from all the different sections in the unit.

Reading the book, working the sections, doing the practice exercises, transcribing the cases—all of this will move students toward their goals in the legal field.

I have taught English-related subjects and machine shorthand at every speed level in court reporter training, and I commend this excellent publication to students and instructors alike.

Margie Wakeman Wells, Online Education Consultant
College of Court Reporting,
Hobart, Indiana
Author of Court Reporting: Bad Grammar☹, Good Punctuation☺
A text on punctuating the reporting transcript; book@margiewakemanwells.com

Preface

Legal Terminology for Transcription and Court Reporting is designed for students studying transcription, court reporting, stenography, legal research, as well as for other careers including legal assisting, captionist, scopist, proofreader, and government agency employee. Until you become expert in one of these careers, "Knowing what you don't know" is the key to advancing in your chosen profession. Why? Successful people know what they don't know and avoid mistakes such as misusing words, mispronouncing words, and misspelling terms.

Employers form judgments about a prospective employee's intelligence and abilities during a telephone call, at an interview, or from an e-mail or resume. Job candidates who use the correct terms, pronounce words correctly, or submit resumes with no spelling errors are most likely to be selected for the jobs they seek. How do job seekers who "know what they don't know" acquire the knowledge for a career as a transcriptionist, court reporter, or any other occupation that requires the correct use of legal terminology and the related English skills to produce accurate records and documents?

Objectives of Text

Legal Terminology for Transcription and Court Reporting offers the reader a self-paced language immersion course of study—in the language of law. Nineteen areas of law, Administrative Law through Wills, Trusts, and Estates, are represented with over 1900 terms in concise and easy-to-master definitions.

No matter what case is on the docket or the areas of law a firm specializes in, the reader of this book will be prepared to use the terms correctly. Never will the reader be embarrassed by misusing terms and mispronouncing them. The book transforms the reader into someone who is confident using legal terms as a listener and speaker with judges, attorneys, witnesses, jurors, government agencies, experts, court officers, and the parties in court. The reader will learn the legal terminology and English skills necessary to produce a record that accurately reflects court proceedings, depositions, legal stipulations, hearings, and law office meetings. The book's explanation of legal terms is enhanced with examples and over 2000 exercises that test the reader's understanding of definitions, usages, pronunciations, grammar, punctuation, and proofreading. Hence, the book is a comprehensive work-text for anyone studying transcription and court reporting. The main take-away for the reader is the confidence to use legal terminology for professional transcription and court reporting in law offices, the courts, and one's own court reporting business.

The accompanying CD-ROM of electronic flashcards with terms, definitions, audio pronunciations, and transcription exercises allows a self-paced learning format suitable for learners at all levels.

Features and Benefits to the Reader

The Mistakes Court Reporters Make and How to Avoid Them

The opening feature of all 19 units shows that learning from other's mistakes makes them easier to avoid. "The Mistakes Court Reporters Make and How to

Avoid Them" illustrates actual blunders that have occurred to reporters at work. Some are relatively minor mishaps while others are so severe that they warranted disciplinary action. Both examples demonstrate that anything can happen (and will) and are resolved with positive "how to avoid" sections that show the lesson learned.

Unit Introduction

Areas of law are introduced concisely and with more legal subjects in nineteen units than any other book of its kind. From Administrative Law to Intellectual Property to Wills, Trusts, and Estates, the reader is treated to quick coverage of the most widely-practiced areas of law.

Unit-by-unit the book isolates each area of law into its own domain, allowing the reader to focus on the meanings of terms within that area. Sometimes the meanings of terms change in a different area of law, and again the book allows the reader to focus on that area and the meanings of terms being studied within just that unit. Unique to this book, learning the terms is easier because the reader is only concerned with one set of terms at a time.

Unit Objectives

Seven clearly stated objectives are declared to reflect the intended outcomes of studying each unit. Using the dictionary/thesaurus to complete the exercises in the unit is emphasized as an effective learning feature. Note: the same terms and definitions are on the CD-ROM, allowing the reader use of an automated flash card feature to quickly learn the terms in each unit.

Dictionary/Thesaurus

The dictionary/thesaurus feature provides the whole universe of terms related to the unit's area of law. Each term appears with a phonetic spelling to ensure the correct pronunciation of the word. There is at least one complete definition and often alternative definitions for added clarity. Other features include: parts of speech (noun, verb, etc.), "see" and "compare" references to related terms and synonyms where appropriate. All terms, with audio pronunciations, appear with definitions on the CD-ROM.

Different learning formats are represented with over 100 exercises per unit as follows:

Missing Words: Sentence completion is accomplished with a missing legal term found by referencing the dictionary/thesaurus.

Matching: Match the appropriate definition to the legal term.

Multiple Choice: The best answer from several choices completes the definition.

True/False: A correct or incorrect definition appears for each term.

Synonyms: Exercises where one synonym, or similar term, is matched to the correct term.

Self-Test: Terms are listed to fill in where appropriate in a paragraph with missing terms.

This one is also featured on the CD-ROM in audio format for practice transcription purposes and is designated with a CD-ROM icon in the book.

Defining Words: This is an open-ended exercise that requires the definition to be written for each term.

The following exercises are preceded by rules of English that require study in the unit before completion:

Capitalization: Identify any errors in capitalization.

Word Pairs: Choose the correct word for the sentence provided.

Is It One Word or Two? An Apostrophe? A Hyphen?: Choose the correct form of the word for the sentence provided.

Proofreading: Make the necessary corrections in the sentences provided based on the rules presented in the unit.

Case: All units have a case brief pertaining to one area of law for transcription. It is in audio format on the CD-ROM as well.

CD-ROM Transcription Exercises: For high success in testing your knowledge, use the accompanying CD-ROM after learning all the terms and the English rules presented. For practice transcription only, use the CD-ROM simply where prompted by the CD-ROM icon in the book.

The following sections of the book, indicated by CD icons, are on the CD-ROM in audio format at 80 wpm and 120 wpm for different skill levels:

1. Terms with pronunciations allow you to "See the term, hear the term, key or transcribe the term," with a quick and easy way to familiarize yourself with each one.

2. Self-Test allows you to complete full paragraphs of transcription and learn the answers to the same exercises that appear in the book, hence the name "self-test!"

3. Adaptions from real cases with the facts, procedural history, issue, rationale, and ruling in each unit offer another opportunity to transcribe at length as well as learn more about each area of law.

Supplemental Teaching Materials

Instructor's Manual and Test Bank

The Instructor's Manual and Test Bank is available online at www.paralegal. delmar.cengage.com in the Instructor's Corner. Written by the author of the text, the Instructor's Manual contains answers to the text exercises and a test bank of all the legal terms.

Online Companion

The Online Companion provides the students with additional support materials in the form of 19 challenging "Term Search" puzzles and solutions (one for each unit), testing spellings of terms; and 19 complete cases (one for each unit) for additional transcription practice. Nineteen model answers appear to compare your work against suggested "corrected" cases. The Online Companion can be found at www.paralegaldelmar.cengage.com in the Online Companion section of the website.

Web Page

Come visit our web site at www.paralegal.delmar.cengage.com where you will find valuable information such as hot links and sample materials to download, as well as other Delmar Cengage Learning products.

Acknowledgments

Many thanks to Shelley Esposito, Acquisitions Editor; Melissa Riveglia, Product Manager; Lyss Zaza, Editorial Assistant; Steven Couse, Content Project Manager; Jonathan Sheehan, Marketing Coordinator; and all the staff at Delmar Cengage Learning as well as the reviewers:

Kolleen Barnes
Cuyahoga Community College
Cleveland, OH

Rollie Cox
Madison Area Technical College
Madison, WI

Kathleen Fisher
National Center for Paralegal Training
Atlanta, GA

Vicki Morgan
Cerritos College
Norwalk, CA

How to Use a Legal
Dictionary/Thesaurus

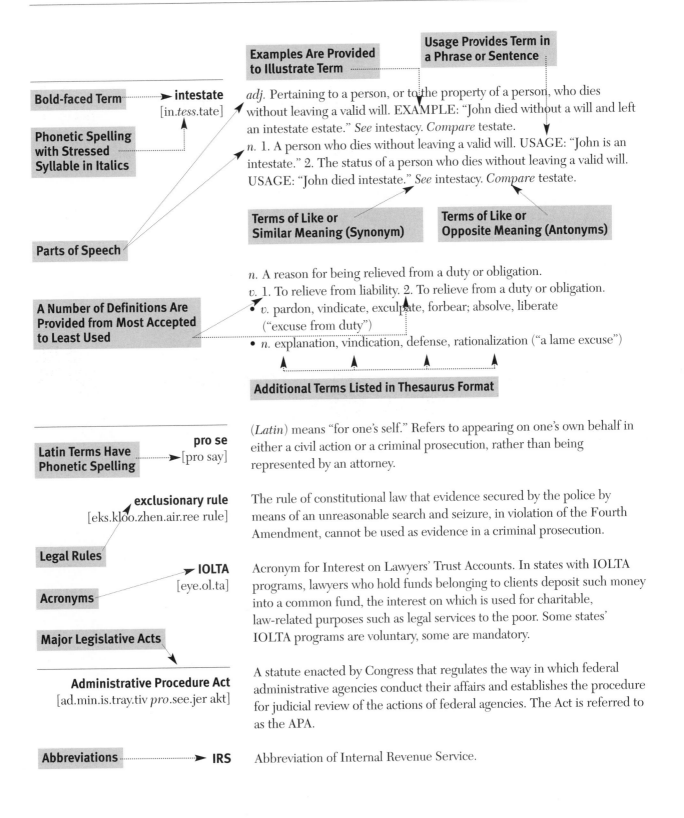

Examples Are Provided to Illustrate Term

Usage Provides Term in a Phrase or Sentence

Bold-faced Term

intestate
[in.*tess*.tate]

Phonetic Spelling with Stressed Syllable in Italics

adj. Pertaining to a person, or to the property of a person, who dies without leaving a valid will. EXAMPLE: "John died without a will and left an intestate estate." *See* intestacy. *Compare* testate.

n. 1. A person who dies without leaving a valid will. USAGE: "John is an intestate." 2. The status of a person who dies without leaving a valid will. USAGE: "John died intestate." *See* intestacy. *Compare* testate.

Parts of Speech

Terms of Like or Similar Meaning (Synonym)

Terms of Like or Opposite Meaning (Antonyms)

n. A reason for being relieved from a duty or obligation.

v. 1. To relieve from liability. 2. To relieve from a duty or obligation.

A Number of Definitions Are Provided from Most Accepted to Least Used

- *v.* pardon, vindicate, exculpate, forbear; absolve, liberate ("excuse from duty")

- *n.* explanation, vindication, defense, rationalization ("a lame excuse")

Additional Terms Listed in Thesaurus Format

Latin Terms Have Phonetic Spelling

pro se
[pro say]

(*Latin*) means "for one's self." Refers to appearing on one's own behalf in either a civil action or a criminal prosecution, rather than being represented by an attorney.

exclusionary rule
[eks.klōō.zhen.air.ree rule]

The rule of constitutional law that evidence secured by the police by means of an unreasonable search and seizure, in violation of the Fourth Amendment, cannot be used as evidence in a criminal prosecution.

Legal Rules

Acronyms

IOLTA
[eye.ol.ta]

Acronym for Interest on Lawyers' Trust Accounts. In states with IOLTA programs, lawyers who hold funds belonging to clients deposit such money into a common fund, the interest on which is used for charitable, law-related purposes such as legal services to the poor. Some states' IOLTA programs are voluntary, some are mandatory.

Major Legislative Acts

Administrative Procedure Act
[ad.min.is.tray.tiv *pro*.see.jer akt]

A statute enacted by Congress that regulates the way in which federal administrative agencies conduct their affairs and establishes the procedure for judicial review of the actions of federal agencies. The Act is referred to as the APA.

Abbreviations

IRS

Abbreviation of Internal Revenue Service.

Administrative Law

The **Mistakes** That Court Reporters Make and *How to Avoid* Them

The Mistake:

Richard McCormick had just gotten a permanent assignment in court. As a new case was called, he recognized that the plaintiff was a buddy that he had not seen since college. At the beginning of the lunch break, Rich hailed his friend, and they had lunch together in the courthouse cafeteria, getting caught up with each other's lives.

When court resumed, the defense attorney, who was also at lunch in the courthouse, brought the meeting between Rich and the plaintiff to the attention of the judge. The judge immediately called a recess and summoned the reporter to his chambers.

How to Avoid It:

When Rich realized that he was acquainted with the plaintiff, he should have spoken to the judge immediately. The reporter must at all times maintain his status as a disinterested person, that is, a person who has no relationship to anyone in the case and no interest whatsoever in the outcome of the case. In this situation, the judge would probably call in another reporter for the duration of the case of Rich's friend and send Rich to another courtroom, where he is once again a neutral person.

Introduction

The United States Constitution divides the power of the government into three branches: the executive, the legislative, and the judicial. Each of the branches has a separate and distinct function. The idea behind the system was to prevent any one system from becoming too powerful.

As life in the United States became increasingly complex in the twentieth century it became clear that the three branches of government could not adequately meet all its peoples' needs. Thus administrative law developed. While technically there are three branches of government, administrative law is informally referred to as the fourth branch of government. Administrative law deals with the creation and operation of agencies. Legislation has created hundreds of agencies by statute. Each agency handles a variety of problems and resolves them through administrative hearings rather than resorting to our court system.

Some of the larger agencies are the Department of Justice, the Equal Employment Opportunity Commission, the Internal Revenue Service, the Social Security Administration, and the Securities and Exchange Commission. Each covers a distinct and separate area or field of law.

Administrative law is composed of the statutes creating the agency, rules and regulations drafted by the agency to carry out its particular purpose, and the decisions and orders of the agency tribunals in resolving individual disputes of citizens against the agency.

Unit Objectives

- ■ Work with a legal dictionary/thesaurus.
- ■ Learn about administrative law.
- ■ Master the similarities and differences in definitions of key terms regarding administrative law.
- ■ Master the pronunciations and spellings of legal terms in this unit.
- ■ Recognize the synonyms and abbreviations used for legal terminology in this unit.
- ■ Practice usage of terms, definitions, and synonyms for administrative law.
- ■ Complete unit exercises in the forms of missing words, matching, multiple choice, true/false, synonyms, self-test, defining words, and also:
  - ● Punctuation/capitalization
  - ● Word pairs
  - ● Transcription of terms, self-test, and case
  - ● Proofreading

📀 Dictionary/Thesaurus

Note: All Dictionary/Thesaurus terms appear on the CD-ROM with audio pronunciations.

Term
[phonetic pronuciation]

abuse of discretion
[a.byooss ov dis.*kresh*.en]

A judicial or administrative decision so grounded in whim or caprice, or against logic, that it amounts to a denial of justice.

adjudicatory
[a.*joo*.di.ka.tore.ee]

Refers to the decision-making or quasi-judicial functions of an administrative agency, as opposed to the judicial functions of a court. Thus, for EXAMPLE, an adjudicatory hearing is a hearing before an administrative agency as opposed to a hearing or trial before a court.

administrative act
[ad.*min*.is.tray.tiv akt]

A routine act by a public official, required by law, as opposed to an act based upon a decision involving a degree of choice; a ministerial act. EXAMPLE: the maintaining of court records by the clerk of the court.

administrative agency
[ad.*min*.is.tray.tiv *ay*.jen.see]

A board, commission, bureau, office, or department of the executive branch of government that implements the law, which originates with the legislative branch. EXAMPLES: the FBI (Federal Bureau of Investigation); a county public assistance office.

administrative discretion
[ad.*min*.is.tray.tiv dis.*kresh*.en]

The power to choose between courses of conduct in the administration of a public office or in carrying out a public duty.

administrative hearing
[ad.*min*.is.tray.tiv *heer*.ing]

A hearing before an administrative agency, as distinguished from a hearing before a court.

administrative law
[ad.*min*.is.tray.tiv law]

1. The body of law that controls the way in which administrative agencies operate. 2. Regulations and decisions issued by administrative agencies.

administrative law judge
[ad.*min*.is.tray.tiv law juj]

A person, generally a civil servant, who conducts hearings held by an administrative agency. An administrative law judge is variously referred to as an ALJ, a hearing examiner, or a hearing officer.

administrative notice
[ad.*min*.is.tray.tiv *no*.tiss]

See official notice.

Administrative Procedure Act (APA)
[ad.*min*.is.tray.tiv pro.*see*.jer akt]

A statute enacted by Congress that regulates the way in which federal administrative agencies conduct their affairs and establishes the procedure for judicial review of the actions of federal agencies. The Act is referred to as the APA.

administrative proceeding
[ad.*min*.is.tray.tiv pro.*see*.ding]

A proceeding before an administrative agency, as distinguished from a proceeding before a court.

administrative remedy
[ad.*min*.is.tray.tiv *rem*.e.dee]

A remedy that the law permits an administrative agency to grant.

advisory opinion
[ad.*vize*.e.ree o.*pin*.yen]

A judicial interpretation of a legal question requested by the legislative or executive branch of government, or by a private individual or corporation.

arbitrary and capricious
[*ar*.bi.trare.ee and ke.*prish*.es]

A reference to the concept in administrative law that permits a court to substitute its judgment for that of an administrative agency if the agency's decision unreasonably ignores the law or the facts of a case.

color
[*kull*.er]

An apparent legal right; a seeming legal right; the mere semblance of a legal right. Although they may also refer to activity by private persons, terms such as color of authority, color of law, and color of right generally refer to actions taken by a representative of government.

color of right
[*kull*.er ov rite]

A right based upon color of authority, color of law, or color of office.

de novo review
[de *no*.vo re.*vyoo*]

(*Latin*) Standard of review under which the reviewing body may find the facts and review all issues without deference to the lower body's findings and conclusions.

declaratory judgment
[de.*klar*.e.toh.ree *juj*.ment]

A judgment that specifies the rights of the parties but orders nothing. Nonetheless, it is a binding judgment and the appropriate remedy for the determination of an actionable dispute when the plaintiff is in doubt as to his legal rights.

declaratory provision
[de.*klar*.e.toh.ree pro.*vizh*.en]

Part of a statute or ordinance that states the need that the legislation was enacted to fulfill, i.e., the statute's purpose. Declaratory provisions often begin with the word "whereas."

declaratory relief
[de.*klar*.e.toh.ree re.*leef*]

See declaratory judgment.

declaratory statute
[de.*klar*.e.toh.ree *stat*.shoot]

A statute enacted to clarify and resolve the law when the correct interpretation has been in doubt.

delegation of powers
[del.e.*gay*.shen ov *pow*.erz]

1. Provisions of the Constitution by which executive powers are delegated to the executive branch of the government, legislative powers to the legislative branch, and judicial powers to the judicial branch. 2. Delegation of constitutional power by one branch of government to another. Such delegation is permissible only if it is consistent with the principle of separation of powers set forth in the Constitution. 3. The transfer of power from the president to an administrative agency.

department
[de.*part*.ment]

An administrative unit within an organization.
• *n.* branch, section, office, agency, bureau, unit, division

department of government
[de.*part*.ment ov *guv*.ern.ment]

1. One of the three divisions into which the Constitution separates the government of the United States. Used in this sense, the term is synonymous with branch of government. 2. A similar division in state government. 3. An administrative unit within a branch of government. EXAMPLES: the Department of Justice (DOJ); the Department of Commerce (DOC).

due process hearing
[dew *pross*.ess *heer*.ing]

An administrative hearing held to comply with the due process clause. EXAMPLE: a parole revocation hearing.

due process of law
[dew *pross*.ess ov law]

Law administered through courts, equally applicable to all, that does not violate principles of fairness. Whether a person has received due process of law can only be determined on a case-by-case basis. In all criminal cases, however, it involves, at the very least, the right to be heard by a fair and impartial tribunal, the defendant's right to be represented by counsel, the right to cross-examine witnesses against him, the right to offer testimony on his own behalf, and the right to have advance notice of trial and of the charge sufficient in detail and in point of time to permit adequate preparation for trial. Due process requirements for criminal prosecutions are considerably more rigorous than those for civil cases. "Due process of law" is guaranteed by both the Fifth Amendment and the Fourteenth Amendment.

Enabling Act
[en.*ay*.bling akt]

A statute that gives the governance the power to enforce other legislation or that carries out a provision of a constitution.

Equal Employment Opportunity Commission (EEOC)
[*ee*.kwel em.*ploy*.ment op.er.*tew*.ni.tee kuh.*mish*.en]

A federal agency whose purpose is to prevent and remedy discrimination based on race, color, religion, national origin, age, or sex with respect to most aspects of employment, including hiring, firing, promotion, and wages. The commission, which is known as the EEOC, enforces many federal Civil Rights Acts and anti-discrimination statutes.

executive
[eg.*zek*.yoo.tiv]

adj. Pertaining to the administration or enforcement of the law.
n. 1. A person who enforces the law, as distinguished from a person who makes the law or a person who interprets the law. 2. A person who manages or administers.
• *n.* chief, supervisor, boss, director, chairperson, president
• *adj.* managerial, presidential, official, administrative

executive agency
[eg.*zek*.yoo.tiv *ay*.jen.see]

See administrative agency.

executive branch
[eg.*zek*.yoo.tiv branch]

1. With the legislative branch and the judicial branch, one of the three divisions into which the Constitution separates the government of the United States. These branches of government are also referred to as departments of government. The executive branch is primarily responsible for enforcing the laws. 2. A similar division in state government.

exhaustion of remedy [eg.*zaws*.chen ov *rem*.e.dee]	The doctrine that when the law provides an administrative remedy, a party seeking relief must fully exercise that remedy before the courts will intervene. 2. The doctrine, applicable in many types of cases, that the federal courts will not respond to a party seeking relief until she has exhausted her remedies in state court.
federal agency [*fed*.er.el *ay*.jen.see]	Any administrative agency, board, bureau, commission, corporation, or institution of the federal government, usually in the executive branch of government. EXAMPLE: The Equal Employment Opportunity Commission is a federal agency whose purpose is to prevent and remedy discrimination based on race, color, religion, national origin, age, or sex with respect to most aspects of employment including hiring, firing, promotion, and wages. The commission, which is known as the EEOC, enforces many federal Civil Rights Acts and anti-discrimination statutes.
Federal Register [*fed*.er.el *rej*.is.ter]	An official publication, printed daily, containing regulations and proposed regulations issued by administrative agencies, as well as other rulemaking and other official business of the executive branch of government. All regulations are ultimately published in the Code of Federal Regulations (CFR).
Freedom of Information Act (FOIA) [*free*.dum ov in.fer.*may*.shen akt]	A federal statute that requires federal agencies to make available to the public, upon request, material contained in their files, as well as information on how the agencies function. The act contains various significant exemptions from disclosure, including information compiled for law enforcement purposes.
hearing [*heer*.ing]	A proceeding in which evidence is introduced and witnesses are examined so that findings of fact can be made and a determination rendered. Although, in a general sense, all trials can be said to be hearings, not all hearings are trials. The difference is in the degree of formality each requires, with the rules of procedure being more relaxed in hearings. A hearing may be conducted by a court, an administrative agency, an arbitrator, or a committee of the legislature, as well as by many other public bodies. • *n.* trial, inquiry, litigation, adjudication, review, legal proceedings
hearing examiner [*heer*.ing eg.*zam*.in.er]	The title of the person who functions as a judge with respect to an administrative hearing. In some states, and in the federal system, the title administrative law judge is used instead. *See also* hearing officer.
hearing officer [*heer*.ing *off*.i.ser]	Same as hearing examiner, although, in some circumstances, a hearing officer, unlike a hearing examiner, does not have the power to adjudicate, her authority being limited to making recommendations to the appropriate administrative agency. *See also* administrative law judge.
in camera [in *kam*.e.ra]	(*Latin*) In chambers; in private. A term, referring to a hearing or any other judicial business conducted in the judge's office or in a courtroom that has been cleared of spectators and certain excepted parties.

inspection laws
[in.*spek*.shen lawz]

Federal, state, and local laws designed to promote health and safety by protecting the public from hazards such as the unsanitary processing of food, the improper packaging of articles for sale, or unsafe working conditions. EXAMPLES: food inspection laws administered by the FDA (Food and Drug Administration).

judicial review
[joo.*dish*.el re.*vyoo*]

1. Review by a court of a decision or ruling of an administrative agency.
2. Review by an appellate court of a determination by a lower court.

license
[*ly*.sense]

1. A special privilege, not a right common to everyone. 2. Permission (EXAMPLES: a marriage license; a fishing license) to do something that, if it were not regulated, would be a right. 3. A privilege conferred on a person by the government to do something she otherwise would not have the right to do. EXAMPLES: the privilege of incorporation; the privilege of operating as a public utility or a common carrier. 4. A requirement imposed as a means of regulating a business. EXAMPLE: a liquor license. 5. Permission to practice a profession, engage in an occupation, or conduct a business. EXAMPLES: a license to practice law; a business license; a real estate license. 6. A certificate evidencing an official grant of permission or authorization. EXAMPLES: a driver's license; a hunting license.
• *n.* privilege, authorization, sanction, permission, entitlement
• *v.* authorize, legitimize, sanction, approve, validate

licensing
[*ly*.sen.sing]

The act or process of granting or issuing a license.

licensor
[*ly*.sen.*sore*]

The grantor of a license. EXAMPLES: a state (Department of Motor Vehicles); a city (health department); a federal agency (FAA).

official notice
[o.*fish*.el *no*.tiss]

The equivalent of judicial notice by an administrative agency; also referred to as administrative notice.

official records
[o.*fish*.el *rek*.erdz]

Records made by an official of the government in the course of performing her official duties. (EXAMPLE: correspondence; memoranda; data; minutes.) Official records are admissible in the federal courts and in federal administrative proceedings, as well as in most state courts, as an exception to the hearsay rule, to prove the transactions they memorialize.

privacy
[*pry*.ve.see]

As used in the law, a reference to the right of privacy. The right of privacy is the right to be left alone. It means that personal information of the kind in the possession of, for EXAMPLE, the government, insurance companies, and credit bureaus may not be made public. The right to privacy, which is implied by the Constitution, is supported, and to some extent enforced, by federal and state privacy acts.
• *n.* confidentiality, noninfringement

promulgate
[*prom*.ul.gate]

1. To publish, announce, or proclaim official notice of a public act.
2. To issue a regulation.

quasi-judicial
[kwazi-joo.*dish*.el]

A term applied to the adjudicatory functions of an administrative agency, i.e., taking evidence and making findings of fact and findings of law.

quasi-legislative
[kwazi-*lej*.is.lay.tiv]

A term applied to the legislative functions of an administrative agency, for EXAMPLE, rulemaking.

rate fixing
[rate *fik*.sing]

See rate making.

rate making
[rate *may*.king]

The process engaged in by a public service commission in establishing a rate to be charged to the public for a public service.

regulation
[reg.yoo.*lay*.shun]

1. The act of regulating. 2. A rule having the force of law, promulgated by an administrative agency; the act of rulemaking. *See* rulemaking. 3. A rule of conduct established by a person or body in authority for the governance of those over whom they have authority.
• *n.* regimentation, conduct, arrangement, standardization, governance, coordination; canon, decree, directive, dictate, ordinance

regulatory
[*reg*.yoo.le.tore.ee]

Pertaining to that which regulates; pertaining to the act of regulation. *See also* regulation.

regulatory agency
[*reg*.yoo.le.tore.ee *ay*.jen.see]

An administrative agency empowered to promulgate and enforce regulations. *See also* regulation.

reporters
[re.*port*.erz]

1. Court reports, as well as official, published reports of cases decided by administrative agencies. 2. Court reporters.

ripeness doctrine
[*ripe*.ness *dok*.trin]

The doctrine that an administrative agency or a trial court will not hear or determine a case, and an appellate court will not entertain an appeal, unless an actual case or controversy exists.

rulemaking
[*rool*.may.king]

The promulgation by an administrative agency of a rule having the force of law, i.e., a regulation.

separation of powers
[sep.ar.*ay*.shun ov *pow*.erz]

A fundamental principle of the Constitution, which gives exclusive power to the legislative branch to make the law, exclusive power to the executive branch to administer it, and exclusive power to the judicial branch to enforce it. The authors of the Constitution believed that the separation of powers would make abuse of power less likely.

statute
[stat.*shoot*]

A law enacted by a legislature; an act.

statutory benefits
[stat.*shoo*.tore.ee *ben*.e.fits]

Benefits that are provided because the law requires it. EXAMPLES: compensation coverage, unemployment insurance, and Social Security.

subpoena [sub.*pee*.nah]	*n.* A command in the form of written process requiring a witness to come to court to testify; short for subpoena ad testificandum. *v.* To issue or serve a subpoena.
substantial evidence [sub.*stan*.shel *ev*.i.dense]	Evidence that a reasonable person would accept as adequate to support the conclusion or conclusions drawn from it; evidence beyond a scintilla. *See also* substantial evidence rule.
substantial evidence rule [sub.*stan*.shel *ev*.i.dense rool]	The rule that a court will uphold a decision or ruling of an administrative agency if it is supported by substantial evidence. *See also* substantial evidence.
substantive due process [*sub*.stan.tiv doo *prah*.ses]	A right grounded in the Fifth Amendment and the Fourteenth Amendment. The very essence of those amendments, as they relate to substantive due process, is the concept that the government may not act arbitrarily or capriciously in making, interpreting, or enforcing the law. A person is entitled to both substantive due process and procedural due process.
sunshine law [*sun*.shine law]	State and federal statutes requiring that meetings and records of administrative agencies be open to the public.

Missing Words

Fill in the blanks below.

1. The promulgation by an administrative agency of a rule having the force of law is _____.

2. State and federal statutes requiring that meetings of administrative agencies be open to the public are called _____.

3. The _____ is a federal statute that requires federal agencies to make available to the public, upon request, material contained in their files.

4. When the law provides an administrative remedy, a party seeking relief must fully exercise _____ before the courts will intervene.

5. A rule having the force of law, promulgated by an administrative agency is a(n) _____.

6. An administrative decision that is grounded in whim or caprice is a(n) _____.

7. When a representative of government has an apparent legal right or semblance of, he or she acts under _____.

8. A(n) _____ is the same as a hearing examiner, but has the power limited to making recommendations.

9. _____ is the power to choose between courses of conduct in the administration of a public office or in carrying out a public duty.

10. A(n) _____ occurs where an administrative decision is so grounded in whim that it amounts to a denial of justice.

11. The _____ is a federal agency whose purpose is to prevent and remedy discrimination.

12. A(n) _____ inspection of documents occurs in a courtroom that has been cleared of all spectators.

13. _____ is the act or process of granting a license.

14. Evidence that is beyond what a reasonable person would accept as adequate to support the conclusion drawn from it is _____.

15. A law enacted by a legislature is a(n) _____.

Matching

Match the letter of the definition to the abbreviation below.

_____ 16. APA

_____ 17. EEOC

_____ 18. FOIA

_____ 19. FDA

_____ 20. ALJ

_____ 21. FCC

_____ 22. NLRB

_____ 23. OSHA

_____ 24. FBI

_____ 25. CFR

_____ 26. DOJ

_____ 27. DOC

_____ 28. IRS

_____ 29. SSA

_____ 30. SEC

A. Department of Commerce

B. Administrative Procedure Act

C. Equal Employment Opportunity Commission

D. Freedom of Information Act

E. Food and Drug Administration

F. Administrative law judge

G. Federal Communications Commission

H. National Labor Relations Board

I. Occupational Safety and Health Administration

J. Federal Bureau of Investigation

K. Code of Federal Regulations

L. Department of Justice

M. Social Security Administration

N. Internal Revenue Service

O. Securities and Exchange Commission

Multiple Choice

Select the best choice.

_____ 31. An adjudicatory hearing is:
   a. the commencement of legal action
   b. the settlement of legal action
   c. a hearing before an administrative agency as opposed to a court
   d. when a new trial is requested

_____ 32. The process engaged in by a public service commission in establishing a rate to be charged to the public for a public service is known as:
   a. rate of exchange
   b. rate of interest
   c. rate of return
   d. rate making

_____ 33. Federal, state, and local laws designed to promote health and safety by protecting the public from hazards such as unsafe working conditions are called:
   a. sunshine laws
   b. judicial review
   c. de novo review
   d. inspection laws

_____ 34. The body of law that controls the way in which administrative agencies operate is:
   a. common law
   b. administrative law
   c. Federal Claims Act
   d. none of the above

_____ 35. A rule made by an administrative agency is also known as:
   a. decision
   b. order
   c. opinion
   d. regulation

_____ 36. An official publication printed daily containing regulations and proposed regulations issued by administrative agencies is:
   a. Federal Report
   b. Federal Register
   c. Administrative News
   d. Agency News

_____ 37. This branch of government is responsible for enforcing the laws:
   a. judicial
   b. executive
   c. legislative
   d. bipartisan

_____ 38. In camera hearings are hearings held:
   a. in public with press coverage
   b. at the employers' place of business
   c. in a courtroom cleared of spectators
   d. with photographers

_____ 39. A court will uphold a decision or ruling of an administrative agency if it is supported by:
   a. substantial evidence
   b. proof beyond a reasonable doubt
   c. a preponderance of evidence
   d. a scintilla of evidence

_____ 40. When de novo review is performed by the agency it:
   a. may review facts and redecide all issues
   b. must uphold facts found by the administrative law judge
   c. is the final step in the administrative process
   d. none of the above

_____ 41. The Exhaustion of Remedies Doctrine provides that:
   a. all parties seeking administrative relief are entitled to seek at least two different kinds of remedies
   b. a claimant has the option of taking their problem to the agency or the courts
   c. a party must pursue all avenues of agency action before resorting to the court system
   d. all of the above

_____ 42. A judicial interpretation of a legal question is:
   a. an administrative act
   b. color of right
   c. rate making
   d. advisory opinion

True/False

Mark the following T or F.

_____ 43. An administrative hearing is a hearing before an administrative agency.

_____ 44. The body of law that controls the way in which administrative agencies operate is called admiralty law.

_____ 45. An administrative remedy is a remedy that the law permits an administrative agency to grant.

_____ 46. When a court reviews a decision or ruling of an administrative agency this is called inspection laws.

_____ 47. Courts will uphold a decision of an administrative agency if it is supported by substantial evidence.

_____ 48. A person who conducts hearings held by an administrative agency is called a justice.

_____ 49. A remedy that the law permits an administrative agency to grant is called judicial review.

_____ 50. A court can never substitute its judgment for that of an administrative agency, even if the agency's decision is arbitrary and capricious.

_____ 51. An administrative agency is a board, commission, bureau, office, or department of the executive branch of government that implements the law, which originates with the legislative branch.

_____ 52. Administrative notice or official notice is the equivalent of judicial notice.

_____ 53. A judgment that specifies the rights of the parties but orders nothing is called a declaratory judgment.

_____ **54.** An enabling act is a statute that gives the government the power to enforce other legislation.

_____ **55.** An administrative judge can issue a regulation.

Synonyms

Select the correct synonym in parentheses for each numbered item.

___

56. EXECUTIVE AGENCY
    (administrative agency, agency by estoppel, implied agency)

57. SUBPOENA
    (summons, complaint, answer)

58. FOIA
    (Freedom of Interstate Agencies, Freedom of Information Act, Full Office
    Information Advice)

59. RATE MAKING
    (antitrust, rate of exchange, rate fixing)

60. ADMINISTRATIVE LAW JUDGE
    (hearing examiner, justice of the peace, arbitrator)

61. APA
    (Administrative Precedent Act, Administrative Procedure Act, Administrative Policy Act)

62. ADMINISTRATIVE HEARING
    (administrative proceeding, court hearing, deposition)

63. STATUTE
    (constitution, act, regulation)

64. SUNSHINE LAW
    (closed meetings, monitored meetings, open meetings)

65. ARBITRARY AND CAPRICIOUS
    (abuse of discretion, rational basis, ripeness doctrine)

66. RIPENESS DOCTRINE
    (hypothetical case, proposed case, actual case)

67. COLOR OF RIGHT
    (color of authority, color of interest, color of remedy)

68. ENABLING ACT
   (carries out a provision of a constitution, enables the right to privacy, acts on a promulgation by a public officer)

69. PROMULGATE
   (to proclaim official notice, to summon, to abuse one's office)

Self-Test

Place the number of the correct term in the appropriate space.

70. Judicial review

71. Due process

72. Official notice

73. Administrative law hearings

74. De novo

75. Exhaustion of administrative remedies

76. Agencies

77. Separation of powers

78. Administrative Procedure Act

79. Administrative

80. Substantial evidence

81. Administrative law judge

82. Substantive due process

83. Arbitrary and capricious

As modern life gets more and more complex, the court system, Congress, and the executive branch of government can no longer handle all of the problems that arise. Accordingly, _____ are set up to provide specific types of services to the public. Informally, agencies are known as the fourth branch of government. _____ law sets up and regulates the manner in which agencies operate. Unlike the other branches of government, agencies do not have _____, and each agency performs acts of a legislative, judicial, and executive nature. The _____ sets up procedures for judicial review of federal agencies. Although agencies act much like courts in some instances, it should be remembered that they are not courts. It is important that citizens' rights be protected nonetheless. A person's right to _____ and a fair hearing, commonly referred to as _____, should be protected. It is also important that laws bear some relationship to their objective; this is known as _____. A(n) _____ presides over _____ and issues a decision. If a party is not happy with the decision, they may appeal to the agency. The agency may perform a(n) _____ review and refind the facts or redecide the issues without regard to the administrative law judge's findings. When a party is unhappy with an agency's actions they can go directly to the court system for _____. First, a(n) _____ is required. An agency's decision should not be _____; it should be supported by _____ to be upheld.

Defining Words

Complete the definition.

84. Administrative agency _____

85. Licensing _____

86. Rulemaking _____

87. Hearing _____

88. Official notice _____

89. Inspection laws _____

90. Arbitrary and capricious _____

91. De novo review _____

92. Ripeness doctrine _____

93. Adjudicatory _____

94. Department _____

95. Color of right _____

_____

96. Promulgate _____

_____

97. Enabling Act _____

_____

98. Freedom of Information Act _____

_____

99. Abuse of discretion _____

_____

100. Sunshine law _____

_____

Punctuation/Capitalization

Capitalization: Names of parties to a lawsuit.

Words that name parties to a lawsuit—*defendant, plaintiff, claimant, petitioner*—follow the rules for capitalizing titles in general:

Rule 1: If the word is used before the name as a title, it is capitalized.

I worked with Petitioner Davis before the hearing.

He is sitting at the table with Defendant Marvin.

He said that Claimant Bagdazarian has filed an amended form.

Rule 2: If the word were to be used in direct address—that is, using a name when talking directly to a person—it would be capitalized. Though this happens with other titles, it is not common to use the names of the parties to the lawsuit in direct address. We do not say, "I want to know, Plaintiff, when you arrived."

Rule 3: If the word is used in general context, it is not capitalized.

The defendant wishes to speak at this time.

We had a conference with respondent this morning.

I have spoken to the plaintiff regarding this matter.

Directions: Correct any errors in capitalization.

1. I think she represents only defendant Andrews.

2. There are three plaintiffs present at this time.

3. I believe that the Petitioner requested that you produce that document.

4. He said that the defendant was at the scene.

5. I am sure that Plaintiff Marsden will agree.

Word Pairs

allowed/aloud

allowed = permitted. This is the past tense form of the verb *to allow*.

That behavior is not allowed in the courtroom.
He was allowed to get up and walk on the day of surgery.
She had been allowed only limited access.

aloud = audibly, not silent.

He spoke aloud without regard to who was present.
You need to answer aloud, not nod or shake your head.
There were several hurtful things spoken aloud.

base/bass (rhymes with *case*)/bass (rhymes with *sass*)/basis

base = several meanings. The plural form is *bases*, pronounced BAIS/UZ.

- military installation, as in *the Los Angeles Air Force Base.*
- foundation, as in *a crack at the base of the statue.*
- main support, as in *the base of his fan support.*
- as opposed to an acid, as in *a chemical base.*
- starting point, as in *the base camp for a climb.*
- low, immoral, as in *base desires.*

He used them as his base of support.
The base had a construction flaw.
What do you base that on?

bass = lowest musical range. It is a homophone (pronounced the same, spelled differently) for *base* above. It rhymes with *case*. The plural form is *basses*.

He has a stunning bass voice.
She plays bass guitar.
The bass control is not functioning.

bass = kind of fish. It is a homonym (pronounced differently, spelled the same) for *bass* above. It rhymes with *sass*. The plural form is *bass*.

He likes to fish for bass.
I do not like the smell of bass.
He caught seven bass.

basis = grounding, beginning, core, source. The plural is bases, pronounced BAY/SEEZ.

That is the basis of his whole presentation.
There is no basis for his thinking that way.
What is the basis for his reasoning?

based/baste

based = located, headquartered. This is the past tense of *base*.

She based that on past experience.
He was based out of Houston.
It is based on a chemical formula.

baste = sewn with very large stitches; moisten meat as it is cooking.

Did he baste the meat several times as he was talking?
She said she would baste the hem in until the final fitting.
She did baste it; it was not permanent.

fair/fare

fair = several meanings.

- without bias, as in *a fair judge.*
- light complexioned, as in *fair and blond.*
- acceptable, as in *a fair settlement.*
- so-so, as in *feeling fair.*
- reasonably large, as in *a fair number of votes.*
- meeting with exhibits, rides, et cetera, as in *the county fair.*

I had a fair chance but messed it up.
The baby was fair complexioned despite having dark hair.
How fair is it for him to compete?

fare = several meanings.

- meal, as in *the fare at that restaurant.*
- person in a cab, as in *looking for a fare.*
- amount paid for a ticket, as in *airfare.*
- how someone is doing, as in *to fare well.*

He fared well in the competition.
What is the fare for the evening?
The cab fare was exorbitant.

ordinance/ordnance

ordinance = law, usually referring to a local jurisdiction.

There is a noise abatement ordinance in effect after midnight.
He had violated a local parking ordinance.
I was unaware of the new ordinance regarding trash disposal.

ordnance = military term referring to ammunition and weaponry. This is generally as opposed to *materiel*, which is everything else for the military—general support supplies and equipment.

The missile hit the ordnance depot.
The sergeant was in charge of ordnance.
He was too inexperienced to handle work in ordnance.

statue/statute/stature

statue = sculpted, cast, or carved image.

We admired the statue every day as we entered the building.
The statue sits right in the middle of the square.
There was a crack at the base of the statue.

statute = law enacted by a legislature, an act. The adjective form is *statutory*.

It was an issue with the statute of limitations.
According to the applicable statutes, it was within the law.
Your claim is in violation of the statutes.

stature = a person's standing or height.

More is expected of a man of his stature.
His stature alone was intimidating.
She is of large stature.

Directions: Circle the correct word.

1. It is built on a solid base/bass/basis of stone.

2. It is really not fair/fare that he is here.

3. He was in charge of the ordinance/ordnance depot.

4. I enjoy trying to hit those base/bass/basis notes.

5. Did you based/baste it enough to be moist?

6. That type of behavior is not allowed/aloud here.

7. We attended the fair/fare with her sisters.

8. I regret that I spoke allowed/aloud about that.

9. Is that based/baste on how he performed his job?

10. Does that follow the statue/statute to the letter of the law?

11. Those are the length of based/baste stitches.

12. His voice really is not suited to the base/bass/basis part.

13. He has a fair/fare amount to accomplish before week's end.

14. Is that the base/bass/basis for his argument in this case?

15. Do you believe he has been allowed/aloud too much leeway?

16. It came to rest near the statue/statute/stature in the center of the square.

17. He succumbed to the base/bass/basis desires.

18. She did not fair/fare well in the competition.

19. Is a man of his statue/statute/stature going to be in charge?

20. Was it based/baste in reality or in fiction?

Is It One Word or Two? An Apostrophe? A Hyphen?

anymore/any more

anymore = from this time forward, no longer.

I don't want to do that anymore.
He doesn't have that anymore.
Anymore, there is nothing one can do.

any more = anything or anyone additional.

I don't need any more to do.
There is not any more that anyone can do.
He doesn't have any more money to invest.

everyday/every day

everyday = usual, ordinary, habitual. The word is used only as a direct adjective—that is, right before the noun—and does not refer to each individual day.

It is one of his everyday responsibilities.
I do not want this as an everyday job.
Was it just an everyday thought for you?

every day = each individual day. Always remember that, if it is not before a noun, it must be two words.

I saw him every day that week.
They have low prices every day.
They fly to Japan four times every day.

Directions: Circle the correct form of the word.

1. I never see him anymore/any more.

2. It is an everyday/every day job for me.

3. She said she does not need anymore/any more responsibilities for this.

4. Do you think there is anymore/any more room there?

5. He has to do that everyday/every day.

Proofreading

Directions: Make necessary corrections, based on the material presented in the unit. If the sentence has no errors, write the word *correct* after the sentence.

1. Is the defendant aloud to base this on the statue in Section 5? _____

2. We enjoyed the bases but didn't think the parts were distributed farely to all the singers, including Plaintiff Azarian. _____

3. Because of the new stature, she will not fare well any more if she decides to sue about the unfairness of the ordinance. _____

4. The testimony of the defendant was baste on what was allowed, and he testified that there was not anymore that he could do. _____

5. The condition of the Claimant was fare after the injury at the ordinance base. _____

6. It is an every day responsibility of the legislature to monitor the effectiveness of the statues. _____

7. The attorney for defendant Martino was asked to read the statute allowed. _____

8. The ordnance seemed fair to all the participants at the convention. _____

9. The five defendants sat quietly everyday without showing any emotion. _____

10. I felt that he based his argument on something that was a rare occurrence, not an everyday happening, in the household. _____

An Adaptation from an Administrative Law Case

Facts:

The San Francisco Library Commission held its regular monthly meeting. The Commission's president announced at the start of the meeting that the public comment on the meeting would be limited to two minutes per speaker instead of three minutes. The president did this because he had four items on the agenda for the meeting that he knew would be lengthy. There were a total of twelve items on the agenda. Meetings generally last between two and a half and three hours, and on this particular night, the meeting went on for more than four hours.

Procedural History:

In this case, Claimant Charles Foster brought an action that claimed that his rights had been violated under the Sunshine Ordinance of the San Francisco Administrative Code and a section of the state code by not allowing him and others who spoke to have public comment for at least three minutes. The defendant was granted summary judgment. The claimant has now appealed this matter.

Issue:

Was the trial court correct in granting the San Francisco Library Commission summary judgment?

Rationale:

The Sunshine Ordinance is meant to regulate public comment at meetings, and Claimant Foster claims both state and local law required that he be given at least three minutes for comment. This ordinance, on the one hand, provides for open meetings and that each person who wishes to comment on a subject is allowed to do so. On the other hand, in order to do this, the amount of time each person gets to speak must be limited in some manner so that everyone who wants to speak will have a chance to speak. Time limits must be applied uniformly to all people so that they are fair. The question of what "up to three minutes" should mean is based upon a review of the legislative history in drafting the code. It was designed to allow some flexibility so that governmental bodies could impose reasonable shorter time limits that, in their discretion, were necessary.

Ruling:

The appellate court affirmed the finding of the trial court.

Directions for CD-ROM Transcription Exercises

In audio format are:

1. Terms for the unit with pronunciations from the thesaurus/dictionary feature.

2. Self-Test that appears in the book at mid-unit.°

3. Case that appears at the unit end.°

°speeds are 80 wpm/120 wpm for differing skill levels

CD-ROM icons appear where the three above are located within each unit.

Readers may practice transcription by listening to the CD-ROM where prompted by the icons in the book. However, for high success in testing your transcription skills, mastering all the terms and English skills in the unit is recommended before attempting the CD-ROM.

For Keyboard Transcriptionists: Listen to the CD-ROM audio file for this unit at 80 wpm or 120 wpm and transcribe from the dictation on your computer. Edit and proofread your work against the printed copy in the book.

For Reporting Writers: Listen to the CD-ROM audio file at 80 wpm or 120 wpm and take down the dictation on your writer. Either transcribe from your notes and proofread your work or edit and proofread your CAT (computer-aided transcription) transcript. Always check your work against the printed copy in the book.

Student CD-ROM
For additional materials, please go to the CD in this book.

Online Companion™
For additional resources, please go to http://www.paralegal.delmar.cengage.com

Unit 2 | Agency

The **Mistakes** That Court Reporters Make and *How to Avoid* Them

The Mistake:

The deposition began a little after 10:00 in the morning, and it was now late afternoon. There was a break, and there were refreshments available. Maria Martinez, a veteran reporter, opted for a soda. She was sitting at her machine and placed her drink on the conference table, and the deposition continued.

A little later, as the attorneys were having a discussion off the record, Maria sipped her soda. When testimony abruptly resumed and she put her soda can down to begin writing, disaster struck. She inadvertently set the can on the edge of a binder on the table, and the soda spilled—all over the exhibits she had been so carefully marking since the start of the deposition.

How to Avoid It:

Though this had never happened to Maria in all of her years of reporting, it takes just once. The best rule to follow is "no liquids." If you never have anything liquid near your machine or the documents, this disaster cannot happen. And though the sugar in the soda is a nightmare, water can cause just as much damage to valuable documents. Use breaks in the proceedings to consume any liquid you might need, but do not bring it back to your place at the conference table.

Introduction

Gone are the days when you dealt face to face with each and every person who provided you with a service or sold goods to you. More typically, instead of going into Brownell's Realty and meeting Brownell, you will be served by an employee with no relation to Brownell. Businesses are becoming larger and more impersonal.

One person, a corporation, or partnership might own several real estate companies. While Brownell might have built his reputation and business on individual customer service, it is physically impossible for Brownell to be in all of his offices at the same time. Thus, the law of agency comes into play. Brownell needs people who can act on his behalf. Brownell can't single-handedly run three offices at once.

In an agency relationship, one person gives another person the authority to act and contract on his behalf. The use of an agent is common in buying and selling real estate and people are oftentimes represented by an agent. A large corporation like Century 21 may appoint an agent to represent it in transactions. Likewise an insurance agent may represent several companies as a broker. This unit explores the terminology associated with agency.

Unit Objectives

- Work with a legal dictionary/thesaurus.
- Learn about the law of agency.
- Master the similarities and differences in definitions of key terms regarding agency.
- Master the pronunciations and spellings of legal terms in this unit.
- Recognize the synonyms used for legal terms in this unit.
- Practice usage of terms, definitions, and synonyms for agency.
- Complete unit exercises in the forms of missing words, matching, multiple choice, true/false, synonyms, self-test, defining words, and also:
  - Punctuation/capitalization
  - Word pairs
  - Transcription of terms, self-test, and case
  - Proofreading

 Dictionary/Thesaurus

Note: All Dictionary/Thesaurus terms appear on the CD-ROM with audio pronunciations.

Term [phonetic pronunciation]	
agency [*ay*.jen.see]	A relationship in which one person acts for or on behalf of another person at the other person's request. *See also* implied agency.
agency by estoppel [*ay*.jen.see by es.*top*.el]	An agency created by appearances that lead people to believe that the agency exists. It occurs when the principal, through negligence, permits her agent to exercise powers she never gave him, even though she has no knowledge of his conduct. *See also* estoppel; apparent authority; implied agency; implied authority.
agency by ratification [*ay*.jen.see by rat.i.fi.*cay*.shen]	A relationship in which one misrepresents one's self as an agent to a principal, when in fact one is not, while the principal accepts the unauthorized act.
agency coupled with an interest [*ay*.jen.see *cup*.ld with an *in*.trest]	*See* power coupled with an interest.
agency in fact [*ay*.jen.see in fakt]	An agency created by the agreement of the principal and the agent, as distinguished from an agency created by operation of law. EXAMPLE: an agency by estoppel.
agency relationship [*ay*.jen.see re.*lay*.shun.ship]	The relationship that exists in law between a principal and an agent.
agent [*ay*.jent]	One of the parties to an agency relationship, specifically, the one who acts for and represents the other party, who is known as the principal. The word implies service as well as authority to do something in the name of or on behalf of the principal. (EXAMPLE: a person who represents a business person in contract negotiations.) Although one can be both an employee and an agent, the usual distinction between the two is that the manner in which an employee does his work is controlled and directed by his employer; in contrast, an agent is free to use independent skill and judgment, his principal's concern being the results he produces, not how he does his work. *See also* del credere agent; general agent; managing agent; special agent; universal agent. • *n.* assistant, delegate, emissary, assignee, deputy, functionary, proxy, representative
apparent agent [a.*par*.ent *ay*.jent]	One who is, in law, an agent because she has obvious authority. EXAMPLE: a nurse in uniform working at a doctor's office, who greets patients in the waiting room.

apparent authority
[a.*par*.ent aw.*thaw*.ri.tee]

Authority that an agent is permitted to exercise, although not actually granted by the principal. *See also* agency by estoppel.

consignee
[ken.sine.*ee*]

The person to whom a carrier is to deliver a shipment of goods; the person named in a bill of lading to whom the bill promises delivery; the person to whom goods are given on consignment, either for sale or safekeeping. *Compare* consignor. *See also* factor.
• *n.* receiver, salesperson, representative, seller
• *ant.* consignor

consignment
[ken.*sine*.ment]

The entrusting of goods either to a carrier for delivery to a consignee or to a consignee who is to sell the goods for the consignor.
• *n.* entrusting, distribution, committal, transmittal

consignment contract
[ken.*sine*.ment *kon*.trakt]

A consignment of goods to another (the consignee) with the understanding either that she will sell them for the consignor and forward the proceeds, or, if she does not, that she will return them to the consignor. A consignment is also known as a bailment for sale.

consignor
[ken.sine.*or*]

A person who sends goods to another on consignment; the person named in a bill of lading as the person from whom goods have been received for shipment. *Compare* consignee.
• *n.* shipper, sender
• *ant.* consignee

del credere agent
[*del kreh.de.reh ay.jent*]

(*Italian*) An agent who guarantees his principal against the default of those with whom he contracts.

deviation doctrine
[dee.vee.*ay*.shen *dok*.trin]

The rule that if an agent has digressed only slightly from the instructions of the principal, the principal is not excused from liability for the agent's negligence.

employee
[em.*ploy*.ee]

A person who works for another for pay in a relationship that allows the other person to control the work and direct the manner in which it is done. The earlier legal term for employee was servant. *Compare* independent contractor. *Also compare* agent. *Note* that statutory definitions of "employee" may differ, depending upon the purpose of the statute. For EXAMPLE, although the distinctions between the definitions of employee in the Social Security Act, the Fair Labor Standards Act, and the National Labor Relations Act may seem insignificant, they may, in any given instance, be critical.
• *n.* servant, worker, agent, laborer, helper, personnel, jobholder

employer
[em.*ploy*.er]

A person who hires another to work for her for pay in a relationship that allows her to control the work and direct the manner in which it is done. The earlier legal term for employer was master.
• *n.* master, contractor, director, boss, chief
• *ant.* employee

estoppel
[es.*top*.el]

A prohibition imposed by law against uttering what may actually be the truth. A person may be estopped by his own *acts or representations* (that is, not be permitted to deny the truth or significance of what he said or did) if another person who was entitled to rely upon those statements or acts did so to her detriment. This type of estoppel is also known as equitable estoppel or estoppel in pais.
• *n.* impediment, prohibition, restraint, ban, bar

factor
[*fak*.ter]

A person employed to receive goods from a principal and to sell them for compensation, usually in the form of a commission referred to as factorage. A factor is a bailee who is sometimes called a consignee or commission merchant, e.g., sale of right to collect accounts in exchange for a commission.
• *n.* ingredient, determinant, consideration, instrumentality, point; bailee, consignee, commission, merchant

frolic and detour
[*froll*.ik and *de*.tur]

The negligent conduct of an employee or agent who has departed from doing the employer's or principal's business to do something unrelated to work, for which the employer/principal is not liable.

general agent
[*jen*.e.rel *ay*.jent]

An agent authorized to perform all acts connected with the business of his principal. *Compare* special agent. *See also* agent; managing agent.

implied agency
[im.*plide ay*.jen.see]

An actual agency, the existence of which is proven by deductions or inferences from the facts and circumstances of the situation, including the words and conduct of the parties. *Compare* estoppel; apparent authority.

implied authority
[im.*plide* aw.*thaw*.ri.tee]

The authority of an agent to do whatever acts are necessary to carry out her express authority. EXAMPLE: an attorney retained to commence a legal action has the implied authority to file such pleadings as she feels are appropriate.

imputed
[im.*pew*.ted]

1. That which is attributed to a person, not because she personally performed the act (or personally had knowledge or notice), but because of her relationship to another person for whose acts, omissions, knowledge, or notice she is legally responsible. USAGE: "The neglect by his paralegal in this matter will be imputed to attorney Jones." *See also* agency.
2. Blamed; implicated; ascribed; charged.
• *adj.* attributed, blamed, implicated, ascribed, charged ("The paralegal's neglect is the attorney's imputed neglect.")

imputed knowledge
[im.*pew*.ted *nawl*.edj]

1. An agent's knowledge that is binding upon his principal because of their agency relationship. 2. Knowledge of facts charged to a person because anyone of ordinary common sense would know them. 3. That which a person has a duty to know and the means of knowing.

imputed negligence
[im.*pew*.ted *neg*.li.jenss]

The negligence of one person that, by reason of her relationship to another person, is chargeable to the other person. EXAMPLE: an employer is liable for the negligence of his employee that occurs within the scope of employment.

independent contractor
[in.de.*pen*.dent *kon*.trak.ter]

As distinguished from an employee, a person who contracts to do work for another person in her own way, controlling the means and method by which the work is done but not the end product. An independent contractor is the agent of the person with whom she contracts. *Compare* employee.

managing agent
[*man*.e.jing *ay*.jent]

A person to whom a corporation has given general powers involving the exercise of judgment and discretion in conducting the corporation's business. *See* agent. *See also* general agent.

master
[*mas*.ter]

adj. Dominant; principal, main; controlling.
n. 1. An outdated term for employer. *See also* employer; master; servant.
2. A person who has control or authority over others.
• *n.* officer, official, employer, boss, director, leader, commandant, head ("office master")

power coupled with an interest
[*pow*.er *cup*.ld with an *in*.trest]

1. A power of appointment that includes an interest in the thing itself.
2. A power that gives an agent an interest in the subject of the agency. EXAMPLE: the power and interest of a partner in a business who is given the right to manage the business as security for loans he has made to the partnership.

power of attorney
[*pow*.er ov a.*tern*.ee]

A written instrument by which a person appoints another as his agent or attorney in fact and confers upon her the authority to perform certain acts. A power of attorney may be "full" (a general power of attorney) or "limited" (a special power of attorney). The power to sell property without specifying which property, or to whom, is an EXAMPLE of a general power of attorney; the power to sell a particular piece of property to a particular person is an EXAMPLE of a special power of attorney.

principal
[*prin*.sipl]

n. In an agency relationship, the person for whom the agent acts and from whom the agent receives her authority to act. *See also* undisclosed principal.

respondeat superior
[res.*pon*.dee.at soo.*peer*.ee.or]

(*Latin*) Means "let the master respond." The doctrine under which liability is imposed upon an employer for the acts of its employees committed in the course and scope of their employment. Similarly, respondeat superior makes a principal liable for a tort committed by her agent, and a master responsible for the negligence of his servant.

servant
[*ser*.vent]

An outdated term for employee. *See also* master. *See also and compare* agent; employee; independent contractor.
• *n.* assistant, attendant, domestic

special agent
[spesh.el *ay*.jent]

An agent authorized to perform a particular or specific act connected with the business of her principal. *Compare* general agent.

third party
[thurd *par*.tee]

A person who is not a party to an agreement, instrument, or transaction, but who may have an interest in the transaction. *See also* third person.

third-party beneficiary
[thurd-*par*.tee ben.e.*fish*.er.ee]

The intended beneficiary of a contract made between two other persons. A third-party beneficiary may sue to enforce such a contract: e.g., the child of a couple who signed a separation agreement guaranteeing college tuition for the child.

third person
[thurd *per*.sen]

As the term is used in the law, either a person who has an interest in a transaction or a person who has an interest in an action (i.e., a party or a third party).

undisclosed agency
[un.dis.*klozed ay*.jen.see]

A situation where a person who is in fact an agent for another deals with a third person as if he were the principal, the fact that he is an agent being unknown or hidden. *See also* undisclosed principal.

undisclosed principal
[un.dis.*klozed prin*.sipl]

The unrevealed principal in a situation involving an undisclosed agency.

universal agent
[yoon.i.*ver*.sel *ay*.jent]

An agent who is authorized to do everything her principal is entitled to delegate.

vicarious liability
[vy.*kehr*.ee.us ly.e.*bil*.i.tee]

Liability imposed upon a person because of the act or omission of another. EXAMPLES: the liability of an employer for the conduct of its employees; the liability of a principal for the conduct of her agent. *See also* respondeat superior.

Missing Words

Fill in the blanks below.

1. A(n) _____ is a relationship in which one person acts for or on behalf of another.

2. A(n) _____ is a person who sends goods to another on consignment.

3. An agent authorized to perform all acts connected with the business of his principal is a(n) _____.

4. An actual agency, the existence of which is proven by deductions or inferences is a(n) _____.

5. A(n) _____ is an agent authorized to perform a particular act for a principal.

6. A written instrument by which a person appoints another as his agent and confers upon her the authority to perform certain acts is a(n) _____.

7. A(n) _____ is a situation where a person who is in fact an agent for another deals with a third person as if he was a principal, the fact that he is an agent being unknown.

8. The person for whom the agent acts is called a(n) _____.

9. Liability imposed upon a person because of the act or omission of another is _____.

10. A(n) _____ is an agency created by appearances that lead people to believe that the agency exists.

11. The relationship that exists in law between a principal and an agent is a(n) _____.

12. A(n) _____ is one of the parties to an agency relationship, specifically the one who acts for and represents the other party.

13. A(n) _____ is an agent authorized to perform all acts connected with the business of his principal.

14. A power of appointment that includes an interest in the thing itself is called _____.

15. A person who contracts to do work for another in her own way, controlling the method and means by which the work is done (but not the end product) is a(n) _____.

16. An agent's knowledge that is binding upon his principal because of his agency relationship is _____.

Matching

Match the letter of the definition to the term below.

_____ **17.** Implied authority

_____ **18.** Factor

_____ **19.** Servant

_____ **20.** Power of attorney

_____ **21.** Principal

_____ **22.** Agency

_____ **23.** Universal agent

_____ **24.** Consignment

_____ **25.** Undisclosed agent

_____ **26.** Agent

_____ **27.** Respondeat superior

_____ **28.** Third party

_____ **29.** Special agent

_____ **30.** Vicarious liability

_____ **31.** Consignee

_____ **32.** Frolic and detour

_____ **33.** Deviation doctrine

A. One who acts for and represents a principal

B. Written instrument giving another authority to perform a certain act

C. Entrusting of goods to a carrier for delivery to a consignee

D. Authority of an agent to do whatever acts are necessary to carry out express authority

E. Person who is not a party to an agreement, but who might have an interest in the transaction

F. An agent who hides the fact that he is an agent to a third party

G. Person for whom an agent acts

H. Doctrine that an employer is responsible for acts of an employee

I. An agent who is authorized to do everything the principal is entitled to delegate

J. A bailee who is sometimes called a consignee

K. An employee

L. Relationship in which one person acts for or on behalf of another person

M. Liability imposed upon a person because of the act or omission of another

N. Agent authorized to perform a specific act

O. A negligent agent is responsible when departing from doing the principal's business

P. The principal is not excused from liability for the agent's negligence

Q. The person to whom a carrier is to deliver a shipment of goods

Multiple Choice

Select the best choice.

_____ 34. A person employed to receive goods from a principal and to sell them for compensation, usually in the form of a commission referred to as factorage is:
    a. an employer
    b. a factor
    c. a general agent
    d. a managing agent

_____ 35. An agent's knowledge that is binding upon his principal because of their agency relationship is:
    a. power coupled with an interest
    b. respondeat superior
    c. imputed knowledge
    d. implied authority

_____ 36. A person who is not a party to an agreement, but who may have an interest in the transaction is a(n):
    a. third party
    b. undisclosed agency
    c. universal principal
    d. power of attorney

_____ 37. A person who contracts to do work for another person in her own way, controlling the means and method by which work is done but not the end product, is:
    a. a master
    b. an independent contractor
    c. an employee
    d. a third party

_____ 38. The intended beneficiary of a contract made between two other persons is a:
    a. third-party beneficiary
    b. second-party beneficiary
    c. first-party beneficiary
    d. fourth-party beneficiary

_____ 39. A power of appointment that includes an interest in the thing itself, such as the power and interest of a partner in a business who is given the right to manage the business as security for loans he has made to the partnership, is:
    a. a power coupled with an interest
    b. an implied authority
    c. an undisclosed agency
    d. respondeat superior

_____ 40. The entrusting of goods either to a carrier for delivery to a consignee or to a consignee who is to sell the goods for the consignor is:
    a. a power of attorney
    b. an undisclosed agency
    c. an undisclosed principal
    d. a consignment

_____ 41. Authority that, although not actually granted by the principal, she permits her agent to exercise is:
    a. insurance agency
    b. agency by estoppel
    c. implied agency
    d. agency by law

_____ 42. The doctrine under which liability is imposed upon an employer for the acts of its employees committed in the course and scope of their employment is:
    a. third-party beneficiary
    b. apparent agency
    c. respondeat superior
    d. consignment contract

_____ 43. The authority of an agent to do whatever acts are necessary to carry out her express authority is called:
    a. implied authority
    b. partial authority
    c. apparent authority
    d. undisclosed authority

_____ 44. An agent who is authorized to do everything the principal is entitled to delegate is a:
    a. third person
    b. universal agent
    c. agent in fact
    d. implied agent

True/False

Mark the following T or F.

_____ 45. There is a fully disclosed agency when an agent reveals he is acting for a principal and gives the name of the principal he represents.

_____ 46. An agent commits an unauthorized act when he does exactly as the principal instructs.

_____ 47. A man negotiates a fantastic movie role for a star. The star never hired the man to do this but thinks it's a great opportunity and wishes to sign the contract. This is an example of agency by ratification.

_____ 48. An insurance agency hires an outside consulting firm to come in and evaluate how to make the insurance company more efficient. It's up to the consulting firm how they'll accomplish this job. This is an example of an independent contractor.

_____ 49. When a hospital administrator orders a nurse to paint the outside of the hospital, this is an example of work that is outside the scope of the nurse's employment.

_____ 50. A power of attorney is used to allow another to sign your checks or conduct business on your behalf.

_____ 51. When an agent is told to negotiate a contract for the sale of diamonds and follows instructions exactly, this is known as an unauthorized act.

_____ 52. When an agent acts on a principal's behalf but does not reveal that he is acting as an agent or the name of the principal, this is known as an undisclosed agency.

_____ 53. Employers are liable for acts of their employees committed in the scope of their employment. This is known as respondeat superior.

_____ 54. When an ice cream seller drives around a neighborhood wearing a uniform, operating a company truck, and offers to mow peoples' lawns, this is an example of apparent agency.

Synonyms

Select the correct synonym in parentheses for each numbered item.

55. CONSIGNMENT
(entrusting, donation, implied authority)

56. AGENT
(impostor, spy, representative)

57. CONSIGNEE
(obligation, alter ego, receiver)

58. IMPUTED
(denied, blamed, ratified)

59. SERVANT
(third party, principal, employee)

60. VICARIOUS LIABILITY
(conflict of interest, duty of loyalty, respondeat superior)

61. IMPLIED AUTHORITY
(incidental authority, express agency, exclusive agency)

62. POWER OF ATTORNEY
(unauthorized act, express agency, frolic and detour)

63. AGENCY COUPLED WITH AN INTEREST
(power coupled with an interest, agency by ratification, respondeat superior)

64. APPARENT AGENCY
(obvious authority, vicarious liability, coming and going rule)

Self-Test

Place the number of the correct term in the appropriate space.

65. Fully disclosed agency

66. Agent

67. Third persons

68. Agency

69. Express

70. Undisclosed agency

71. Agency by ratification

72. Principal

73. General agent

74. Special agent

75. Deviation doctrine

An owner of a successful fast-food chain wishes to start up a second restaurant at another location. The business owner visits her attorney and tells her of her plans. The lawyer advises:

"Certain situations repeat themselves over and over. The law responds with various solutions. When a person needs an alter ego, a(n) _____ can be set up with the _____ acting on behalf of a(n) _____. Typically the principal wishes to delegate certain duties to the agent. When the principal spells out in detail all acts required by the agent, this is known as a(n) _____ agency. Occasionally the agent acts beyond the scope of his agency. Should the principal approve of the actions notwithstanding, a(n) _____ develops. A lot is expected of an agent. Some of the agent's duties are the duty of obedience and a duty of performance. Slightly digressing from a principal's instructions by an agent does not excuse the principal of liability of the agent's negligence under the _____. Sometimes, outsiders known as _____ aren't aware of the existence of an agency relationship between agent and principal. This is known as a(n) _____. In contrast, an agent may tell third persons about her relationship and reveal the principal's name. This is known as a(n) _____. An agent authorized to perform all acts connected with the business of the principal is a(n) _____, whereas a(n) _____ can only perform a particular or specific act connected with the business of the principal."

Defining Words

Complete the definition.

76. Agent _____

_____

77. Principal _____

_____

78. Agency _____

_____

79. Consignment _____

_____

80. Special agent _____

_____

81. Implied agency _____

_____

82. Power of attorney _____

_____

83. Universal agent _____

_____

84. Respondeat superior _____

_____

85. Imputed knowledge _____

_____

86. Power coupled with an interest _____

_____

87. General agent _____

_____

88. Estoppel _____

_____

89. Deviation doctrine _____

_____

90. Frolic and detour _____

_____

Punctuation/Capitalization

Possessive forms.

In order to form a possessive, it is important to know the correct singular and plural forms of the word first. Check a good English source for how to make words plural. Note that the pronunciation of the word should not affect the written possessive form.

Rule 1: Singular possessive: Add an apostrophe *s* to the singular form of the word—no exceptions.

the lady is . . .	the lady's wallet is . . .
Mr. Wells is . . .	Mr. Wells's property is . . .
the witness is . . .	the witness's story is . . .
Ms. Hodges is . . .	Ms. Hodges's car is . . .

Mr. Brownell is a real estate agent.
Mr. Brownell's motivations are in question.

Mr. Riggs owns the property.
Mr. Riggs's property did not sell.

Rule 2: Plural possessive: Add an apostrophe alone to a plural word that ends in *s*. (Most of them do.) If the plural ends in other than an *s*, add an apostrophe *s*.

the ladies are . . .	the ladies' wallets are . . .
the Wellses are . . .	the Wellses' property is . . .
the witnesses are . . .	the witnesses' stories are . . .
the Hodgeses are . . .	the Hodgeses' car is . . .

The Brownells live in Michigan.
The Brownells' car was stolen.

The Riggses were not in town.
The Riggses' house was sold.

Making Words Plural in Brief: Normally, English adds an *s* to make a word plural. A word ending in *s*, *z*, *x*, *ch*, or *sh* adds *es* to make it plural. Proper names follow the same rules.

Brown	Browns	Boggs	Boggses
Fox	Foxes	Sanchez	Sanchezes
Williams	Williamses	Ruiz	Ruizes

Rule 3: Plural Possessive: When the plural does not end in *s*, an apostrophe *s* is added to the plural form of the word.

The children were watching television.
The children's television programming was not good.

The men were meeting at 10:00.
The men's group was in a different room.

Directions: Write the correct singular possessive form for these words after the word.

1. witness

2. Mr. Adams

3. boy

4. Ms. Hess

5. teenager

6. Mr. Nelson

7. plaintiff

8. Ms. Andrews

9. defendant

10. Jess

Directions: First, write the plural form after the word. Then write the correct plural possessive form.

1. witness
2. Wilson
3. child
4. lady
5. Rodriguez
6. Gibbs
7. man
8. Ruiz
9. mother
10. White

Word Pairs

perspective/prospective

The root of these two words is *spect*, which means "to see." The words *spectacles* and *spectator* and *inspect* come from this root. The prefix *pro-* means "for, toward"; the prefix *per-* means "through."

perspective = point of view. It literally means "to see through one's eyes."

From my perspective, this is not a reasonable settlement.
He can deal with it only through his own perspective.
His perspective cannot be changed by any sort of logic.

prospective = upcoming, potential, likely. It literally means "to see toward."

She appears to be a prospective client.
He declined to discuss his prospective purchase.
It involved his prospective father-in-law.

principle/principal

principle = rule. Notice the *-le* of *principle* matches the *-le* of *rule*. *Principle* means "standard, belief, tenet"; and those all relate to a rule. This word alone can never be an adjective before a noun.

He was unprincipled in his dealings with the company.
The defendant showed a lack of the basic principles of decency.
I stand on principle in this matter.

principal = all the other meanings. The *-pal* spelling means "chief, main." Think of the *a* in *principal* and the *a* in *main*.

- main person in the school, as in *sent to the principal*.
- people suing and/or being sued in the lawsuit, as in *one of the principals*.
- stars of the play, as in *the principal in the red suit*.

- money borrowed from the bank, as in *owe money on the principal*.
- main or chief reason or ingredient or thing, as in *the principal choice* (used as an adjective).

Mr. Jones was a principal in the proceedings.
The principal reason she took the classes is she wanted to be a principal.
We need to pay down the principal to continue to afford the loan.

profit/prophet

profit = gain, return, income.

He stood to profit financially from the scheme.
We will need to see a profit and loss statement.
I have not profited from her presence in the corporation.

prophet = person who predicts the future.

He was deemed a prophet for the new era.
The prophet turned out to be a fake.
He did not want to be thought of as a prophet.

rational/rationale

rational = logical, reasonable.

He made a very rational decision.
That is the most rational thinking I have heard.
His behavior was often irrational.

rationale = reason for doing something.

That is based on a faulty rationale.
She already had the rationale for her actions.
Please tell me your rationale for your position.

Directions: Circle the correct form of the word.

1. The principals/principles he claims to live by are questionable.

2. That is the principal/principle reason I talked to him.

3. The rational/rationale for that has not been established.

4. I did not consider him to be a perspective/prospective client.

5. Have you paid on the principal/principle since you lost your job?

6. Have you given any consideration to paying down the principal/principle?

7. The company predicted a profit/prophet for our department.

8. From my perspective/prospective, this was not a good deal.

9. It is my opinion that he is not capable of rational/rationale thought.

10. His unprincipaled/unprincipled conduct was called into question.

11. There were several perspective/prospective jobs he was qualified for.

12. It cannot be measured in terms of profits/prophets and losses alone.

13. I think I told you the principal/principle reasons for it.

14. It is a perspective/prospective that is not shared in the company.

15. It operates in accordance with the principals/principles of physics.

16. Her views are those of a profit/prophet.

17. Let's look at this from a different perspective/prospective.

18. Is the CEO one of the principals/principles in this action?

19. The problem is he had no perspective/prospective buyers for the property.

20. I just know I will never be able to pay off the principal/principle.

Is It One Word or Two? An Apostrophe? A Hyphen?

anyone/any one

anyone = any person at all, no specific person. This form is an indefinite pronoun.

I did not see anyone who I knew at that meeting.
We will take anyone who has the qualifications for the job.
Is there anyone who can help you at home?

any one = one of several things or persons. This is always two words when followed by a prepositional phrase that begins with *of*.

There are three cars I like. I would be happy with any one.
He said any one of the three could have done it.
He had many ideas for solutions to the problem. Any one might work.

everyone/every one

everyone = each individual, nonspecific person. This form is an indefinite pronoun.

I saw everyone last week at the conference.
The defendant looked everyone in the eye.
Does the list include everyone who participated?

every one = all of a number of things or persons, all things included. This is always two words when followed by a prepositional phrase that begins with *of*.

The books were there. Every one looked helpful.
Every one of the checks she wrote bounced.
I saw three plays. Every one was excellent.

someone/some one

someone = any individual, nonspecific person. This form is an indefinite pronoun.

Was there someone to explain it to you?
How is it that someone did not assist you?
The plaintiff says he knows someone who might have been there.

some one = a few, a selected one. This is always two words when followed by a prepositional phrase that begins with *of*.

There had to be some one of them who could do it.
There were three schedules. Some one of them could have been adapted.
I know that some one of the nurses was responsible.

no one

no one = not one. There is no one-word form.

I saw no one from the organization.
He testified that no one was present at the time.
Was there no one who could offer any ideas?

Directions: Circle the correct form of the word.

1. I wanted everyone/every one to participate in the project.

2. Is it true that anyone/any one of the men was capable of that?

3. He had given it to someone/some one of the assistants to finish.

4. The defendant testified that everyone/every one of the cars belonged to her.

5. Are you aware that noone/no one from your office attended that conference?

Proofreading

Directions: Make necessary corrections, based on the material presented in the unit. If the sentence has no errors, write the word *correct* after the sentence.

1. There were several perspective clients with the Stewart's when I saw them.   _____

2. We sent the memo to all the board member's secretaries, but Mrs. Harris' secretary obviously did not give the information to anyone of her colleagues.   _____

3. We were told that someone of the aides would be at a restaurant named Joes' Pizza.   _____

4. The principals involved in the negotiations walked together to the Harrison's place from the Harrises' house, and when they arrived, everyone of them wanted to speak first.   _____

5. The Lewises were concerned about the profits from the sale of the house also because Mrs. Lewises' car had been broken into right in front of the house.   _____

6. The principle reason he wrote the letter to Mr. Hillis' company was to inform everyone of the merger.   _____

7. From her perspective, no one should be in the company of the Hodges's son.   _____

8. The childrens' program was of great benefit to everyone of the kids in the principal program.   _____

9. His lack of principals was a problem for everyone in the company.   _____

10. It was a prospective look at how anyone involved would fare in the new program.   _____

An Adaptation from an Agency Case

Facts:

Plaintiff Riggs's property did not sell for over one and one half years while he had it listed with his real estate broker, Brownell. The listing had expired and had been renewed several times. Each time the price was reduced. Finally, Riggs agreed to sell to Brownell. After they had signed the contract but before the closing, Brownell found a buyer for the property and resold the property for a profit. Brownell did not tell Riggs about the prospective buyer until after the sale. Brownell claimed that Riggs could not prove that Brownell met the buyer before signing the contract with Riggs. Brownell also claimed that he had no duty to disclose information that he received after signing the real estate sales contract but before the closing took place. Riggs claimed that Brownell was an agent for Century 21 and they had a duty to supervise his actions under respondeat superior.

Procedure:

Riggs brought a complaint against both Brownell, the real estate broker, and Century 21, his alleged employer, in the Circuit Court. The court decided, on a motion for summary judgment, that there was no breach of fiduciary duty by the defendants and that Century 21 was not vicariously liable for Brownell's actions.

Issue:

Did the trial court err in granting the defendants' motion for summary judgment?

Rationale:

There was sufficient evidence to show there was an agency relationship in this case with Riggs and both defendants even after the written agreements had expired. Both defendants collected a commission from the sale of Riggs's property. Clearly, both defendants would not have collected a commission from the sale of the property if an agency relationship did not exist. A real estate agent serves as an agent of the owner of property, who bargains or negotiates on behalf of his principal in relation to the purchase or sale of property. As an agent, Brownell owed the general duties of good faith, loyalty, and trust to Riggs. The broker had the obligation to inform the seller of the buyer's offer. The facts show that Century 21 consented or knowingly acquiesced in Brownell acting on behalf of them as an agent. Accordingly, Century 21 had an obligation to supervise the acts of its agent Brownell.

Ruling:

Reversed and remanded for trial.

Directions for CD-ROM Transcription Exercises

In audio format are:

1. Terms for the unit with pronunciations from the thesaurus/dictionary feature.

2. Self-Test that appears in the book at mid-unit.°

3. Case that appears at the unit end.°

°speeds are 80 wpm/120 wpm for differing skill levels

CD-ROM icons appear where the three above are located within each unit.

Readers may practice transcription by listening to the CD-ROM where prompted by the icons in the book. However, for high success in testing your transcription skills, mastering all the terms and English skills in the unit is recommended before attempting the CD-ROM.

For Keyboard Transcriptionists: Listen to the CD-ROM audio file for this unit at 80 wpm or 120 wpm and transcribe from the dictation on your computer. Edit and proofread your work against the printed copy in the book.

For Reporting Writers: Listen to the CD-ROM audio file at 80 wpm or 120 wpm and take down the dictation on your writer. Either transcribe from your notes and proofread your work or edit and proofread your CAT (computer-aided transcription) transcript. Always check your work against the printed copy in the book.

Student CD-ROM
For additional materials,
please go to the CD in this book.

Online Companion™
For additional resources, please go to
http://www.paralegal.delmar.cengage.com

Area of Law

Bankruptcy

The **Mistakes** That Court Reporters Make and *How to Avoid* Them

The Mistake:

Carol Sharipova had been a reporter for two years and was planning her first major vacation. She had to be at the airport at 5:00 on Friday afternoon for her flight to Hawaii. At the last minute, she was offered a Friday afternoon job that was supposed to go a little over an hour. Because it would be some extra spending money on the trip, she decided to take the job. At 4:00 there seemed to be no end in sight, and at 4:15 Carol had to ask for a break to find out how much longer they were going to go—only to find out that she was going to have to stop the proceedings, call her office, and try to get another reporter to do the job or miss her trip. Rather than miss her trip, she told the attorneys that she had to leave and that they would have to wait for another reporter.

How to Avoid It:

Carol should never, no matter how tempted by any details of the job, have agreed to take this job. Having to stop in the middle of the deposition to wait for another reporter is sure to anger the attorneys and your agency. You never take a job when there is any possibility that you cannot stay to finish it. This includes being sure you have babysitting arrangements in place for that deposition that goes four hours when it was scheduled to be only two.

Introduction

An individual who petitions for straight bankruptcy files under Chapter 7 of the Bankruptcy Code. Chapter 11 (reorganization) allows a business to repay creditors and continue in business pursuant to a plan filed with the bankruptcy court. Wage earners may pay all or part of their debt to creditors under protection of the court over an approved period of time. This is known as Chapter 13, or consumer debt adjustment. Now there is a bankruptcy provision for family farmers, known as Chapter 12. From time to time, federal legislation updates the Bankruptcy Code to keep pace with inflation, current business conditions (the endangered American family farm), and standards of living.

Under the new law, the bankruptcy court can convert a Chapter 7 (straight bankruptcy) case to either a Chapter 11 or Chapter 13 case with a debtor's consent. Previously, a debtor needed to request such a conversion. Now, the court on its own motion, or that of any party in interest, can move for the dismissal of a case. Previously, any party in interest could not bring such a motion. The standard of substantial abuse is no longer needed for dismissal or conversion of a case, only simple abuse need be shown. The previous presumption in favor of granting relief to a debtor has now been changed, with a new presumption that abuse exists if the debtor's monthly income exceeds a certain monthly figure. In order to file a bankruptcy petition, you must now first receive a briefing from a budget and credit counseling service. All Chapter 7 and Chapter 13 discharges are conditioned upon the debtor's completion of an approved instructional course concerning personal finance management. Clearly it is the intent to prevent some of the abuse that has occurred under the prior laws, which were aimed at granting everyone a "fresh start."

Unit Objectives

- Work with a legal dictionary/thesaurus.
- Learn about the law of bankruptcy.
- Master the similarities and differences in definitions of key terms.
- Master the pronunciations and spellings of legal terms in the unit.
- Recognize the synonyms used for legal terminology in bankruptcy.
- Practice usage of terms, definitions, and synonyms in bankruptcy law.
- Complete unit exercises in the forms of missing words, matching, multiple choice, true/false, synonyms, self-test, defining words, and also:
  - Punctuation/capitalization
  - Word pairs
  - Transcription of terms, self-test, and case
  - Proofreading

Dictionary/Thesaurus

Note: All Dictionary/Thesaurus terms appear on the CD-ROM with audio pronunciations.

Term
[phonetic pronunciation]

---

arrangement with creditors
[a.*raynj*.ment with *kred*.i.terz]

1. A proceeding, also called a composition, by which a debtor who is not insolvent may have her failing finances rehabilitated by a bankruptcy court under an agreement with her creditors. *See also* composition with creditors. 2. The plan worked out by the bankruptcy court; also referred to as an arrangement for the benefit of creditors. *See also* bankruptcy.

---

assets
[*ass*.ets]

Property of any value.

---

bankrupt
[*bank*.rupt]

1. A person who is unable to pay her debts as they come due; an insolvent person. 2. A person who is entitled to the protection of the Bankruptcy Code.
• *adj.* insolvent, indigent, wiped out, penniless, destitute, broke, out of business

---

bankruptcy
[*bank*.rupt.see]

1. The circumstances of a person who is unable to pay his debts as they come due. 2. The system under which a debtor may come into court (voluntary bankruptcy) or be brought into court by his creditors (involuntary bankruptcy), either seeking to have his assets administered and sold for the benefit of his creditors and to be discharged from his debts (a straight bankruptcy), or to have his debts reorganized (a business reorganization or a wage earner's plan). A straight bankruptcy is called a Chapter 7 proceeding because it is conducted under Chapter 7 of the Bankruptcy Code. Under Chapter 11, the debtor is permitted to continue business operations until a reorganization plan is approved by two-thirds of his creditors. Under a Chapter 13 proceeding, an individual debtor who is a wage earner and who files a repayment plan acceptable to his creditors will be given additional time in which to meet his obligations. Chapter 12 proceedings regard family farms.
• *n.* insolvency, failure, disaster, defaulting
• *ant.* solvency

Bankruptcy Abuse Prevention and Consumer Protection Act
[*bank*.rupt.see a.*byooss* pre.*vent*. shen and kon.*soo*.mer *pro*.tek.shen act]

Enacted in 2005, it is a significant overhaul in bankruptcy and less favorable for debtors.

Bankruptcy Code
[*bank*.rupt.see code]

Federal bankruptcy legislation. There have been six major statutes, enacted respectively in 1800, 1841, 1867, 1898, 1978, and 2005. The last of these is the Bankruptcy Abuse Prevention and Consumer Protection Act.

bankruptcy courts [*bank*.rupt.see kortz]	Federal courts that hear and determine only bankruptcy cases.
bankruptcy estate [*bank*.rupt.see es.*tate*]	All of the property of the debtor at the time the petition in bankruptcy is filed.
bankruptcy judge [*bank*.rupt.see juj]	A judge of a bankruptcy court.
bankruptcy proceedings [*bank*.rupt.see pro.*see*.dings]	Any proceedings under the Bankruptcy Code; any proceedings relating to bankruptcy.
bankruptcy trustee [*bank*.rupt.see trus.*tee*]	*See* trustee in bankruptcy.
composition with creditors [kom.po.*zish*.en with *kred*.i.terz]	1. An agreement between a debtor and her creditors under which, in exchange for prompt payment, the creditors agree to accept amounts less than those actually owed in satisfaction of their claims. *See also* arrangement with creditors. 2. Proceedings under Chapter 13 of the Bankruptcy Code for debt readjustment.
creditor [*kred*.it.er]	A person to whom a debt (secured by collateral or unsecured) is owed by a debtor. *See also* general creditor, secured creditor, and unsecured creditor. • *n.* lender, assignee
creditor beneficiary [*kred*.it.er ben.e.*fish*.ee.ar.ee]	A creditor who is the beneficiary of a contract made between the debtor and a third person.
creditors' meeting [*kred*.it.erz *meet*.ing]	The first meeting of creditors of a debtor, required for the purpose of allowing the claims of creditors, questioning the debtor under oath, and electing a trustee in bankruptcy.
debtee [*det*.ee]	A person who lends to a debtor. • *n.* creditor, lender
debtor [*det*.er]	1. A person who owes another person money. 2. A person who owes another person anything. *See also* debtee. • *n.* borrower, buyer, deadbeat
debtor in possession [*det*.er in po.*zesh*.en]	A debtor who continues to operate his business while undergoing a business reorganization under the jurisdiction of the bankruptcy court. *See also* bankruptcy.
discharge in bankruptcy [dis.*charj* in *bank*.rupt.see]	The release of a debtor from an obligation to pay, pursuant to a bankruptcy proceeding. • *v.* To perform an obligation or duty; to satisfy a debt. USAGE: "All his debts were discharged by bankruptcy."

dismissal [dis.*miss*.el]	The release of the debtor's case in totality from protection and jurisdiction of the bankruptcy court.
exemptions [eg.*zemp*.shenz]	Earnings and property allowed to be retained by a debtor free from claims of creditors in bankruptcy.
fraudulent conveyance [*fraw*.je.lent ken.*vay*.ense]	1. The act of a debtor in making payment to one of her creditors by paying him with the intention of defrauding other creditors. 2. Under the Bankruptcy Code, a transfer of property to a creditor that gives him an advantage over other creditors. Although such a transfer may be disallowed by the trustee in bankruptcy, it is not necessarily a criminal act. *See also* preference.
garnishment [*gar*.nish.ment]	Attachment of debtor's wages by a creditor.
general creditor [*jen*.e.rel *kred*.it.er]	One who is not entitled to priority because the creditor's claim is not secured by a mortgage or other lien.
homestead exemption [home.sted eg.*zemp*.shen]	Under homestead exemption statutes, the immunity of real property from execution for debt, provided the property is occupied by the debtor as the head of the family. This can vary by state law, with some states allowing for 100 percent immunity even for mansions.
involuntary bankruptcy [in.*vol*.en.te.ree *bank*.rupt.see]	A bankruptcy initiated by one's creditors. *See also* bankruptcy; bankruptcy proceedings. *Compare* voluntary bankruptcy.
lien [leen]	A claim on personal or real property for the payment of a debt or mortgage.
liquidation [lik.wi.*day*.shen]	1. The extinguishment of a debt by payment or straight bankruptcy. 2. The ascertainment of the amount of a debt or demand by agreement or by legal proceedings. *See also* bankruptcy; receivership. • *n.* elimination, abolition, rescission
moratorium [more.e.*toh*.ree.um]	A period during which a person, usually a debtor, has a legal right to postpone meeting an obligation. An individual creditor may declare a moratorium with respect to her debtor, or a moratorium may be imposed by legislation and apply to debtors as a class. • *n.* grace period
nondischargeable debt [non.dis.*charj*.ebl det]	Any voidable or fraudulent preferences, taxes, child support, or other debts that cannot be legally discharged in bankruptcy. *See also* voidable preference, fraudulent preference.
petition in bankruptcy [pe.tish.en in *bank*.rupt.see]	A document filed in a bankruptcy court initiating bankruptcy proceedings. *See also* bankruptcy, petitioning creditor.

petitioner
[pe.*tish*.en.er]

A person seeking relief by a petition.
• *n.* pleader, litigant, applicant, asker, supplicant ("The petitioner asked for relief")
• *ant.* respondent

petitioning creditor
[pe.*tish*.en.ing *kred*.it.er]

A creditor who initiates proceedings against his debtor in a bankruptcy court. *See also* bankruptcy proceedings; petition in bankruptcy.

preference
[*pref*.e.rense]

1. The act of a debtor in paying one or more of his creditors without paying the others. "Preference" is often confused with priority. However, a priority exists by operation of law; a preference is a transaction that, depending upon the circumstances, the law may consider voidable. *See also* priority. 2. Under the Bankruptcy Code, a transfer of property by an insolvent debtor to one or more creditors to the exclusion of others, enabling such creditors to obtain a greater percentage of their debt than other creditors of the same class. Such a transaction may constitute a voidable preference and be disallowed by the trustee in bankruptcy. *See also* fraudulent preference. 3. The right of one person over other persons. *See also* voidable preference.
• *n.* partiality, election, advantage; priority, prejudice, promotion, upgrading, precedence

preferential assignment
[*pref*.e.*ren*.shel a.*sine*.ment]

An assignment for the benefit of creditors by which the assignor gives a preference to certain of her creditors; any assignment that prefers one creditor over another.

preferential debts
[*pref*.e.*ren*.shel detz]

Debts that, under the Bankruptcy Code, are payable before all other debts. EXAMPLE: wages owed employees.

preferential transfer
[*pref*.e.*ren*.shel *tranz*.fer]

See preference.

priority
[pry.*aw*.ri.tee]

1. In bankruptcy law, the right of a secured creditor to receive satisfaction before an unsecured creditor. 2. The status of that which is earlier or previous in point of time, degree, or rank; precedence. *See also* preference.
• *n.* lead, order, superiority, primacy, preference, precedence, right, seniority, rank

proof of claim
[proof ov klam]

In bankruptcy, a statement in writing, signed by a creditor, setting forth the amount owed and the basis of the claim.

receiver
[re.*seev*.er]

A person appointed by the court to take custody of property in a receivership. In the case of the assets or other property of an insolvent debtor, whether an individual or corporation, the duty of a receiver is to preserve the assets for sale and distribution to the creditors. In the case of assets or other property that is the subject of litigation, the duty of a receiver is to preserve the property or fund in litigation, receive its rent or profits, and apply or dispose of them as the court directs. Such a receiver is called a pendente lite receiver. If the property in dispute is a business, the receiver may have the additional responsibility of operating the business as a going concern.
• *n.* trustee, supervisor, administrator, depository, overseer, manager, collector

receivership
[re.*seev*.er.ship]

A proceeding by which the property of an insolvent debtor, or property that is the subject of litigation, may be preserved and appropriately disposed of by a person known as a receiver, who is appointed and supervised by the court. A corporation as well as an individual may be "in receivership." *See also* receiver.

schedule in bankruptcy
[*sked*.jool in *bank*.rupt.see]

A schedule filed by a bankrupt listing, among other things, all of his property, its value, his creditors, and the nature of their claims.

secured creditor
[se.*kyoord kred*.it.er]

One who has security for a debt owed in the form of an encumbrance on the property of the person in bankruptcy.

stay
[stay]

The Bankruptcy Code provides for automatic stops to further proceedings, usually temporarily; to restrain; to hold back; to suspend foreclosures or executions on certain types of debts upon filing of bankruptcy petition. *See also* moratorium.
• *v.* arrest, hinder, postpone, intermit, obstruct, suspend ("stay the creditor's foreclosure")
• *n.* deferment, halt, remission, reprieve, standstill, suspension

trustee in bankruptcy
[trust.*ee* in *bank*.rupt.see]

A person appointed by a bankruptcy court to collect any amounts owed the debtor, sell the debtor's property, and distribute the proceeds among the creditors.

unsecured creditor
[un.se.*kyoord kred*.it.er]

One who has received no security for the debt owed by the person in bankruptcy.

voidable preference
[*void*.ebl *pref*.rense]

Under the Bankruptcy Code, a preference is voidable if it takes place within a specified number of days before the filing of the petition in bankruptcy and if it allows the creditor to obtain more than she would have received from the bankruptcy court.

voluntary bankruptcy
[*vol*.en.ter.ee *bank*.rupt.see]

A bankruptcy that the petitioner himself initiates, as opposed to an involuntary bankruptcy.

wage earner's plan
[wayj *ern*.erz plan]

Under Chapter 13 of the Bankruptcy Code, a debtor who is a wage earner and who files a repayment plan acceptable to his creditors and the court will be given additional time in which to meet his obligations.

Missing Words

Fill in the blanks below.

1. A(n) _____ is the act of a debtor in making payment to one of her creditors by paying him with the intention of defrauding other creditors.

2. Under _____ statutes real property is immune from execution for debt.

3. The _____ is federal bankruptcy legislation.

4. A(n) _____ is any voidable or fraudulent preference, taxes, child support, or other debts that cannot be legally discharged in bankruptcy.

5. A(n) _____ is a statement in writing signed by a creditor, setting forth the amount owed and the basis of the claim.

6. The right of a secured creditor to receive satisfaction before an unsecured creditor is _____.

7. The attachment of a debtor's wages by a creditor is _____.

8. A(n) _____ is the release of a debtor's case in totality from protection and jurisdiction of a bankruptcy court.

9. _____ of the Bankruptcy Code is also called the wage earner's plan.

10. A(n) _____ is a creditor who initiates proceedings against his debtor in a bankruptcy court.

11. A(n) _____ is a person who is unable to pay her debts as they come due.

12. The right to have one's claim against a debtor's estate satisfied out of the assets of the estate before other claimants is called _____.

13. Any proceedings under the Bankruptcy Code are known as _____.

14. An assignment that gives advantage to one creditor over another is a(n) _____.

15. _____ is the extinguishment of a debt by payment or straight bankruptcy.

16. Property of any value is called a(n) _____.

17. One who is not entitled to priority because her claim is not secured by a lien is a(n) _____.

Matching

Match the letter of the definition to the term below.

_____ 18. Composition with creditors

    A. An agreement between a debtor and her creditors under which, in exchange for prompt payment, the creditors accept less than actually owed

_____ 19. Preferences

    B. They can file an involuntary petition in bankruptcy

_____ 20. Nondischargeable debt

    C. Child support is an example of this. It is a debt that must be paid and can't be discharged in a bankruptcy proceeding.

_____ 21. Chapter 7

    D. Frequently, creditors are successful in attaching unpaid judgments by garnishing a debtor's wages prior to bankruptcy

_____ 22. Chapter 11 reorganization plan

    E. All the debtor's assets are not sold to pay off debts; debts are paid over time

_____ 23. Creditors

    F. Payments made by the debtor to particular creditors

_____ 24. Petition in bankruptcy

    G. A bankruptcy proceeding is commenced with the filing of forms

_____ 25. Receiver

    H. Person who might be appointed by the court to collect rents and profits and preserve the property involved, if a landlord of an apartment building filed for bankruptcy

_____ 26. Garnishment

    I. Straight bankruptcy

_____ 27. Stay

    J. Person appointed by a bankruptcy court to sell the debtor's property

_____ 28. Lien

    K. Claim on personal or real property for the payment of a debt

_____ 29. Trustee

    L. Automatic stop to further proceedings

_____ 30. 2005 law

    M. Bankruptcy Abuse Prevention and Consumer Protection Act

_____ 31. Fraudulent conveyance

    N. A creditor not entitled to priority in bankruptcy

_____ 32. General creditor

    O. A creditor who has security for a debt

_____ 33. Secured creditor

    P. A creditor who has received no security for debt

_____ 34. Unsecured creditor

    Q. A transfer of property to a creditor that gives her an advantage over other creditors

Multiple Choice

Select the best choice.

_____ 35. A person seeking relief by a petition is a:
   a. bankruptcy trustee
   b. trustee in bankruptcy
   c. petitioner
   d. bankruptcy judge

_____ 36. Under Chapter 13 of the Bankruptcy Code, a debtor who is a wage earner and who files a repayment plan acceptable to his creditors and the court will be given additional time to meet his obligations. This is called:
   a. friends and family plan
   b. wage earner's plan
   c. head of household plan
   d. receivership

_____ 37. All of the property of the debtor at the time the petition in bankruptcy is filed is called the:
   a. bankruptcy estate
   b. bankruptcy collection
   c. bankruptcy holdings
   d. homestead exemption

_____ 38. The release of a debtor from an obligation to pay pursuant to a bankruptcy proceeding is a:
   a. probation in bankruptcy
   b. parole in bankruptcy
   c. discharge in bankruptcy
   d. merger in bankruptcy

_____ 39. A person appointed by a bankruptcy court to collect any amounts owed the debtor, sell the debtor's property, and distribute the proceeds among the creditors is the:
   a. adjuster
   b. insurer
   c. administrative law judge
   d. trustee in bankruptcy

_____ 40. When a debtor comes into court seeking to have his assets administered and sold for the benefit of his creditors and to be discharged from his debts, this is called straight bankruptcy or:
   a. Chapter 5
   b. Chapter 6
   c. Chapter 7
   d. Chapter 8

_____ 41. A document filed in a bankruptcy court initiating bankruptcy proceedings is the:
   a. summons
   b. subpoena
   c. petition in bankruptcy
   d. bankruptcy complaint

_____ 42. A schedule filed by a bankrupt listing, among other things, all of his property, its value, his creditors and the nature of their claims is a:
   a. W-2 form
   b. proof of claim
   c. moratorium
   d. schedule in bankruptcy

_____ 43. The business reorganization plan, where the debtor is permitted to continue business operations until a reorganization plan is approved by two-thirds of his creditors, is:
   a. Chapter 10
   b. Chapter 11
   c. Chapter 12
   d. Chapter 13

_____ **44.** Under the Bankruptcy Code, a preference that takes place within a specified number of days before the filing of the petition in bankruptcy that allows a creditor to receive more than she would have received from the bankruptcy court is a(n):
 a. voluntary bankruptcy
 b. voidable preference
 c. priority
 d. arrangement with creditors

_____ **45.** A written statement by the creditor with amount owed by the debtor is called:
 a. preference
 b. priority
 c. wage earner's plan
 d. proof of claim

_____ **46.** Preferred term for person unable to pay debts:
 a. broke
 b. penniless
 c. bankrupt
 d. wiped out

True/False

Mark the following T or F.

_____ **47.** Chapter 7 is frequently referred to as the Business Reorganization Plan.

_____ **48.** Chapter 13 is also called a Liquidation Plan.

_____ **49.** The automatic stay prevents creditors from contacting the debtor after commencing a bankruptcy proceeding.

_____ **50.** Exemptions are property that is included in the debtor's estate when calculating those assets available to pay debtor's claims.

_____ **51.** When a debtor receives a discharge in bankruptcy he is relieved from the obligation of paying certain debts.

_____ **52.** The purpose of the Bankruptcy Code is to give individuals and businesses a fresh start after becoming deeply indebted.

_____ **53.** A creditor is a person who owes another person money.

_____ **54.** Under the homestead exemption statutes, real property is immune from execution for debt.

_____ **55.** A debtor may file a repayment plan under Chapter 13 of the Bankruptcy Code.

_____ **56.** A stay is used to continue with further proceedings in a bankruptcy case.

Synonyms

Select the correct synonym in parentheses for each numbered item.

---

57. CHAPTER 7
    (straight bankruptcy, reorganization, receivership)

58. PREFERENCE
    (priority, garnish, dismissal)

59. DISCHARGE
    (foreclosure, lien, release)

60. MORATORIUM
    (luxury, security, grace period)

61. LIEN
    (claim, retain, surrender)

62. DEBT
    (prize, obligation, homestead)

63. CREDITOR
    (lender, buyer, borrower)

64. ARRANGEMENT WITH CREDITORS
    (maintain, increase, composition)

65. GARNISHMENT
    (interest, allowance, attachment)

66. PRIORITY
    (strategic, proportional, precedence)

67. BANKRUPT
    (frugal, insolvent, conversion)

68. LIEN
    (sale, claim, exemption)

69. PETITIONER
    (litigant, respondent, defendant)

70. RECEIVER
    (debtor, bankruptcy judge, trustee)

Self-Test

Place the number of the correct term in the appropriate space.

---

71. Creditors

72. Assets

73. Bankruptcy

74. Debt

75. Bankruptcy Code

76. Debtors

77. Wage earner's plan

78. Liquidation

79. Reorganization

80. Trustee

81. Discharge in bankruptcy

82. Voluntary bankruptcies

83. Involuntary bankruptcies

84. Bankruptcy Abuse Prevention and Consumer Protection Act

All day long, people hear on the radio and the television, buy now, pay later. Credit card companies call and write to people telling them they can make the purchases they have been dreaming about if they apply for a certain credit card. Stores invite people to make major appliance purchases with no payments for the first six months after the purchase. The end result is that there are lots of people who are heavily in _____. Since the writing of the U.S. Constitution, Congress has realized that there comes a time when _____ need a fresh start, erasing payments so they may go on with their lives. A common sign that a person has economic problems is when stores and other _____ report to credit bureaus about a person's delinquent payments.

A creditor might threaten to repossess a car that's the subject of a loan, or even foreclose on a home. At this point, a debtor will most likely consult an attorney. The attorney will look at the client's complete financial picture, adding up all _____, deducting all liabilities, distinguishing between luxuries and necessities, such as tools of the trade needed by the debtor to continue to earn a living. The attorney will counsel the client about the different options available from Chapter 7, known as _____ or straight bankruptcy, to Chapter 11, a business _____ plan, or Chapter 13, a _____.

Whatever is decided, the matter will be handled by a(n) _____ court. A(n) _____ will be appointed to monitor the case and the bankruptcy proceeding will be handled under the _____ until a(n) _____ is granted. Most bankruptcy filings are _____. However, under the _____, bankruptcies initiated by creditors are called _____.

Defining Words

Complete the definition.

85. Debtee _____

_____

86. Creditor _____

_____

87. Debtor _____

_____

88. Bankruptcy court _____

_____

89. Bankruptcy _____

_____

90. Bankruptcy Code _____

_____

91. Bankruptcy proceeding _____

_____

92. Discharge _____

_____

93. Exemption _____

_____

94. Preference _____

_____

95. Nondischargeable debt _____

_____

96. Preferential debts _____

_____

97. Composition with creditors _____

_____

98. Schedule in bankruptcy _____

_____

99. Fraudulent conveyance _____

_____

100. General creditor _____

_____

Punctuation/Capitalization

Capitalization of words in titles.

Rule 1: The specific name of a code is capitalized.

We were following the provisions of the Bankruptcy Code.
She made reference to the Penal Code.
The Business and Professions Code governs that instance.

Rule 2: The specific name of an act or bill is capitalized.

This involves the Taft-Hartley Act of 1947.
It was a vote on the Wheatley Farm Appropriations Bill.
The Peace and Freedom Act gave us new hope.

Rule 3: The specific name of a committee or company or school is capitalized.

The Ways and Means Committee is considering the measure.
I worked for Production Machinery Tool Company.
It is a policy of the College of Court Reporting.

Rule 4: When any of these words are used alone without the full name, they are not capitalized.

The committee is considering the bill.
The company does not follow the code.
I decided to attend the college near my home.

Directions: Correct any errors in capitalization.

1. I could not vote for the Kennedy Tax Cut bill of 2006.

2. This does not seem to be in compliance with the code involved.

3. She worked for the Company for several years.

4. Is there any way to use the sections of that act in your argument?

5. He served on the committee on Homeland Security.

Word Pairs

accede/exceed

accede = give in to, assent to, reach power. This word is often followed by the word *to*.

He acceded to the wishes of the judge.
Elizabeth acceded to the throne of England.
Did he accede to your demands in the contract?

exceed = go beyond, surpass, outdo.

Did she exceed your expectations on the job?
The approaching car was exceeding the speed limit.
She did not exceed the accomplishments of her predecessor.

access/excess

access = entry, right or opportunity to use, call up.

We gained access to the building through the guard.
The password gave them access to his files.
No one else had access to that information.

excess = more than enough, surplus, extra.

We had an excess of merchandise in the warehouse.
He tended to do everything to excess.
Did you recognize the excess weight he was carrying?

ensure/insure

When the word *guarantee* can be substituted into the sentence, use the word *ensure*.

When the word *protect* can be substituted into the sentence, use the word *insure*.

ensure = guarantee.

I want to ensure that he comes with her to the trial hearing.
This ensures his participation in the meeting.
Was it your intention to ensure that you were elected?

insure = protect.

He decided to insure his business with State Farm.
She intends to insure her family by purchasing a term policy.
I did my best to insure it for the highest dollar value.

lean/lien

lean = thin, slant or move toward something, economical, not productive.

It was a lean year as he was out of work for seven months.
It is said that he was lean and mean.
The tower seemed to lean slightly to the east.

lien = claim on property for the payment of a debt or mortgage.

We discovered the lien on her home when she tried to sell it.
The bank placed a lien on the main building of the company headquarters.
He denied there was a lien on his house.

peace/piece

peace = contentment, without turmoil, quiet.

I just want to live in peace.
He exudes an aura of peace.
The treaty was intended to create peace between the two nations.

piece = portion, one thing in a group.

He was looking for a piece of the action.
That is the last missing piece to the puzzle.
His piece is larger than mine.

personal/personnel

personal = private, individual.

It is a personal issue that I cannot discuss with you.
He tried to claim it was a matter of a personal nature.
It involved my personal property.

personnel = people employed in an organization, workers, staff.

He was part of the personnel office.
We determined that we needed more personnel to handle the work.
She was the director of personnel for the organization.

Directions: Circle the correct form of the word.

1. I need one more small peace/piece of evidence to ensure/insure that the case will come to trial.

2. Is this in access/excess of what you already have?

3. I was told he was fired because of personal/personnel issues that he had at home and the access/excess number of employees.

4. Things were lean/lien that month after his access/excess of speed earned him a $500 ticket.

5. It was necessary to accede/exceed to her demands in order to prevent a lean/lien on our home.

6. How long has this acceded/exceeded the limits?

7. Did you ensure/insure the property for the full value?

8. Was it a personal/personnel decision, or did you discuss it with your colleagues?

9. It is a peace/piece initiative that I can fully support.

10. She seems to be leaning/liening toward a school on the East Coast.

11. Did you accede/exceed to his wishes on that project?

12. That is definitely in access/excess of anything I asked for.

13. This ensures/insures that he will accede/exceed output from prior years.

14. The personal/personnel involved had very little experience in these situations.

15. Did you lean/lien toward or away from her as you rounded the corner?

16. He wanted a peace/piece of the action but wasn't willing to make peace/piece with her to get it.

17. Her performance did not accede/exceed his on this task.

18. We placed the access/excess near the bundles that were ensured/insured by the company.

19. Does this ensure/insure more than two buildings?

20. We need to ensure/insure that he will be present in court.

Is It One Word or Two? An Apostrophe? A Hyphen?

alot/a lot

alot = never a correct form.

a lot = piece of property, used for "much/very much" as a substandard form.

There remained a lot to do in the case.
I don't have a lot of information for you.
He owns a lot near the bridge on the highway.

alright/allright

alright = never a correct form. Think about *alwrong*!

all right = always the correct form.

She said it was all right to park there.
Is that all right with you?
It is all right to leave it out on the counter.

awhile/a while

awhile = adverb: an indefinite period of time.

a while = noun: an indefinite period of time. This is the correct form as the object of the preposition or with *ago* and *back*.

Because of a specific construction in English grammar (called an adverbial objective), you are always correct to make this two words. There are many instances where grammar demands that it be two words, but there is never an instance where it has to be one word.

It took a while for me to discover the problem.
We were together a while to talk about it.
I have not seen him for a while.

Directions: Circle the correct form of the word.

1. It is alright/all right to leave it here.

2. Have you seen him in awhile/a while?

3. He has alot/a lot to do before he finishes the job.

4. Was it alright/all right to leave early?

5. I am not sure there was alot/a lot he could do.

Proofreading

Directions: Make necessary corrections, based on the material presented in the unit. If the sentence has no errors, write the word *correct* after the sentence.

1. He acceded to his colleagues' wishes in passing the Bill in this session. _____

2. There has been a lean on his property for awhile. _____

3. The committee wants to insure that this bill makes it to the House of Representatives. _____

4. It was a personal decision to accede the limit of ten pieces of jewelry. _____

5. It is alright for you to access the Internet from here. _____

6. I wrote to the personal section a lot about my position with the Company. _____

7. My excess baggage is limited to one small peace of luggage. _____

8. A while ago I ensured my house with that company. _____

9. He did not want to ensure that I would be all right with that medication. _____

10. There is a lot of excess material in that article from the committee. _____

An Adaptation from a Bankruptcy Case

Facts:

The debtor, Sullivan, obtained a bond from O'Hara Bonding Company, which was in connection with a required court appearance for his son, to ensure his son's presence in court. When the debtor's son failed to appear in court as required, Sullivan forfeited the return of his money, and O'Hara Bonding obtained a judgment against Sullivan for $100,000 plus interest. Two years later, Sullivan filed a Chapter 7 Bankruptcy Petition. O'Hara Bonding sought to deny the debtor's discharge and was seeking a judgment against Sullivan.

Procedural History:

The Bankruptcy Court granted summary judgment to Creditor O'Hara Bonding Company for debtor's failure to maintain adequate records. Debtor had appealed this ruling.

Rationale:

There was not one piece of paper offered by the debtor relating to his financial actions, nothing concerning his wages or his expenses and no income tax returns or other documents. Debtor claims that he provided an earnings summary from Social Security and various other checks. The debtor submitted a cursory affidavit that stated he never made more than $1,000 in any month in the year prior to bankruptcy, that he did not transfer or conceal any assets before or after bankruptcy, and that he has not filed tax returns because his accountant said he did not earn enough to qualify. The Bankruptcy Code does not require creditors to take a debtor's word that his income is insubstantial. Creditors are entitled to see it for themselves from accurate and reliable records that the debtor is required to maintain.

Ruling:

Judgment affirmed for O'Hara Bonding Company. Debtor was denied a discharge in bankruptcy. Under the new Bankruptcy Abuse Prevention and Consumer Protection Act, which went into effect in 2005, there has been a significant overhaul in the bankruptcy laws, making them less favorable toward debtors. Accordingly, it will take some time for the new appellate cases that deal with these issues to become available. Some of the key provisions of the new act are as follows: Under the new law the Bankruptcy Court can convert a Chapter 7 case to either a Chapter 11 or Chapter 13 case with a debtor's consent. Previously, a debtor needed to request such a conversion. Now the court, on its own motion or that of any party in interest, can move for the dismissal of a case. Previously any party in interest could not bring such a motion. The standard of substantial abuse is no longer needed for dismissal or conversion of a case. Only simple abuse need be shown. The previous presumption in favor of granting relief to a debtor has now been changed and has a new presumption that abuse exists if the debtor's monthly income exceeds a certain monthly figure. In order to file a bankruptcy petition, you must now first receive a briefing from a budget and credit counseling service. All Chapter 7 and Chapter 13 discharges are conditioned upon the debtor's completion of an approved instructional course concerning personal finance management. Clearly, it is the intent to prevent some of the abuse that has occurred under the prior laws, which were aimed at granting everyone a "fresh start."

Directions for CD-ROM Transcription Exercises

In audio format are:

1. Terms for the unit with pronunciations from the thesaurus/dictionary feature.

2. Self-Test that appears in the book at mid-unit.*

3. Case that appears at the unit end.*

*speeds are 80 wpm/120 wpm for differing skill levels

CD-ROM icons appear where the three above are located within each unit.

Readers may practice transcription by listening to the CD-ROM where prompted by the icons in the book. However, for high success in testing your transcription skills, mastering all the terms and English skills in the unit is recommended before attempting the CD-ROM.

For Keyboard Transcriptionists: Listen to the CD-ROM audio file for this unit at 80 wpm or 120 wpm and transcribe from the dictation on your computer. Edit and proofread your work against the printed copy in the book.

For Reporting Writers: Listen to the CD-ROM audio file at 80 wpm or 120 wpm and take down the dictation on your writer. Either transcribe from your notes and proofread your work or edit and proofread your CAT (computer-aided transcription) transcript. Always check your work against the printed copy in the book.

 Student CD-ROM
For additional materials,
please go to the CD in this book.

 Online Companion™
For additional resources, please go to
http://www.paralegal.delmar.cengage.com

Unit 4 | Civil Litigation (Pretrial)

The **Mistakes** That Court Reporters Make and *How to Avoid* Them

The Mistake:

Joanne Politano had five exhibits from her morning job. She slipped them into the side pocket of her purse as she left the deposition and set out for her afternoon job. That evening, as she was putting everything away, the exhibits from the morning deposition were nowhere to be found. She had lost them. She would have to call her office and reveal that she had lost the exhibits.

How to Avoid It:

Joanne should have put the exhibits in a secure place: her briefcase, her steno case. It is unforgivable to lose exhibits. You must put them in a very secure place. The outside pocket on a purse probably does not qualify.

Introduction

When parties fail to resolve their differences privately, the process of resolving such disputes through the court system is known as civil litigation. Unlike criminal litigation, which is brought by the government against the accused, civil litigation is brought by one party (the plaintiff) against another party (the defendant). Distinguishing a civil matter from a criminal case is key. Civil procedure is very different from criminal procedure and the damages sought in a civil case are usually monetary in nature.

Prior to trial, litigation attorneys and their teams of assistants engage in time-consuming tasks of discovery for trial: investigating the facts, interviewing witnesses, researching the law, and drafting legal documents (briefs, interrogatories, memoranda of law, as well as pleadings). In the case at the end of the unit, discovery demands were not met.

Before the evidence ever reaches a judge or jury in the courtroom, years may be spent by the legal teams in preparation for trial or settlement before trial.

At any point in a lawsuit, or even prior thereto, a party might make a request to the court for the purpose of obtaining an order or rule directing that something be done in favor of the applicant. This is called a motion. There are many different kinds of motions. A motion might be made orally or in writing. A party might bring a motion to dismiss a lawsuit without having to proceed to trial, or for a protective order limiting a party's discovery requests. In the case herein, the court denied the motion for relief.

The unit following this one will examine litigation during trial and appeal.

Unit Objectives

■ Work with a legal dictionary/thesaurus.

■ Learn about civil litigation.

■ Master the similarities and differences in definitions of key terms in the pretrial phase of civil litigation.

■ Master the pronunciations and spellings of legal terms in this unit.

■ Recognize the synonyms used for legal terminology in this unit.

■ Practice the usage of terms, definitions, and synonyms for pretrial civil litigation.

■ Complete unit exercises in the forms of missing words, matching, multiple choice, true/false, synonyms, self-test, defining words, and also:

- Punctuation/capitalization
- Word pairs
- Transcription of terms, self-test, and case
- Proofreading

💿 Dictionary/Thesaurus

Note: All Dictionary/Thesaurus terms appear on the CD-ROM with audio pronunciations.

Term
[phonetic pronunciation]

---

acknowledgment
[ak.*naw*.lej.ment]

1. The signing of a document, under oath, whereby the signer certifies that he is, in fact, the person who is named in the document as the signer.
2. The certificate of the person who administered the oath, for EXAMPLE, a clerk of court, justice of the peace, or notary.
• *n.* confirmation, admission, ratification, declaration, endorsement ("acknowledgment of paternity")

---

action
[*ak*.shen]

A judicial or administrative proceeding for the enforcement or protection of a right; a lawsuit. It is important to distinguish a civil action from a criminal action.
• *n.* legal proceeding, lawsuit, dispute, litigation ("an action for divorce")

---

action at common law
[*ak*.shen at *kom*.en law]

A lawsuit governed by the common law rather than by statutes.

---

action at law
[*ak*.shun at law]

A lawsuit brought in a court of law as opposed to a court of equity. *Compare* equitable action.

---

adversary
[*ad*.ver.sa.ree]

1. An opponent; an enemy. 2. The opposite party in a lawsuit.
• *n.* opponent, enemy, competitor, foe, challenger, litigant, opposing party, adverse party

---

adversary proceeding
[*ad*.ver.sa.ree pro.*see*.ding]

A trial or other proceeding in which all sides have the opportunity to present their contentions; a proceeding involving a contested action.

---

adversary system
[*ad*.ver.sa.ree *sis*.tem]

The system of justice in the United States. Under the adversary system, the court hears the evidence presented by the adverse parties and decides the case.

---

affidavit
[a.fi.*day*.vit]

Any voluntary statement reduced to writing and sworn to or affirmed before a person legally authorized to administer an oath or affirmation (EXAMPLE: a notary public). A sworn statement. *See also* verification.
• *n.* affirmation, oath, statement, testimony, avowal, averment, declaration, sworn statement

---

affidavit of service
[a.fi.*day*.vit ov *ser*.viss]

An affidavit that certifies that process (EXAMPLES: a summons; a writ) has been served upon the parties to the action in a manner prescribed by law.

affirmation
[a.fer.*may*.shen]

A formal statement or declaration, made as a substitute for a sworn statement, by a person whose religious or other beliefs will not permit him to swear. 2. A positive statement.
• *n.* statement, oath, declaration, assertion, avowal, confirmation ("out-of-court affirmation")

affirmative defense
[a.*fer*.ma.tiv de.*fense*]

A defense that amounts to more than simply a denial of the allegations in the plaintiff's complaint. It sets up a new matter that, if proven, could result in a judgment against the plaintiff even if all the allegations of the complaint are true. EXAMPLES of affirmative defenses in civil cases include accord and satisfaction, act of God, estoppel, release, and statute of limitations. EXAMPLES of affirmative defenses in criminal cases include alibi, double jeopardy, insanity, and self-defense.

allegation
[al.e.*gay*.shen]

A statement in a pleading of a fact that the party filing the pleading intends to prove.
• *n.* assertion, accusation, avowal, claim, charge

amend
[a.*mend*]

To improve; to make better by change or modification; to correct; to adjust. Thus, a motion to amend is a motion by which a party seeks the court's permission to correct an error or omission in a pleading or to modify allegations and supply new ones. *See also* amendment of pleading.
• *v.* correct, remedy, adjust, change, revise, alter, modify

amendment of pleading
[a.*mend*.ment ov *plee*.ding]

Although every jurisdiction imposes different restrictions, all jurisdictions permit pleadings to be amended for the purpose of correcting errors and omissions and to modify allegations and supply new ones. *See also* amend.

amicus curiae
[a.*mee*.kes *koo*.ree.eye]

(*Latin*) "Friend of the court." A person who is interested in the outcome of the case, but who is not a party, whom the court permits to file a brief for the purpose of providing the court with a position or a point of view that it might not otherwise have; often referred to simply as an amicus.

amount in controversy
[a.*mount* in *kon*.tre.ver.see]

A term relevant to determining a court's jurisdiction, when jurisdiction is based upon either a minimum dollar amount with which the court is permitted to concern itself or a maximum amount that represents the upper limit of its jurisdiction.

answer
[*an*.ser]

n. A pleading in response to a complaint. An answer may deny the allegations of the complaint, demur to them, admit to them, or introduce affirmative defenses intended to defeat the plaintiff's lawsuit or delay it. One may also assert counterclaims against the plaintiff.
v. 1. To reply. 2. In pleading, to respond to the plaintiff's complaint by denying its allegations or by introducing affirmative defenses containing new matter.
• *n.* defense, reply, denial, rebuttal, refutation, counterclaim ("file an answer to a complaint")
• *v.* reply, respond, defend, controvert ("He answered the plaintiff's complaint by denying the allegations")

appear [a.*peer*]	To enter an appearance in a case. • *v.* surface, attend, arrive, come in, materialize ("appear in court")
appearance [a.*peer*.ense]	1. The action of an attorney in declaring to the court that he represents a litigant in a case before the court (also referred to as "entering an appearance"). 2. The act by which a party comes into court. EXAMPLES: the filing of a complaint by a plaintiff; the filing of an answer by a defendant. • *n.* actualization, entrance, exhibition, materialization, emergence ("The appearance of his attorney was timely")
appearance docket [a.*peer*.ense *dok*.et]	A docket kept by the clerk of court in which appearances are entered.
bill of particulars [bill ov per.*tik*.yoo.lerz]	In civil actions, a more detailed statement of the pleading. An adverse party is entitled to be informed of the precise nature of the opposite party's cause of action or defense, in order to be able to prepare for trial and to protect himself against surprise at the trial.
caption [*kap*.shen]	A heading. As applied in legal practice, when "caption" is used to mean "heading," it generally refers to the heading of a court paper. EXAMPLE:

Miriam Brown   In the Court of Common
Plaintiff   Pleas of Bucks County,
v. Stanley Brown,   Pennsylvania
Scott Lang,
Defendants   Civil Action No. 1234
                             September Term, 1994

• *n.* heading, title, inscription ("the caption of the case")

cause of action [koz ov *ak*.shen]	Circumstances that give a person the right to bring a lawsuit and to receive relief from a court. *See also* complaint.
change of venue [chanj ov *ven*.yoo]	Moving the trial of a case from one county or judicial district to another county or judicial district. The most common reason for a court to permit a change in the venue of a criminal trial is the defendant's inability to receive a fair trial, usually as the result of undue or unfair publicity. The issue is put before the court by means of a motion for change of venue.
civil law [*siv*.el law]	1. Body of law that determines private rights and liabilities, as distinguished from criminal law. 2. The entire body of law adopted in a country or a state, as distinguished from natural law (sometimes called moral law) and from international law (the law governing relationships between countries). 3. The law of the Roman Empire, or modern law that has been handed down from Roman Law. 4. The name of the body of law by which the State of Louisiana is governed.
civil procedure [*siv*.el pro.*see*.jer]	The rules by which private rights are enforced by the courts and agencies. There are both Federal Rules of Civil Procedure, followed in the federal courts, and rules of civil procedure of each of the states.

claimant
[*clay*.ment]

One who claims or makes a claim; an applicant for justice; a plaintiff.
• *n.* petitioner, challenger, plaintiff, appellant, litigant, party, pleader

class action
[klas *ak*.shen]

An action brought by one or several plaintiffs on behalf of a class of persons. A class action may be appropriate when there has been injury to so many people that their voluntarily and unanimously joining in a lawsuit is improbable and impracticable. In such a situation, injured parties who wish to do so may, with the court's permission, sue on behalf of all. A class action is sometimes referred to as a representative action.

clear and convincing evidence
[kleer and kon.*vinss*.ing *ev*.i.denss]

A degree of proof required in some civil cases, higher than the usual standard of preponderance of the evidence.

complaint
[kom.*playnt*]

The initial pleading in a civil action, in which the plaintiff alleges a cause of action and asks that the wrong done to him be remedied by the court.
• *n.* petition, charge, pleading, indictment, accusation ("Susan was served with a complaint")

concurrent jurisdiction
[kon.*ker*.ent joo.ris.*dik*.shen]

Two or more courts having the power to adjudicate the same class of cases or the same matter. *See also* jurisdiction.

counterclaim
[*kown*.ter.klame]

A cause of action on which a defendant in a lawsuit might have sued the plaintiff in a separate action. Such a cause of action, stated in a separate division of a defendant's answer, is a counterclaim. *See also* cross-action; cross-claim; cross-complaint.

court of equity
[kort ov *ek*.wi.tee]

A court having jurisdiction of non-money or equitable actions; a court that administers remedies that are equitable in nature. *Compare* court of law.

court of general jurisdiction
[kort ov *jen*.e.rel joo.ris.*dik*.shen]

Generally, another term for trial court; that is, a court having jurisdiction to try all classes of civil and criminal cases except those that can be heard only by a court of limited jurisdiction.

court of inferior jurisdiction
[*kort* ov in.*feer*.ee.er joo.ris.*dik*.shen]

A court of original or limited jurisdiction.

court of law
[kort ov law]

1. A court having jurisdiction of actions at law, as distinguished from equitable actions. 2. Any court that administers the law of a state or of the United States. *Compare* equitable action.

court of limited jurisdiction
[kort ov *lim*.i.ted joo.ris.*dik*.shen]

A court whose jurisdiction is limited to civil cases of a certain type (EXAMPLE: probate court) or that involve a limited amount of money (EXAMPLE: small claims court), or whose jurisdiction in criminal cases is confined to petty offenses and preliminary hearings.

cross-action
[*kross*-ak.shen]

1. An action brought by a defendant in a lawsuit against another named defendant based upon a cause of action arising out of the same transaction on which the plaintiff's suit is based. *See also* counterclaim. 2. An independent action brought by a defendant in a lawsuit against the plaintiff.

cross-claim [*kross*-klame]	A counterclaim against a plaintiff or a codefendant.
cross-complaint [*kross*-kem.*plaint*]	A complaint a defendant in an action may file: (a) against the *plaintiff*, based upon *any* cause of action she has against him; or (b) against *anyone* (including persons not yet involved in the lawsuit) if she alleges a cause of action based upon the same transactions as those upon which the complaint against her is based.
defendant [de.*fen*.dent]	The person against whom an action is brought. • *n.* accused, respondent, responding litigant, the party charged • *ant.* plaintiff
deposition [dep.e.*zish*.en]	1. The transcript of a witness's testimony given under oath outside of the courtroom, usually in advance of the trial or hearing, upon oral examination or in response to written interrogatories. *See also* discovery. 2. In a more general sense, an affidavit, a statement under oath. • *n.* testimony, sworn testimony, testimony under oath, affidavit, declaration
discovery [dis.*kuv*.e.ree]	1. A means for providing a party, in advance of trial, with access to facts that are within the knowledge of the other side, to enable the party to better try her case. A motion to compel discovery is the procedural means for compelling the adverse party to reveal such facts or to produce documents, books, and other things within his possession or control. *See also* deposition; interrogatories. • *n.* exposure, uncovering, disclosure, investigation, finding, breakthrough, pretrial device
dismiss [dis.*miss*]	To order a case, motion, or prosecution to be terminated. A party requests such an order by means of a motion to dismiss.
diversity jurisdiction [di.*ver*.se.tee joo.ris.*dik*.shen]	The jurisdiction of a federal court arising from diversity of citizenship where parties are residents of different states and the jurisdictional amount has been met.
diversity of citizenship [di.*ver*.se.tee ov *sit*.i.zen.ship]	A ground for invoking the original jurisdiction of a federal district court, the basis of jurisdiction being the existence of a controversy between citizens of different states.
equitable action [*ek*.wi.tebl *ak*.shen]	Although the distinction between a suit in equity and an action at law has been abolished in most states, all actions now being simply civil actions, the concept of an equitable action still exists with respect to the remedy sought, as historically certain types of relief were available only in a court of equity (EXAMPLES: an injunction; specific performance). Equitable actions are designed to remedy injuries that cannot adequately be redressed by an action at law.

in personam action
[in peer.*soh*.nam *ak*.shen]

A legal action whose purpose is to obtain a judgment against a person, as opposed to a judgment against property. Most lawsuits are in personam actions. *See also* jurisdiction in personam. *Compare* in rem action; quasi in rem action.

in rem action
[in rem *ak*.shen]

A legal action brought against property (EXAMPLES: an action to quiet title; a civil forfeiture), as opposed to an action brought against the person.

injunction
[in.*junk*.shen]

A court order that commands or prohibits some act or course of conduct. It is preventive in nature and designed to protect a plaintiff from irreparable injury to his property or property rights by prohibiting or commanding the doing of certain acts. An injunction is a form of equitable relief.
• *n.* ban, stay, order, enjoinder, interdiction, restraint, mandate, prohibition

interplead
[in.ter.*pleed*]

To file an interpleader in a lawsuit.

interpleader
[in.ter.*pleed*.er]

A remedy that requires rival claimants to property held by a disinterested third party (EXAMPLES: a stakeholder; a person who is in debt to the claimants) to litigate their demands without entangling him in their lawsuits.

interrogatories
[in.te.*raw*.ge.toh.reez]

Written questions put by one party to another, or, in limited situations, to a witness in advance of trial. Interrogatories are a form of discovery and are governed by the rules of civil procedure. They must be answered in writing. *Compare* deposition.
• *n.* questions, inquiries

judgment
[*juj*.ment]

1. In a civil action, the final determination by a court of the rights of the parties, based upon the pleadings and the evidence; a decision or decree. 2. In a criminal prosecution, a determination of guilt; a conviction.

jurisdiction
[joo.ris.*dik*.shen]

A term used in several senses: 1. In a general sense, the power and authority of a court to decide lawsuits and bind the parties. EXAMPLES: the right of juvenile courts to hear cases involving juvenile offenders; the power of federal courts to adjudicate federal questions. 2. In a specific sense, the right of a court to determine a particular case; in other words, the power of the court over the subject matter of, or the property involved in, the case at bar. 3. In a geographical sense, the power of a court to hear cases only within a specific territorial area (EXAMPLES: a state; a county; a federal judicial district). *See also* venue. 4. Authority; control; power. 5. District; area; locality. *See also* diversity jurisdiction; subject matter jurisdiction.
• *n.* capacity, authority, authorization, right, charter, judicature, license, sovereignty; territory, region, domain, district, circuit, state, quarter, field, province ("The matter has not been decided in this jurisdiction")

jurisdiction in personam
[joo.ris.*dik*.shen in per.*soh*.nam]

The jurisdiction a court has over the person of a defendant. It is acquired by service of process upon the defendant or by her voluntary submission to jurisdiction. Voluntary submission may be implied from a defendant's conduct within the jurisdiction, for EXAMPLE, by doing business in a state or by operating a motor vehicle within a state. Jurisdiction in personam is also referred to as personal jurisdiction. *See also and compare* jurisdiction in rem; jurisdiction quasi in rem.

jurisdiction in rem
[joo.ris.*dik*.shen in rem]

The jurisdiction a court has over property situated in the state. *See also and compare* jurisdiction in personam; jurisdiction quasi in rem. *See also* in rem action.

jurisdiction quasi in rem
[joo.ris.*dik*.shen *kway*.sye in rem]

The jurisdiction a court has over the defendant's interest in property located within the jurisdiction. *See also and compare* jurisdiction in personam; jurisdiction in rem.

jurisprudence
[joor.is.*proo*.dense]

The science of law; legal philosophy.
• *n.* philosophy, theory, legal foundation, philosophy of law, system of laws

lis pendens
[liss *pen*.denz]

A pending suit or pending action. The doctrine of lis pendens states that a pending suit is notice to all, so buying real estate subject to suit binds the purchaser.

litigation
[lit.i.*gay*.shen]

A legal action; a lawsuit.
• *n.* judicial contest, prosecution, action, lawsuit, case, cause ("Massive amounts of litigation have backlogged the courts")

long arm statutes
[long arm *stat*.shoots]

State statutes providing for substituted service of process on a nonresident corporation or individual. Long arm statutes permit a state's courts to take jurisdiction over a nonresident if she has done business in the state (provided the minimum contacts test is met), or has committed a tort or owns property within the state.

memorandum of law
[mem.o.*ran*.dum ov law]

A written statement submitted to a court for the purpose of persuading it of the correctness of one's position. Similar to a brief, although usually not as extensive, it cites case law and other legal authority.

motion
[*moh*.shen]

1. An application made to a court for the purpose of obtaining an order or rule directing something to be done in favor of the applicant. (EXAMPLE: a defendant's motion to dismiss is a formal request to the court that the plaintiff's lawsuit be terminated without further consideration.) The types of motions available to litigants, as well as their form and the matters they appropriately address, are set forth in detail in the Federal Rules of Civil Procedure and the rules of civil procedure of the various states. Motions may be written or oral, depending on the type of relief sought and on the court in which they are made. Some common motions are motion to produce, motion for entry upon land, and motion to dismiss.
• *n.* request, petition, proposition, plan, demand, offering ("motion to dismiss")

motion for summary judgment
[*mo*.shen for *sum*.e.ree *juj*.ment]

A method of disposing of an action without further proceedings. Under the Federal Rules of Civil Procedure, and the rules of civil procedure of many states, a party against whom a claim, counterclaim, or cross-claim is asserted, or against whom a declaratory judgment is sought, may file a motion for summary judgment seeking judgment in her favor if there is no genuine issue as to any material fact. *See also* motion.

motion to dismiss
[*moh*.shen to dis.*miss*]

Motion requesting a case, motion, or prosecution to be terminated.

order
[*or*.der]

1. A determination made by a court; an order of court. 2. A determination made by an administrative agency.
• *v.* dictate, require, rule, demand, ordain, prescribe
• *n.* decree, command, mandate, demand, judgment ("order of the court")

order to show cause
[*or*.der to show koz]

An order of court directing a party to appear before the court and to present facts and legal arguments showing cause why the court should not take a certain action adversely affecting that party's interests. Orders to show cause are often granted ex parte. A party's failure to appear, or having appeared, his failure to show cause, will result in a final judgment unfavorable to him.

petition
[pe.*tish*.en]

1. A formal request in writing, addressed to a person or body in a position of authority (EXAMPLES: a city council; an administrative agency), signed by a number of persons or by one person. 2. The name given in some jurisdictions to a complaint or other pleading that alleges a cause of action. 3. An application made to a court ex parte. 4. A prayer; a request; an appeal.
• *n.* appeal, request, plea, prayer, motion, application
• *v.* plead, seek, solicit, ask, urge, entreat, apply for ("We petitioned the court for mercy")

plaintiff
[*plain*.tif]

A person who brings a lawsuit.
• *n.* complainant, accuser, suitor, petitioner, opponent, litigant

pleadings
[*plee*.dingz]

Formal statements by the parties to an action setting forth their claims or defenses. EXAMPLES of pleadings include: a complaint; a cross-complaint; an answer; a counterclaim. The various kinds of pleadings, and the rules governing them, are set forth in detail in the Federal Rules of Civil Procedure and, with respect to pleading in state courts, by the rules of civil procedure of several states. *See also* amendment of pleading.

preponderance of the evidence
[pre.*pon*.der.ense ov the *ev*.i.dense]

The degree of proof required in most civil actions. It means that the greater weight and value of the credible evidence, taken as a whole, belongs to one side in a lawsuit rather than to the other side. In other words, the party whose evidence is more convincing has a "preponderance of the evidence" on its side and must, as a matter of law, prevail in the lawsuit because she has met her burden of proof. The expression "preponderance of the evidence" has nothing to do with the number of witnesses a party presents, only with the credibility and value of their testimony.

pretrial [pree.*try*.el]	Prior to trial. "Pretrial" is applied to any aspect of litigation that occurs before the trial begins. USAGE: "pretrial proceedings"; "pretrial motions"; "pretrial conference."
pretrial conference [pree.*try*.el *kon*.fer.ense]	A conference held between the judge and counsel for all parties prior to trial, for the purpose of facilitating disposition of the case by, among other actions, simplifying the pleadings, narrowing the issues, obtaining stipulations to avoid unnecessary proof, and limiting the number of witnesses. Often leads to resolution or settlement of case.
pretrial motions [pree.*try*.el *moh*.shenz]	Motions that may be filed prior to the commencement of a trial. EXAMPLES: a motion to suppress; a motion to dismiss.
procedural law [pro.*seed*.jer.el law]	The means or method by which a court adjudicates cases (EXAMPLES: the Federal Rules of Civil Procedure; the Federal Rules of Criminal Procedure; rules of court), as distinguished from the substantive law by which it determines legal rights. • *n.* process, system, method, policy, routine, action, operation ("Federal Rules of Civil Procedure")
proceeding [pro.*seed*.ing]	1. In one sense, every procedural aspect of a lawsuit, from beginning to end, including all means or process by which a party is able to cause a court to act; a suit; an action. 2. In another sense, any procedural aspect of a lawsuit undertaken to enforce rights or achieve redress. EXAMPLE: a hearing on a motion. 3. A specific course of action. • *n.* undertaking, course, happening ("The divorce proceeding took longer than I thought"); records, minutes, report, account, transactions ("The proceeding from GALA are kept in a file")
quasi in rem action [*kway*.zye in rem *ak*.shen]	An action that adjudicates only the rights of the parties with respect to property, not the rights of all persons who might have an interest in the property. *See also and compare* in personam action; in rem action.
reply [re.*ply*]	1. In pleading, the plaintiff's response to the defendant's setoff or counter-claim. 2. A response; an answer. • *n.* rejoinder, replication, retort, refutation, retaliation, response, answer • *v.* answer, counter, acknowledge, react, return
request for admission [re.*kwest* for ad.*mish*.shen]	Written statements concerning a case, directed to an adverse party, that must be admitted or denied. All will be treated by the court as having been established and need not be proven at trial.
service [*ser*.viss]	The delivering of process; short for service of process. • *n.* notice, notification ("service by mail" or "service by posting")
service by mail [*ser*.viss by mail]	In circumstances where permitted by statute, service of process by mailing a copy to the party to be served at his last known address or by mailing it to his attorney.

service by publication
[ser.*viss* by pub.li.*kay*.shen]

In circumstances where permitted by statute, service of process by publishing it in a newspaper of general circulation in that region.

service of process
[ser.*viss* ov *pross*.ess]

Delivery of a summons, writ, complaint, or other process to the opposite party, or other person entitled to receive it, in such manner as the law prescribes, whether by leaving a copy at her residence, by mailing a copy to her or her attorney, or by publication.

statutes of limitations
[*stat*.shootz ov lim.i.*tay*.shenz]

Federal and state statutes prescribing the maximum period of time during which various types of civil actions and criminal prosecutions can be brought after the occurrence of the injury or the offense.

subject matter jurisdiction
[*sub*.jekt *mat*.er joo.ris.*dik*.shen]

The jurisdiction of a court to hear and determine the type of case before it. EXAMPLE: the jurisdiction of a family court to try cases involving matters of family law.

substantive law
[*sub*.sten.tiv law]

Area of the law that defines rights and responsibilities, law, and facts, as opposed to procedural law, which governs the process by which rights are adjudicated.

summons
[*sum*.enz]

In a civil case, the process by which an action is commenced and the defendant is brought within the jurisdiction of the court.
• *n.* citation, mandate, process, notification, command, direction

third-party complaint
[third-*par*.tee kum.*plaint*]

A complaint filed by the defendant in a lawsuit against a third person whom he seeks to bring into the action because of that person's alleged liability to the defendant.

trial court
[*try*.el kort]

A court that hears and determines a case initially, as opposed to an appellate court; a court of general jurisdiction.

venue
[*ven*.yoo]

The county or judicial district in which a case should be tried. In civil cases, venue may be based on where the events giving rise to the cause of action took place or where the parties live or work. Venue is distinguishable from jurisdiction because it is an issue only if jurisdiction already exists and because, unlike jurisdiction, it can be waived or changed by consent of the parties.
• *n.* county, district, zone, area, neighborhood, place of jurisdiction

verification
[vehr.i.fi.*kay*.shen]

A sworn statement certifying the truth of the facts recited in an instrument or document. Thus, for EXAMPLE, a verified complaint is a pleading accompanied by an affidavit stating that the facts set forth in the complaint are true.
• *n.* confirmation, proof, evidence, corroboration

verified
[*vehr*.i.fide]

Sworn; sworn to; stated under oath.
• *adj.* sworn, sworn to, authenticated

verify
[*vehr*.i.fy]

1. To certify the accuracy or truth of a statement under oath; to make a verification. 2. To establish the accuracy or truth of anything, whether or not by oath.

• *v.* attest, authenticate, confirm, debunk, document, justify, establish, certify; swear, declare, state, avow

Missing Words

Fill in the blanks below.

1. A(n) _____ motion is a method of disposing of an action without further proceedings.

2. A(n) _____ is a sworn statement certifying the truth of the facts recited in an instrument or document.

3. A(n) _____ is an affidavit that certifies that process has been served.

4. A(n) _____ action is designed to remedy injuries that cannot adequately be redressed by an action at law.

5. _____ are statutes prescribing the maximum period of time during which various types of actions can be brought.

6. A(n) _____ is a court that hears and determines a case initially.

7. A(n) _____ is the action of an attorney in declaring to the court that he represents a litigant in a case.

8. In a civil action the final determination by a court of the rights of the parties is _____.

9. A remedy that requires rival claimants to property held by a disinterested third party to litigate their demands without involving the third party in their lawsuit is called _____.

10. A(n) _____ is the plaintiff's answer to the defendant's setoff or counterclaim.

11. A(n) _____ is a defense that amounts to more than simply a denial of the allegations of the plaintiff's complaint.

12. _____ is a means for providing a party, in advance of trial, with access to facts that are within knowledge of the other side, to enable the party to better try the case.

13. A(n) _____ is a cause of action on which a defendant in a lawsuit might have sued a plaintiff in a separate action.

14. A(n) _____ is a counterclaim against a plaintiff or a codefendant.

15. Service of process is the delivery of a(n) _____.

16. A(n) _____ is the person against whom an action is brought.

17. Written statements directed to an adverse party that must be either admitted or denied are called _____.

18. A degree of proof required in some civil cases is _____.

Matching

Match the letter of the definition to the term below.

____ 19. Preponderance of the evidence

____ 20. Interrogatories

____ 21. Summons

____ 22. Motion

____ 23. Litigation

____ 24. Affidavit

____ 25. Judgment

____ 26. Jurisdiction in personam

____ 27. Cross-claim

____ 28. Interpleader

____ 29. Jurisdiction

____ 30. Affirmation

____ 31. Trial court

____ 32. Petition

A. Lawsuit

B. Sworn statement

C. Request to court for relief

D. Jurisdiction the court has over the person of a defendant

E. The name given in some jurisdictions for a complaint

F. Substitute for sworn statement

G. Written questions put by one party to another

H. The jurisdiction of a court to hear and determine the type of case before it

I. The process by which a civil action is commenced and the defendant is brought within the jurisdiction of the court

J. A remedy that requires rival claimants to property held by a disinterested third party to litigate their demands without entangling the third party in the lawsuit

K. A court order that commands or prohibits some act or course of conduct

L. In a civil action, the final determination by a court of the rights of the parties

M. A counterclaim against a plaintiff or a codefendant

N. In a general sense, the right of a court to adjudicate lawsuits and bind the parties

____ 33. Subject matter jurisdiction

    O. A court that hears and determines a case initially

____ 34. Injunction

    P. The degree of proof required in most civil actions

____ 35. Court of inferior jurisdiction

    Q. A court of original or limited jurisdiction

Multiple Choice

Select the best choice.

____ 36. A means for providing a party with access to facts that are within the knowledge of the other side, to enable the party to better try the case is:
    a. diversity
    b. discovery
    c. injunction
    d. equitable action

____ 37. A person who brings a lawsuit is the:
    a. defendant
    b. respondent
    c. plaintiff
    d. stenographer

____ 38. A caption is:
    a. the heading on a pleading or motion
    b. a cause of action
    c. an affirmation
    d. an action

____ 39. The initial pleading in a civil action in which a plaintiff alleges a cause of action and asks that the wrong done him be remedied by the court is the:
    a. counterclaim
    b. answer
    c. cross-claim
    d. complaint

____ 40. An order of the court directing a party to appear and present facts and legal arguments showing cause why the court should not take a certain action adversely affecting that party's interests is a(n):
    a. deposition
    b. summons
    c. petition
    d. order to show cause

____ 41. A long arm statute provides for:
    a. service on a resident
    b. substituted service on a resident
    c. substituted service on a non-resident
    d. service on a nonresident

____ 42. A written statement submitted to the court for the purpose of persuading it of the correctness of one's position is a(n):
    a. memorandum of law
    b. interrogatory
    c. bill of particulars
    d. verification

____ 43. The means or method by which a court adjudicates cases, as distinguished from the substantive law by which it determines legal rights is:
    a. substantive law
    b. procedural law
    c. long arm statute
    d. statute of limitations

_____ **44.** The jurisdiction of a federal court arising from a controversy between citizens of different states is:
  a. jurisprudence
  b. personal jurisdiction
  c. diversity jurisdiction
  d. in personam jurisdiction

_____ **45.** A formal request to the court that the plaintiff's lawsuit be terminated without further consideration is:
  a. interpleader
  b. jurisdiction
  c. order
  d. motion to dismiss

_____ **46.** The county or judicial district in which a case should be tried is:
  a. venue
  b. deposition
  c. caption
  d. class action

_____ **47.** A statement in a pleading of a fact that the party filing the pleading intends to prove is a(n):
  a. affidavit
  b. verification
  c. allegation
  d. action

True/False

Mark the following T or F.

_____ **48.** An action is a judicial proceeding for the enforcement or protection of a right.

_____ **49.** An application to the court for the purpose of obtaining an order or rule is a motion.

_____ **50.** A more detailed statement of the pleadings is the summons.

_____ **51.** The person who brings a lawsuit is the defendant.

_____ **52.** A class action is an action brought by one or several plaintiffs on behalf of a class of persons.

_____ **53.** A counterclaim is a cause of action on which the defendant might have sued the plaintiff in a separate action.

_____ **54.** Litigation is a term for a legal action.

_____ **55.** Civil law is from the law of the Roman Empire.

_____ **56.** A court order that commands or prohibits some act or course of conduct is an injunction.

_____ **57.** A court's jurisdiction is the right of a court to adjudicate lawsuits of a certain kind.

_____ **58.** A deposition is the transcript of a witness's testimony given under oath outside of the courtroom, usually in advance of trial.

_____ **59.** The process by which an action is commenced and the defendant is brought within the jurisdiction of the court is called an affidavit.

_____ **60.** Statutes of limitations detail the maximum period of time during which various types of actions can be brought.

_____ **61.** A verification is a sworn statement certifying the truth of facts recited in an instrument or document.

_____ **62.** An equitable action is brought to remedy injuries that cannot be resolved by an action at law.

Synonyms

Select the correct synonym in parentheses for each numbered item.

63. ACTION
   (proceeding, motion, interpleader)

64. ANSWER
   (demand, inquiry, response)

65. ORDER
   (determination, complaint, reply)

66. PLEADINGS
   (allegations, venue, action)

67. PLAINTIFF
   (respondent, claimant, interpleader)

68. MOTION
   (summons, request, judgment)

69. AFFIDAVIT
   (appearance, discovery, statement)

70. DEFENDANT
   (respondent, petitioner, juror)

71. LITIGATION
   (jurisdiction, lawsuit, reply)

72. VENUE
   (place, caption, pleadings)

73. DISCOVERY
   (order, cross-claim, disclosure)

74. PETITION
    (answer, complaint, reply)

75. AFFIRMATIVE DEFENSE
    (interrogatories, action, excuse)

76. AMENDMENT OF PLEADING
    (correction, appearance, equitable relief)

77. ADVERSARY
    (complaint, opponent, judge)

Self-Test

Place the number of the correct term in the appropriate space.

78. Motion

79. Plaintiff

80. Litigation

81. Counterclaim

82. Summons

83. Complaint

84. Affirmative defenses

85. Answer

86. Civil procedure

87. Discovery

88. Defendant

89. Order

90. Allegations

91. Proceeding

_____ is the rules of procedure by which private rights are enforced. Usually, a dispute or problem arises. In most instances, the parties work their differences out. If not, an attorney might be consulted. Sometimes a simple letter or telephone call is all that is needed. Where the parties refuse to budge from their positions, _____ might be needed, and a judge or jury resolves the dispute. The _____, the person who brings the action, will need to supply the attorney with a set of facts supporting one or more causes of action entitling him to relief. A(n) _____ and _____ will then be drafted and served upon the defendant to start the action or _____.

The _____ must then respond to the _____ contained in the complaint. The defendant usually responds with a(n) _____ denying the plaintiff's claims, and sometimes sets forth new issues. The defendant might allege a new matter that, if proven, could result in a judgment against the plaintiff. These are called _____. Occasionally, defendants will have a(n) _____ in their answer, a cause of action on which a defendant in a lawsuit might have sued the plaintiff in a separate action.

At any point, the parties could still decide to settle their dispute. If not, the case proceeds toward trial. Both sides usually conduct _____ to obtain facts within the knowledge of the other side. A(n) _____, or request to the court for an order or ruling, may be needed if the parties do not voluntarily reply to discovery requests. The judge will then issue a(n) _____ or determination resolving the request.

Defining Words

Complete the definition.

92. Answer _____

_____

93. Plaintiff _____

_____

94. Venue _____

_____

95. Motion _____

_____

96. Jurisdiction _____

_____

97. Litigation _____

_____

98. Affidavit _____

_____

99. Summons _____

_____

100. Interpleader _____

_____

101. Order _____

_____

102. Discovery _____

_____

103. Counterclaim _____

_____

104. Trial court _____

_____

105. Appearance _____

_____

106. Order to show cause _____

_____

Punctuation/Capitalization

Punctuating a series.

In English grammar, a series has three or more members.

the principal and the interest and the penalties
books, magazines, newspapers
laptop, steno machine, and briefcase

Depending upon the configuration of the series, these are the rules:

Rule 1: If there is a coordinate conjunction—*and, but, or, nor*—between each member of the series, there are no commas anywhere in the series.

I paid the light bill and the gas bill and the phone bill from my account.
He had a television and a radio and a CD player in his room.
They amounted to $336 and $429 and $152.

Rule 2: If there are no conjunctions between any members of the series, there is a comma between each member of the series.

I paid the light bill, the gas bill, the phone bill from my account.
He had a television, a radio, a CD player in his room.
They amounted to $336, $429, $152.

The standard series is the listing of the members of the series with a conjunction only before the last member.

a car, a truck, and a van
Nelson, Martino, or Van Deventer
ballpoint, fountain pen, or pencil

Rule 3: When there are no conjunctions between the members of a series except before the last member, there are commas between each member of the series and a comma in front of the conjunction for the last member.

I applied for work at a bank, a savings and loan, and a credit union.
She read Willa Cather, Edgar Allen Poe, and Herman Melville.
We were considering at the time a Toyota, a Honda, or a Ford.

Though some authorities might recommend leaving out the comma before the conjunction at the end of a series, the standard in court reporting is to use the comma before the conjunction. Using the comma ensures that a distinction can be made between two elements that might be separate and two elements that might form a unit. Look at this sentence.

I offered him tuna, ham and cheese.

How many sandwiches are being offered? Is it a tuna sandwich and a ham and cheese sandwich? Or are there three? To always make it clear, use the comma before the conjunction in a series to show the last two members are separate; leave out the comma when the last two members form a unit.

I offered him tuna, ham and cheese.   (two sandwiches)
I offered him tuna, ham, and cheese.   (three sandwiches)

Directions: Make necessary punctuation changes.

1. I was in the positions of VP in charge of sales and VP in charge of marketing and VP in charge of human relations.

2. He was looking to find a home in Los Angeles Seattle or Phoenix.

3. Was she there at 5:00 5:30 or 6:00?

4. Hanson normally sent e-mails faxes snail mail.

5. She needed to take classes in math science and language.

Word Pairs

adverse/averse

adverse = harmful, injurious, hurtful. This word is not usually used to describe a person.

I feel I am working under adverse conditions.
That will be adverse to her interests in the case.
He sent the report under adverse circumstances.

averse = reluctant, unwilling, opposed to. This word is used most frequently after a form of the verb *to be:* i.e., *is, are, was, were.*

He is averse to the new policies.
I am averse to what you want to do with that document.
I think she is averse to that policy.

deposition/disposition

deposition = testimony given under oath outside the courtroom.

The deposition is scheduled for 10:00 A.M.
They think the deposition will go for about two hours.
It was clear she did not understand the nature of the deposition.

disposition = temperament, outcome.

What do you think the disposition of this case will be?
Part of the problem in the relationship is her foul disposition.
I question the ultimate disposition of this.

equable/equitable

equable = even, calm, not extreme. This word usually describes someone's manner.

I always appreciate his equable manner.
Her equable nature makes her easy to be around.
He maintains an equable temperament even during adversity.

equitable = fair, equal.

There was an equitable distribution of the funds.
She argues that it is not equitable.
I am looking for an equitable solution to this dilemma.

plaintiff/plaintive

plaintiff = person who brings the lawsuit.

As the plaintiff in the case, he is trying to collect for the damage to his property.
I want to see whether the plaintiffs can prove their allegations.
It is recommended that the plaintiffs drop the suit.

plaintive = mournful, sad, nostalgic.

We heard the plaintive cry of the dove.

He told the story with a plaintive tone.

Did you hear the plaintive sound in his voice?

procedures/proceedings

procedures = means or method by which a court adjudicates cases.

You need to know more about the procedures used.

She took a course in deposition procedures.

He must learn to follow the procedures that had been set in place.

proceeding = every procedural aspect of a lawsuit. This refers to what is actually going on in a session.

He was not present at the proceedings today.

The proceedings commenced right on time.

A substitute judge presided over the proceedings.

Directions: Circle the correct form of the word.

1. I heard his plaintiff/plaintive cry in response to hearing the news.

2. He did not think it was an equable/equitable solution.

3. I am adverse/averse to anything he might have to say on this.

4. Do you know what the deposition/disposition of the case was?

5. His temper erupted during the procedures/proceedings.

6. My information is that her deposition/disposition is tomorrow.

7. He had an adverse/averse reaction to her stated opinions.

8. The procedures/proceedings were conducted behind closed doors.

9. It is easy to admire his equable/equitable manner.

10. I did not like his combative deposition/disposition.

11. There were some adverse/averse opinions stated in court.

12. Do you think he followed the appropriate procedures/proceedings?

13. The rumor is that she is adverse/averse to the new policies.

14. How do you know it came from the plaintiff/plaintive?

15. The procedures/proceedings were delayed for more than a week.

16. Do you remember when the deposition/disposition was?

17. Those procedures/proceedings have to be followed to the letter.

18. His adverse/averse reaction to the drug almost cost him his life.

19. I was attracted to his equable/equitable nature.

20. A plaintiff/plaintive cry went up from the crowd.

Is It One Word or Two? An Apostrophe? A Hyphen?

it's/its

it's = the contraction for "it is."

I believe it's here in this folder.
It's not a problem unless it's perceived as one.
It's from a blog that he read online.

its = the possessive form of the word.

The company has invested its money wisely.
The United States has its national interest at stake.
The animal caught its foot in the trap that was set.

you're/your

you're = the contraction of "you are."

I think you're the next one in line.
You're not able to participate in the day-to-day activities.
Is there a reason you're still not interested?

your = the possessive form of the word.

I have your credentials here to look at.
Do you have your CV with you today?
She does not have your permission to do that.

they're/their/there

they're = the contraction of "they are."

Do you know whether they're coming with us?
They're not able to access the computer files in that department.
He said they're on the table.

their = the possessive form of the word.

I have their information in my folder.
Their home was ransacked by a burglar.
Do you know whether their employees are paid overtime?

there = an adverb meaning "in that location." This word is also a structure word in the expressions *there is, there are,* et cetera.

I have placed it there on the table for you to see.
There were 150 people involved in the case.
We were sitting there in the middle of the intersection.

Directions: Circle the correct form of the word.

1. You need to accept it's/its effect within the company.

2. Are you sure you're/your car was in good repair?

3. They're/their/there jobs were in jeopardy they're/their/there.

4. Do you know whether it's/its a good idea that you're/your leaving?

5. I know you're/your leaving was intentional.

Proofreading

Directions: Make necessary corrections, based on the material presented in the unit. If the sentence has no errors, write the word *correct* after the sentence.

1. It is clear that it was not an equitable, fair and just decision to release her from prison. _____

2. He is adverse to having you're car left in his driveway overnight. _____

3. They're singing brought a plaintive cry from the neighbors. _____

4. There are openings for the day shift and the swing shift, and the graveyard shift. _____

5. The case and it's disposition is in question at this time because the plaintiff is ill. _____

6. The procedures were followed though there was an adverse reaction to them. _____

7. I know that it is an equitable solution to the situation your facing. _____

8. Jose, Franklin and Richard had there dispositions taken their. _____

9. Your leaving is causing an averse reaction among your colleagues. _____

10. The proceedings were postponed in order to ensure an equable trial for all. _____

An Adaptation from a Civil Litigation/Pretrial Case

Facts:

Jerry's Shell and 21 other complainants sued Equilon, which does business in the United States under the name Shell Oil. The Complaint alleges that Equilon, a joint enterprise of Shell and Texaco, is trying to force independent franchise dealers into company-operated stations who are considered "favored" dealers. Those stations that did not become favored dealers would have difficulty competing through pricing, delayed credit card payments, and failure to make station repairs and improvements. On December 6 of last year, Equilon had served 58 interrogatories directed toward Jerry's Shell and one set of 112 document requests directed to all parties. Counsel for Equilon wrote to appellants and requested an answer to the discovery requests. Equilon filed a motion to compel responses to the interrogatories and the requests for documents as there was no response to the discovery demands. Appellants were ordered to reply and to pay a fine of $1,483.20. Appellants failed to comply, and a second motion to compel was brought. Appellants failed to respond to this motion. Appellants' case was dismissed as a sanction for failure to respond to discovery demands and to the motion to compel.

Issue:

Was the court correct in dismissing appellants' case?

Procedural History:

The court denied the motion for relief from the judgment dismissing appellants' case.

Rationale:

Repeated failure to respond to discovery requests and to comply with court orders compelling discovery provides ample grounds for the imposition of the ultimate sanction of dismissal of a case. When a party is unwilling or counsel is incapable of performing the obligations of litigation with diligence, they should not be surprised when they are no longer allowed to proceed with a case.

Ruling:

Affirm.

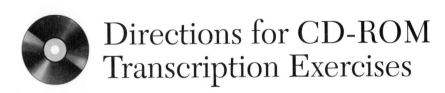

Directions for CD-ROM Transcription Exercises

In audio format are:

1. Terms for the unit with pronunciations from the thesaurus/dictionary feature.

3. Self-Test that appears in the book at mid-unit.°

3. Case that appears at the unit end.°

°speeds are 80 wpm/120 wpm for differing skill levels

CD-ROM icons appear where the three above are located within each unit.

Readers may practice transcription by listening to the CD-ROM where prompted by the icons in the book. However, for high success in testing your transcription skills, mastering all the terms and English skills in the unit is recommended before attempting the CD-ROM.

For Keyboard Transcriptionists: Listen to the CD-ROM audio file for this unit at 80 wpm or 120 wpm and transcribe from the dictation on your computer. Edit and proofread your work against the printed copy in the book.

For Reporting Writers: Listen to the CD-ROM audio file at 80 wpm or 120 wpm and take down the dictation on your writer. Either transcribe from your notes and proofread your work or edit and proofread your CAT (computer-aided transcription) transcript. Always check your work against the printed copy in the book.

Student CD-ROM
For additional materials,
please go to the CD in this book.

Online Companion™
For additional resources, please go to
http://www.paralegal.delmar.cengage.com

Unit 5 | Civil Litigation (Trial and Appeal)

The **Mistakes** That Court Reporters Make and *How to Avoid* Them

The Mistake:

It was Thursday, and Jim Rudetski had arrived at the deposition. This was the fourth day of all-day depositions that Jim had reported in the same case, and he was tired. He opened his trunk to get out his machine—and it was not there. He was panicked. He remembered putting it into the trunk the night before—or did he? Was that the night before last? He had 15 minutes before the deposition was set to begin. He called his office to see whether anyone could get a machine to his location.

How to Avoid It:

Always, always check that you have your machine, laptop, et cetera, before you get into your car to leave for your job—even if you just checked a half hour before. Never leave without checking for your equipment, and you will never be in Jim's position at the deposition.

Introduction

The majority of civil cases are settled before trial. Even fewer cases are appealed than go to trial. Appeals are the exception rather than the rule.

There are separate rules of civil procedure for the federal and state court systems. At the federal level, there are Federal Rules of Civil Procedure, which govern trial practice. At the state level, some states have enacted their own rules of civil procedure, while other states follow a combination of the two sets of rules.

Generally, a trial by jury is not automatic. It is a privilege that must be requested, and is not granted nor permitted in all situations. Some matters are heard by a judge alone and are referred to as bench trials. Even where a jury trial is granted, a judge always remains in the courtroom. The plaintiffs generally have the burden of proof, to demonstrate that they have a cause of action against the defendant at the time of trial.

To avoid the long wait for a trial date, some litigants are selecting alternative dispute resolution (ADR) where methods other than a formal court trial are used to resolve disputes. Some of the methods used are arbitration, conciliation, mediation, and mini-trials. These alternatives are usually quicker, cheaper, and easier for all the parties and do not contribute to the congestion of the courts.

A court that hears and determines cases initially is called a trial court. Sometimes, a party will request that a higher court review the decision of a lower court. This process is called an appeal. Such reconsideration is normally confined to review of the record from the lower court, with no new testimony taken and no new issues raised. Only the judge, or panel of judges (depending on the court), will hear the appeal. A review by a higher court may result in affirmance, reversal, modification, or remand of the lower court's decision. The case at the end of the unit shows how an appeals court affirmed a district court's ruling.

Unit Objectives

- Work with a legal dictionary/thesaurus.
- Learn about the law of civil litigation, particularly trial and appeal.
- Master the similarities and differences in definitions of key terms regarding trial and appeal.
- Master the pronunciations and spellings of legal terms in this unit.
- Recognize the synonyms used for legal terminology in this unit.
- Practice usage of terms, definitions, and synonyms for the trial and appeal stages of civil litigation.
- Complete unit exercises in the forms of missing words, matching, multiple choice, true/false, synonyms, self-test, defining words, and also:
  - Punctuation/capitalization
  - Word pairs
  - Transcription of terms, self-test, and case
  - Proofreading

Dictionary/Thesaurus

Note: All Dictionary/Thesaurus terms appear on the CD-ROM with audio pronunciations.

Term
[phonetic pronunciation]

---

adjudication
[a.joo.di.*kay*.shen]

The final decision of a court, usually made after trial of the case; the court's final judgment.
• *n.* decision, ruling, holding, disposition, pronouncement, verdict, judgment

---

admissible evidence
[ad.*mis*.ibl *ev*.i.dense]

Evidence that a court may admit under the rules of evidence and consider in a case before it.

---

admission
[ad.*mish*.en]

1. A statement of a party to an action that is inconsistent with his claim or position in the lawsuit and which therefore constitutes proof against him.
2. A voluntary statement that something asserted to be true is true. EXAMPLE: the admission of testimony in a trial.
• *n.* confession, acknowledgment, affirmation, declaration, disclosure ("his admission of guilt"); admittance, access, passage ("admission to the bar")

---

affirm
[a.*ferm*]

In the case of an appellate court, to uphold the decision or judgment of the lower court after an appeal.
• *v.* uphold, validate, confirm, ratify ("The decision was affirmed"); declare, assert, maintain, allege ("He affirmed his innocence")

---

alternative dispute resolution
[all.*ter*.ne.tiv dis.*pyoot* res.e.*loo*.shen]

A term for speedier and less costly methods for resolving disputes than going to court. EXAMPLES: arbitration; conciliation; mediation; mini-trial; rent-a-judge; summary jury trial. Also known as ADR.

---

alternative pleading
[all.*ter*.ne.tiv *plee*.ding]

A form of pleading in which the pleader alleges facts that may be inconsistent with each other and contradictory. Such pleading is permissible in most jurisdictions as long as the inconsistent statements, standing alone, are sufficient grounds for a lawsuit.

---

amicus curiae
[a.*mee*.kes *koo*.ree.eye]

(*Latin*) "Friend of the court." A person who is interested in the outcome of the case, but who is not a party, whom the court permits to file a brief for the purpose of providing the court with a position or a point of view that it might not otherwise have. An amicus curiae is often referred to simply as an amicus.

---

appeal
[a.*peel*]

1. The process by which a higher court is requested by a party to a lawsuit to review the decision of a lower court. Such reconsideration is normally confined to a review of the record from the lower court, with no new testimony taken nor new issues raised. Review by a higher court may result in affirmance, reversal, modification, or remand of the lower court's decision.
2. The process by which a court or a higher level administrative body is asked to review the action of an administrative agency. *See also* cross-appeal.
• *n.* petition, review, reexamination ("his appeal to a higher court")

appeal bond [a.*peel* bond]	Security furnished by the party appealing a case to guarantee that the appeal is bona fide.
appellant [a.*pel*.ent]	A party who appeals from the lower court to a higher court. • *n.* appealer, litigant, petitioner, party
appellate court [a.*pel*.et kort]	A higher court to which the appeal is taken from a lower court.
appellate jurisdiction [a.*pel*.et joo.ris.*dik*.shen]	The authority of one court to review the proceedings of another court or of an administrative agency. USAGE: "In our system, the Supreme Court of the United States has ultimate appellate jurisdiction."
appellate review [a.*pel*.et re.*vyoo*]	Review of facts by an appellate court of a case appealed to it from a lower court.
appellee [a.pel.*ee*]	A party against whom a case is appealed from a lower court to a higher court. • *n.* respondent, defendant
arbitration [ar.bi.*tray*.shen]	A method of settling disputes by submitting a disagreement to a person (an arbitrator) or a group of individuals (an arbitration panel) for decision instead of going to court. If the parties are required to comply with the decision of the arbitrator, the process is called binding arbitration; if there is no such obligation, the arbitration is referred to as nonbinding arbitration. Compulsory arbitration, arbitration required by law, most notably in labor disputes. *See also* alternative dispute resolution. *Compare* conciliation; mediation.
award [a.*ward*]	*n.* 1. The decision, decree, or judgment of an arbitrator or administrative law judge. 2. A jury's determination with respect to damages. 3. A court's order for the payment of damages or costs. *v.* To confer, grant, or give.
bar [bar]	*n.* 1. The attorneys permitted to practice before a particular court, taken collectively. 2. The court itself, when one speaks of the "case at bar" or the "bar of justice." *v.* To prevent; EXAMPLE: The case was barred by the statute of limitations.
below [be.*loh*]	1. The court below; a lower court. USAGE: "The appeals court may not uphold the judgment of the court below." 2. In a position of lower rank; inferior. • *adv.* beneath, down, underneath
bench trial [*bench try*.el]	A trial before a judge without a jury; a nonjury trial.
bifurcated trial [*by*.fer.kay.ted *try*.el]	A trial that is divided into two parts to provide separate hearings for different aspects of the same matter, for EXAMPLE, guilt and punishment, guilt and sanity, or liability and damages.

brief
[breef]

1. A written statement submitted to a court for the purpose of persuading it of the correctness of one's position. A brief argues the facts of the case and the applicable law, supported by citations of authority. 2. A text that an attorney prepares to guide her in the trial of a case. Called a trial brief, it can include lists of questions to be asked of various witnesses, points to be covered, and arguments to be made. 3. An outline of the published opinion in a case, made by an attorney or a paralegal for the purpose of understanding the case.
• *n.* legal argument; summary, abstract, digest, outline, synopsis, review, abridgement, restatement

bringing suit
[*bring*.ing sut]

Beginning a lawsuit by filing papers that will result in the court's issuing process compelling the defendant to appear in court.

burden of proof
[*bir*.den ov pruf]

The duty of establishing the truth of a matter; the duty of proving a fact that is in dispute. In most instances the burden of proof, like the burden of going forward, shifts from one side to the other during the course of a trial as the case progresses and evidence is introduced by each side. *See also* prima facie case.

calendar
[*kal*.en.der]

A list of cases ready for the court to dispose of, whether by trial or otherwise; a court calendar. A court calendar is also referred to as a docket. *See also* trial calendar.
• *n.* diary, journal, register, schedule, lineup, program, chronology

calendar call
[*kal*.en.der kol]

The reading aloud of the calendar in court, to determine whether the cases listed are ready for trial or to set trial dates.

certification of record on appeal
[ser.tif.i.*kay*.shen ov *rek*.erd on a.*peel*]

The trial judge's signed acknowledgment of the questions to be decided on appeal. *See also* appeal.

certiorari
[ser.sho.*rare*.ee]

(*Latin*) "To be informed." A writ issued by a higher court to a lower court requiring the certification of the record in a particular case so that the higher court can review the record and correct any actions taken in the case that are not in accordance with the law. The Supreme Court of the United States uses the writ of certiorari to select the state court cases it is willing to review. *See also* certification of record on appeal.

challenge for cause
[*chal*.enj for koz]

An objection, for bias, prejudice, or other stated reason, to a juror being allowed to hear a case. *Compare* peremptory challenge.

conciliation
[kon.sil.ee.*ay*.shen]

The voluntary resolution of a dispute in an amicable manner. One of the primary uses of conciliators, also called mediators, is in settling labor disputes. Professional conciliators are available for that purpose through the Federal Mediation and Conciliation Service. Conciliation differs from arbitration in that a conciliator, unlike an arbitrator, does not render a decision. *See also* alternative dispute resolution; mediation.

confession of judgment [ken.*fesh*.en ov *juj*.ment]	The entry of a judgment upon the admission and at the direction of the debtor, without the formality, time, or effort involved in bringing a lawsuit.
court [kort]	1. A part of government, consisting of a judge or judges, and, usually, administrative support personnel, whose duty it is to administer justice; the judicial branch of government. 2. A place where justice is judicially administered. 3. All judges of the same jurisdiction. For EXAMPLE, all persons who sit as judges of the United States District Court for the Southern District of Texas, taken collectively, constitute "the court" for that judicial district. *Note* that in many instances the words "court" and "judge" are used interchangeably and, in context, have the same meaning. • *n.* unit of government, forum, chamber, panel, bench, bar, justice, judge, session
court below [kort be.*loh*]	A term used by an appellate court, or by attorneys appearing before an appellate court, to refer to the trial court.
court costs [kort kostz]	1. Court fees. 2. The expenses involved in litigating an action (EXAMPLES: witness fees; filing fees, the cost of a transcript), including court fees but excluding attorney fees.
court fees [kort feez]	The charges for the services of a public officer, particularly the clerk of court, rendered in connection with litigation. These are fixed by law. EXAMPLES: the fee for a certified copy of a document; filing fees.
court of appeals [kort ov a.*peelz*]	Often abbreviated as CA, C.A., or Ct. App. 1. A Court of Appeals. 2. The intermediate appellate court in most states, although it is the highest appellate court in some, including New York. 3. A court in which appeals from a lower court are heard.
Court of Appeals of the United States [kort ov a.*peelz* ov the yoo.*ny*.ted states]	The intermediate appellate court in the federal court system, which is divided into 12 geographical circuits (each designated the United States Court of Appeals for that circuit), plus the United States Court of Appeals for the Federal Circuit, which hears appeals in patent, copyright, and customs cases, as well as some appeals from lower courts.
court of record [kort ov *rek*.erd]	Generally, another term for trial court.
court order [kort *or*.der]	1. An adjudication by a court. 2. A ruling by a court with respect to a motion or any other question before it for determination during the course of a proceeding.
court reporter [kort re.*port*.er]	A person who stenographically (*see also* stenographic notes) or by "voice writing" records court proceedings, from which, when necessary, he prepares a transcript that becomes a part of the record in the case.
court reports [kort re.*ports*]	Official, published reports of cases decided by courts, filing the opinions rendered in the case, with headnotes prepared by the publisher.

cross-appeal [kros-a.*peel*]	An appeal filed by the appellee from the same judgment, or some portion of the same judgment, as the appellant has appealed from. A cross-appeal is generally made as part of the review proceedings set in motion by the original appeal.
cross-examination [kross-eg.zam.in.*ay*.shen]	The interrogation of a witness for the opposing party by questions designed to test the accuracy and truthfulness of the testimony the witness gave on direct examination.
defendant in error [de.*fen*.dent in *err*.er]	The party against whom an appeal is taken to a higher court; an appellee.
dicta [*dik*.ta]	Plural of dictum, which is short for the Latin term obiter dictum. Dicta are expressions or comments in a court opinion that are not necessary to support the decision made by the court; they are not binding authority and have no value as precedent. If nothing else can be found on point, an advocate may wish to attempt to persuade by citing cases that contain dicta.
direct examination [de.*rekt* eg.zam.in.*ay*.shen]	The first or initial questioning of a witness by the party who called her to the stand. *Compare* cross-examination.
directed verdict [de.*rek*.ted *ver*.dikt]	A verdict that a jury returns as directed by the judge. A judge directs a verdict when the party who has the burden of proof has failed to meet that burden. A motion for directed verdict is the procedural means by which a litigant requests the court to direct a verdict.
dismissal [dis.*miss*.el]	An order for the termination of a civil action without a trial of its issues, or without further trial. Whether a dismissal is a final judgment against the plaintiff depends upon whether it is a dismissal with prejudice or a dismissal without prejudice. • *n.* termination, discharge
exhibit [eg.*zib*.it]	1. Any paper or thing offered in evidence and marked for identification. 2. A document attached to and made a part of a pleading, transcript, contract, or other legal paper.
expert witness [*eks*.pert *wit*.nes]	A person who is so qualified, either by actual experience or by careful study, as to enable him to form a definite opinion of his own respecting a subject about which persons having no particular training, experience, or special study are incapable of forming accurate opinions.
fact finding body [*fakt* fine.ding *bod*.ee]	A board or body, usually an administrative agency that is empowered to make findings of fact, a conclusion with respect to disputed facts. The finding of fact is reasoned or inferred from the evidence.
high court [hi kort]	An informal way of referring to the Supreme Court of the United States or the highest court in a state judicial system. *See also* highest court.

highest court
[hi.est kort]

The highest court of a state; the Supreme Court of the United States; a court whose decisions are not subject to review by a higher court.

hung jury
[hung *joo*.ree]

A jury that cannot reach a unanimous verdict.

impanel
[im.*pan*.el]

To enroll; to list. The act of the clerk of the court in listing the names of persons who have been selected for jury duty. *See also* jury panel.
• *v.* list, enroll, enter, schedule, docket

impartial juror
[im.*par*.shel *joo*.rer]

A juror who will render a verdict solely on the basis of the evidence.

judgment
[*juj*.ment]

In a civil action, the final determination by a court of the rights of the parties, based upon the pleadings and the evidence; a decision. *See also* confession of judgment.

judgment notwithstanding the verdict
[*juj*.ment not.with.*stan*.ding the *ver*.dikt]

Also referred to as a judgment NOV, a judgment rendered by the court in favor of a party, notwithstanding the fact that the jury has returned a verdict against that party.

judgment NOV
[*juj*.ment en.oh.vee]

Short for judgment non obstante verdicto (judgment notwithstanding the verdict).

judgment on the merits
[*juj*.ment on the *mehr*.its]

A judgment based on the substantive rights of the parties, as distinguished from a judgment based upon procedural points.

judgment on the pleadings
[*juj*.ment on the *plee*.dingz]

A judgment rendered in favor of the defendant when the plaintiff's complaint fails to state a cause of action, or in favor of the plaintiff when the defendant's answer fails to state a legally sufficient defense.

juror
[*joor*.er]

A person on a jury.
• *n.* factfinder, trier of fact, appraiser, arbiter

jury
[*joor*.ee]

A group of women and men selected according to law to determine the truth. Juries are used in various types of legal proceedings, both civil and criminal. *See also* hung jury, petit jury, polling the jury.
• *n.* factfinder, trier of fact, reviewers, panel, veniremen, array, arbiters

jury challenge
[*joor*.ee *chal*.enj]

See challenge for cause; peremptory challenge.

jury instructions
[*joor*.ee in.*struk*.shenz]

Directions given to the jury by the judge just before she sends the jurors out to deliberate and return a verdict, explaining the law that applies in the case and spelling out what must be proven and by whom.

jury panel
[*joor*.ee *pan*.el]

1. The jury list. 2. The jury impaneled for the trial of a particular case. *See also* impanel.

jury trial
[*joor*.ee *try*.el]

A trial in which the jurors are the judges of the facts and the court is the judge of the law. Trial by jury is guaranteed in all criminal cases by the Sixth Amendment, and in many civil cases by the Seventh Amendment. *Compare* bench trial.

leading question
[*lee*.ding *kwes*.chen]

A question put to a witness that suggests the answer the questioner desires. (EXAMPLE: "You did as you were told, didn't you?") Leading questions are generally not allowed on direct examination, but are permitted on cross-examination.

mediation
[mee.dee.*ay*.shen]

The voluntary resolution of a dispute in an amicable manner. One of the primary uses of mediators, also called conciliators, is in settling labor disputes. Professional mediators are available for that purpose through the Federal Mediation and Conciliation Service. Mediation differs from arbitration in that a mediator, unlike an arbitrator, does not render a decision. *See also* alternative dispute resolution; conciliation.

mistrial
[*mis*.try.el]

A trial that has been terminated by the judge prior to its conclusion because the jury is unable to reach a verdict (*see also* hung jury), because of prejudicial error that cannot be corrected or eliminated by any action the court might take (EXAMPLE: the plaintiff's use of racial slurs), or because of the occurrence of some event that would make it pointless to continue (EXAMPLE: the death of a juror). A mistrial is the equivalent of no trial having been held.

notice of appeal
[*noh*.tess ov a.*peel*]

The process by which appellate review is initiated; specifically, written notice to the appellee advising her of the appellant's intention to appeal.

oral argument
[*ohr*.el *ar*.gyoo.ment]

A party, through her attorney, usually presents her case to an appellate court on appeal by arguing the case verbally to the court, in addition to submitting a brief. Oral argument may also be made in support of a motion.

out-of-court settlement
[out-ov-kort *setl*.ment]

1. The ending of a controversy by agreement, before it gets to court.
2. The settlement of a lawsuit after the complaint has been served, and without obtaining or seeking judicial approval.

peremptory challenge
[per.*emp*.ter.ee *chal*.enj]

A challenge to a juror that a party may exercise without having to give a reason. *Compare* challenge for cause.

perfecting an appeal
[per.*fek*.ting an a.*peel*]

Completing all of the steps required by statute for obtaining appellate court review of a judgment.

petit jury
[*pet*.eet *joo*.ree]

The jury in a trial court.

polling the jury
[*pole*.ing the *joo*.ree]

Individually examining the jurors who participated in a verdict to ascertain whether they unanimously support the verdict.

preliminary injunction
[pre.*lim*.i.ner.ee in.*junk*.shen]

An injunction granted prior to a full hearing on the merits. Its purpose is to preserve the status quo until the final hearing. A preliminary injunction is also referred to as a provisional injunction or temporary injunction. *See also* temporary restraining order.

prima facie case
[*pry*.muh *fay*.shee case]

A cause of action or defense that is sufficiently established by a party's evidence to justify a verdict in her favor, provided the other party does not rebut that evidence; a case supported by sufficient evidence to justify its submission to the trier of fact and the rendition of a compatible verdict.

rebuttal
[re.*but*.el]

The stage in a trial or hearing at which a party introduces rebuttal evidence. It occurs after the opposite party has rested her case.

record on appeal
[*rek*.erd on a.*peel*]

The papers a trial court transmits to the appellate court, on the basis of which the appellate court decides the appeal. The record on appeal includes the pleadings, all motions made before the trial court, the official transcript, and the judgment or order appealed from.

reversal
[re.*ver*.sel]

1. The act of an appellate court in setting aside, annulling, or vacating a judgment or order of a lower court. 2. The act of turning a thing or person around, or being turned around.

settlement
[*set*.el.ment]

The ending of a lawsuit by agreement. *See also* out-of-court settlement.
• *n.* resolution, termination ("to reach a settlement")

subpoena
[sub.*peen*.ah]

n. A command in the form of written process requiring a witness to come to court to testify; short for subpoena ad testificandum.
v. To issue or serve a subpoena. *See also* subpoena (noun).
• *v.* order, command, summon, beckon, demand
• *n.* order, command, mandate, citation, summons, writ, call, directive

subpoena ad testificandum
[sub.*peen*.ah ad *tes*.te.fe.*kan*.dem]

(*Latin*) The term ad testificandum means "testify under penalty." A subpoena ad testificandum is a subpoena to testify. *Compare* subpoena duces tecum.

subpoena duces tecum
[sub.*peen*.ah *doo*.ses *tee*.kum]

(*Latin*) The term duces tecum means "bring with you under penalty." A subpoena duces tecum is a written command requiring a witness to come to court to testify and at that time to produce for use as evidence the papers, documents, books, or records listed in the subpoena.

summary jury trial (SJT)
[*sum*.e.ree *joor*.ee *try*.el]

A court-ordered form of alternative dispute resolution sometimes used by the federal courts in complex cases that would otherwise require a lengthy jury trial. An SJT is a kind of nonbinding capsule trial that allows the parties to obtain the thoughts of jurors with respect to the merits of the case. The facts are presented in simplified form to a reduced jury, questions of admissibility of evidence are decided with the judge in advance, and counsel interview the jurors after the verdict. Although the verdict is nonbinding, the parties may agree to be bound by it, or they may settle the case based upon the reactions of the jurors.

summary proceeding
[*sum*.e.ree pro.*seed*.ing]

A proceeding in which a case is disposed of or a trial is conducted in a prompt and simple manner without a jury and without many of the ordinary requirements (such as complaint, summons, indictment, or information). EXAMPLES: a contempt proceeding; trial before a magistrate or a justice of the peace; trial in a small claims court.

summary remedy
[*sum*.e.ree *rem*.e.dee]

In a civil action, a remedy obtainable in a summary proceeding.

temporary restraining order (TRO)
[*tem*.pe.rer.ee re.*strane*.ing *or*.der]

The court is empowered to grant injunctive relief to one party, without notice to the opposite party, if the result would cause "immediate and irreparable harm or loss."

transcript
[*tran*.skript]

A typewritten copy of the court reporter's stenographic notes of a trial, i.e., a record of the proceedings.

transcript of the record
[*tran*.skript ov the *rek*.erd]

The complete record of a case as furnished to the appellate court when an appeal is taken.

trial
[*try*.el]

1. A hearing or determination by a court of the issues existing between the parties to an action; an examination by a court of competent jurisdiction, according to the law of the land, of the facts or law at issue in either a civil case or a criminal prosecution, for the purpose of adjudicating the matters in controversy. *See also* bench trial; bifurcated trial; jury trial; mistrial.
• *n.* citation, hearing, litigation, prosecution, suit ("trial by jury")

trial by jury
[*try*.el by *joor*.ee]

A trial in which the jurors are the judges of the facts and the court is the judge of the law. Trial by jury is guaranteed in all criminal cases by the Sixth Amendment, and in most civil cases by the Seventh Amendment. *Compare* trial by the court. *Also compare* bench trial; *see also* jury trial.

trial by the court
[*try*. el by the kort]

A trial held before a judge sitting without a jury. A trial by the judge alone is also referred to as a judge trial, a bench trial, or a nonjury trial. *Compare* trial by jury.

trial calendar
[*try*.el *kal*.en.der]

A list of cases awaiting trial.

trial court
[*try*.el kort]

A court that hears and determines a case initially, as opposed to an appellate court; a court of general jurisdiction.

trial de novo
[*try*.el deh *noh*.voh]

A new trial, a retrial, or a trial on appeal from a justice's court or a magistrate's court to a court of general jurisdiction. A trial de novo is a trial in which the matter is tried again as if it had not been heard before and as if no decision had previously been rendered.

trial judge
[*try*.el juj]

The judge who presides at the trial of a case.

trial jury [*try*.el *joor*.ee]	A jury for the trial of a case, as distinguished from a grand jury.
verdict [*ver*.dikt]	The final decision of a jury concerning questions of fact submitted to it by the court for determination in the trial of a case. In a civil case, the jury may be required to return either a general verdict or a special verdict. *See also* judgment notwithstanding the verdict. • *n.* adjudication, arbitration, conclusion, decision, decree
verdict against the evidence [*ver*.dikt a.*genst* the *ev*.i.dense]	A verdict that is contrary to the evidence, or to the weight of the evidence, or that is not supported by sufficient evidence.
verdict contrary to law [*ver*.dikt *kon*.trare.ee to law]	The verdict of a jury that has failed to follow the instructions of the judge with respect to matters of law.
voir dire examination [vwa deer eg.zam.i.*nay*.shen]	Examination of a potential juror for the purpose of determining whether she is qualified and acceptable to act as a juror in the case. A prospective juror who a party decides is unqualified or unacceptable may be challenged for cause or may be the subject of a peremptory challenge.
witness [*wit*.nes]	*n.* 1. A person who testifies or gives evidence before a court or at an administrative hearing with respect to something she has observed or of which she has knowledge. *See also* expert witness. 2. A person who is asked to be present at a transaction (for EXAMPLE, the signing of a contract) in order to attest that it took place. *v.* 1. To see or observe. 2. To attest; to act as an observer for the purpose of attesting.

Missing Words

Fill in the blanks below.

1. _____ is a person who is not a party to a case, whom the court permits to file a brief.

2. The first or initial questioning of a witness by the party who called her to the stand is _____.

3. Any paper or thing offered in evidence and marked for identification is called a(n) _____.

4. A group of women and men selected according to law to determine the truth is a(n) _____.

5. Directions given to the jury by the judge just before sending jurors out to deliberate are _____.

6. A(n) _____ is a challenge to a juror that a party may exercise without having to give a reason.

7. The jury in a trial court is known as the _____, as distinguished from the grand jury.

8. Written notice to the appellee advising of appellant's intention to appeal is called a(n) _____.

9. The _____ is a written list of cases awaiting trial.

10. The judge who presides at the trial of a case is known as _____.

11. _____ is when jurors who participated in a verdict are examined to see whether they unanimously support the verdict.

12. A person who is qualified, either by actual experience or by careful study, to form a definite opinion of his own respecting a subject is a(n) _____.

13. A(n) _____ is a written command requiring a witness to come to court to testify and at that time to bring documents listed in the subpoena.

14. A(n) _____ occurs where a trial is terminated by the judge because the jury cannot reach a verdict.

15. _____ is the voluntary resolution of a dispute in an amicable manner through the use of mediators who do not render a decision.

16. A(n) _____ is a judgment notwithstanding the verdict. A judgment is rendered by the court in favor of a party, notwithstanding the fact that the jury has returned a verdict against the party.

17. A(n) _____ is a writ issued by a higher court to a lower court requiring the certification of the record, so the higher court can review the record and correct any actions not in accordance with the law.

18. In a civil case, a remedy obtainable in a summary proceeding is called _____.

19. A case on appeal is verbally presented to the appellate court by _____.

20. A(n) _____ is empowered to make findings of fact, a conclusion with respect to disputed facts in a legal action.

Multiple Choice

Select the best choice.

_____ 21. The process by which a higher court is requested by a party to a lawsuit to review the decision of a lower court is:
   a. an amicus curiae
   b. an appeal
   c. a peremptory challenge
   d. a challenge for cause

_____ 22. A jury that cannot reach a unanimous verdict is:
   a. a hung jury
   b. a petit jury
   c. a grand jury
   d. none of the above

_____ 23. Any papers or things offered in evidence and marked for identification are called:
   a. expert witnesses
   b. oral argument
   c. exhibits
   d. amicus curiae

_____ 24. Arbitration, conciliation, mediation, and mini-trials are speedier and less costly methods for resolving disputes than going to court. These are examples of:
   a. certiorari
   b. impaneling the jury
   c. voir dire
   d. alternative dispute resolution

_____ 25. A written statement submitted to the court for the purpose of persuading it of the correctness of one's position is a:
   a. brief
   b. judgment
   c. rebuttal
   d. challenge for cause

_____ 26. The act of the clerk of the court in listing the names of persons who have been selected for jury duty is called:
   a. affirm
   b. impanel
   c. appeal
   d. reversal

_____ 27. The final decision of a jury concerning questions of fact submitted to it by the court for determination in the trial of a case is the:
   a. verdict
   b. judgment
   c. judgment NOV
   d. mistrial

_____ 28. A subpoena duces tecum is a written command requiring:
   a. a witness to tell the truth
   b. a witness to come to court to testify
   c. a witness to come to court to testify and bring records listed in the subpoena
   d. a witness to plead the Fifth Amendment and refuse to testify

_____ 29. Leading questions that suggest the answer the questioner desires are usually used during:
   a. direct examination
   b. cross-examination
   c. rebuttal
   d. jury instructions

_____ 30. A prospective juror whom a party decides is unqualified or unacceptable may be challenged for cause or may be the subject of a peremptory challenge during:
   a. an out-of-court settlement
   b. voir dire
   c. oral argument
   d. jury instructions

_____ 31. In a civil action, the final determination by a court of the rights of the parties based upon the pleadings and evidence is the:
   a. appeal
   b. notice of appeal
   c. judgment
   d. verdict

_____ 32. A trial that has been terminated by a judge prior to its conclusion because of a hung jury, or prejudicial error, is called:
   a. a mistrial

   b. arbitration
   c. alternative dispute resolution
   d. confession of judgment

_____ 33. A person who is interested in the outcome of the case, but who is not a party, whom the court permits to file a brief for the purpose of providing the court with a position that it might not otherwise have is a(n):
   a. prima facie case
   b. appellant
   c. appellee
   d. amicus curiae

_____ 34. The process by which appellate review is initiated is:
   a. oral argument
   b. rebuttal
   c. voir dire
   d. notice of appeal

Matching

Match the letter of the definition to the term below.

_____ 35. Record on appeal

A. The duty of establishing the truth of a matter; the duty of proving a fact that is in dispute

_____ 36. Leading question

B. A question put to a witness that suggests the answer the questioner desires

_____ 37. Settlement

C. The stage in a trial or hearing at which a party introduces rebuttal evidence

_____ 38. Burden of proof

D. A command requiring a witness to come to court and testify

_____ 39. Verdict

E. A case is presented to the appellate court by arguing the case verbally to the court

_____ 40. Reversal

F. The ending of a lawsuit by agreement

_____ 41. Rebuttal

G. The final decision of a jury concerning questions of fact submitted to it by the court in the trial of a case

_____ 42. Alternative dispute resolution

H. Examination of a potential juror for the purpose of determining whether she is qualified to act as a juror

_____ 43. Confession of judgment

   I. The act of an appellate court in setting aside, annulling, or vacating a judgment or order of a lower court

_____ 44. Transcript

   J. A typewritten copy of the court reporter's stenographic notes of a trial

_____ 45. Subpoena

   K. A final determination by a court of the rights of the parties

_____ 46. Judgment

   L. An objection, for a stated reason, to a juror being allowed to hear a case

_____ 47. Challenge for cause

   M. Entry of judgment upon admission and at the direction of the debtor, without bringing a lawsuit

_____ 48. Oral argument

   N. The papers a trial court transmits to the appellate court, on the basis of which the appellate court decides the appeal

_____ 49. Voir dire

   O. A term for speedier and less costly methods for resolving disputes than going to court

True/False

Mark the following T or F.

_____ 50. The process by which a higher court reviews the decision of a lower court is called an appeal.

_____ 51. The ending of a controversy through a court trial is called an out-of-court settlement.

_____ 52. Arbitration is a method of settling disputes by submitting a disagreement to a person, or group of individuals, for decision instead of going to court.

_____ 53. A witness is a person who testifies or gives evidence before a court or at an administrative hearing with respect to something observed or of which he has knowledge.

_____ 54. Jury instructions are the papers the trial court transmits to the appellate court, on the basis of which the appellate court decides the appeal.

_____ 55. A confession of judgment is the stage in a trial or hearing at which a party introduces rebuttal evidence.

_____ 56. The act of an appellate court in setting aside, annulling, or vacating a judgment or order of a lower court is called certiorari.

_____ 57. The appellee is a party against whom a case is appealed from a lower court to a higher court.

____ 58. An appeal bond is security furnished by the party appealing a case to guarantee that the appeal is bona fide.

____ 59. Direct examination is the first or initial questioning of a witness by the party who called her to the stand.

____ 60. Mediation is the same as arbitration; a mediator resolves a dispute by issuing a decision.

____ 61. The final determination by a jury of the rights of the parties is called a judgment.

____ 62. When an appellate court sets aside a judgment of the lower court, this is a reversal.

Synonyms

Select the correct synonym in parentheses for each numbered item.

63. AFFIRM
    (uphold, compare, reverse)

64. JURY
    (factfinders, witness, expert)

65. SUBPOENA
    (play, command, certiorari)

66. JUDGMENT
    (transcript, mediation, ruling)

67. EXHIBIT
    (document, appeal, rebuttal)

68. APPEAL
    (reverse, review, settle)

69. TRIAL COURT
    (higher court, appellate court, court below)

70. DISMISSAL
    (termination, continuation, change)

71. SETTLEMENT
    (reversal, resolution, continuation)

72. HUNG JURY
    (unanimous, undecided, concerned)

73. BENCH TRIAL
    (jury trial, nonjury trial, arbitration)

74. TRIAL
    (verdict, mediation, hearing)

75. APPELLANT
    (respondent, petitioner, defendant)

76. IMPANEL
    (to list, to accuse, to defend)

77. MISTRIAL
    (jury instructions, hung jury, polling the jury)

78. REVERSAL OF JUDGMENT
    (to sustain, to restrain, to vacate)

79. ADJUDICATION
    (disposition, summons, petition)

Self-Test

Place the number of the correct term in the appropriate space.

80. Appeal

81. Verdict

82. Subpoena duces tecum

83. Petit jury

84. Challenges for cause

85. Jury

86. Burden of proof

87. Direct examination

88. Judgment

89. Witnesses

90. Trial

91. Leading questions

92. Voir dire examination

93. Peremptory challenges

94. Expert witness

95. Proceedings

A(n) _____ is a hearing by a court of the issues existing between the parties to an action. A case might be heard solely by a judge, or a dispute might be heard by a(n) _____ , which is called a(n)

_____ to distinguish it from a grand jury proceeding. In order to select a fair and impartial group of jurors to try a matter, the attorneys first proceed with a(n) _____ to determine if jurors are qualified and acceptable to act as jurors in a particular case. Attorneys can exercise _____ to eliminate some jurors without reason, and _____ to eliminate biased or prejudiced jurors.

After a group of jurors is determined to be acceptable by both sides, the jurors will be sworn in to hear the case.

The party with the _____ will generally try their side of the case first. This is done through the introduction of various _____ who will testify about what they said and observed.

A(n) _____ may be used to command a witness to bring documents to court. Sometimes a(n) _____ is needed to testify about matters concerning his particular field of expertise or training. Information is initially brought out through _____ of the witnesses. Thereafter, the attorney for the opposing party will usually conduct cross-examination by use of _____ to narrow the issues in dispute and pinpoint the weakness in a witness's testimony or recall.

At the end of the trial, the jury will issue a(n) _____. Then a(n) _____ will be entered by the court. It is then up to the losing party to decide if they wish to continue with litigation and take a(n) _____ or accept the result of the _____.

Defining Words

Complete the definition.

96. Appeal _____
_____

97. Settlement _____
_____

98. Alternative dispute resolution _____
_____

99. Jury _____
_____

100. Voir dire _____
_____

101. Witness _____

_____

102. Expert _____

_____

103. Subpoena _____

_____

104. Appellant _____

_____

105. Transcript _____

_____

106. Rebuttal _____

_____

107. Challenge for cause _____

_____

108. Mistrial _____

_____

109. Arbitration _____

_____

110. Fact finding body _____

_____

Punctuation/Capitalization

Punctuating the compound sentence.

One of the most basic rules in all of punctuation is the rule for the comma in a compound sentence. To understand this rule, you need to know a couple of basic definitions:

A *coordinate conjunction* links grammatically equal parts. The most common coordinate conjunctions are *and, but, or, nor.*

not where to go but what to do
on the table or on the counter
to read and to sleep

An *independent clause* has a subject and verb and stands alone as a complete thought.

He was standing near the intersection of the two streets.
Did you go with her to the doctor?
The boss always thought that about me.

A *dependent clause* has a subject and verb but does not stand alone to express a complete thought.

while you were with her
because he had nowhere to go
that she didn't want to stay

A *compound sentence* is two independent clauses that are linked by a coordinate conjunction.

I talked to her that morning, and we had dinner that night.
The driver seemed to be incoherent, but I am not sure about the passenger.
Will you bring it to my office, or will you deliver it to headquarters?

Rule 1: When two independent clauses are joined by a coordinate conjunction, there is a comma before the coordinate conjunction. In the following examples, focus on the independent subject and verb after the coordinate conjunction to determine whether a comma goes before the conjunction.

I called the manager early about the issue, but I got no response.
The car was coming from the left, and it didn't seem to be slowing down.
Did you deposit it into your personal account, or did you give it to her?

Rule 2: When there is not a subject and a verb that can stand alone after a coordinate conjunction, there is no comma before the conjunction. When there is no subject for the verb after the conjunction, the comma is no longer correct because there is not an independent clause after the conjunction.

Did you meet with the CEO or talk to him on the phone?
He had contracted a rare virus in Africa but had not returned home at that time.
I was traveling in an easterly direction and was encountering little traffic.

Notice that in these sentences it is simply the grammatical construction that makes the difference in the punctuation. When there is a subject and verb in a complete sentence after a coordinate conjunction, there is a comma; when there is not a subject and verb in a complete sentence after a coordinate conjunction, there is not a comma.

I called the manager early about the issue, but I got no response.
I called the manager early about the issue but got no response.

The car was coming from the left, and it didn't seem to be slowing down.
The car was coming from the left and didn't seem to be slowing down.

Did he mail the copy to you, or did he give it to you personally?
Did he mail the copy to you or give it to you personally?

Directions: Make necessary punctuation changes.

1. Was he contributing to the problem or trying to solve it?

2. We were driving northbound in the left lane, and we turned left at the intersection.

3. The bank had foreclosed on the house and was taking it away from us.

4. Did you want to move up in the company or did you want to stay where you were?

5. He called upon us to speak up about the issues but he didn't seem to take us seriously.

Word Pairs

alternate/alternative

alternate = off and on, fluctuate, take turns, every other, substitute.

The father will have the child on alternate weekends.
His alternate filled in for the evening.
Her moods alternated between hysteria and calm.

alternative = different choice, option, nontraditional.

He enjoys an alternative lifestyle that is not acceptable to his parents.
There seemed to be no alternatives for her.
We offered him alternatives to having the meeting.

appellant/appellate

appellant = party who appeals from the lower court to a higher court.

There are four appellants in this matter.
The case was decided on behalf of the appellants.
He is the appellant in the case before the court.

appellate = higher court to which the appeal is taken from a lower court.

The case was appealed to the appellate level.
She is a judge in an appellate court.
The appellate case gave her the opportunity to express her views.

calendar/calender/colander

calendar = chart, timetable, schedule.

Put that date on your calendar so that you do not forget.
I intend to calendar that for next week.
One of my jobs was to keep her calendar.

calender = rollers for treating cloth or paper. This word is both the name of the machine and the verb that describes the process.

It was calendered as the concluding step in the process.
He caught his hand underneath the calender.
The calendering process took a long while.

colander = strainer.

I bought a colander for his new kitchen.
The colander could not hold the entire batch of noodles.
It is a colander I saw on television.

mediation/meditation

mediation = voluntary resolution of a dispute in an amicable manner. The verb form is *mediate*.

We submitted the case to mediation.
The mediation proved to be ineffective.
All parties to the mediation seemed to want to work it out amicably.

meditation = quiet contemplation. The verb form is *meditate*.

He says his daily meditation is important to him.
She sat in quiet meditation during the worst of the trial.
I know that the meditation helped get me through the problems.

pole/poll

pole = several meanings

- endpoints of the earth, as in *the North Pole*.
- end of a magnet, as in *opposite poles*.
- object that is long and straight, as in *used a pole to reach it*.
- first position in a car race, as in *the pole position*.

They are at opposite ends of the pole politically.
He was the first to arrive at the South Pole.
She aspired to be a pole vaulter.

poll = take a tally or census or survey.

The judge decided to poll the jury individually.
The polls indicated he would be soundly defeated.
I was asked to participate in a public opinion poll.

suit/suite/sweet

suit = case brought to a court of law, matching clothing, be right or convenient to someone.

He brought suit in Superior Court over the fence issue.
The new accommodations do not suit me.
It is necessary for you to wear a suit and tie.

suite = set of rooms, matching furniture, collection of application programs on the computer.

The suite was too expensive for us.
We used the Microsoft Office Suite in our firm.
They needed a suite to fit the entire group.

sweet = tasting of sugar, not salty or bitter, pleasant.

She enjoys sweets after each meal.
She is a really sweet child.
It is the sweet taste that appeals to everyone.

Directions: Choose the correct form of the word.

1. I need a new suit/suite/sweet to make a good impression at the job interview.

2. Do you know that they did alternate/alternative during the spring?

3. She is an appellate/appellant in this part of the proceeding.

4. He was an alternate/alternative juror on the death penalty case.

5. I use that suit/suite/sweet on my laptop at home but not on my PC at work.

6. He was involved in the calendaring/calendering/colandering process in the factory.

7. You have left me with no alternate/alternative but to leave.

8. Did they pole/poll everyone in the company on that?

9. He did not think that mediation/meditation would solve their differences in the case.

10. Did he believe you had the pole/poll position for the race?

11. In the situation that existed, I felt I had no alternate/alternative but to quit.

12. He has worked his way up to serve at the appellate/appellant level in the court system.

13. The issue was the calendaring/calendering/colandering of the trial dates.

14. I believe in going to alternate/alternative medicine for a cure.

15. Did you believe the length of the pole/poll was the problem in the construction?

16. How far did you go to find an alternate/alternative to replace you?

17. The case was decided in favor of the appellates/appellants.

18. He sat quietly in mediation/meditation as he waited for the verdict.

19. The children will be with each parent on alternate/alternative weeks in the summer.

20. It does not suit/suite/sweet her purposes to be so antagonistic.

Is It One Word or Two? An Apostrophe? A Hyphen?

always/all ways

always = forever, for all times. The form is an adverb.

He is always with her.
I always wanted to work in a bank.
It was always a problem in the office when she was around.

all ways = by every method, by any means. This form is the adjective *all* as it modifies the noun *ways*.

It satisfied my creative desires in all ways.
She was a good worker in all ways that mattered.
We tried all ways we knew to convince her.

maybe/may be

maybe = possibly, perhaps. This form is an adverb.

He said maybe he would join us later.
Maybe you can read that back to us if we need it.
I know that he maybe will be joining us.

may be = possible, it could be. This form is the helping verb *may* with a main verb *be*.

He may be here with us later.
It may be that she is lying to you.
He thinks they may be in his desk at work.

Directions: Choose the correct form of the word.

1. It maybe/may be that he cannot attend.

2. I am looking for always/all ways to work on the issue.

3. He can maybe/may be see you in about ten minutes.

4. Is he always/all ways so pleasant?

5. It is my thought that he maybe/may be able to help us.

Proofreading

Directions: Make necessary corrections, based on the material presented in the unit. If the sentence has no errors, write the word *correct* after the sentence.

1. Did the alternate arrive in time or did you have to delay the proceedings? _____

2. The pole indicated that there would all ways be dissenters. _____

3. I spoke to the appellate, and told him he would have to alter his suit somewhat. _____

4. The meditation proceeding is calendared for Friday but it maybe postponed. _____

5. She is meditating in the office suite on company time, and it irritates everyone. _____

6. His alternative lifestyle really bothers his mother but is okay with his father. _____

7. The poll was too short to support the weight of the calendering machine. _____

8. There may be a chance, but I doubt the validity of the pole they took among the voters. _____

9. It was decided by the appellate court, and overruled by the higher court. _____

10. His job was to mediate the situation between the appellate and his opponent. _____

An Adaptation from a Trial/Appeal Case

Facts:

Elena Granada worked for Allstate Insurance as a marketing business consultant (MBC). Allstate set a deadline of October 31 for all of the MBCs to pass certain required exams for licensing. Of the 31 MBCs, Granada was the only one who did not pass the exams and obtain her license by the deadline. Granada's employment was terminated, and she was replaced by a male employee. She claimed sex discrimination and retaliation.

Procedural History:

During a trial of this matter, the employer Allstate made a motion for summary judgment, which was granted. The Court found that Granada could not establish a prima facie case of sex discrimination because she was not qualified as a MBC and that further she had not proved that Allstate's reason for discharging her—failure to pass the examination by the October deadline—was a pretext for discrimination. The matter is now on appeal to the Court of Appeals.

Issue:

Did the District Court err in failing to grant Allstate's motion for summary judgment?

Rationale:

The appeals court reviewed the District Court's grant of summary judgment de novo. "We will affirm if, viewing the record in the light most favorable to the nonmoving party, there are no genuine issues of material fact; then the moving party is entitled to judgment, as a matter of law." In order to establish a genuine issue of fact, it is not enough for the moving party to merely rest on the pleading or rely on conclusory statements. You must point to specific evidence in the record to raise a genuine issue for trial.

Ruling:

We affirm the ruling of the District Court.

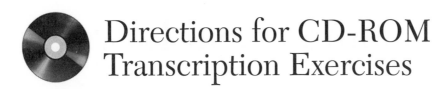

Directions for CD-ROM Transcription Exercises

In audio format are:

1. Terms for the unit with pronunciations from the thesaurus/dictionary feature.

2. Self-Test that appears in the book at mid-unit.*

3. Case that appears at the unit end.*

*speeds are 80 wpm/120 wpm for differing skill levels

CD-ROM icons appear where the three above are located within each unit.

Readers may practice transcription by listening to the CD-ROM where prompted by the icons in the book. However, for high success in testing your transcription skills, mastering all the terms and English skills in the unit is recommended before attempting the CD-ROM.

For Keyboard Transcriptionists: Listen to the CD-ROM audio file for this unit at 80 wpm or 120 wpm and transcribe from the dictation on your computer. Edit and proofread your work against the printed copy in the book.

For Reporting Writers: Listen to the CD-ROM audio file at 80 wpm or 120 wpm and take down the dictation on your writer. Either transcribe from your notes and proofread your work or edit and proofread your CAT (computer-aided transcription) transcript. Always check your work against the printed copy in the book.

Student CD-ROM
For additional materials,
please go to the CD in this book.

Online Companion™
For additional resources, please go to
http://www.paralegal.delmar.cengage.com

Area of Law

Commercial Law

The **Mistakes** That Court Reporters Make and *How to Avoid* Them

The Mistake:

As a fairly new deposition reporter, Joshua Schneider decided he wanted to make more money and would work more. He put his name out there and got calls every day. He went out for two weeks straight on a total of 14 jobs. Because he was working so much, he had postponed doing the scoping* work on the transcripts. The first jobs were due in the office, and he had not even begun to work on them. By the end of the third week, he had to take himself off calendar because he was so far behind. And his good name was damaged because he was late with the work for so many clients.

How to Avoid It:

The job is the complete package: going to the deposition and taking it down, getting it scoped and proofread, and turning it in to the office. There is usually a ten-day to two-week turnaround on getting the job to the client. It is crucial to pace yourself. Set a time limit to begin scoping a job. When you begin to get backlogged, do something right then to get yourself out of the hole. Temporarily cut back on social activities. Take fewer jobs. Pacing is everything to maintain your sanity and your reputation in this job.

Scoping is the editing of the transcript: that is, fixing nontranslates, putting in or removing punctuation, changing word errors. This prepares the transcript for proofreading.

Introduction

A person who regularly trades in a particular type of goods is called a merchant. Years ago most merchants depended on their family, friends, and relatives who lived nearby to purchase their goods. Most transactions were informal transactions, conducted face to face and settled with a handshake. A merchant usually knew the financial standing of purchasers and might even accept a barter or trade arrangement to help out friends who were short on cash.

Now business transactions are much more impersonal. Usually a merchant will not be familiar with the person or corporation that wishes to purchase goods. A field of law has developed that relates to shipping, insurance, the exchange of money, brokerage, drafts, promissory notes, and other matters of concern to merchants; this is called commercial law. To protect merchants who are involved in interstate commerce, the Uniform Commercial Code (UCC) was developed, which deals with most areas of commercial transactions and has been adopted in much the same form in most states.

Article 3 of the Uniform Commercial Code regulates commercial paper, also known as negotiable instruments. These include checks, drafts, certificates of deposit, and promissory notes. The Uniform Commercial Code defines a negotiable instrument as a signed writing that orders or promises payment of money if: it is unconditional, it is in a fixed amount, it is payable on demand to bearer or to order or at a definite time, and it "does not state any undertaking or instruction by the person promising or ordering payment to do any act in addition to the payment of money."

Commercial paper helps facilitate commercial transactions. It's both a substitute for cash and can be used as a device to extend credit.

Unit Objectives

- Work with a legal dictionary/thesaurus.
- Learn about commercial law and commercial paper.
- Master the similarities and differences in definitions of key terms regarding commercial law and commercial paper.
- Master the pronunciations and spellings of legal terms in this unit.
- Practice usage of terms, definitions, and synonyms for commercial law and commercial paper.
- Complete unit exercises in the forms of missing words, matching, multiple choice, true/false, synonyms, self-test, defining words, and also:
  - Punctuation/capitalization
  - Word pairs
  - Transcription of terms, self-test, and case
  - Proofreading

⊙ Dictionary/Thesaurus

Term
[phonetic pronunciation]

---

acceptance
[ak.*sep*.tense]

1. With respect to negotiable instruments, the agreement of the bank or other drawer to honor a draft, check, or other negotiable instrument. Acceptance, which must be indicated on the instrument, in writing, is an acknowledgment by the drawee that the drawer has sufficient funds on deposit to cover the draft. *See also* certified check. 2. In the law of sales, the acceptance of the goods that are the subject of the sale has an important bearing upon the passage of title from the buyer to the seller per the contract.
• *n.* acquisition, reception, adoption, compliance, consent, acknowledgment
• *ant.* rejection, opposition

---

acceptor
[ak.*sep*.tor]

A drawee who has accepted a draft. *See also* acceptance.

---

accommodation loan
[a.kom.o.*day*.shen loan]

A loan made as a favor, without consideration or without adequate consideration.

---

accommodation paper
[a.kom.o.*day*.shen *pay*.per]

A bill or note signed as a favor to another person, known as the accommodated party, to enable that person to receive a loan. The person who grants the favor is the accommodation party or accommodation maker. If the accommodated party and the accommodation party sign jointly, they are known as co-makers. If the accommodated party defaults on the note, the accommodation party is fully liable.

---

alteration
[al.ter.*ay*.shen]

An erasure, writing, or typing that modifies the content of an instrument or document. EXAMPLE: changing the date on a check (as opposed to securing or writing a new check). Because an instrument can be altered by a person entitled to do so, an alteration is not necessarily a forgery.
• *n.* change, modification, conversion, reshaping, shift, switch, correction

---

asset
[*ass*.et]

Anything of value owned by a person or an organization. Assets include not only all real property and personal property, but intangible property such as bills, notes, stock, and accounts receivable.

---

assignment
[a.*sine*.ment]

A transfer of property, or a right in property, from one person to another.
• *n.* responsibility, task, appointment, commission, authorization

assignment for the benefit of creditors
[a.*sine*.ment for the *ben*.e.fit ov *kred*.it.terz]

An assignment and transfer by a debtor of all her property to a trustee to collect any amounts owned, to sell the property, and to distribute the proceeds among her creditors.

attachment
[a.*tach*.ment]

The process by which a person's property is figuratively brought into court to ensure satisfaction of a judgment that may be rendered against him. In the event judgment is rendered, the property may be sold to satisfy the judgment.
• *n.* seizure, confiscation, garnishment, dispossession, affixation, appending, securing ("the attachment of the seal on the document")

attachment lien
[a.*tach*.ment *leen*]

A lien that arises when property is attached; it is perfected when judgment is entered.

bearer
[*bare*.er]

1. The holder of a negotiable instrument payable to "bearer" or to "cash," i.e., a negotiable instrument not payable to a named person. The Uniform Commercial Code defines a bearer as the person in possession of an instrument, document of title, or certificated security payable to bearer or indorsed in blank.
• *n.* carrier, recipient, courier, possessor, holder, payee

bearer instrument
[*bare*.er *in*.stroo.ment]

A negotiable instrument payable to bearer or to cash, or that is in any form that does not specify a payee.

bearer paper
[*bare*.er *pay*.per]

Commercial paper payable to bearer or to cash, or in any other form that does not designate a specific payee.

cash
[kash]

Coin, money; money in hand, either in coin, currency, or other legal tender. A cashier's check or a certified check is the equivalent of cash, because payment is essentially guaranteed.
• *n.* coin, money, funds, currency, notes, legal tender
• *v.* make change, pay, draw, liquidate, redeem ("to cash a check")

cashier's check
[kash.*eerz chek*]

A bill of exchange, drawn by a bank upon bank funds, and accepted by virtue of the act of issuance. The bank's insurance of the check is a guaranty that it will be honored. A cashier's check is the equivalent of cash. *Compare* certified check.

certificate of deposit
[ser.*tif*.i.ket ov de.*poz*.it]

A voucher issued by a bank acknowledging the receipt of money on deposit that the bank promises to repay to the depositor. There are two kinds of certificates of deposit: demand certificates and time certificates. Demand certificates are ordinary savings accounts; the deposit can be withdrawn at any time, without penalty. Time certificates, which pay a higher rate of interest, are designed not to be cashed for a specified number of months or years. A certificate of deposit is often referred to simply as a CD. A treasury certificate is a form of certificate of deposit issued by the United States Treasury.

certified check
[*ser*.ti.fide chek]

A check upon which the bank has stamped the words "certified" or "accepted," certifying that the check is drawn upon sufficient funds and will be honored when it is presented for payment. A certified check is the equivalent of cash. *See also* acceptance. *Compare* cashier's check.

chattel paper
[*chat*.el *pay*.per]

As defined by the Uniform Commercial Code, a document that reflects both a debt and a security interest in specific goods. *See also* secured transaction.

check
[chek]

A written order ("pay to the order of") directed to a bank to pay money to the person named. *See also* cashier's check; certified check; traveler's check; draft; negotiable instrument.
• *n.* draft, note, negotiable instrument, bank note, inspection, examination

collateral
[ko.*lat*.er.el]

Stocks, bonds, or other property that serve as security for a loan or other obligation; property pledged to pay a debt.
• *n.* deposit, security, endorsement, pledge, promise

commercial paper
[ke.*mer*.shel *pay*.per]

Negotiable instruments, including checks, drafts, certificates of deposit, and promissory notes. Commercial paper is regulated by Article 3 of the Uniform Commercial Code.

consignment
[ken.*sine*.ment]

The entrusting of goods either to a carrier for delivery to a consignee or to a consignee who is to sell the goods for the consignor.
• *n.* entrusting, distribution, committal, transmittal

consumer
[kon.*soo*.mer]

A person who buys and uses products or services and who is affected by their cost, availability, and quality, as well as by laws regulating their manufacture, sale, and financing.
• *n.* buyer, client, patron, purchaser, vender, customer

consumer credit protection acts
[kon.*soo*.mer *kred*.it pro.*tek*.shen aktz]

Also known as truth in lending acts; federal and state statutes that require, among other things, that contracts for the sale of consumer goods involving credit be written in plain language, that the finance charges be stated as a uniform annual percentage rate, and that goods purchased on credit or with credit cards be returnable within specified periods of time. *See also* credit.

consumer goods
[kon.*soo*.mer gudz]

As defined by the Uniform Commercial Code, articles used primarily for personal, family, or household purposes.

credit
[*kred*.it]

Trust placed in a person's willingness and ability to pay when the obligation to pay is extended over a period of time without security.
• *n.* rating, trust, standing, authority, loan, mortgage ("He has good credit")

credit bureau
[*kred*.it *byoo*.roh]

A company that collects information concerning the financial standing, credit, and general reputation of others, which it furnishes to subscribers for a fee.

credit card
[*kred*.it kard]

A card issued for the purpose of enabling the owner to obtain goods, services, or money on credit.

creditor
[*kred*.it.or]

A person to whom a debt is owed by a debtor.

debt
[det]

An unconditional and legally enforceable obligation for the payment of money (EXAMPLES: a mortgage; an installment sale contract) and obligations imposed by law without contract (EXAMPLES: a judgment, unliquidated damages). A debt not presently due is nonetheless a debt.
• *n.* obligation, liability, debit, dues, commitment, encumbrance

defense
[de.*fense*]

With respect to commercial paper, a legal basis for denying one's liability on an instrument.

deficiency
[de.*fish*.en.see]

1. The amount still due the creditor after foreclosure of a mortgage or other security. 2. Shortage, undersupply, lack.
• *n.* insufficiency, lack, shortage, inadequacy, absence, scantiness, want
• *ant.* adequacy

demand loan
[de.*mand* lone]

A loan that is callable (total payment is demanded) at any time.

demand note
[de.*mand* note]

A promissory note payable when payment is demanded.

demand paper
[de.*mand pay*.per]

Commercial paper payable when payment is demanded.

dishonor
[dis.*on*.er]

To refuse to accept or pay a negotiable instrument when it is duly presented for acceptance or payment, or when presentment is excused and the instrument is not accepted or paid.
• *ant.* accept

draft
[draft]

n. An order in writing by one person on another (commonly a bank) to pay a specified sum of money to a third person on demand or at a stated future time. EXAMPLE: a check.
v. To make a preliminary version of a document.
• *n.* money order, check, banknote, negotiable paper ("a bank draft"); version, attempt ("first draft of my brief")

draw
[draw]

v. 1. To create, make, or sign a negotiable instrument. 2. To take or accept an advance. 3. To withdraw money from a bank account.
• *v.* draft, prepare, make, compose ("draw up the papers"); extract, deplete, exhaust, withdraw ("Do you wish to draw on your savings account?")
• *ant.* deposit
• *n.* extraction, withdrawal, depletion, advance ("I made a draw on my checking account")

drawee
[draw.*ee*]

The person upon whom a draft is drawn; the person to whom a draft is presented for acceptance and payment. The drawee of a check is always a bank. *Compare* drawer.

drawer
[draw.*er*]

The maker of a draft. *Compare* drawee.

execution
[ek.se.*kyoo*.shen]

1. A writ of process for the enforcement of a judgment. 2. The act of an officer in serving a writ or process. 3. The signing of a document or instrument.
• *n.* fulfillment, achievement, performance, conclusion ("The execution of a contract")

filing
[*file*.ing]

The act of depositing a document with a public officer to preserve it as one of the records of his office.

filing laws
[*file*.ing lawz]

Statutes that require the filing of an instrument as a condition of its complete effectiveness.

financing statement
[*fine*.an.sing *state*.ment]

A notice of the existence of a security interest in goods, which a creditor is entitled to file with the appropriate public officer, usually the secretary of state. The designated public office varies from state to state. Note that "financing statement" is not "financial statement."

forge
[forj]

To commit a forgery; to make falsely with intent to defraud or injure any writing that, if genuine, might appear to be legally effective or the basis for legal liability. Forgery is a crime.
• *v.* counterfeit, design, duplicate, imitate, reproduce, construct, invent, build, manufacture

garnishment
[*gar*.nish.ment]

A proceeding by a creditor to obtain satisfaction of a debt from money or property of the debtor that is in the possession of a third person or is owed by such a person to the debtor. EXAMPLE: Because Ron owes back taxes, the IRS (the creditor, also called the garnishor or plaintiff) initiates a garnishment against Ron (the debtor, also called the defendant) by serving a notice of garnishment of Ron's wages upon his employer, the ABC Company (the garnishee). Note that a garnishment is distinguished from an attachment by the fact that the money or property reached by the garnishment remains in the hands of the third party until there is a judgment in the action involving the basic debt.
• *n.* attachment, levy, appropriation, collection

holder
[*hole*.der]

A person who has the legal right to enforce a negotiable instrument or who is entitled to receive, hold, and dispose of a document of title and the goods to which it pertains. With respect to an instrument payable to or in the name of "bearer," the person in possession is the holder; with respect to an instrument payable to or in the name of an identified person, that person is the "holder" if she is in possession of the instrument.
• *n.* owner, possessor, bearer, keeper, recipient

holder for value
[*hole*.der for *val*.yoo]

A person who has given consideration for a negotiable instrument that he holds.

holder in due course [*hole*.der in dew kors]	A holder of a negotiable instrument who gave value for it and took it in good faith and without notice of any claim or defense against it.
holder in good faith [*hole*.der in good faith]	A person who takes or holds property, including a negotiable instrument, without knowledge of any defect in title.
honor [*on*.er]	To pay or accept a negotiable instrument when it is duly presented. *Compare* dishonor. *See also* acceptance. • *v.* credit, redeem, make good ("The store honors personal checks.")
indorse [in.*dorse*]	To sign one's name on the back of a document, especially a check. *See also* indorsement.
indorsee [in.dor.*see*]	The person to whom a negotiable instrument is indorsed by name. *Compare* bearer. *See also* indorse.
indorsee in due course [in.dor.*see* in dew korss]	A person who in good faith, in the ordinary course of business, for value, acquires a negotiable instrument duly indorsed to her, indorsed generally, or payable to bearer.
indorsement [in.*dorse*.ment]	The writing of one's name on the back of a negotiable instrument, by which a person transfers title to the paper to another person.
indorser [in.*dor*.ser]	The person who indorses a negotiable instrument. *Compare* indorsee.
installment payments [in.*stall*.ment *pay*.ments]	Payments at fixed intervals until the entire principal and interest on an obligation are satisfied. Installment payments are made under installment contracts, installment notes, or installment sale contracts, as well as other types of agreements. Commercial installment sales and installment loans are regulated by consumer credit protection acts.
judgment [*juj*.ment]	In a civil action, the final determination entered by a court after it renders its decision on the rights of the parties, based upon the pleadings and the evidence. • *n.* decree, holding, ruling, conclusion, opinion, award, sentence, finding, adjudication, verdict, arbitration ("the judgment of the court"), decision
lien [*leen*]	A claim or charge on, or right against, personal property, or an encumbrance on real property, for the payment of a debt. A lien may be created by statute (EXAMPLES: a tax lien, an attachment lien) or by agreement between the parties (EXAMPLES: a mortgage on real estate; a security agreement covering personal property). In some instances, a lien permits the creditor to retain the debtor's property in his possession until the debt is satisfied. Such a lien is called a possessory lien. • *n.* debt, obligation, mortgage, interest ("The mortgage is a lien on the house")

lien creditor [*leen kred*.i.tor]	A creditor whose debt is secured by a lien. EXAMPLES: an execution creditor; a judgment creditor.
liquidated debt [*lik*.wi.day.ted det]	A debt that has been paid or for which it is certain as to how much is due. *See also* debt.
maker [*may*.ker]	A person who obligates himself by executing a check, promissory note, draft, or other negotiable instrument. *See also* drawer.
merchant [*mer*.chent]	1. A person who regularly trades in a particular type of goods. 2. Under the Uniform Commercial Code, "a person who deals in goods of the kind or otherwise by his occupation holds himself out as having knowledge or skill peculiar to the goods involved in the transaction." The law holds a merchant to a higher standard than it imposes upon a casual seller.
mortgage [*more*.gej]	*n.* 1. A pledge of real property to secure a debt. Which one of at least three possible legal principles defines the rights of the parties to a given mortgage depends upon the state in which the mortgaged property is located. In states that have adopted the lien theory, the mortgagee (creditor) has a lien on the property; the mortgagor (debtor) retains legal title and is entitled to possession unless his interest is terminated by a foreclosure decree. In title theory states, a mortgage transfers title and a theoretical right of possession to the mortgagee; title reverts to the mortgagor upon full payment of the mortgage debt. A third group of states employs hybrid versions of the lien and title theories, with characteristics of both. 2. A written agreement pledging real property as security. *v.* 1. To place real property under a mortgage. (*n.*) 2. To obligate; to pledge.
negotiable [ne.*go*.shebl]	Transferable by indorsement or delivery. EXAMPLE: a negotiable instrument. • *adj.* transferable, assignable, alienable, open, undetermined, malleable • *ant.* nonnegotiable, fixed
negotiable instrument [ne.*go*.shebl *in*.stroo.ment]	Under the Uniform Commercial Code, a signed writing that orders or provides payment of money if: it is unconditional, it is in a fixed amount, it is payable on demand to bearer or to order or at a definite time, and it "does not state any undertaking or instruction by the person promising or ordering payment to do any act in addition to the payment of money." (EXAMPLES: a check; a money order; a certificate of deposit; a bond; a note, a bill of lading; a warehouse receipt.) Negotiable instruments are also referred to as commercial paper or negotiable paper. • *n.* draft, check, bond, note, money order, instrument
negotiate [ne.*go*.shee.ate]	To transfer a negotiable instrument to a third person by indorsement or delivery.

negotiation [ne.go.shee.*ay*.shen]	The act of transferring a negotiable instrument to a third person by indorsement or delivery. • *n.* agreement compromise, mediation, discussion
nonnegotiable [non.ne.*go*.shebl]	1. A document or instrument not transferable by indorsement or delivery. EXAMPLES: a lease, a deed; a mortgage. 2. Not subject to negotiation. • *adj.* nontransferable, nonassignable
nonnegotiable instrument [non.ne.*go*.shebl *in*.stroo.ment]	An instrument that is not negotiable.
note [note]	A written promise by one person to pay another person a specified sum of money on a specified date; a term used interchangeably with promissory note. A note may or may not be negotiable, depending upon its form. *See also* negotiable instrument.
order paper [*or*.der *pay*.per]	A negotiable instrument; i.e., an instrument that recites an unconditional promise to pay a fixed amount of money, and that is payable to order and meets all the other requirements of negotiability.
payor [pay.*or*]	1. A person who makes a payment or is obligated to make a payment. 2. The person who makes a check, bill, or note.
perfection of a security interest [per.*fek*.tion ov a se.*kyoo*.ri.tee *in*.trest]	Under the Uniform Commercial Code, a method of protecting a security interest in goods against the claims of other creditors by filing a financing statement with the appropriate public officer (usually the secretary of state). However, a security interest in consumer goods is perfected without such filing.
possession [poh.*zesh*.en]	Occupancy and dominion over property; a holding of land legally, by one's self (actual possession) or through another person such as a tenant (constructive possession). The holding may be by virtue of having title or an estate or interest of any kind. One need not have a resident on the land to be in actual possession of it. • *n.* dominion, proprietorship, ownership, holding, guardianship, keeping ("I have possession of my family's land")
presentment [pre.*zent*.ment]	A demand to accept (presentment for acceptance) or to pay (presentment for payment) a negotiable instrument, made to the drawee by a person, usually the payee or holder, entitled to enforce the instrument.
primary liability [*pry*.mer.ee ly.e.*bil*.i.tee]	The liability of a person who, by the terms of the instrument he has executed, or because of some other legal obligation he has incurred, or by virtue of his legal relationship to an injured party, is absolutely required to make payment, satisfy the obligation, or assume full responsibility for the injury; the liability of a maker or principal, as distinguished from that of a guarantor or indorser. *Compare* secondary liability.

promissory note
[*prom*.i.sore.ee note]

A written promise to pay a specific sum of money by a specified date or on demand. A promissory note is negotiable if, in addition, it is payable to the order of a named person or to bearer. *See also* negotiable instrument.

purchase money security interest
[*per*.ches *mun*.ee se.*kyoo*.ri.tee *in*.trest]

A security interest created when a security agreement is executed by a purchaser of personal property.

repossession
[ree.po.*zesh*.en]

1. A remedy of the seller upon default by the buyer under a conditional sale contract or other security agreement. 2. A taking of possession by the owner of real estate after the occupant relinquishes possession or forfeits the right to possession.
• *n.* recapture, restoration, retrieval, seizure, reacquisition, recovery

secondary liability
[*sek*.en.dare.ee ly.e.*bil*.i.tee]

Liability that does not come about until the primary obligor fails to meet her obligation; the liability of a guarantor or indorser as distinguished from that of a maker or principal. *Compare* primary liability.

secured
[se.*kyoord*]

1. Made certain of payment; given security. 2. Guaranteed against a risk or peril. 3. Protected. 4. Obtained. *Compare* unsecured.
• *adj.* guaranteed, protected, insured, sheltered ("a secured debt")

secured creditor
[se.*kyoord kred*.it.er]

A creditor who has a perfected security lien for a debt in the form of an encumbrance on property of the debtor. EXAMPLES: a mortgagee; a lienee.

secured transaction
[se.*kyoord* tranz.*ak*.shen]

A transaction that creates or provides for a security interest in personal property. EXAMPLES: a secured loan.

security
[se.*kyoor*.i.tee]

1. Singular of securities. 2. Collateral; a pledge given to a creditor by a debtor for the payment of a debt or for the performance of an obligation. EXAMPLES: a mortgage; a lien; a deposit.
• *n.* warranty, bail, surety, escrow, collateral, debenture, assurance ("security for the mortgage")

security interest
[se.*kyoor*.i.tee *in*.trest]

1. Under the Uniform Commercial Code, "an interest in personal property or fixtures which secures payment or performance of an obligation." *See also* purchase money security interest. 2. With respect to real property, a mortgage or other lien.

sight draft
[site draft]

A bill of exchange or draft payable upon presentment to the drawee. It is the equivalent of a check that is payable on demand.

special indorsement
[*spesh*.el in.*dors*.ment]

An indorsement that specifies the person to whom or to whose order the instrument is to be payable, e.g., "Pay to the order of Lisa Whitney."

time draft
[time draft]

A draft payable at a fixed or determinable future time.

traveler's check
[*trav*.lerz chek]

An instrument, usually one of a set, purchased from a bank or other financial institution and similar in many respects to a cashier's check. Traveler's checks must be signed by the purchaser at the time of purchase and countersigned when cashed.

Uniform Commercial Code (UCC)
[*yoon*.i.form ke.*mersh*.el kode]

One of the Uniform Laws, which have been adopted in much the same form in every state. It governs most aspects of commercial transactions, including sales, leases, negotiable instruments, deposits and collections, letters of credit, bulk sales, warehouse receipts, bills of lading and other documents of title, investment securities, and secured transactions.

unsecured
[un.se.*kyoord*]

A term describing debts or obligations for which no security has been given or no perfected security lien exists.

Missing Words

Fill in the blanks below.

1. A card issued for the purpose of enabling the owner to obtain goals, services, or money on credit is a(n) _____.

2. A(n) _____ debt is a debt for which it is certain how much is due.

3. A promissory note payable when payment is demanded is a(n) _____.

4. The act of depositing a document with a public officer is known as _____.

5. A person who regularly trades in a particular type of goods is known as a(n) _____.

6. Money one owes another person is a(n) _____.

7. A security interest created when a security agreement is executed by a purchaser of personal property is a(n) _____.

8. When the contents of a document are modified by erasure this is called _____.

9. A voucher issued by a bank acknowledging the receipt of money on deposit that the bank promises to repay is a(n) _____.

10. A(n) _____ is the amount still due a creditor after foreclosure of a mortgage.

11. A(n) _____ is the transfer of property, or a right in property, from one person to another.

12. A(n) _____ is an encumbrance on real property or a claim on personal property for payment of a debt.

13. A pledge of real property to secure a debt is called a(n) _____.

14. _____ is a method of protecting a security interest in goods against the claims of their creditors by filing a financing statement.

15. A(n) _____ is the holder of a negotiable instrument who gave value for it and took it in good faith and without notice of any claim or defense against it.

16. The _____ is the maker of a draft.

17. Checks, certificates of deposit, drafts, and notes are all examples of _____.

18. Statutes that require the filing of an instrument as a condition of its complete effectiveness are _____.

19. Payments made at fixed intervals until the entire principal and interest on an obligation are satisfied are _____.

Matching

Match the letter of the definition to the term below.

_____ 20. Assignment

_____ 21. Repossession

_____ 22. Consumer

_____ 23. Filing

_____ 24. Judgment

_____ 25. Demand note

_____ 26. Promissory note

_____ 27. Possession

_____ 28. Perfection of a security interest

_____ 29. Uniform Commercial Code

_____ 30. Financing statement

_____ 31. Attachment

_____ 32. Check

_____ 33. Certificate of deposit

A. Deposit a document with a public officer

B. A person's property is used to satisfy a judgment

C. Promissory note payable when payment is demanded

D. Transfer of property or a right in property

E. Written promise to pay a sum of money

F. Method of protecting a security interest in goods

G. Remedy of seller upon default by buyer

H. A notice of the existence of a security interest in goods that a creditor files

I. Occupancy and dominion over property

J. Person who buys or uses services

K. A uniform law that governs most aspects of commercial transactions

L. Final determination by a court of the rights of the parties

M. Voucher issued by a bank acknowledging the receipt of money on deposit that the bank promises to repay to the depositor

N. Material alteration of a writing

____ 34. Forgery

O. Written order directed to bank to pay money to the person named

____ 35. Sight draft

P. Draft payable at a fixed time

____ 36. Time draft

Q. The equivalent of a check that is payable on demand

Multiple Choice

Select the best choice.

____ 37. Commercial law is the branch of law that is related to matters of concern to:
   a. merchants
   b. farmers
   c. food service workers
   d. wallpaper hangers

____ 38. An unconditional and legally enforceable obligation for the payment of money is known as:
   a. filing
   b. asset
   c. perfection of a security interest
   d. debt

____ 39. The process by which a person's property is figuratively brought into court to ensure satisfaction of a judgment is known as:
   a. promissory note
   b. attachment
   c. assignment
   d. UCC

____ 40. The amount still due a creditor after foreclosure of a mortgage is known as:
   a. deficiency
   b. lis pendens
   c. default
   d. possession

____ 41. A financing statement is a notice of the existence of a security interest in goods, which a creditor is entitled to file with the appropriate public officer, usually the:
   a. court
   b. bank
   c. secretary of state
   d. creditor

____ 42. Unsecured debt is a debt for which:
   a. there has been no security given
   b. there has been no lien given
   c. there has been no contract given
   d. there has been no writ of execution given

____ 43. A consumer loan is a loan made to a consumer for the purpose of purchasing consumer goods usually under a conditional sales contract involving:
   a. assignment
   b. attachment
   c. installment payments
   d. filing

____ 44. In a civil action, the final determination by a court of the rights of the parties is known as:
   a. repossession
   b. perfection of a security interest
   c. writ of execution
   d. judgment

____ 45. A claim on or right against personal property or an encumbrance on real property for the payment of a debt is known as:
   a. lien
   b. garnishment
   c. consumer loan
   d. demand note

____ 46. A secured transaction creates or provides a security interest in:
   a. real property
   b. personal property
   c. luxury goods
   d. farm land

_____ 47. A company that collects information concerning the credit and general reputation of others is known as a:
   a. court
   b. debtor
   c. creditor
   d. credit bureau

_____ 48. When a demand is made to accept or pay a negotiable instrument this is called:
   a. overdraft
   b. presentment
   c. cancellation
   d. alteration

_____ 49. Negotiable instruments, including checks, drafts, certificates of deposit, and promissory notes are called:
   a. business paper
   b. demand paper
   c. commercial paper
   d. working paper

_____ 50. An order in writing by one person on another to pay a specified sum of money to a third person on demand or at a stated future time is called a(n):
   a. draft
   b. presentment
   c. certificate of deposit
   d. indorsement

True/False

Mark the following T or F.

_____ 51. An unsecured debt is a debt for which no security has been given.

_____ 52. Time draft is when a buyer has paid off a debt in full.

_____ 53. An interest in personal property or fixtures that secures the payment or performance of an obligation is known as a security interest.

_____ 54. A person who owes another person money is known as a secured creditor.

_____ 55. An agreement to do or refrain from doing a particular thing is known as perfection of a security interest.

_____ 56. An obligation for the payment of money is called debt.

_____ 57. A security agreement is filed with the court in foreclosure proceedings to give notice that the property listed in the notice is the subject of litigation.

_____ 58. An asset is anything of value owned by a person or organization.

_____ 59. A deficiency is the amount still due a debtor after foreclosure.

_____ 60. An installment payment is a lump sum payment.

_____ 61. Primary liability is the liability of a person who is absolutely required to make payment to satisfy an obligation.

_____ **62.** A certified check is a check upon which the bank has stamped the words "certified" or "accepted," certifying that the check is drawn on sufficient funds and will be honored when presented for payment.

_____ **63.** The writing of one's name on the back of a negotiable instrument is called an indorsement.

_____ **64.** The payor is the person to whom a payment is made.

_____ **65.** A mortgage is an example of a security interest.

_____ **66.** A maker or principal has secondary liability.

_____ **67.** The holder of a negotiable instrument not payable to a named person is the bearer.

Synonyms

Select the correct synonym in parentheses for each numbered item.

68. DRAWER
(buyer, maker, consumer)

69. DEBT
(obligation, perfection, possession)

70. HOLDER ·
(owner, possessor, seller)

71. INDORSE
(sign, attach, breach)

72. NEGOTIATE
(transfer, bargain, collect)

73. POSSESSION
(ownership, execution, judgment)

74. BEARER
(holder, payer, seller)

75. FORGE
(counterfeit, expose, default)

76. DRAFT
(check, note, certificate of deposit)

77. CONSUMER
(buyer, seller, creditor)

78. HONOR
(refuse, copy, pay)

79. NOTE
(order to pay, promise to pay, intention to pay)

80. MERCHANT
(purchaser, consumer, seller)

81. CHECK
(order to pay, promise to pay, intention to pay)

82. MAKER
(payer, possessor, drawer)

83. ALTERATION
(attachment, repossession, modification)

84. ASSIGNMENT
(to transfer, to perfect, to present)

85. EXECUTION
(termination, signing, filing)

86. LIQUIDATED
(paid, owed, refunded)

Self-Test

Place the number of the correct term in the appropriate space.

87. Checks

88. Contract

89. Defaults

90. Uniform Commercial Code (UCC)

91. Judgment

92. Unsecured debt

93. Negotiable instruments

94. Creditor

95. Secured debt

96. Repossess

97. Commercial law

98. Debt

99. Drafts

100. Certificates of deposit

_____ is the area of law that relates to concerns of merchants. A uniform law that has been adopted in much the same form in most states and governs most aspects of commercial transactions is known as the _____. Generally, some form of an agreement is reached called a(n) _____ to do or refrain from doing a particular thing. A debtor/ _____ relationship may be established with one person owing a(n) _____ to another.

Depending on the particulars of the transaction, different legal documents will be needed to protect the interests of each party. To protect the creditor, collateral gives him a(n) _____. Should this fail, the creditor will find himself with _____, leaving the creditor little protection.

Filing a security interest is just one of the many ways a creditor might protect his interests. In the event a debtor _____ on a loan or other agreement, a creditor needs to know the remedies available to him. A court action might be needed to foreclose on real estate, or _____ personal property such as cars or boats. Eventually a(n) _____ may be entered against the debtor after a court action. Even this does not insure that a creditor will be paid, and further legal action might still be required by the creditor to collect against a debtor.

Commercial paper is a term used to refer to _____, which are relied on in business to conduct commercial transactions. These are signed writings that order or promise payment of money. Examples of commercial paper are _____, _____, promissory notes, and _____.

Defining Words

Complete the definition.

101. Debt _____

_____

102. Credit _____

_____

103. Draft _____

_____

104. Honor _____

_____

105. Forge _____

_____

106. Drawer _____

_____

107. Possession _____

_____

108. Negotiate _____

_____

109. Perfection _____

_____

110. Maker _____

_____

111. Holder in due course _____

_____

112. Check _____

_____

113. Cash _____

_____

114. Promissory note _____

_____

115. Secured transaction _____

_____

Punctuation/Capitalization

Punctuating the dependent adverb clause.

A dependent clause that begins with words like *because, when, where, as, since, before, after* is used as an adverb in the sentence; that is, it answers one of the questions *when, where, why,* or *how.*

Rule 1: When an adverb dependent clause comes at the end of the sentence, it takes no punctuation.

I called him before I left the office that day.
He was late to the office that day because there was a thunder and lightning storm.
She did not contact me after the accident happened.

Rule 2: When an adverb dependent clause comes at the beginning of the sentence, it is always followed by a comma.

Before I left the office that day, I called him.
Because there was a thunder and lightning storm, he was late to the office that day.
After the accident happened, she did not contact me.

Notice that the only difference is the placement of the clause within the sentence and that it is the placement that determines the punctuation.

Directions: Make necessary punctuation changes.

1. Before you leave please call everyone you are responsible for on that list.

2. I was there, while he was having the surgery.

3. After the earthquake happened, did you immediately see any obvious damage?

4. Since he had been so traumatized, we tried to calm him down, before the paramedics took him away.

5. We were able to leave with a clear conscience because we had done the work.

Word Pairs

accept/except

accept = take, believe, endure, agree to, receive, understand.

I accept your invitation to the luncheon.
Did he accept your views on the issue?
He accepted a gift from one of the vendors.

except = but, excluding, object.

There was nothing to do except believe him.
Everyone except Herb was there.
I except, Your Honor, on the grounds of relevance.

altar/alter

altar = raised, flat area where religious ceremonies are performed.

Fire damaged the altar area of the church.
It is out there on the altar of public opinion.
She left him at the altar.

alter = change, revise, modify, adjust.

It was a mind-altering drug.
That does not alter my opinion in any way.
It is clear it is an altered document.

cache/cash

cache = hidden supply, special kind of computer memory, secret hiding place.

It is stored in the cache memory.
She had a cache of chocolate in her office.
There was a rumored cache of weapons.

cash = coin, money, money in hand.

There were several uncashed checks in his belongings.
The check cannot be cashed without two forms of identification.
He never has cash with him.

filing/filling

filing = depositing a document with a public officer to preserve it, tiny metal particle, cutting down. The noun and verb form is *file*.

There will be further filings in this matter.
The filing was not made within the time limit.
He was filing down the edge on the shelf.

filling = heavy, satisfying, food mixture. The noun and verb form is *fill*.

It was a filling meal.
He seemed to be filling his own pockets with company profits.
The room was filling up as the flood waters rose.

loan/lone

loan = money given to someone, advance.

It is a loan with very high interest.
She was on loan from the parent company.
I asked him for a personal loan, but he refused.

lone = single, only, solitary.

He was the lone resident in the boarding house.
It is thought there was a lone gunman.
There was a lone dissenter on the jury.

Directions: Choose the correct form of the word.

1. Did you accept/except yourself from the decision because of your bias?

2. The error message was that there was not enough cache/cash memory.

3. The filing/filling was done in a different county.

4. It was thought that there was a loan/lone gunman involved.

5. Did he somehow altar/alter his appearance?

6. He accepted/excepted the position as the loan/lone officer for the real estate company.

7. He was the loan/lone dissenter to the bill.

8. He had nothing he could convert to the much-needed cache/cash.

9. He had his file/fill of her attitude.

10. She was told to file/fill it with the court no later than Friday.

11. Someone in the office regularly raided her cache/cash of printer cartridges.

12. The prospect of the promotion filed/filled me with excitement.

13. Everyone accept/except Juan was included in the decision.

14. The loan/lone did not cover the entire expense of the trip.

15. It is suspected the problem occurred in the altar/alter area.

16. I think the list included all of the past presidents accept/except Mitchell.

17. He wanted to cache/cash in on his success of the moment.

18. There was a loan/lone palm tree on the grounds.

19. He tried to altar/alter his behavior to fit the rather formal circumstances.

20. The filing/filling cabinet held no recent documents.

Is It One Word or Two? An Apostrophe? A Hyphen?

With only a few exceptions, the general rule for prefixes is to add them to the front of the word and form a solid word.

dissatisfied	unnecessary
postsurgery	nonnegotiable
prenatal	sublease

With the prefix *re-*, meaning "again," there is a potential problem. If we are going to go back to the bank and sign papers again, we cannot add the prefix *re-* directly to the word *sign* because we already have a word *resign*, meaning "to quit a job." Therefore, the word *re-sign*, meaning "to sign again," must be hyphenated. There are approximately 25 words beginning with *re-* where there is a conflict.

Rule 1: When adding the prefix *re-*, hyphenate it to the word when there is already a word beginning with *re-* that has another meaning.

resign = leave a job.
re-sign = sign again.

redress = equalize, rectify.
re-dress = dress again.

recreate = spend leisure time.
re-create = create again.

reform = change for the better, improve.
re-form = form again.

Rule 2: If there is no other word with a different definition, add the prefix *re-* and make it a solid word. Notice that two *e*'s in a word are not a problem.

redo
rework
reemphasize
reenter

Directions: Choose the correct form of the word.

1. We need to rework/re-work our agreement in order to regain/re-gain the equitable distribution of the workload.

2. The company was reformed/re-formed from the ground up after the president resigned/re-signed and left for a bigger opportunity.

3. The witness tried to recreate/re-create the mood at the scene of the accident.

4. We will redo/re-do the contract as soon as he is willing.

5. The check was reissued/re-issued at least twice.

Proofreading

Directions: Make necessary corrections, based on the material presented in the unit. If the sentence has no errors, write the word *correct* after the sentence.

1. When he called that Friday I was the loan person in the office and was swamped with work.   _____

2. The computer seemed to have too little cache memory because it kept tying up.   _____

3. I filed out the loan application and listed no one accept myself as the income source.   _____

4. Because there was an incompetent person at the bank I had to return and resign the papers for the lone.   _____

5. When he called a second time, she altered her story about the events of the evening.   _____

6. His early return resulted in his restraining the muscle in his leg.   _____

7. As the workmanship was faulty we had to re-side the house, before winter set in.   _____

8. After the tennis referee called a let ball McEnroe reserved the ball.   _____

9. We intended to file the suit, before the courts closed on Friday.   _____

10. He cashed in his life savings after he had the surgery.   _____

An Adaptation from a Commercial Law Case

Facts:

Ronald Moreno opened a small sawmill operation under the name Hollander Cut, Inc. He engaged the services of Randolph as a consultant to arrange for finances and related activities. Randolph was to receive a 20 percent interest in the new business venture. Moreno eventually turned over control of the corporate checkbook to Randolph. Moreno would sometimes give Randolph blank signed checks so he could pay bills, but Randolph had no authority to sign checks. When Moreno discovered that some of the bills were not being paid, he reviewed the company's bank records and found unauthorized payments—some were on blank checks he had signed and others with a signature he did not recognize—that Randolph used to pay his own personal expenses. Moreno claimed that, when Randolph improperly signed or issued checks, he had stolen thousands of dollars from the company.

Procedural History:

This case is before the Court of Appeals to decide whether the decision of the Appellate Division was correct.

Issue:

Was the conviction against Randolph for forgery by the Appellate Division correct?

Rationale:

Only in rare instances can one commit a forgery by signing one's own name, which is precisely what Randolph has done. However, if you sign your name to deceive others so that they think you are a third party, an issue of forgery might come up. In most jurisdictions, a forger must act without authority and sign someone else's name. Usually the forger signs the check in someone else's name with the intent of having another believe he is someone else. This is to mislead the payee to believe that the forger is really someone else, that the maker is a real person, and that the document is authentic. But where the alleged maker and the actual maker of the draft are one and the same, there can be no forgery. Forgery is a crime because of the need to protect commercial instruments and make them freely negotiable.

Ruling:

The order of the Appellate Division should be reversed and the indictment dismissed.

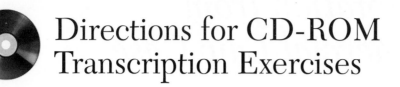

Directions for CD-ROM Transcription Exercises

In audio format are:

1. Terms for the unit with pronunciations from the thesaurus/dictionary feature.

2. Self-Test that appears in the book at mid-unit.*

3. Case that appears at the unit end.*

*speeds are 80 wpm/120 wpm for differing skill levels

CD-ROM icons appear where the three above are located within each unit.

Readers may practice transcription by listening to the CD-ROM where prompted by the icons in the book. However, for high success in testing your transcription skills, mastering all the terms and English skills in the unit is recommended before attempting the CD-ROM.

For Keyboard Transcriptionists: Listen to the CD-ROM audio file for this unit at 80 wpm or 120 wpm and transcribe from the dictation on your computer. Edit and proofread your work against the printed copy in the book.

For Reporting Writers: Listen to the CD-ROM audio file at 80 wpm or 120 wpm and take down the dictation on your writer. Either transcribe from your notes and proofread your work or edit and proofread your CAT (computer-aided transcription) transcript. Always check your work against the printed copy in the book.

 Student CD-ROM
For additional materials,
please go to the CD in this book.

 Online Companion™
For additional resources, please go to
http://www.paralegal.delmar.cengage.com

Unit 7 | Constitutional Law

The **Mistakes** That Court Reporters Make and *How to Avoid* Them

The Mistake:

Ana Ramirez was on a new health kick and was trying to drink at least 80 ounces of water a day. On Thursday she had consumed her goal and went off to her late-afternoon deposition. The inevitable happened. She had to ask for a break six times during the two-hour deposition. The next day the attorney called her office and said that he would prefer not to use Ana again because she was too disruptive.

How to Avoid It:

Do not take the chance of having to interrupt the deposition often because you drank a lot of water or coffee or soda before the session. Most attorneys will take a break about every hour to hour and a half. You need to plan to take advantage of those and not frequently ask for other breaks. Obviously, it is okay for you to ask for a break if you need to. It is the frequency of your requests that could make a difference.

Introduction

The American system of government is set forth in the United States Constitution. Each individual state has its own state constitution as well. Generally, when reference is made to "the Constitution," the federal Constitution is intended. In 1787, the U.S. Constitution came into effect and is composed of seven articles that cover the organization and running of the government.

In time, various amendments to the Constitution have been adopted. The first 10 amendments to the Constitution, which were made to further protect the rights of individual citizens, are known as the Bill of Rights. There have been a mere 27 amendments to the Constitution, the last in 1992.

Much respect is due the Constitution, a document enacted over 200 years ago, yet flexible enough to withstand the great changes in American society and in the world at large. When the Constitution was drafted there was no technology or advanced communications. Yet the Constitution was written to deal with many of the legal problems encountered daily, to wit: separation of church and state, election of the government, freedom of assembly and religion, and illegal search and seizure. Those stated are but a few that will be examined in this unit on constitutional law, including the First Amendment freedom in the case that ends this unit.

Unit Objectives

■ Work with a legal dictionary/thesaurus.

■ Learn about the United States Constitution and constitutional law.

■ Master the similarities and differences in key terms concerning constitutional law.

■ Master the pronunciations and spellings of the terms in this unit.

■ Recognize the synonyms used for terminology in this unit.

■ Practice usage of terms, definitions, and synonyms related to constitutional law.

■ Complete unit exercises in the forms of missing words, matching, multiple choice, true/false, synonyms, self-test, defining words, and also:

- Punctuation/capitalization
- Word pairs
- Transcription of terms, self-test, and case
- Proofreading

💿 Dictionary/Thesaurus

Note: All Dictionary/Thesaurus terms appear on the CD-ROM with audio pronunciations.

Term
[phonetic pronunciation]

---

amendment of constitution
[a.*mend*.ment ov kon.sti.*too*.shen]

A process of proposing, passing, and ratifying amendments to the United States Constitution or a state or other constitution.

American Civil Liberties Union
[a.*mare*.i.ken *siv*.il *lib*.er.tees *yoon*.yun]

A nonprofit organization, commonly called the ACLU, which is concerned with constitutional rights, particularly individual liberties, and engages in litigation and lobbying.

---

articles
[*ar*.tiklz]

Plural of article. Distinct divisions, parts, clauses, or provisions that, taken as a whole, make up a constitution, charter, statute, contract, or other written statement of principles or mutual understandings.

---

balancing test
[*bal*.en.sing test]

A principle of constitutional law that declares that the constitutional rights of each citizen must in each instance be balanced against the danger that their exercise presents to others or to the state. EXAMPLE: freedom of speech does not include the right "to cry fire in a crowded theater" if there is no fire.

---

bicameral
[by.*kam*.er.el]

Two-chambered, referring to the customary division of a legislature into two houses (a Senate and a House of Representatives).

Bill of Rights
[bil ov ritz]

The first 10 amendments to the United States Constitution. The Bill of Rights is the portion of the Constitution that sets forth the rights that are the fundamental principles of the United States and the foundation of American citizenship.

---

commerce clause
[*kom*.erss kloz]

The clause in Article I, Section 8, of the Constitution that gives Congress the power to regulate commerce between the states and between the United States and foreign countries. Federal statutes that regulate business and labor (EXAMPLES: the Fair Labor Standards Act; the Occupational Safety and Health Act) are based upon this power. *See also* interstate commerce.

---

constitution
[kon.sti.*too*.shen]

1. The system of fundamental principles by which a nation, state, or corporation is governed. A nation's constitution may be written (EXAMPLE: the Constitution of the United States) or unwritten (EXAMPLE: the British Constitution). A nation's law must conform to its constitution. A law that violates a nation's constitution is unconstitutional and therefore unenforceable. 2. The document setting forth the fundamental principles of governance. 3. The Constitution of the United States.

Constitution
[kon.sti.*too*.shen]

The Constitution of the United States.
• *n.* charter, code, formation, written law, supreme law

Constitution of the United States
[kon.sti.*too*.shen ov the yoo.*nie*.ted states]

The fundamental document of American government, as adopted by the people of the United States through their representatives in the Constitutional Convention of 1787, as ratified by the states, together with the amendments to the Constitution.

constitutional
[kon.sti.*too*.shen.el]

1. In accordance with the Constitution of the United States; consistent with the Constitution; not in conflict with the Constitution.
2. In accordance with, consistent with, or not in conflict with a constitution, for EXAMPLE, a state constitution or the constitution of an organization, such as a union or a fraternal benefit society.
3. In, grounded in, based upon, contained in, or relating to a constitution.
• *adj.* approved, chartered, lawful, democratic, enforceable
• *ant.* unconstitutional

constitutional amendment
[kon.sti.*too*.shen.el a.*mend*.ment]

An amendment to a constitution. *See also* amendment of constitution.

constitutional convention
[kon.sti.*too*.shen.el ken.*ven*.shen]

1. A representative body that meets to form and adopt a constitution. (EXAMPLE: The convention that met in Philadelphia in 1787 to draft and adopt the Constitution of the United States.) 2. A representative body that meets to consider and adopt amendments to an existing constitution. Article V of the United States Constitution provides for the calling of a convention as a means of amending the Constitution.

constitutional courts
[kon.sti.*too*.shen.el kortz]

Courts directly established by the Constitution, which are therefore beyond the power of Congress to abolish or alter. EXAMPLE: the Supreme Court of the United States.

constitutional law
[kon.sti.*too*.shen.el law]

The body of principles that apply in the interpretation, construction, and application of the Constitution to statutes and to other governmental action. Constitutional law deals with constitutional questions and determines the constitutionality of state and federal laws and of the manner in which government exercises its authority.

constitutional limitations
[kon.sti.*too*.shen.el lim.i.*tay*.shenz]

The provisions of a constitution that limit the legislature's power to enact laws.

constitutional questions
[kon.sti.*too*.shen.el *kwes*.chenz]

See constitutional law.

constitutional right
[kon.sti.*too*.shen.el ryt]

A right guaranteed by the Constitution of the United States or by a state constitution; a fundamental right. A constitutional right cannot be abrogated or infringed by Congress or by a state legislature.

due process clause
[dew *pross*.ess kloz]

Actually a reference to two due process clauses, one in the Fifth Amendment and one in the Fourteenth Amendment. The Fifth Amendment requires the federal government to accord "due process of law" to citizens of the United States; the Fourteenth Amendment imposes a similar requirement upon state governments. *See also* due process of law.

due process of law
[dew *pross*.ess ov law]

Law administered through courts of justice, equally applicable to all under established rules that do not violate fundamental principles of fairness. Whether a person has received due process of law can only be determined on a case-by-case basis. In all criminal cases, however, it involves, at the very least, the right to be heard by a fair and impartial tribunal, the defendant's right to be represented by counsel, the right to cross-examine witnesses against him, the right to offer testimony on his own behalf, and the right to have advanced notice of trial and of the charge sufficient in detail and in point of time to permit adequate preparation for trial. Due process requirements for criminal prosecutions are considerably more rigorous than those for civil cases. "Due process of law" is guaranteed by both the Fifth Amendment and the Fourteenth Amendment. *See also* due process clause.

enumerated powers
[e.*nyoo*.me.ray.ted *pow*.erz]

Powers specifically granted by the Constitution to one of the three branches of government. Another term for enumerated powers is express powers.

equal protection clause
[*ee*.kwel pro.*tek*.shen kloz]

The clause in the Fourteenth Amendment that dictates that no state may "deny to any person within its jurisdiction the equal protection of the laws." *See also* equal protection of the laws.

equal protection of the laws
[*ee*.kwel pro.*tek*.shen ov the lawz]

Constitutional guarantee that specifies that the rights of all persons must rest upon the same rules under the same circumstances. Put another way, every state must give equal treatment to every person who is similarly situated or to persons who are members of the same class. "Equal protection of the laws" is a requirement for the Fourteenth Amendment. *See also* equal protection clause.

Equal Rights Amendment
[*ee*.kwel rytz a.*mend*.ment]

A proposed constitutional amendment, passed by Congress in 1972, that failed for lack of ratification by three-fourths of the states. The proposed amendment, generally referred to as the ERA, provided that "equality of rights under the law shall not be abridged by the United States or any state on account of sex."

establishment clause
[es.*tab*.lish.ment kloz]

The provision of the First Amendment that states that "Congress shall make no law respecting an establishment of religion, or prohibiting the free exercise thereof." It means that neither a state nor the federal government can set up a state religion; neither can it pass laws that aid one religion, aid all religions, or prefer one religion over another; neither can it force or influence a person to go to or remain away from a church, synagogue, mosque, or other place of worship, or force him to proclaim a belief or disbelief in any religion.

executive branch
[eg.*zek*.yoo.tiv branch]

1. With the legislative branch and the judicial branch, one of the three divisions into which the Constitution separates the government of the United States. These branches of government are also referred to as departments of government. The executive branch is primarily responsible for enforcing the laws. 2. A similar division in state government.

executive privilege
[eg.*zek*.yoo.tiv *priv*.i.lej]

The privilege of the president of the United States to refuse to make certain confidential communications available to public scrutiny or to review by any branch of government other than the executive branch.

federalism
[*fed*.er.el.izm]

1. Pertaining to a system of government that is federal in nature.
2. The system by which the states of the United States relate to each other and to the federal government.

Fifteenth Amendment
[*fif*.teenth a.*mend*.ment]

An amendment to the Constitution that provides that "the right of citizens of the United States to vote shall not be denied or abridged by the United States or by any state on account of race, color, or previous condition of servitude."

Fifth Amendment
[fifth a.*mend*.ment]

An amendment to the Constitution that guarantees the right to grand jury indictment if one is accused of having committed a serious crime, the right not to be placed in double jeopardy, the right not to be compelled to incriminate oneself, the right to due process of law, and the right not to have one's private property taken by the government without just compensation. The Fifth Amendment applies only to the federal government. Its requirements are made applicable to state and local government through the Fourteenth Amendment.

First Amendment
[first a.*mend*.ment]

An amendment to the Constitution that guarantees freedom of religion, freedom of speech, and freedom of the press, as well as freedom of association (the right "peaceably to assemble") and the right to petition the government for redress of grievances.

Fourteenth Amendment
[*four*.teenth a.*mend*.ment]

An amendment to the Constitution that requires the states (as opposed to the federal government—*compare* Fifth Amendment) to provide due process of law, and to ensure equal protection of the laws, "to any person within (their) jurisdiction." The Fourteenth Amendment also prohibits states from abridging "the privileges and immunities of citizens." *See also* due process clause; equal protection clause; privileges and immunities clause.

Fourth Amendment
[fourth a.*mend*.ment]

An amendment to the Constitution prohibiting searches without search warrants and requiring that search warrants be issued only upon probable cause.

free exercise clause
[free *ek*.ser.size kloz]

The clause in the First Amendment that prevents Congress from prohibiting the "free exercise" of religion. *See also* freedom of religion.

freedom of expression
[*free*.dum ov eks.*presh*.en]

A term that covers religious freedom, freedom of speech, and freedom of the press, all of which are protected by the First Amendment.

freedom of religion
[*free*.dum ov re.*lij*.en]

The First Amendment stipulates that "Congress shall make no law respecting an establishment of religion, or prohibiting the free exercise thereof." This provision guarantees the freedom to believe or not believe and, subject to law, the right to act upon one's religious belief or lack of belief. It also prohibits financial assistance to religion from public funds.

freedom of speech and of the press
[*free*.dum ov speech and ov the press]

The First Amendment provides that "Congress shall make no law . . . abridging the freedom of speech or of the press." It embraces the concept that the expression or publication of thought and belief, free from government interference, is essential to the well-being of a free society, and should be limited only to prevent abuse of that right.

interstate commerce
[*in*.ter.state *kawm*.ers]

Commerce between states; that is, from a given point in one state to a given point in another. Most federal statutes dealing with business or labor (EXAMPLES: consumer credit protection acts; the Fair Labor Standards Act), as well as many other federal statutes, are based upon the commerce clause of the Constitution, which gives Congress the power "to regulate commerce . . . among the several states." The term "commerce" is often used as a short reference for "interstate commerce." For EXAMPLE, "affecting commerce" means "affecting interstate commerce" and "engaged in commerce" means "engaged in interstate commerce." *See also* commerce clause. *Compare* intrastate commerce.

intrastate commerce
[*in*.tra.state *kawm*.ers]

Commerce that takes place within the boundaries of one state. *Compare* interstate commerce.

judicial branch
[joo.*dish*.el branch]

With the legislative branch and the executive branch, one of the three divisions into which the Constitution separates the government of the United States. These branches of government are also referred to as departments of government. The judicial branch is primarily responsible for interpreting the laws. 2. The similar division in state government.

legislation
[lej.is.*lay*.shen]

Laws (EXAMPLES: statutes, ordinances) enacted by a legislative body (EXAMPLES: Congress; a state legislature; a city council).
• *n.* law, regulation, statute, ordinances, ruling, measure, act

legislative branch
[lej.is.*lay*.tiv branch]

1. With the judicial branch and the executive branch, one of the three divisions into which the Constitution separates the government of the United States. These branches of government are also referred to as departments of government. The legislative branch is primarily responsible for enacting the laws. 2. A similar division in state government.

legislature
[*lej*.is.lay.cher]

The branch of government that enacts statutory law, usually consisting of two houses, a Senate and a House of Representatives, made up of members representing districts and elected by the voters of those districts. Congress is the national legislature.
• *n.* house, chamber, assembly, parliament, senate, council

Magna Carta
[*mag*.na *car*.ta]

(*Latin*) "Great charter," a document that was issued by King John of England in 1215 and is the basis of English and American constitutional protections. Its guarantees relating to life, liberty, and property are embedded in the Constitution of the United States and in every state constitution in the United States.

police power
[po.*leess pow*.er]

1. The power of the government to make and enforce laws and regulations necessary to maintain and enhance the public welfare and to prevent individuals from violating the rights of others. 2. The sovereignty of each of the states of the United States that is not surrendered to the federal government under the Constitution. *See also* Tenth Amendment.

preemption
[pree.*emp*.shen]

The doctrine that once Congress has enacted legislation in a given field, a state may not enact a law inconsistent with the federal statute. Thus, for EXAMPLE, a state may not enact a wage and hour law, applicable to employers who are in commerce, that is inconsistent with the provisions of the Fair Labor Standards Act. A similar doctrine also governs the relationship between the state government and local government.
• *n.* appropriation, substitution, usurpation, replacement, annexation ("preemption doctrine")

prior restraint
[pry.er re.*straynt*]

The imposition by the government, in advance of publication, of limits that prohibit or restrain speech or publication, as opposed to punishing persons for what they have actually said or written.

privileges and immunities clause
[*priv*.i.lejz and im.*yoon*.i.teez kloz]

1. Section 2 of Article IV of the Constitution, which provides that "[t]he citizens of each state shall be entitled to all privileges and immunities of citizens in the several states." 2. The clause of the Fourteenth Amendment that provides that "[n]o state shall make or enforce any law which shall abridge the privileges or immunities of citizens of the United States. . . ." These provisions represent a constitutional requirement that a state give out-of-state residents the same fundamental rights as it gives its own citizens.

procedural due process
[pro.*seed*.jer.el doo *pross*.ess]

The implication that a person has the right to a proceeding to protect one's rights.

rational basis
[rash.en.el *bay*.sis]

A reasonable basis, under the law. The courts will not invalidate a statute or overrule an order of an administrative agency that has a "rational basis" in law.

referendum
[ref.e.*ren*.dum]

Under some state constitutions, the process by which an act of the legislature or a constitutional amendment is referred to the voters at an election for their approval.
• *n.* proposition, proposal, election, questions, mandate, plebiscite

Senate
[*sen*.et]

The upper house of Congress. Its 100 members, two from each state, are elected for six-year terms; one-third of the Senate's members are elected every two years.

separate but equal doctrine [*sep*.ret but *ee*.kwel *dok*.trin]	A doctrine (overruled by *Brown v. Board of Education*), under which the separation of the races in places of public accommodation, including public schools, had been previously held constitutional.
separation of powers [sep.e.*ray*.shen ov *pow*.erz]	A fundamental principle of the Constitution, which gives exclusive power to the legislative branch to make the law, exclusive power to the executive branch to administer it, and exclusive power to the judicial branch to enforce it. The authors of the Constitution believed that the separation of powers would make abuse of power less likely.
strict scrutiny test [strikt *skrew*.ten.ee test]	A term the Supreme Court uses to describe the rigorous level of judicial review to be applied in determining the constitutionality of legislation that restricts a fundamental right or legislation based upon a suspect classification: age, sex, etc.
substantive due process [*sub*.sten.tiv doo *pross*.ess]	A right grounded in the Fifth and Fourteenth Amendments, the concept that government may not act arbitrarily or capriciously in making, interpreting, or enforcing the law.
supremacy clause [soo.*prem*.e.see kloz]	The provision in Article VI of the Constitution that "this Constitution and the laws of the United States . . . shall be the supreme law of the land, and the judges in every state shall be bound thereby."
supreme court [soo.*preem* kort]	1. The United States Supreme Court. The United States Supreme Court is the highest court in the federal court system. It is established by the Constitution and has both original jurisdiction and appellate jurisdiction. 2. In most states, the highest appellate court of the state. 3. In some states, a trial court.
taxing power [*tak*.sing pow.er]	The power of government to levy, assess, and collect taxes.
Tenth Amendment [tenth a.*mend*.ment]	An amendment to the Constitution that provides that the powers not delegated to the federal government by the Constitution are reserved to the states or to the people.

Missing Words

Fill in the blanks below.

1. The _____ branch of government is primarily responsible for interpreting the laws.

2. The process by which a constitutional amendment is referred to the voters at an election for their approval is known as _____.

3. _____ is the power of government to levy, assess, and collect taxes.

4. There is a(n) _____ clause in both the Fifth and Fourteenth Amendments to the Constitution.

5. The _____ branch is the branch of government that enacts statutory law.

6. The _____ is a nonprofit organization that is concerned with constitutional rights.

7. The courts will not invalidate a statute so long as the statute has a(n) _____ in law.

8. The _____ is the highest court in the federal court system.

9. The president of the United States may rely on _____ and refuse to make confidential communications available to public scrutiny.

10. _____ pertains to a system of government that is federal in nature.

11. _____ of powers makes the abuse of power by one branch of government less likely.

12. The _____ clause guarantees that citizens of each state shall be entitled to the same equal rights.

13. The _____ is the fundamental document of American government.

14. The _____ branch of government is primarily responsible for enforcing the law.

15. When an act of the legislature is referred to the voters at an election, this is called a(n) _____.

16. The _____ provides that the powers not delegated to the federal government are reserved to the states.

17. _____ is commerce that takes place within the borders of one state.

18. The _____ is the document that is the basis of both English and American constitutional protections.

Matching

Match the letter of the definition to the term below.

_____ 19. Freedom of expression

_____ 20. Fifth Amendment

_____ 21. Supremacy clause

_____ 22. Fourth Amendment

_____ 23. Police power

_____ 24. Articles

_____ 25. Magna Carta

_____ 26. Free exercise clause

_____ 27. Interstate commerce

_____ 28. Constitutional courts

_____ 29. Bicameral

_____ 30. Constitution

_____ 31. Enumerated powers

_____ 32. Fifteenth Amendment

_____ 33. Substantive due process

_____ 34. Procedural due process

A. Right not to be compelled to incriminate oneself

B. Commerce between states

C. Freedom of religion

D. Courts directly established by the Constitution

E. Freedom of speech

F. Power of government to make laws maintaining public welfare

G. This amendment prohibits searches without search warrants

H. The Constitution is the supreme law of the land

I. The Constitution is divided into seven of these distinct parts

J. A document that is the basis of English and American constitutional protections

K. Powers specifically granted by the Constitution

L. Right to vote shall not be denied based on race, color, or servitude

M. Two-chambered

N. Written law

O. Prohibits the government from acting arbitrarily or capriciously

P. A person has the right to a proceeding to protect one's rights, per the Fifth and Fourteenth Amendments

Multiple Choice

Select the best choice.

_____ 35. The first 10 amendments to the Constitution are known as the:
   a. Magna Carta
   b. Bill of Rights
   c. preemption doctrine
   d. supremacy clause

_____ 36. The executive branch of government is primarily responsible for:
   a. enforcing the laws
   b. interpreting the laws
   c. making the laws
   d. changing the laws

_____ 37. The principle that requires rights of individual citizens to be balanced against the dangers that their exercise presents to others is called:
   a. strict scrutiny
   b. equal protection
   c. due process
   d. balancing test

_____ 38. Powers specifically granted by the Constitution to one of the three branches of government are called:
   a. secret powers
   b. enumerated powers
   c. springing powers
   d. police powers

_____ 39. A representative body that meets to form and adopt a constitution is called:
   a. legislature
   b. judicial branch
   c. bicameral
   d. convention

_____ 40. This doctrine provided for the separation of races in places of public accommodation:
   a. separate but equal
   b. equal but adequate
   c. separate and apart
   d. separation of powers

_____ 41. The clause in the Constitution prohibiting federal government from setting up a state religion is called the:
   a. establishment clause
   b. due process clause
   c. equal protection clause
   d. privileges and immunities clause

_____ 42. Freedom of speech and expression is a right granted under which amendment to the Constitution?
   a. First Amendment
   b. Fourth Amendment
   c. Fifth Amendment
   d. Fourteenth Amendment

_____ 43. A guarantee in the Constitution that each state will give equal treatment to all persons similarly situated:
   a. due process
   b. equal protection
   c. privileges and immunities
   d. strict scrutiny

_____ 44. The legislature is divided into two houses. It is known as:
   a. separate but equal doctrine
   b. articles
   c. commerce clause
   d. bicameral

_____ 45. Once Congress has enacted legislation in a given field, a state may not enact a law inconsistent with federal statute. This is called:
   a. preemption
   b. prior
   c. separation of powers
   d. rational basis

_____ 46. The upper house of Congress with 100 members, two from each state, is the:
   a. Senate
   b. House of Representatives
   c. General Court
   d. Legislative assembly

True/False

Mark the following T or F.

_____ **47.** The judicial branch of government is primarily responsible for enforcing the laws.

_____ **48.** A document setting forth the fundamental principles of governance is known as a constitution.

_____ **49.** Freedom of speech and the press is covered under the Fourth Amendment to the Constitution.

_____ **50.** Enumerated powers are the government's powers to make laws maintaining the public welfare.

_____ **51.** The executive branch is the branch of government responsible for interpreting the laws.

_____ **52.** The legislature consists of four houses.

_____ **53.** The first 10 amendments to the Constitution are known as the Magna Carta.

_____ **54.** Strict scrutiny test is a term the Supreme Court uses to describe a rigorous level of judicial review.

_____ **55.** If a law is found to be in accordance with the Constitution, it is said to be constitutional.

_____ **56.** The establishment clause prevents the government from setting up a state religion.

_____ **57.** An amendment is a change to the Constitution.

Synonyms

Select the correct synonym in parentheses for each numbered item.

58. FIFTH AMENDMENT
(equal protection clause, due process clause, privileges and immunities clause)

59. ENUMERATED POWERS
(express, implied, changed)

60. AMENDMENT
(correction, protection, preservation)

61. FIRST AMENDMENT
(freedom of expression, double jeopardy, due process)

62. ARTICLE
(part, total, version)

63. CONSTITUTION
(oral law, written law, proposed law)

64. ARTICLES
(provisions, changes, additions)

65. PRIOR RESTRAINT
(freedom, advertising, censorship)

66. EXECUTIVE BRANCH
(president, courts, legislature)

67. SEPARATION OF POWERS
(division, blending, masking)

68. BICAMERAL
(one-chambered, two-chambered, three-chambered)

69. INTRASTATE COMMERCE
(within a state, between states, between nations)

70. DUE PROCESS
(fairness, supremacy, preemption)

71. CONSTITUTIONAL
(lawful, unfair, unenforceable)

Self-Test

Place the number of the correct term in the appropriate space.

72. Executive

73. Legislative

74. Constitution

75. Articles

76. Separation of powers

77. Enumerated

78. Supremacy clause

79. Amendments

80. Bill of Rights

81. Judicial

82. Fourth Amendment

84. Fifth Amendment

83. Tenth Amendment

85. First Amendment

The fundamental document of American government is the _____. The Constitution is composed of 7 _____ and 27 _____. According to Article VI of the Constitution, which is also known as the _____, the Constitution is the supreme law of the land. By setting up a system of _____, each branch of government, the _____ branch, the _____ branch, and the _____ branch, each have their own role in government. This prevents any one branch of government from becoming too powerful. These powers specifically granted to each branch of government are called _____ powers.

After the Constitution was ratified, the people were still concerned with protecting their individual liberties. The enactment of the first ten amendments to the Constitution, also known as the _____, was done to ensure that fundamental rights of citizens were protected.

Included in the Bill of Rights is the _____, which guarantees free speech, the _____, which prohibits warrantless searches, the _____, which protects against double jeopardy, and the _____, which provides that the powers not delegated to the federal government are reserved to the states.

Defining Words

Complete the definition.

_____

86. Legislature _____

_____

87. Amendment _____

_____

88. Federalism _____

_____

89. Preemption _____

_____

90. Enumerated powers _____

_____

91. Referendum _____

_____

92. Separation of powers _____

_____

93. Due process clause _____

_____

94. Constitution of the United States _____

_____

95. Bicameral _____

_____

96. Privileges and immunities clause _____

_____

97. Balancing test _____

_____

98. Strict scrutiny test _____

_____

99. Substantive due process _____

_____

100. Procedural due process _____

_____

Punctuation/Capitalization

Capitalization: the words amendment *and* constitution *and parties to the lawsuit.*

Rule 1: Capitalize the word *amendment*, and write out and capitalize the number of the amendment in front of it. Without the number, the word amendment is not capitalized.

This violates her Fourteenth Amendment rights.

He claimed the Fifth Amendment.

The reporter affirmed there was an amendment on the right to free speech.

Rule 2: Capitalize the word *constitution* when it refers to the United States Constitution. When the word refers to any other constitution, it is capitalized only when it has the full name with it.

It is part of the Bill of Rights of the Constitution.
The state assembly is proposing an amendment to the constitution.
He pointed out that it is a part of the United States Constitution.

Rule 3: The words representing governmental entities—e.g., *county, city, state, government*—are capitalized when they are parties to the lawsuit.

I want the City to take responsibility for the problem with the sidewalks.
The State will prove that this defendant was present at the scene.
This is a Government exhibit that we want marked.

Rule 4: These words are not capitalized when they represent the physical, geographical features.

I live in the city of Long Beach, California.
The crime occurred in the state of Utah.
We decided to locate our company in an unincorporated area of the county.

Directions: Correct any punctuation/capitalization errors in these sentences.

1. The law makes reference to the 8th amendment to the Constitution.

2. He is suing the city because of the accident.

3. The constitution used by this organization is not adequate.

4. He claimed the Fifth Amendment throughout his testimony.

5. How far is it to your city from the airport?

Word Pairs

ban/band/banned/banded

ban = forbid, deny access to.
The government has imposed a ban on the use of that substance.
The ban goes into effect at midnight.
There is a ban on that, as I understand it.

band = rim, musical group, group with similar purposes, ring, radio frequency.
He plays in the band.
She lost her wedding band.
There was a band of thieves operating in the area.

banned = forbidden. This is the past tense of the word *ban*.
That substance has been banned for several years.
The city council banned drinking in public buildings.
My impression is that that behavior was banned at school functions.

banded = having a rim or strap around it.

The bales were banded with wire.
The hat was banded in bright red.
It was banded with contrasting fabric.

clause/claws

clause = section, phrase, passage.

He wants a new clause added to his contract.
I think that clause is very restrictive.
There is a clause that prohibits payment for that service.

claws = nails, scratches, examines thoroughly.

The idea is that he claws his way to the top.
The claws were particularly sharp.
She claws through the material on a daily basis.

dew/do/due

dew = moisture, usually on outdoor surfaces during the night.

He is claiming he slipped on the dew.
The dew covered the entire area.
I didn't realize that the dew was on the grass.

do = accomplish, take action, use, be busy with, work at something.

What do you do for a living?
He intends to do his homework this evening.
The claim is she was doing drugs.

due = owed, expected, appropriate.

The rent check was due on the 5th of each month.
Her delay was due to the severe weather.
The baby is due in June.

moral/morale/mortal

moral = ethical, honest, according to accepted standards, involved with right and wrong.
The opposite form is *immoral*, "without values."

To her, it was a moral decision not to participate.
She lives according to strict morals.
In addition to being illegal, that act was immoral.

morale = spirit, how someone feels emotionally.

The morale at the company was at an all-time low.
It was his job to keep morale up in the group.
How did morale get to such a low level?

mortal = capable of dying. The opposite form is *immortal*, "living forever."

It was a mortal wound.

I believed he was in mortal danger in that house.

He did not want to admit that he is mortal.

sole/soul

sole = lone, only, bottom of the foot or shoe.

He is a sole practitioner in the firm.

Is she solely responsible for the damage here?

The injury was to the sole of his foot.

soul = spirit, private feelings, nonphysical, vital part.

He is the heart and soul of this team.

My feeling is that she is a very soulful person.

He felt the turbulence in his soul.

Directions: Choose the correct form of the word.

1. This attorney is not the sole/soul of brevity.

2. I believe that person has been band/banned/banded from the proceedings.

3. It was a morally/mortally reprehensible act.

4. We needed to do something to lift moral/morale.

5. The clause/claws were sharp as they dug into her skin.

6. When is the plane dew/do/due to arrive?

7. The cartons were band/banned/banded with a heavy twine.

8. He is the sole/soul operator of the business.

9. The feeling is that this is a moral/mortal wound to the project.

10. Moral/Morale was really low after the round of firings.

11. I don't think it is in his sole/soul to commit such an act.

12. He is a part of the moral/morale majority movement in the country.

13. The ban/band will be in effect until further notice.

14. It is obvious that that clause/claws was added to the policy much later.

15. Was she solely/soully at fault for the accident?

16. A band/banned of renegades led the opposition to it.

17. It was necessary to complete the dew/do/due diligence before the sale.

18. This act is immoral/immortal and reprehensible.

19. The band/banned/banded bales of cardboard arrived at the docks.

20. Most people believed that the soles/souls were defective, which led to the recall.

Is It One Word or Two? An Apostrophe? A Hyphen?

thereon/there on

thereon = on that, on there.

He based his argument against the motion thereon.
The judge made a ruling thereon.
There were several items in the bill with the appropriate encumbrances thereon.

there on = from there forward.

From there on, he refused to listen to anything she had to say.
She had a difficult time from there on.
It was understood she was in charge from there on.

overall/ over all

overall = generally, totally, on the whole. In the plural, *overalls*, the word refers to a garment that is used to protect other clothing.

We have the overall responsibility for the project.
Overall, it has been a very good convention.
It is the overall look that she was going for in the design.

over all = in charge of everything.

She was made the manager over all the production staff.
He saw himself as over all the others.
It is thought that she triumphed over all the odds against her.

Directions: Choose the correct form of the word.

1. He was in charge overall/over all the design aspects of the car.

2. She was recovering nicely overall/over all.

3. Did you see him regularly from thereon/there on?

4. Did you base your argument for the bill thereon/there on?

5. Overall/over all, how did you fare?

Proofreading

Directions: Make necessary corrections, based on the material presented in the unit. If the sentence has no errors, write the word *correct* after the sentence.

1. He was claiming his rights under a clause in the 6th amendment to the U.S. constitution. _____

2. For me, it was a moral decision about promoting the over all effectiveness of the product. _____

3. It was band because it contained words in direct opposition to the state constitution. _____

4. After she was admonished, she was the sole of brevity from thereon. _____

5. Overall, our rights under the Fifth Amendment were honored. _____

6. The state attempted to prove that the do diligence was faulty. _____

7. He lives in the City and has banded together with his neighbors to get the ordinance enacted. _____

8. The bill suffered a moral blow when it was declared it violated the 1st Amendment. _____

9. Morale had been low for several months because he was in charge overall the employees. _____

10. The band of the substance from all public buildings was illegal, and I based my argument against it there on. _____

Adaptation from a Constitutional Law Case

Facts:

John Doe, a convicted sex offender with a criminal history of convictions for child molestation, was banned for life from all park property in the city of Lafayette, Indiana. The city of Lafayette has an extensive park system that includes several large parks, many small neighborhood parks, a zoo, a golf course, sports complexes, and pools. Doe's last conviction was ten years before this litigation. This ban occurred after Doe reported to his psychologist and to a self-help group he attended that he had been watching children in a park for about 15 to 30 minutes and thought about having sexual contact with them. An anonymous source reported this to Doe's former probation officer. The City did not provide notice or a hearing before instituting the ban, nor did it allow Doe to appeal the decision.

Procedural History:

Doe filed suit against the City, arguing that the ban violated his First Amendment right to freedom of thought and a right under the Fourteenth Amendment to loiter in public parks. The District Court granted summary judgment in favor of the City.

Issue:

Was the District Court's decision correct? Can you ban a person from public property for having immoral thoughts?

Rationale:

Typically, orders which ban people are directed against those who vandalize a particular location and are for a particular period of time. Generally, at the heart of the First Amendment of the Constitution is the proposition that the right of freedom of thought is protected as is the right to refrain from speaking. The fear that thoughts alone may encourage action is not enough to curb protected thinking. The First Amendment draws a vital distinction between words and deeds. No one is punishable solely for his thoughts. This is the heart of the American criminal justice system. If it were not so restricted, "all mankind would be criminals."

Ruling:

The decision is reversed. The ban violates the First Amendment.

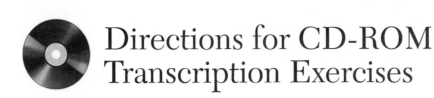

Directions for CD-ROM Transcription Exercises

In audio format are:

1. Terms for the unit with pronunciations from the thesaurus/dictionary feature.

2. Self-Test that appears in the book at mid-unit.*

3. Case that appears at the unit end.*

*speeds are 80 wpm/120 wpm for differing skill levels

CD-ROM icons appear where the three above are located within each unit.

Readers may practice transcription by listening to the CD-ROM where prompted by the icons in the book. However, for high success in testing your transcription skills, mastering all the terms and English skills in the unit is recommended before attempting the CD-ROM.

For Keyboard Transcriptionists: Listen to the CD-ROM audio file for this unit at 80 wpm or 120 wpm and transcribe from the dictation on your computer. Edit and proofread your work against the printed copy in the book.

For Reporting Writers: Listen to the CD-ROM audio file at 80 wpm or 120 wpm and take down the dictation on your writer. Either transcribe from your notes and proofread your work or edit and proofread your CAT (computer-aided transcription) transcript. Always check your work against the printed copy in the book.

Student CD-ROM
For additional materials,
please go to the CD in this book.

Online Companion[TM]
For additional resources, please go to
http://www.paralegal.delmar.cengage.com

Area of Law

Contracts

The **Mistakes** That Court Reporters Make and *How to Avoid* Them

The Mistake:

Marlene McCarthy went to her state reporting convention and bought two necklaces at the jewelry vendor booth. They were in good taste, and she wore them to the job in court the next day. After reading back a rather lengthy section to the jury, Marlene straightened up to begin writing again, only to have her new necklaces intertwined in the keys of her machine. As the judge talked away, Marlene was trying to untangle the necklaces. She had to ask the judge to stop talking until she could get her jewelry problem solved.

How to Avoid It:

It is a simple problem to solve—no long necklaces. Any jewelry, no matter how tasteful, that hangs down low enough to get caught in the keys must be avoided.

Introduction

The law of contracts provides an orderly method for conducting business. People can negotiate and haggle over terms, trying to get the best bargain. When both parties are content and wish to make a binding agreement, they can draft a contract. Contrary to popular belief, it need not always be in writing. For some matters, oral contracts are permissible, but three elements must exist: offer, acceptance, and consideration. In the case at the end of the unit, the court held there was no oral contract.

There are two different kinds of contracts. There are two-sided or bilateral contracts, where a promise for a promise is made: John says, "I promise to mow your lawn on Tuesday for $30." Cindy responds, "I promise to pay you $30 for mowing my lawn on Tuesday." In unilateral or one-sided contracts, only one promise is made. A person promises to perform some act. One can only accept a unilateral contract by performing the act requested. An example of this is a reward situation: "I'll pay $20 to the person who finds my wallet." In order to accept, you don't make any promises. To accept, you must find the wallet and return it as required by the offeror.

Unit Objectives

- ▥ Work with a legal dictionary/thesaurus.
- ▥ Learn about the law of contracts.
- ▥ Master the similarities and differences in definitions of key terms regarding contracts.
- ▥ Master the pronunciations and spellings of legal terms in this unit.
- ▥ Recognize the synonyms used for legal terminology in this unit.
- ▥ Practice usage of terms, definitions, and synonyms for contracts.
- ▥ Complete unit exercises in the forms of missing words, matching, multiple choice, true/false, synonyms, self-test, defining words, and also:
  - ● Punctuation/capitalization
  - ● Word pairs
  - ● Transcription of terms, self-test, and case
  - ● Proofreading

Dictionary/Thesaurus

Note: All Dictionary/Thesaurus terms appear on the CD-ROM with audio pronunciations.

Term [phonetic pronunciation]	
acceptance [ak.*sep*.tens]	The assent by the person to whom an offer is made, to the offer as made by the person making it. This is necessary for a binding contract. *See also* offer and acceptance.
accord and satisfaction [a.*kord* and sat.is.*fak*.shen]	An agreement between two persons, one of whom is suing the other, in which the claimant accepts a compromise in full satisfaction of his claim (usually a lesser amount).
adhesion contract [ad.*hee*.zhen *kon*.trakt]	A contract prepared by the dominant party (usually a form contract) and presented on a take-it-or-leave-it basis to the weaker party, who has no real opportunity to bargain about its terms. *See also* contract.
age of majority [aj ov ma.*jaw*.ri.tee]	The age at which a person may legally engage in conduct in which she could not previously engage because she was a minor. EXAMPLES: entering into a binding contract; enlisting in the military service; voting; making a valid will.
agreement [a.*gree*.ment]	1. A contract. 2. A concurrence of intention; mutual assent. *See also* meeting of the minds. 3. A coming together of parties with respect to a matter of opinion. • *n.* contract, bargain, compact, arrangement, pact; concurrence, compliance, alliance
anticipatory breach [an.*tiss*.i.pe.tore.ee breech]	The announced intention of a party to a contract that she does not intend to perform her obligations under the contract; an announced intention to commit a breach of contract. *Compare* repudiation.
bargain [*bar*.gen]	*n.* An agreement between two or more persons; a contract. *v.* To negotiate; to talk about the terms of a contract. • *n.* treaty, pact, settlement, deal, agreement, transaction, contract, covenant, stipulation
bilateral [by.*lat*.er.el]	1. Involving two interests. 2. Having two sides.
bilateral contract [by.*lat*.er.el *kon*.trakt]	A contract in which each party promises performance to the other, the promise by the one furnishing the consideration for the promise from the other. EXAMPLE: a contract for home heating oil (the dealer promises to deliver, the homeowner promises to pay). *Compare* unilateral contract.

boilerplate language
[*boy*.ler.plate *lang*.wej]

Language common to all legal documents of the same type. Attorneys maintain files of such standardized forms for use where appropriate.

breach of contract
[breech ov *kon*.trakt]

Failure, without legal excuse, to perform any promise that forms a whole or a part of a contract, including the doing of something inconsistent with its terms.

capacity
[ke.*pass*.i.tee]

Competency in law. USAGE: "Generally, a minor does not have the capacity to enter into contracts."

competent
[*kom*.pe.tent]

1. Having legal capacity. 2. Capable; qualified. 3. Sufficient; acceptable.
• *adj.* eligible, qualified, capable, fit, polished, efficient, responsible, able
• *ant.* uncapable

consideration
[ken.sid.e.*ray*.shen]

1. The reason a person enters into a contract; that which is given in exchange for performance or the promise to perform; the price bargained and paid; the inducement. Consideration is an essential element of a valid and enforceable contract. A promise to refrain from doing something one is entitled to do also constitutes consideration. 2. Motivation, incentive, inducement.
• *n.* value, incentive, recompense, inducement, reward, benefit ("Consideration is an essential element of a valid and enforceable contract")

contract
[*kon*.trakt]

n. An agreement entered into, for adequate consideration, to do, or refrain from doing, a particular thing. The Uniform Commercial Code defines a contract as the total legal obligation resulting from the parties' agreement. In addition to adequate consideration, the transaction must involve an undertaking that is legal to perform, and there must be mutuality of agreement and obligation between at least two competent parties. *See also* adhesion contract; bilateral contract; breach of contract; executed contract; executory contract; express contract; implied contract; quasi contract; third-party beneficiary contract; unilateral contract; void contract; voidable contract.
v. To enter into a contract.
• *n.* agreement, understanding, bargain, compact, mutual promise, covenant, accord, arrangement, promise, assurance
• *v.* agree, promise, engage, undertake, covenant, bargain, obligate, pledge; condense, shrink, recede, lessen

counteroffer
[*koun*.ter off.er]

A position taken in response to an offer, proposing a different deal.

cure
[kyur]

1. Under the Uniform Commercial Code, a seller has the right to correct ("cure") his failure to deliver goods that conform to the contract if he does so within the period of the contract. 2. To remedy.
• *n.* recovery, improvement, remedy, restoration, correction, palliative, panacea, antidote, elixir

damages
[*dam*.e.jez]

The sum of money that may be recovered in the courts as financial reparation for an injury or wrong suffered as a result of breach of contract or a tortious act.
• *n.* restoration, compensation, restitution, repayment, recovery, reparation, expenses, expiation

disaffirm
[dis.e.*ferm*]

To disclaim; to repudiate; to renounce; to disavow; to deny.
• *v.* disavow, recant, negate, veto, rescind, renege, renounce, deny, repudiate
• *ant.* affirm

enforceable
[en.*forss*.ebl]

That which can be put into effect or carried out, referring to legal rights. EXAMPLES: a contract; a judgment.
• *adj.* binding, lawful, effective
• *ant.* unenforceable

entire output contract
[in.*tire out*.put *kon*.trakt]

A contract in which the seller binds herself to the buyer to sell to the buyer the entire output of a product she manufactures, and the buyer binds himself to buy all of the product. *See also* requirement contract.

equity
[*ek*.wi.tee]

A system for ensuring justice in circumstances where the remedies customarily available under the conventional law are inadequate; a system of jurisprudence less formal and more flexible than the common law, available in particular types of cases to better ensure a fair result.

executed contract
[ek.se.*kyoot*.ed *kon*.trakt]

A contract whose terms have been fully performed. *Compare* executory contract.

executory contract
[ek.se.kyoo.*tor*.ee *kon*.trakt]

A contract yet to be performed, each party having bound to do or not to do a particular thing. *Compare* executed contract.

express contract
[eks.*press kon*.trakt]

A contract whose terms are stated by the party.

formal contract
[*for*.mel *kon*.trakt]

1. A signed, written contract, as opposed to an oral contract. 2. A contract that must be in a certain form to be valid. EXAMPLE: a negotiable instrument. *Compare* informal contract.

implied contract
[im.*plide kon*.trakt]

Implied contracts are of two types: contracts implied in fact, which the law infers from the circumstances, conduct, acts, or the relationship of the parties rather than from their spoken words; and contracts implied in law, which are quasi contracts or constructive contracts imposed by the law, usually to prevent unjust enrichment.

impossibility
[im.poss.i.*bil*.i.tee]

That which cannot be done. *Compare* impracticability.
• *n.* futility, insurmountability, infeasibility, unattainability, failure, unfeasibility, difficulty, failure

impracticability
[im.prak.ti.ke.*bil*.i.tee]

A legal term unique to the Uniform Commercial Code, from the provision of the UCC that excuses a seller from the obligation to deliver goods when delivery has become unrealistic because of unforeseen circumstances. *Compare* impossibility. *See also* Uniform Commercial Code.

incompetency
[in.*kawm*.pe.ten.see]

1. The condition, state, or status of an incompetent person. 2. Lack of capability. *Compare* competency.

infancy
[*in*.fen.see]

1. The status of a person who has not reached the age of majority and who therefore is under a civil disability; nonage; minority. 2. A civil disability resulting from the fact that one has not yet attained one's majority. 3. The period of life during which one is a very young child.
• *n.* childhood; inception, start, conception, genesis

informal contract
[in.*for*.mel *kon*.trakt]

A contract not in the customary form, often an oral contract. *Compare* formal contract.

intention
[in.*ten*.shen]

Purpose; plan; object; aim; goal. The intention of the parties is the most important factor in interpreting a contract.
• *n.* course, proclivity, purpose, route, propensity, purpose, plan, object, aim, goal ("the intention of the parties"); penchant, bias, leaning, impetus, current

lapse
[laps]

n. A termination or extinguishment, particularly of a right or privilege; a forfeiture caused by a person's failure to perform some necessary act or by the nonoccurrence of some contingency.
v. To cease; to expire; to terminate.
• *n.* termination, extinguishment, forfeiture; break, pause, recess
• *v.* cease, expire, terminate, discontinue, abate

liquidated damages
[*lik*.wi.dated *dam*.e.jez]

A sum agreed upon by the parties at the time of entering into a contract as being payable by way of compensation for loss suffered in the event of a breach of contract; a sum similarly determined by a court in a lawsuit resulting from breach of contract.

mailed
[maled]

Describes an item when it is appropriately enveloped or packaged, addressed, and stamped, and deposited in a proper place for the receipt of mail. In contract law, acceptance of an offer takes place when the acceptance is mailed, unless the parties have made another arrangement or a statute provides otherwise. This is sometimes referred to as the "mailbox rule."

majority
[ma.*jaw*.ri.tee]

Legal age; full age; the age at which a person acquires the capacity to contract; the age at which a person is no longer a minor. The age of majority varies from state to state and differs depending upon the purpose.
• *n.* legal age, full age, age of responsibility

meeting of the minds
[*meet*.ing ov the mindz]

The mutual assent of the parties to a contract with respect to all of the principal terms of the contract. A meeting of the minds is essential to the creation of a legally enforceable contract.

misrepresentation
[mis.rep.re.zen.*tay*.shen]

The statement of an untruth; a misstatement of fact designed to lead one to believe that something is other than it is; a false statement of fact designed to deceive.
• *n.* fraud, deception, deceit, distortion, fabrication, exaggeration

mistake
[mis.*take*]

1. An erroneous mental conception that influences a person to act or to decline to act; an unintentional act, omission, or error arising from ignorance, surprise, imposition, or misplaced confidence. "Mistake" is a legal concept especially significant in contract law because, depending upon the circumstance, it may warrant reformation or rescission of a contract. 2. An error; a misunderstanding; an inaccuracy.
• *n.* misconception, inaccuracy, lapse, slip, confusion, erratum ("a mistake of identity")

mutual mistake
[*myoo*.choo.el mis.*take*]

Both sides of a transaction or contract have different perceptions of fact or law.

offer
[*off*.er]

n. 1. A proposal made with the purpose of obtaining an acceptance, thereby creating a contract. *See also* acceptance, mailed. 2. A tender of performance. 3. A statement of intention or willingness to do something. 4. A proposal; a proposition; a bid. *See also* counteroffer.
v. 1. To propose for acceptance or rejection. USAGE: "I offered him the choice of going with me or staying home."
• *v.* present, advance, propose, provide, award, suggest
• *n.* proposal, suggestion, endeavor, proposition, submission, bid

offer and acceptance
[*off*.er and ak.*sep*.tense]

Essential elements in the creation of a legally enforceable contract, reflecting mutual assent or a meeting of the minds. In the case of a bilateral contract, acceptance is the offeree's communication that she intends to be bound by the offer; in the case of a unilateral contract, the offeree accepts by performing in accordance with the terms of the offer.

offeree
[off.er.*ree*]

A person to whom an offer is made. *Compare* offeror.

offeror
[off.er.*ror*]

A person who makes an offer.

option
[*op*.shen]

An offer, combined with an agreement supported by consideration not to revoke the offer for a specified period of time; a future contract in which one of the parties has the right to insist on compliance with the contract, or to cancel it, at his election. In other words, "option" is short for option contract.
• *n.* advantage, offer, choice, preference, prerogative ("option to purchase")

oral contract [*ohr*.el *kon*.trakt]	A contract that is not in writing. Unless the subject of an oral contract is covered by the statute of frauds, it is just as valid as a written contract; often, however, its enforceability is limited because its terms cannot be proven. *See also* contract, informal contract. • *n.* parol contract
performance [per.*form*.ense]	1. The doing of that which is required by a contract at the time, place, and in the manner stipulated in the contract, that is, according to the terms of the contract. 2. Fulfilling a duty in a manner that leaves nothing more to be done. • *n.* fulfillment, effort, production
promise [*prom*.iss]	*n.* 1. In contract law, an undertaking that binds the promisor to cause a future event to happen; an offer that, if supported by consideration, and if accepted, is a contract. 2. In contract law, an assurance that a thing will or will not be done. It gives the person to whom it is made the right to demand the performance or nonperformance of the thing if she acted in reliance and to her detriment. 3. Under the Uniform Commercial Code, "a written undertaking to pay money signed by the person undertaking to pay." 4. A pledge; a warrant; a covenant; a contract. *v.* To pledge oneself to performance, to covenant. • *v.* affirm, warrant, bargain, swear, vow, pledge, covenant, vouch ("I promise I will do this for you") • *n.* oath, declaration, affirmation, vow, pledge, assurance, endorsement, covenant, hope, warrant ("I have her promise of loyalty")
promisee [prom.i.*see*]	A person to whom a promise is made.
promisor [prom.i.*sore*]	A person who makes a promise.
quantum meruit [*kwan*.tum *mehr*.oo.it]	(*Latin*) Literally, it means "as much as is deserved." This doctrine makes a person liable to pay for goods or services she accepts, while knowing the other party expects to be paid, even if no contract exists.
quasi contract [*kway*.zye *kon*.trakt]	An obligation imposed by law to achieve equity, usually to prevent unjust enrichment. A quasi contract is a legal fiction that a contract exists where there has been no express contract. EXAMPLE: a contract implied on the theory of quantum meruit.
ratify [*rat*.i.fy]	To give approval, to confirm. • *v.* sanction, embrace, confirm, acquiesce, countersign, agree, affirm, authorize • *ant.* repudiate
reformation [ref.er.*may*.shun]	An equitable remedy available to a party to a contract provided she can prove that the contract does not reflect the true agreement.

rejection
[re.*jek*.shun]

1. Any act or word of an offeree, communicated to an offeror, conveying her refusal of an offer. 2. The act of rejecting.
• *n.* abandonment, disallowance, denial, snub, slight, proscription, abnegation, contempt, eviction, refusal, waiver

repudiation
[re.pyoo.dee.*ay*.shun]

A denial of the validity of something; a denial of authority.
• *n.* denial, rejection, renunciation, repeal, retraction, nullification, spurning, disaffirmation

requirement contract
[re.*kwire*.ment *kon*.trakt]

A contract under which one party agrees to furnish the entire supply of specified goods or services required by the other party for a specified period of time, and the other party agrees to purchase his entire requirement from the first party exclusively. *See also* entire output contract.

rescission
[ree.*sizh*.en]

The abrogation, annulment, or cancellation of a contract by the act of a party. Rescission may occur by mutual consent of the parties, pursuant to a condition contained in the contract, or for fraud, failure of consideration, material breach, or default. It is also a remedy available to the parties by a judgment or decree of the court. More than mere termination, rescission restores the parties to the status quo existing before the contract was entered into.
• *n.* unmaking, termination, withdrawal, vitiation, voidance, extricating

restitution
[res.ti.*tew*.shen]

In both contract and tort, a remedy that restores the status quo. Restitution returns a person who has been wrongfully deprived of something to the position he occupied before the wrong occurred; it requires a defendant who has been unjustly enriched at the expense of the plaintiff to make the plaintiff whole, either, as may be appropriate, by returning property unjustly held, by reimbursing the plaintiff, or by paying compensation. *See also* unjust enrichment.
• *n.* compensation, repayment, amends, dues, recompense, reparation, squaring, remitter, redress

revocation of offer
[rev.e.*kay*.shen ov *off*.er]

The withdrawal of an offer by an offeror before it has been accepted.

statute of frauds
[*stat*.shoot ov frawdz]

A statute, existing in one form or another in every state, that requires certain classes of contract to be in writing and signed by the parties. Its purpose is to prevent fraud or reduce the opportunities for fraud. A contract to guarantee the debt of another is an EXAMPLE of an agreement that the statute of frauds requires to be in writing.

third-party beneficiary contract
[third-*par*.tee ben.e.*fish*.er.ee *kon*.trakt]

A contract made for the benefit of a third person.

unconscionable
[un.*kon*.shen.ebl]

Morally offensive, reprehensible, or repugnant. An unconscionable contract is a contract in which a dominant party has taken unfair advantage of a weaker party, who has little or no bargaining power, and has imposed terms and conditions that are unreasonable and one-sided. A court may refuse to enforce an unconscionable contract.
• *adj.* excessive, preposterous, exorbitant, unscrupulous, inexcusable, unequal, grossly unfair

undue influence
[*un*.dew *in*.flew.ense]

Inappropriate pressure exerted on a person for the purpose of causing him to substitute his will with the will or wishes of another.

Uniform Commercial Code (UCC)
[*yoon*.i.form ke.*mersh*.el kode]

One of the Uniform Laws, which have been adopted in much the same form in every state. It governs most aspects of commercial transactions, including sales, leases, negotiable instruments, deposits and collections, letters of credit, bulk sales, warehouse receipts, bills of lading and other documents of title, investment securities, and secured transactions.

unilateral contract
[yoon.i.*lat*.er.el *kon*.trakt]

A contract in which there is a promise on one side only, the consideration being an act or something other than another promise. In other words, a unilateral contract is an offer that is accepted not by another promise but by performance. EXAMPLE: The Acme Ball Bearing Company promises Sam that if he buys advertising material from Acme he will be the sole Chicago distributor of Acme's ball bearings. *Compare* bilateral contract.

unilateral mistake
[yoon.i.*lat*.er.el mis.*take*]

A misconception by one, but not both, parties to a contract with respect to the terms of the contract.

unjust enrichment
[un.*just* en.*rich*.ment]

The equitable doctrine that a person who unjustly receives property, money, or other benefits that belong to another may not retain them and is obligated to return them. The remedy of restitution is based upon the principle that equity will not permit unjust enrichment.

valid
[*val*.id]

Effective; sufficient in law; legal; lawful; not void; in effect. USAGE: "Valid contract"; "valid marriage"; "valid defense."
• *adj.* attested, compelling, irrefutable, proven, substantial ("a valid transcript"); effective, legal, lawful ("valid contract")

void contract
[voyd *kon*.trakt]

A contract that creates no legal rights; the equivalent of no contract at all. *Compare* voidable contract.

voidable
[*voyd*.ebl]

Avoidable; subject to disaffirmance; defective but valid unless disaffirmed by the person entitled to disaffirm.
• *adj.* avoidable, reversible, revocable, nullifiable ("a voidable contract")

voidable contract
[*voyd*.ebl *kon*.trakt]

A contract that may be avoided or disaffirmed by one of the parties because it is defective, for EXAMPLE, a contract induced by fraud.

Missing Words

Fill in the blanks below.

1. A(n) _____ can be either implied in fact based on the conduct of the parties or implied in law to prevent unjust enrichment.

2. A contract that must be in a certain form to be valid is a(n) _____ contract.

3. A system for ensuring fairness in circumstances where the remedies customarily available under conventional law are inadequate is known as _____.

4. _____ is the announced intention of a party to a contract that he doesn't intend to perform his obligation under the contract.

5. A contract where one party agrees to furnish the entire supply of specified goods or services required by another is known as a(n) _____.

6. An agreement between two people, one of whom has a cause of action against the other, in which the claimant accepts a compromise in full satisfaction of a claim, is called _____.

7. A contract that has been _____ has been approved.

8. The _____ is the person to whom a promise is made.

9. When an offer is withdrawn by an offeror before it has been accepted, this is a(n) _____.

10. A(n) _____ is a contract where a dominant party has taken unfair advantage of a weaker party.

11. An offer that _____ is terminated or no longer in force.

12. Any act or word of an offeree communicated to an offeror conveying the refusal of an offer is a _____.

13. A remedy that restores the status quo, that returns a person who has been wrongfully deprived of something to their prior position, is known as _____.

14. Language common to all legal documents of the same type is known as _____.

15. A(n) _____ is a contract made for the benefit of a third person.

16. A sum agreed upon by the parties at the time of entering the contract to be payable in the event of a breach is called _____.

17. A minor must wait until reaching the age of _____ before entering into a binding contract.

Matching

Match the letter of the definition to the term below.

_____ 18. Cure

_____ 19. Performance

_____ 20. Unjust enrichment

_____ 21. Equity

_____ 22. Incompetency

_____ 23. Breach

_____ 24. Infancy

_____ 25. Meeting of the minds

_____ 26. Contract

_____ 27. Unilateral

_____ 28. Restitution

_____ 29. Rejection

_____ 30. Mutual mistake

_____ 31. Quantum meruit

A. One who has not reached the age of majority

B. Failure without legal excuse to perform promises that form a contract

C. System for ensuring justice where conventional laws are inadequate

D. Mutual consent of the parties to a contract

E. Agreement entered into, for adequate consideration, to do, or refrain from doing, a particular thing

F. Right of seller to correct his failure to deliver goods

G. Equitable doctrine that a person who unjustly receives property of another is obligated to return it

H. Doing of that which is required by a contract

I. Legal disability that makes a person incapable of understanding the nature of his acts

J. Contract in which there is a promise on one side only

K. A remedy that restores the status quo

L. Both sides of contract have different perceptions of fact

M. When an offeree refuses an offer

N. "As much as is deserved" is the literal meaning

Multiple Choice

Select the best choice.

_____ 32. When a person refuses an offer, this is known as:
   a. rejection
   b. acceptance
   c. revocation
   d. termination

_____ 33. Consideration is where:
   a. you are thinking over the offer
   b. there is a bargained-for exchange
   c. there is quantum meruit
   d. there is a novation

_____ 34. A valid contract is:
   a. an enforceable contract
   b. an unenforceable contract
   c. a void contract
   d. where there is an illusory promise

_____ 35. In an express contract, the terms are:
   a. oral only
   b. written only
   c. implied
   d. oral or written

_____ 36. When a lawyer drafts an agreement for his client selling a multimillion dollar business to the attorney for $10, the court will most likely find there was:
   a. material breach
   b. impossibility
   c. minority
   d. undue influence

_____ 37. A realtor shows a house to a prospective buyer. When asked about a giant water ring on a ceiling, the realtor lies and says it's just some artwork the owners drew. This is an example of:
   a. misrepresentation
   b. unilateral contract
   c. quasi contract
   d. merger clause

_____ 38. When a contract has a liquidated damages clause:
   a. the amount of damages is left to an arbitrator to compute
   b. the parties at the time of entering a contract agree upon a sum payable in the event of a breach
   c. this is an example of an exculpatory clause
   d. the parties seek accord and satisfaction

_____ 39. Under the mailbox rule, an offer is accepted when:
   a. 24 hours elapse
   b. 50 hours elapse
   c. the offer is mailed
   d. the offer is received

_____ 40. A breach of contract occurs when:
   a. both parties carry out the terms of the contract
   b. there is a bargained-for exchange of performances
   c. there is a merger clause
   d. a party fails to perform a promise that is part of a contract

_____ 41. Scott offers to sell his automobile for $8,000. John says, "I'll take it if you'll accept $6,000, not a penny more."
   a. John has accepted the contract
   b. John has used duress
   c. John has disaffirmed the contract
   d. John has made a counteroffer

_____ 42. A contract not in writing is:
   a. illegal
   b. unenforceable
   c. oral
   d. incomplete

_____ 43. The statute that requires certain types of contracts to be in writing is called:
   a. statute of frauds
   b. restitution statute
   c. adhesion contract
   d. boilerplate statute

True/False

Mark the following T or F.

_____ **44.** A void contract is the same as no contract at all.

_____ **45.** An implied contract is imposed by the court to prevent unjust enrichment.

_____ **46.** A voidable contract is a defective but valid contract unless disaffirmed.

_____ **47.** A requirement contract is where one party agrees to furnish the entire supply of specified goods required by the other party.

_____ **48.** The promisor is the party to whom a promise is made.

_____ **49.** UCC is the abbreviation for Uniform Contract Conditions.

_____ **50.** A third-party beneficiary is one of the original parties to a contract.

_____ **51.** A reward is an example of a bilateral contract.

_____ **52.** An offer is made by the promisor.

_____ **53.** An express contract is implied from the conduct of the parties.

_____ **54.** A contract that has been repudiated has been rejected.

Synonyms

Select the correct synonym in parentheses for each numbered item.

55. PROMISE
(vow, cover, cure)

56. OFFER
(accept, propose, guarantee)

57. EXECUTED
(completed, lapsed, rejected)

58. RATIFICATION
(rescission, insanity, confirmation)

59. PERFORMANCE
    (cure, effort, agreement)

60. INFORMAL
    (casual, implied in law, equity)

61. REVOCATION
    (termination, emancipation, best efforts rule)

62. DIVISIBLE
    (best efforts rule, implied term, severable)

63. IMPOSSIBILITY
    (futility, covenant, mistake)

64. MAJORITY
    (infancy, adulthood, capacity)

65. RESCISSION
    (cancellation, illusory promise, accord and satisfaction)

66. CAPACITY
    (merger, lapse, competency)

67. OFFEROR
    (promisor, promisee, beneficiary)

68. LAPSE
    (continue, terminate, divide)

69. CONTRACT
    (problem, plan, agreement)

70. INFANCY
    (competency, minority, majority)

Self-Test

Place the number of the correct term in the appropriate space.

71. Rejection

72. Voidable contract

73. Agreement

74. Unilateral contracts

75. Offer

76. Executory contract

77. Consideration

78. Contract

79. Enforceable

80. Void contract

81. Counteroffer

82. Implied contract

83. Acceptance

84. Bilateral contract

A(n) _____ between two or more people with the binding effect of the law is known as a(n) _____. Several elements are needed to complete a valid and _____ contract.

You need a party to make a(n) _____ and you need a(n) _____ without qualification. Should the acceptance have contingencies added, this is really a(n) _____ and a(n) _____. That which is given in exchange for performance of the contract is called _____. It is important to remember that a contract need not be in writing. A contract might be oral, or in writing, or even a(n) _____, a contract that the law infers from the parties' conduct. Some contracts are one-sided contracts called _____, while others consist of a promise for a promise and are called _____. Should a contract not be completed, it is called a(n) _____. Once completed, a contract is called executed. A contract to do something in violation of a statute would be illegal and is referred to as a(n) _____. Should a contract be executed by an infant, the contract is called a(n) _____, a contract that is valid but may be disaffirmed.

Defining Words

Complete the definition.

85. Contract _____

_____

86. Offer _____

_____

87. Acceptance _____

_____

88. Consideration _____

_____

89. Promise _____

_____

90. Executory _____

_____

91. Enforceable _____

_____

92. Void _____

_____

93. Mistake _____

_____

94. Misrepresentation _____

_____

95. Revocation _____

_____

96. Informal contract _____

_____

97. Express contract _____

_____

98. Damages _____

_____

99. Quantum meruit _____

_____

100. Majority _____

_____

Punctuation/Capitalization

Titles after names and the word however.

Rule 1: Titles and designations after names are surrounded by commas.

I went to Monica Harrison, M.D., for the problem.
We consulted with DeWitt Tool Company, Inc., for several months.
She was referred to as Harriett Hartley, Ph.D., to all of us.

Rule 2: Titles such as "the second" and "the third" are transcribed without the word *the* and as a Roman numeral, and they do not have commas around them.

Henry VIII had several wives.
We hired Ross Heathcliffe IV to fill the position.
He is loyal to Queen Elizabeth II.

Rule 3: The word *however* has a comma after it at the beginning of the sentence, commas around it in the middle of the sentence, and a comma before it at the end of the sentence.

However, I am not sure he was with the firm at that time.
He was leaving, however, in order to take a job in Denver.
There were several of them in the same group, however.

Rule 4: There is a special English construction when the word *however* comes before an adjective or adverb as a modifier. There is a single comma before the word *however* in this construction.

I will be with him, however long it may take.
She said she would help us, however hard it might be.
We will travel with you, however far away it may be.

Directions: Correct the punctuation.

1. Charles Chandler the III, was not with us however.

2. We were assisted by Will Johnson, R.N. on the procedure.

3. However, he worked for Chapman Manufacturing Inc., for just two months.

4. We however, sent Jonathan Martinez, M.D., to the convention.

5. I told him I would be here however late it was when he returned.

Word Pairs

aural/oral

aural = relating to the ear and hearing.

The doctor reported that it was an aural problem.
He lacked good aural skills.
I am not sure how that affects his aural ability.

oral = not written, said.

He felt they had an oral contract.
The psychiatrist feels she does not do well with oral speech.
I heard his oral recitation of his platform.

conscientious/conscious

conscientious = diligent, hardworking, according to one's conscience.

The jurors are asked to be conscientious in making their decision.
Do you think he conscientiously performed this job?
He did not seem to be conscientious about his duties on this project.

conscious = awake, aware.

He was unconscious when the paramedics arrived.
I was concerned about his lack of consciousness.
Do you think it was a conscious decision?

laps/lapse

laps = one circle of the track, stage, top of thighs when sitting, wash against a surface.

The water laps against the shore incessantly.
Her effort laps all other efforts.
He was ordered to take three laps around the track.

lapse = termination or extinguishment.

There was a lapse in the coverage of the story.
She allowed the coverage of the policy to lapse.
I think they said she suffered a lapse of memory.

mind/mined

mind = way of thinking, behave, seat of thought, be careful, remember.

Do you mind that he is not going to stay here?
He seems to be out of his mind with worry over where she is.
She told us that her husband would not mind if we did the work.

mined = pulled out ore, found the source.

She mined the information to pull out what she needed.
They had mined everything in the region.
He mined in the West Virginia area.

parcel/partial

parcel = portion of land, package, lot.

He mailed it parcel post.
We owned a parcel near the new shopping center.
There was a parcel that was addressed to you.

partial = not complete, dentures, favoring.

He had been fit for a partial plate.
It was partially complete.
I am partial to chocolate.

poor/pore/pour

poor = having no money, low quality.

He lives in a poorer section of town.
His poor grades are the reason he did not get into the college of his choice.
Her condition was listed as poor.

pore = minute opening; look carefully, examine. This is usually used with the word *over.*

He pored over the books to see whether he could find some extra cash.
I intend to pore over this report to find the flaws.
The pores in her skin in that area were infected.

pour = decant, dispense, discharge.

The rain poured in every window and door in the house.
He proposed a toast as she poured the wine.
All of her emotions came pouring out.

Directions: Choose the correct form of the word.

1. There were aural/oral instructions only, nothing written.

2. We mind/mined the streets for any extra coins we could find.

3. All I heard was the parcel/partial ruling that was issued.

4. I do not believe he was conscientious/conscious when we found him.

5. They are poring/pouring through the transcripts of the trial.

6. There was a laps/lapse in appropriate protocol.

7. It is just a small parcel/partial of land.

8. His poor/pore/pour judgment caused the problem.

9. She stated that she did not mind/mined his interference.

10. He is valued for his conscientious/conscious work on the project.

11. He pored/poured it over the open wound on her leg.

12. She made several laps/lapse around the mall for exercise.

13. She had aural/oral difficulties when the speaker's voice was low.

14. I believe it is a parcel/partial transcript of what happened in there.

15. Do you mind/mined accompanying her to the doctor?

16. The aural/oral report given was not encouraging about the finances for the year.

17. The dentist prepared a parcel/partial for him as a stopgap measure.

18. She was poring/pouring over the checkbook to find the mistake.

19. It was a real laps/lapse in judgment.

20. Do you know how poor/pore/pour the neighborhood really is?

Is It One Word or Two? An Apostrophe? A Hyphen?

anyway/any way

anyway = in any case, no matter what. This word is an adverb.

Anyway, I haven't seen him since the argument.
She is not participating anyway; so it doesn't matter.
He said there was nothing I could do, but I went anyway.

any way = by any method. The word *any* is an adjective that modifies the noun *way*.

There was not any way to do what he wanted.
If there is any way I can help, let me know.
Is there any way to accomplish this before Friday?

apiece/a piece

apiece = each, per person.

We gave them three apiece.
Each child got $100,000 apiece.
I think they were charging $200 apiece for the tickets.

a piece = portion, section.

He wants a piece of the action on this one.

She gave us only a piece of the puzzle about the murder.

Do I assume correctly that you got a piece of the estate?

Directions: Choose the correct words.

1. Did they receive more than $500 apiece/a piece?

2. Has he improved in anyway/any way that you know of?

3. Anyway/Any way, we aren't able to join them.

4. She got apiece/a piece of the profit.

5. There is not anyway/any way that she deserves apiece/a piece of it.

Proofreading

Directions: Make necessary corrections, based on the material presented in the unit. If the sentence has no errors, write the word *correct* after the sentence.

1. It was rumored that Henry Hendricks, IV, was a conscious objector. _____

2. There is not anyway to remedy her laps in judgment. _____

3. However he has lost his mind if he thinks that we are going to do this aurally. _____

4. The heirs were given $10,000 a piece however. _____

5. George Jefferson, M.D. has issued a parcel report on her condition. _____

6. He promised to be conscientious about this job, however long he may be in it. _____

7. They were pouring over a piece of evidence regarding Jeremy Peters, Jr. _____

8. His laps of consciousness is of concern, however, because of the possible damage to his brain. _____

9. There is a parcel that we are looking to buy, but we are concerned about the poor condition it is in. _____

10. I know however that, in his mind, there is not any way to fix it. _____

An Adaptation from a Contracts Case

Facts:

Highland Trade, HT, sued General Stores, Inc., for breach of contract for goods sold in a dispute concerning the alleged failure of General Stores to pay for a large number of decorative reindeer sold to General Stores for resale to the public during the Christmas season. General Stores counterclaimed for breach of contract and fraud. According to General Stores, at least 70 percent of the reindeer, which were manufactured in Haiti, were "scary looking" and unsuitable for sale as Christmas decorations. General Stores marked down the price of the reindeer due to their poor quality. HT denied there was an oral contract as to whether they would give General Stores a $200,000 credit for the defective merchandise and moved for partial summary judgment seeking an award in the sum of $200,000 for the unpaid balance. HT claimed an oral agreement was unenforceable and violated the Statute of Frauds.

Procedural History:

The District Court granted partial summary judgment in favor of HT and submitted the remaining claims to a jury, who found in favor of HT. General Stores moved for a new trial, which motion was denied.

Issue:

Was there an oral contract, and was it confirmed with a writing as is required under the merchants' exception rule?

Rationale:

The Arkansas version of the Uniform Commercial Code, UCC, renders unenforceable any agreement for the sale of goods worth more than $500 unless the agreement is in writing and is signed by the party against whom enforcement is sought. Both parties agree the case falls under the merchants' exception rule to the Statute of Frauds. Under this rule, if the recipient of a writing knows its contents and fails to object in writing within ten days, what is in the writing becomes a confirmation of an oral agreement. However, after a review of all the e-mails between the parties and HT's responses, it was clear that HT never agreed to any agreement about markdowns or changing the contract. In fact, HT continued to demand full payment.

Ruling:

The decision was affirmed.

Directions for CD-ROM Transcription Exercises

In audio format are:

1. Terms for the unit with pronunciations from the thesaurus/dictionary feature.

2. Self-Test that appears in the book at mid-unit.°

3. Case that appears at the unit end.°

°speeds are 80 wpm/120 wpm for differing skill levels

CD-ROM icons appear where the three above are located within each unit.

Readers may practice transcription by listening to the CD-ROM where prompted by the icons in the book. However, for high success in testing your transcription skills, mastering all the terms and English skills in the unit is recommended before attempting the CD-ROM.

For Keyboard Transcriptionists: Listen to the CD-ROM audio file for this unit at 80 wpm or 120 wpm and transcribe from the dictation on your computer. Edit and proofread your work against the printed copy in the book.

For Reporting Writers: Listen to the CD-ROM audio file at 80 wpm or 120 wpm and take down the dictation on your writer. Either transcribe from your notes and proofread your work or edit and proofread your CAT (computer-aided transcription) transcript. Always check your work against the printed copy in the book.

 Student CD-ROM
For additional materials, please go to the CD in this book.

 Online Companion™
For additional resources, please go to http://www.paralegal.delmar.cengage.com

Unit 9

Corporations, Partnerships, and Sole Proprietorships

The **Mistakes** That Court Reporters Make and *How to Avoid* Them

The Mistake:

Georgette Kowalski took a deposition in which the two sides were very combative. She was copied on an e-mail in the case. Her reply included some personal comments about opposing counsel, and inadvertently she hit "Reply to All" when she sent it. Those comments went to all the parties in the case. Opposing counsel lodged a complaint with her agency.

How to Avoid It:

First, it is never a good idea to put "personal comments" into a business e-mail. And, second, always be sure to whom that e-mail is being sent. We have all hit that "Send" button and wished we could retract it.

Introduction

There are different forms of organizations in which to conduct business in the United States. Sometimes a person single-handedly opens and operates a sole proprietorship. Oftentimes people wish to enter a business venture with others.

When two or more individuals carry on a business as co-owners for a profit, this is known as a partnership. The partners must share in the profits as well as losses of the business. Each partner serves as an agent for the partnership, and can perform acts binding on the other partners. Any contracts made by one partner become the responsibility of the partnership even though the other partners weren't involved in making the agreement.

A corporation is a fictitious legal entity created to carry on a business. A corporation is formed pursuant to the particular laws of the state of incorporation. Shareholders invest their money and become owners of the corporation. A shareholder has the opportunity to earn a profit without incurring personal liability for debts of the corporation. Corporations are taxed differently than individuals, and can have perpetual existence.

Unit Objectives

- ▨ Work with a legal dictionary/thesaurus.
- ▨ Learn about the law of business organizations: corporations, partnerships, and sole proprietorships.
- ▨ Master the similarities and differences in definitions of key terms regarding corporations, partnerships, and sole proprietorships.
- ▨ Master the pronunciations and spellings of legal terms in this unit.
- ▨ Recognize the synonyms used for legal terminology in this unit.
- ▨ Practice usage of terms, definitions, and synonyms for corporations, partnerships, and sole proprietorships.
- ▨ Complete unit exercises in the forms of missing words, matching, multiple choice, true/false, synonyms, self-test, defining words, and also:
  - Punctuation/capitalization
  - Word pairs
  - Transcription of terms, self-test, and case
  - Proofreading

Dictionary/Thesaurus

Note: All Dictionary/Thesaurus terms appear on the CD-ROM with audio pronunciations.

Term [phonetic pronunciation]	
accounting [a.*kount*.ing]	An equitable action brought to obtain an adjudication of the respective rights and obligations of the members of a partnership.
agency [*ay*.jen.see]	A relationship in which one person acts for or on behalf of another person at the other person's request.
annual meeting [*an*.yoo.el *meet*.ing]	A regular meeting of the stockholders of a corporation, held once a year.
annual report [*an*.yoo.el re.*port*]	A report issued yearly by a corporation, informing its stockholders, the government, and the public, in some detail, of its operations, particularly its fiscal operations, during the year. The contents of an annual report (also called an annual statement), as well as the report itself, are required by law.
articles of incorporation [*ar*.tiklz ov in.kore.per.*ay*.shen]	The charter or basic rules that create a corporation and by which it functions. Among other things, it states the purposes for which the corporation is being organized, the amount of authorized capital stock, and the names and addresses of the directors and incorporators. *See also* certificate of incorporation; incorporation.
articles of partnership [*ar*.tiklz ov *part*.ner.ship]	*See* partnership agreement.
association [a.so.see.*ay*.shen]	Also called an unincorporated association, a collection of persons who have joined together for the pursuit of a common purpose or design. Unlike a corporation, an association has no legal existence independent of its members. On the other hand, an association that sometimes functions like a corporation may be treated as a corporation for some purposes by the law.
board of directors [bord ov di.*rek*.terz]	The directors of a corporation or association who act as a group in representing the organization and conducting its business, and may be liable for their actions as such.
bond [bond]	1. A debt owed by a corporation or by the government to an investor. 2. The written instrument that evidences a debt. 3. An obligation to pay a sum of money upon the happening of a stated event. Bonds that represent debt and pay interest are called investment bonds. EXAMPLES of investment bonds issued by corporations include convertible bonds, coupon bonds, guaranteed bonds, registered bonds, serial bonds, and term bonds. Unsecured, long-term corporate bonds are called debentures.

business
[*biz*.ness]

The work in which a person is regularly or usually engaged and from which she makes a living.
• *n.* trade, occupation, calling, activity, profession, field ("the cosmetology business"); commerce, manufacture, industry, intercourse, dealings ("doing business")

business corporation
[*biz*.ness kore.per.*ay*.shen]

An ordinary corporation; a commercial corporation; a for-profit corporation. *Compare* nonprofit corporation. *See also* corporation.

business judgment rule
[*biz*.ness *juj*.ment rule]

The principle that courts should be reluctant to second-guess the decisions of corporate directors, even if those decisions are not in the best interests of the stockholders, as long as the decisions are within the power of the directors to make.

business name
[*biz*.ness name]

The name under which a business is operated. In the case of an individual, it may be his real name or a fictitious name. *See also* DBA.

business records
[*biz*.ness *rek*.erdz]

A book of original entry; a book of account; all records kept in the ordinary course of business.

by-laws
[*by*-lawz]

Rules and regulations created by corporations, associations, clubs, and societies for their governance.

C corporation
[see kore.per.*ay*.shen]

Under the Internal Revenue Code, a corporation that has not elected S corporation status. Its income is taxed at the corporate level, its dividends at the shareholder level. *Compare* S corporation.

CEO
[CEO]

Abbreviation of chief executive officer.

certificate of incorporation
[ser.*tif*.i.ket ov in.kore.per.*ay*.shen]

1. In some states, the same as articles of incorporation. 2. In some states, a certificate issued by the secretary of state attesting that articles of incorporation have been filed and that the filing corporation is therefore a legal entity and capable of being sued. *See also* incorporation.

charitable corporation
[char.i.tebl kore.per.*ay*.shen]

A corporation organized and existing solely to engage in charitable activities. It issues no stock and earns no profit. *See also* nonprofit corporation.

chief executive officer (CEO)
[cheef *eg*.sek.yoo.tiv *off*.i.ser]

The officer of a corporation or other organization who has the most responsibility for managing its affairs, commonly referred to as the CEO.

close corporation
[kloz kore.per.*ay*.shen]

1. A corporation in which all the stock is owned by a few persons or by another corporation; sometimes also referred to as a closely held corporation. 2. Another term for a family corporation.

common stock [*kom*.en stok]	Ordinary capital stock in a corporation, the market value of which is based upon the worth of the corporation. Owners of common stock vote in proportion to their holdings, as opposed to owners of other classes of stock that are without voting rights. By contrast, however, common stock earns dividends only after other preferred classes of stock. *Compare* preferred stock. *See also* stock.
corporate agents [*kore*.per.et *ay*.jents]	The officers and employees of a corporation who have the authority to act for the corporation.
corporate directors [*kore*.per.et de.*rek*.terz]	Directors of a corporation; members of the board of directors of a corporation.
corporate domicile [*kore*.per.et *dom*.i.sile]	A corporation is domiciled in the state of its incorporation.
corporate officers [*kore*.per.et *off*.i.serz]	The officers of a corporation. EXAMPLES: the president, the treasurer, the comptroller.
corporate records [*kore*.per.et r*ek*.erdz]	The charter and by-laws of a corporation, the minutes of the meetings of its board of directors and of stockholders' meetings, and the written evidence of its contracts and business transactions.
corporate securities [*kore*.per.et se.*kyoor*.it.eez]	Stock, bonds, notes, and other documentation of indebtedness issued by a corporation to obtain funds to use in the corporation's business. *See also* securities.
corporation [kore.per.*ay*.shen]	An artificial person, existing only in the eyes of the law, to whom a state or the federal government has granted a charter to become a legal entity, separate from its shareholders, with a name of its own, under which its shareholders can act and contract and sue and be sued. A corporation's shareholders, officers, and directors are not normally liable for the acts of the corporation. *See also* charitable corporation; close corporation; de facto corporation; de jure corporation; domestic corporation; foreign corporation; nonprofit corporation. *n.* business, company, enterprise, organization, association, establishment, firm
DBA [DBA]	An abbreviation of, and commonly a short way of saying, "doing business as." A person's DBA is his or her trade name. EXAMPLES: a lawsuit involving a business owned by an individual named Gerri Jones, who does business under the trade name Gerri's Jams, might be captioned Sam Smith v. Gerri Jones DBA Gerri's Jams; a lawsuit involving a business owned by the ABC Corporation, which does business under the trade name Merry Motels, might be captioned ABC Corporation DBA Merry Motels v. Sam Smith.
de facto corporation [dee *fak*.toh kore.per.*ay*.shen]	A corporation in fact, but one that has failed to comply with the formal requirements for incorporation; an apparent corporation, asserted to be a corporation by its members and acting as a corporation under color of law. Such an organization is deemed a corporation with respect to everyone except the state. *Compare* de jure corporation.

de jure corporation [dee *zhoo*.reh kore.per.*ay*.shen]	A corporation created in compliance with all legal requirements, so that its right to exist and to exercise the powers described in its charter are protected against challenge by the state. *Compare* de facto corporation.
derivative action [de.*riv*.e.tiv *ak*.shen]	An action brought by one or more stockholders of a corporation to enforce a corporate right or to remedy a wrong to the corporation, when the corporation itself fails to take action.
dissolution of corporation [dis.e.*loo*.shen ov kore.per.*ay*.shen]	The termination of a corporation's existence and its abolishment as an entity.
dissolution of partnership [dis.e.*loo*.shen ov *part*.ner.ship]	The change in the relation of partners caused by any partner's ceasing to be associated in the carrying on of the business. Any such change brings about the dissolution of the partnership. *See also* partnership; liquidate.
dividend [*div*.e.dend]	A payment made by a corporation to its stockholders, either in cash (a cash dividend), in stock (a stock dividend), or out of surplus earnings. • *n.* profit, benefit, reward, share, allowance, bonus
domestic corporation [de.mest.tick kore.per.*ay*.shen]	A corporation organized under the laws of the state. *Compare* foreign corporation.
fiduciary duty [fi.*doo*.she.air.ee *dew*.tee]	The duty to act loyally and honestly with respect to the interests of another.
foreign corporation [forr.en kore.per.*ay*.shen]	A corporation incorporated under the laws of one state, doing business in another. *Compare* domestic corporation.
general partner [*jen*.e.rel *part*.ner]	A partner in an ordinary partnership, as distinguished from a limited partnership. "General partner" is synonymous with "partner."
general partnership [*jen*.e.rel *part*.ner.ship]	An ordinary partnership, as distinguished from a limited partnership. "General partnership" is synonymous with "partnership."
incorporation [in.kore.per.*ay*.shen]	1. The act of forming a corporation. 2. The act of combining one thing with another.
incorporator [in.*kore*.per.ay.ter]	A person who, alone or with others, forms a corporation.
insider [in.*sy*.der]	An officer or director of a corporation or any other person who is in a position to acquire knowledge of the business and condition of the corporation through his official position. • *n.* officer, director, member, intimate, associate • *adj.* private, protected, nonpublic, undisclosed ("insider information")
issue [*ish*.oo]	Securities offered for sale at a particular time, either for the public or privately, by a corporation or by government; an offering. EXAMPLES: corporate stock (a stock issue); municipal bonds (a bond issue).

limited
[*lim*.i.ted]

1. A word that follows a company's name and indicates that the business is a corporation, especially in England and Canada, although some American corporations also use the term (or its abbreviation, Ltd.) in place of "Inc." EXAMPLE: "Jack and Jill Limited." 2. A word used to signify a partnership other than a general partnership.

limited liability corporation (LLC)
[*lim*.i.ted ly.e.*bil*.i.tee kore.per.*ay*.shen]

The preferred terminology is "limited liability company." A business that has both partnership and corporate qualities. A limited liability corporation offers the tax advantages of a partnership while providing liability protection of a corporation.

limited liability partnership
[*lim*.i.ted ly.e.*bil*.i.tee *part*.ner.ship]

A partnership in which the liability of one or more of the partners is limited to the amount each partner has invested in the partnership. Where the partner takes no part in running the business, the partner incurs no liability beyond that contribution or investment with regard to partnership obligations.

liquidate
[*lik*.wi.date]

To break up, do away with, wind up, or dissolve. USAGE: "After Jim died his partner liquidated the business." *See also* winding up.
• *v.* discharge, clear, cancel, honor, pay off, quit ("liquidate my debts"); cash, convert, exchange, realize ("liquidate the bonds"); remove, wipe out ("liquidate the company")
• *ant.* incur; create

merger of corporations
[*mer*.jer ov kore.per.*ay*.shenz]

A joining of two (or more) corporations in which one goes out of existence, leaving a single survivor that possesses the powers and owns the stock and other property of both (or all). Although the terms "merger" and "consolidation" are often used interchangeably, they are actually quite different. In a merger, one of the combining corporations continues in existence and absorbs the others; in a consolidation, the combining corporations are dissolved and lose their identity in a new corporate entity that takes over the property and powers, as well as the rights and liabilities, of the constituent corporations.

nonprofit corporation
[non.prof.it kore.per.*ay*.shen]

A nonstock corporation organized for purposes other than making a profit, generally for charitable or educational purposes. EXAMPLE: A private college or a private university. *Compare* profit corporation. *See also* charitable corporation.

outstanding stock
[out.*stan*.ding stok]

Shares of stock issued by a corporation. Outstanding stock is an obligation of the corporation.

over-the-counter market
[*oh*.ver-the-*count*.er *mar*.ket]

A market in securities other than the stock exchange; securities transactions directly between brokers. The over-the-counter securities market (the OTC) trades through the NASDAQ system.

par value
[par *val*.yu]

The value of a share of stock or of a bond, according to its face; the named or nominal value of an instrument. The par value and the market value of stock are not synonymous; there is often a wide difference between them. The issuer of a bond is obligated to redeem it at par value upon maturity.

parent company
[*pair*.ent *kum*.pe.nee]

A corporation that owns all or the majority of the stock of another corporation. The corporation owned by the parent company is called a subsidiary or a wholly owned subsidiary.

partner
[*part*.ner]

A member of a partnership. *See also* general partner; limited partnership.
• *n.* participant, associate, confrere, collaborator, confederate, member, teammate

partnership
[*part*.ner.ship]

An undertaking of two or more persons to carry on, as co-owners, a business or other enterprise for profit; an agreement between or among two or more persons to put their money, labor, and skill into commerce or business, and to divide the profit in agreed-upon proportions. Partnerships may be formed by entities as well as individuals; a corporation, for EXAMPLE, may be a partner. For federal income tax purposes, a partnership is a for-profit enterprise that is not a corporation. *See also* articles of partnership; dissolution of partnership; general partnership; limited partnership.
• *n.* federation, alliance, league, association, collaboration, business, enterprise, undertaking

partnership agreement
[*part*.ner.ship a.*gree*.ment]

The agreement signed by the members of a partnership that governs their relationship as partners. It is sometimes referred to as articles of partnership.

partnership assets
[*part*.ner.ship *ass*.ets]

All assets belonging to the partnership, as opposed to the personal assets of the partners.

partnership debts
[*part*.ner.ship detz]

Debts owed by the partnership, as opposed to the personal debts of the partners.

piercing the corporate veil
[*peer*.sing the *kore*.pe.ret vale]

Ignoring the corporate entity to reach or to proceed legally against the corporation's directors, officers, or managers directly and personally. Although a corporation's officers and directors are not normally liable for the acts of the corporation, the courts will hold them responsible for corporate acts if the purpose of organizing the corporation was to perpetrate fraud or if the corporation was a mere shell without substantial assets or capital.

preferred stock
[pre.*ferd* stok]

Corporate stock that is entitled to a priority over other classes of stock, usually common stock, in distribution of the profits of the corporation (i.e., dividends) and in distribution of the assets of the corporation in the event of dissolution or liquidation.

professional corporation
[pro.*fesh*.en.el kore.per.*ay*.shen]

A corporation formed for the purpose of practicing a profession (EXAMPLES: law; medicine; psychotherapy; dentistry) and to secure certain tax advantages. The members of a professional corporation remain personally liable for professional misconduct. Professional corporations often identify themselves by the abbreviation PC. Thus, for EXAMPLE, a professional corporation composed of attorneys Jessica Smith and Sam Smith might be named, "Smith & Smith, Esqs., PC." *See also* corporation.

profit [*prof*.it]	*n.* 1. The excess of gross receipts or gross proceeds over the cost or expenses of a transaction; the excess of receipts over expenditures. 2. Gain realized from the investment of capital. 3. For some purposes, the equivalent of income. 4. Gain; benefit. *v.* To gain or benefit; to realize an advantage.
profit corporation [*prof*.it kore.per.*ay*.shen]	A corporation organized for the purpose of realizing gain (i.e., earning profit) to be distributed among its shareholders; a business corporation. A corporation organized for profit-making purposes is often referred to as a for-profit corporation, as opposed to a nonprofit corporation.
promoter [pro.*mote*.er]	A person who organizes a business venture or is a major participant in organizing the venture. • *n.* organizer, incorporator, planner, backer, patron, sponsor
prospectus [pro.*spek*.tus]	A statement published by a corporation that provides information concerning stock or other securities it is offering for sale to the public. The contents of a prospectus are regulated by the Securities Exchange Commission. • *n.* details, design, list, program, synopsis, statement, résumé ("CSX's prospectus is impressive")
proxy [*prox*.ee]	Authority given in writing by one shareholder in a corporation to another shareholder to exercise her voting rights for her. • *n.* authorization, power ("I gave her my proxy")
quorum [*kwohr*.em]	The number of members of a body (EXAMPLE: a board of directors) who must be present for the body to be able to conduct business.
S corporation [ess kore.per.*ay*.shen]	A corporation electing to be taxed under Subchapter S of the Internal Revenue Code. Its income is taxed to the shareholders rather than at the corporate level. *Compare* C corporation. *See also* corporation.
securities [se.*kyoor*.i.teez]	Certificates that represent a right to share in the profits of a company or in the distribution of its assets, or in a debt owned by a company or by the government. EXAMPLES: stocks; bonds; notes with interest coupons; any registered security. • *n.* stocks, convertible debentures, negotiables, coupons, bills, warranties
Securities and Exchange Commission (SEC) [se.*kyoor*.i.teez and eks.*chaynj* kum.*ish*.en]	The agency that administers and enforces federal statutes relating to securities, including the Securities Act of 1933 and the Securities Exchange Act.
shareholder [*share*.hole.der]	*See* stockholder. • *n.* stockholder, owner, investor
sole proprietorship [sole pro.*pry*.e.ter.ship]	Ownership by one person, as opposed to ownership by more than one person, ownership by a corporation, ownership by a partnership, etc.

stock
[stok]

1. The shares of stock or stock certificates issued by a corporation or a joint-stock company. 2. Shares in a corporation or a joint-stock company owned by shareholders; put another way, the sum of all the rights and duties of the shareholders. 3. The capital of a corporation. *See also* common stock; preferred stock.
• *n.* assets, blue chips, bonds, capital, convertible paper, share ("stock in the company")

stock certificate
[stok ser.*tif*.i.ket]

An instrument issued by a corporation stating that the person named is the owner of a designated number of shares of its stock.

stock market
[stok *mar*.ket]

A market where securities are bought and sold. EXAMPLES: a stock exchange; the over-the-counter market.

stockbroker
[*stok*.bro.ker]

A person employed in buying and selling stock for others.
• *n.* broker, securities broker, agent

stockholder
[*stok*.hole.der]

The owner of one or more shares of stock in a corporation or a joint-stock company; a person who appears on the books of a corporation as the owner of one or more shares of its stock. The terms "stockholder" and "shareholder" are used interchangeably.

stockholders' meeting
[*stok*.hole.derz *mee*.ting]

A meeting of the stockholders of a corporation called for the purpose of electing directors or transacting other business requiring the consent of the stockholders. *See also* annual meeting.

subsidiary corporation
[sub.*sid*.ee.er.ee kore.per.*ay*.shen]

A corporation controlled by another corporation, known as the parent company, which owns all or a majority of its stock.

ultra vires
[ul.tra *vee*.rayz]

(*Latin*) "Beyond the power." A term that the law applies to a contract, transaction, or other act of a corporation that is beyond those powers enumerated or implied in its articles of incorporation, charter, or by-laws.

winding up
[*wine*.ding up]

The dissolution or liquidation of a corporation or a partnership.

Missing Words

Fill in the blanks below.

1. A change in relationship of partners caused by a partner's ceasing to be associated with the partnership is known as _____ of the partnership.

2. An equitable action brought by members of a partnership to resolve their respective rights and obligations is called a(n) _____.

3. A(n) _____ is a person employed in buying and selling stock for others.

4. A corporation is domiciled in the state of its _____.

5. A(n) _____ is an action brought by shareholders to enforce a corporate right or to remedy a wrong of the corporation.

6. _____ occurs when the corporate entity is ignored to reach or proceed directly against the corporation's directors, officers, or managers.

7. _____ is corporate stock that is entitled to a priority over other classes of stock.

8. A(n) _____ is a statement issued by a corporation providing information about stock that is for sale to the public.

9. When a corporation transacts business that is beyond its powers, this is a(n) _____ act.

10. The _____ is an agency that administers and enforces federal statutes relating to securities.

11. _____ is the shares of stock issued by a corporation.

12. A(n) _____ is an instrument issued by a corporation stating that the person named is the owner of a designated number of shares of stock.

13. The _____ is a meeting of the stockholders of the corporation called for the purpose of electing directors or transacting other business requiring stockholder consent.

14. The _____ of a corporation acts as a group in representing the organization and conducting its business.

15. The _____ are the officers of the corporation such as the president, treasurer, and comptroller.

16. A(n) _____ is the person who organizes a business venture.

17. A corporation organized under the laws of a state is a(n) _____ corporation.

18. _____ is a word following a company's name to indicate that a business is a corporation.

Matching

Match the letter of the definition to the term below.

_____ 19. Sole proprietorship

_____ 20. S corporation

_____ 21. Partnership

_____ 22. Corporation

_____ 23. Proxy

_____ 24. Shareholder

_____ 25. Certificate of incorporation

_____ 26. Par value

_____ 27. By-laws

_____ 28. Dividend

_____ 29. Professional corporation

_____ 30. Profit corporation

_____ 31. Annual meeting

A. Ownership of business by one person

B. Payment made by a corporation to its stockholders

C. Value of a share of stock or bond according to its face

D. Artificial person separate from its shareholders, that can act and contract, and sue and be sued

E. In some states it's a certificate issued by the secretary of state attesting that articles of incorporation have been filed

F. Corporation formed to practice a profession such as law

G. Owner of one or more shares of stock in a corporation

H. When two or more people carry on as co-owners of a business for profit

I. Rules and regulations created by corporations

J. Authority given by one shareholder in a corporation to another shareholder to exercise voting rights for them

K. Corporation whose income is taxed to the shareholders rather than at the corporate level

L. A corporation organized to realize a gain

M. Regular meeting of stockholders held once a year

Multiple Choice

Select the best choice.

_____ **32.** Corporate stock that is entitled to a priority over other classes of stock is known as:
  a. common stock
  b. preferred stock
  c. treasury share
  d. stock split

_____ **33.** A market in securities other than the stock exchange:
  a. over-the-counter market
  b. under-the-counter market
  c. all of the above
  d. none of the above

_____ **34.** Certificates that represent a right to share in the profits of a company or in the distribution of assets, or in a debt owed by a company or by the government are known as:
  a. proxies
  b. ultra vires
  c. securities
  d. by-laws

_____ **35.** A corporation organized and existing solely to engage in charitable activities is known as:
  a. a charitable corporation
  b. a private corporation
  c. a close corporation
  d. a publicly held corporation

_____ **36.** Authorization given in writing by one shareholder in a corporation to another shareholder to exercise voting rights is known as:
  a. stock issue
  b. stock dividend
  c. insider trading
  d. proxy

_____ **37.** The directors of a corporation or association who act as a group in representing the organization are known as:
  a. board of directors
  b. stockholders
  c. incorporators
  d. stockbrokers

_____ **38.** The annual meeting of a corporation is a meeting of:
  a. incorporators
  b. promoters
  c. insider traders
  d. shareholders

_____ **39.** A corporation controlled by another corporation, known as the parent corporation, which owns all or a majority of its stock, is known as:
  a. a subsidiary corporation
  b. a charitable corporation
  c. a private corporation
  d. a close corporation

_____ **40.** When the corporate entity is ignored to reach or to proceed directly against the corporation's directors, officers, or managers, this is known as:
  a. the business judgment rule
  b. piercing the corporate veil
  c. stock redemption
  d. stock manipulation

_____ **41.** The president, treasurer, and comptroller of a corporation are examples of:
  a. officers of a corporation
  b. directors of a corporation
  c. shareholders of a corporation
  d. none of the above

_____ 42. A statement published by a corporation that provides information concerning stock or other securities it is offering for sale to the public is called:
    a. proxy
    b. prospectus
    c. stock certificate
    d. stock split

_____ 43. The principle that courts should be reluctant to second-guess the decisions of corporate directors is called:
    a. business judgment rule
    b. insider trading
    c. blue sky laws
    d. piercing the corporate veil

True/False

Mark the following T or F.

_____ 44. A partner is a member of a partnership.

_____ 45. All assets belonging to a partnership are known as partnership assets.

_____ 46. The agreement signed by members of a partnership that governs their relationship as partners is known as the Uniform Partnership Act.

_____ 47. A partner's duty to act loyally and honestly with respect to the interests of the other partners is known as indemnification.

_____ 48. A partnership where the liability of one or more partners is limited to the amount of money they have invested is known as a general partnership.

_____ 49. An artificial person existing only in the eyes of the law, to whom a state or federal government has granted a charter to become a legal entity separate from its shareholders, is a corporation.

_____ 50. A corporation electing to be taxed under Subchapter S of the Internal Revenue Code with income taxed to the shareholders is called a private corporation.

_____ 51. A dividend is a payment made by a corporation to its stockholders.

_____ 52. An equitable action brought to resolve the respective rights and obligations of the members of a partnership is called the annual shareholder meeting.

_____ 53. Insider trading occurs when stock is bought and sold based on information obtained through your position in a company.

_____ 54. The process that takes place when a corporation is broken up or merges with or acquires another corporation is called dissolution.

_____ **55.** A market in securities other than the stock exchange is the over-the-counter market.

_____ **56.** A company that owns all or the majority of the stock of another corporation is a subsidiary corporation.

Synonyms

Select the correct synonym in parentheses for each numbered item.

57. SHAREHOLDER
(stockholder, stockmaker, stockseller)

58. DIVIDEND
(debt, payment, liquidation)

59. STOCK
(share, action, prospectus)

60. FIDUCIARY DUTY
(loyalty, public, dissolution)

61. BY-LAWS
(corporate records, corporate laws, corporate officers)

62. ANNUAL MEETING
(first meeting, regular meeting, last meeting)

63. WINDING UP
(dissolution, ultra vires, merger)

64. PROXY
(prohibition, insider, authorization)

65. PROMOTER
(CEO, incorporator, officer)

66. CHARITABLE CORPORATION
(public corporation, nonprofit corporation, C corporation)

67. STOCKBROKER
(securities broker, registered agent, officer)

68. BOND
(assets, debt, collateral)

69. SECURITIES
(stocks, promoters, insiders)

Self-Test

Place the number of the correct term in the appropriate space.

70. Corporation

71. Partnership

72. Partnership assets

73. Professional corporation

74. Securities and Exchange Commission

75. Nonprofit corporation

76. S corporation

77. Sole proprietorship

78. Partnership agreement

79. DBA

80. Dissolution of corporation

81. Merger of corporations

There are three main forms in which to organize a business. There are pluses and minuses to each of the different types of business organizations. Where a person dreams of having his own business and being his own boss, this is called a(n) _____. However, after working ten-hour days and seven-day weeks, some people decide that this is not the way they want to run a business. They may decide to try a(n) _____, where two or more people agree to carry on a business as co-owners, for a profit. The agreement signed by members of a partnership that governs their relationship as partners is called the _____. All the assets that belong to the partnership, as opposed to the partners' personal assets, is called _____.

You needn't use your own name to form a business. Some businesses file a(n) _____ certificate when they wish to conduct business under an assumed name.

Should business partners wish to protect themselves from unlimited liability as a result of their business affairs, they may wish to form a(n) _____. There are many different types of corporations. Attorneys or doctors might wish to form a(n) _____. A charitable organization that does not seek to earn a profit might form a(n) _____ corporation. Should shareholders desire that the income of the corporation be taxed to the shareholders rather than at the corporate level, they might consider forming a(n) _____.

Sometimes two or more corporations have a(n) _____ and one of the corporations becomes the single survivor. The corporation that goes out of existence will need to undergo a(n) _____.

The _____ is the agency that administers and enforces the federal statutes relating to securities.

Defining Words

Complete the definition.

82. Partnership _____

_____

83. Business _____

_____

84. Profit _____

_____

85. Certificate of incorporation _____

_____

86. De jure corporation _____

_____

87. Stock _____

_____

88. Limited liability partnership _____

_____

89. Dividend _____

_____

90. Fiduciary duty _____

_____

91. Agency _____

_____

92. Corporation _____

_____

93. Sole proprietorship _____

_____

94. Board of directors _____

_____

95. Shareholders _____

_____

96. Officers _____

_____

97. Proxy _____

_____

98. Limited liability corporation _____

_____

Punctuation/Capitalization

Commas and semicolons in series.

Rule 1: When numbers or letters are used to delineate the members of a series—*one, first, in the first place, A*—they are written out and surrounded by punctuation.

Remember the rule that, when there is an *and* connecting each member of the series, there are no commas between the members of the series. The only commas in the following examples are around the numbers or letters.

I have to get the names from the list and make calls to each of them and get their opinions on this bill. I have to, one, get the names from the list and, two, make calls to each of them and, three, get their opinions on this bill.

We sent it to the CEO and the COO and the CFO.
We sent it to, A, the CEO and, B, the COO and, C, the CFO.

There were fliers and pamphlets and bulletins and Google results.
There were, first, fliers and, second, pamphlets and, third, bulletins and, fourth, Google results.

Rule 2: When members of a series are separated by commas and there are internal commas in one or more members of the series, the series itself is separated by semicolons.

Notice that each number or letter has punctuation around it though it is not necessarily a pair of commas. Once the number or letter in the series has commas, the series must have semicolons.

I have to get the names from the list, make calls to each of them, and get their opinions on this bill.
I have to, one, get the names from the list; two, make calls to each of them; and, three, get their opinions on this bill.

We sent it to the CEO, the COO, and the CFO.
We sent it to, A, the CEO; B, the COO; and, C, the CFO.

There were fliers, pamphlets, bulletins, and Google results.
There were, first, fliers; second, pamphlets; third, bulletins; and, fourth, Google results.

Directions: Correct the punctuation in these sentences.

1. We saw first, Gugliano and, second Wilson and, third, Barone.

2. He had accounts with Yahoo Hotmail and Verizon.

3. She thought she would study to be A, a doctor or, B, a lawyer, or C, an engineer.

4. They asked for, 1, tax forms; 2, personnel forms, and, 3, accounts payable.

5. They were scheduled at, first, 1:00 P.M.; second 2:00 P.M., third, 4:30 P.M.

Word Pairs

anal/annual/annul

anal = relating to the anus, overly devoted to detail (short for *anal retentive*).
The tumor was in the anal area.
I told her not to be so anal.
Part of his problem is that he is anal retentive.

annual = yearly.
We had our annual convention in Seattle this year.
There are annual dues of $200.
He was elected at the annual meeting.

annul = declare void.
The marriage was annulled after just a few days.
We will attempt to annul it.
There was a decision to annul the union.

board/bored

board = piece of wood, panel, get into a vehicle.
He is a member of several boards that govern these groups.
She tripped on a board that was lying in the pathway.
They tried to board the plane early with the baby.

bored = not interested, made a hole. This is the past tense of the verb *bore*.

We were bored with his constant haranguing.
The termites bored into the wood.
The movie bored us to tears.

cent/scent/sent

cent = one penny.

He had 37 cents in his pocket.
I do not have one red cent.
She would not give him one cent more.

scent = smell, odor.

My favorite movie is *Scent of a Woman*.
It was a scent I could not identify.
There was a trace of the scent of marijuana.

sent = caused to go, referred, transmitted. This is the past tense of the word *send*.

I sent the reply without giving it much thought.
They sent me to Dallas to work on the project.
She was sent several transcripts to read.

imply/infer

imply = suggest. The noun form is *implication*. Writers and speakers imply.

The president implied that he would not be involved in the merger.
The article implies that the prices have dropped dramatically.
There was an implication that the couple is to divorce.

infer = assume. The noun form is *inference*. Readers and listeners infer. This word is often followed by the word *from*.

I inferred from what was said that the company was in trouble.
His inference from reading the book is that there was no scandal involved.
She infers from that discussion that he will not be promoted.

vale/veil

vale = valley, gorge.

The house was hidden in the vale.
The vale afforded protection from the winds.
They wandered off into the vale.

veil = covering, hide or disguise.

They hid their suspicious behavior behind the corporate veil.
There was a veil of secrecy surrounding their activities.
The veil covered most of her face.

waist/waste

waist = middle section, body between hips and ribs.

Her waist was very small.
She had a sweatshirt tied around her waist.
The waist area is where he carried the weight.

waste = spend foolishly, throw away.

He wasted his opportunity to get an education.
Waste disposal in the area is a problem.
The money spent on that is a waste.

Directions: Choose the correct form of the word.

1. He was usually fairly anal/annual/annul about anyone touching his keyboard.

2. She was adamant about not waisting/wasting natural resources.

3. We drove through a thick, dense vale/veil.

4. The cent/scent/sent drifted upwards to our apartment.

5. He said the e-mail was cent/scent/sent early in the day.

6. He seemed to be on board/bored with the decision.

7. It was implied/inferred but not stated directly that she would get the job.

8. There seemed to be little waist/waste in that office.

9. The dogs picked up the cent/scent/sent up the river.

10. The coastline was valed/veiled in fog.

11. He decided to skip the anal/annual/annul meeting of the board/bored.

12. What do you think he would imply/infer from what you stated?

13. It was a mutual decision to anal/annual/annul the marriage.

14. I believe he implied/inferred from that that it was cent/scent/sent from corporate.

15. His anal/annual/annul personality caused him great difficulties on the job.

16. The teenagers seemed board/bored, but everyone else had a good time.

17. The implication/inference of the author was clear, in my mind.

18. It is weight around the waist/waste area that the doctor feels is dangerous.

19. The activities were well disguised behind the corporate vale/veil.

20. I believe it is estimated at just a few cents/scents/sents on the dollar.

Is It One Word or Two? An Apostrophe? A Hyphen?

There are many words in English where the letter *a* stands separately from a word and serves as an article and those where the letter *a* combines with the word. It is important to know which word the context requires.

array/a ray
abridge/a bridge
align/a line

acute/a cute
ahead/a head
arise/a rise

There is not a way to do it with him away.
He began a round of golf around 10:00 A.M.
She had a bout of the flu in about November.

Directions: Choose the correct form of the word.

1. Did they apprise/a prize you of apprise/a prize in the contest?

2. He tried to assure/a sure me it was assure/a sure thing.

3. We sat apart/a part from them as we did not want to be apart/a part of that.

4. They were in accord/a cord that accord/a cord needed to be attached.

5. They were alike/a like in their appeal/a peal to the others.

Proofreading

Directions: Make necessary corrections, based on the material presented in the unit. If the sentence has no errors, write the word *correct* after the sentence.

1. The members of the bored were aligned on the side of management.   _____

2. He inferred in his speech that the problems were, one, inflation, two, high prices, and three, high interest rates.   _____

3. Did he a sure you that corporate waist was a target of his campaign?   _____

4. I implied from what they said that appropriate attire for the mourners is black clothing and a veiled hat.   _____

5. Apart from the books she had the chance to read, she was clearly bored with one, the classes themselves and two, the discussion groups.   _____

6. At the annul meeting, they apprised us of the new scent that was to be debuted in the fall.   _____

7. Several people stepped up to a peal the annulment of the union.   _____

8. The areas of concern were, A, the thighs; B, the hips; C, the waste.   _____

9. He was sent a head on a very important mission for the board.   _____

10. The veil of secrecy has not been lifted in order to assure them about the results.   _____

An Adaptation from a Corporations, Partnerships, and Sole Proprietorships Case

Facts:

Sinatra, a stockholder, filed an action pursuant to Section 220 of the Delaware General Corporation Law, seeking to compel an inspection of the books and records related to the three senior executives' compensation that he claims is excessive and wasteful. Sinatra had sent a written demand as is required. He claimed all three executives were functioning in the same job and were paid amounts above the minimum in their contracts. Sinatra claimed that for three executives to earn total compensation of $205 million as co-chief executive officers running one enterprise and receiving such extraordinary compensation during a two-year period is unusual.

Procedural History:

Sinatra filed suit after Verizon refused his demand to review the books. Sinatra moved for summary judgment. Defendant Verizon cross-moved for summary judgment.

Issue:

Did Sinatra have a credible basis to imply there was excessive compensation?

Rationale:

Section 220 of the Delaware General Corporation Law sets out a procedure for a stockholder to follow in order to be entitled to inspect books and records. Such stockholders must establish that, one, he/she is a stockholder; two, he/she has complied with the form and manner required for making a demand; three, the inspection must be for a proper purpose. Mere curiosity is not enough. The stockholder must present evidence based on some credible basis from which the court can infer that waste or mismanagement may have occurred. While a stockholder does not have to prove actual wrongdoing, a statement of purpose to investigate possible general mismanagement is not sufficient. All Sinatra could say when questioned at a deposition was that he had no basis to allege that the executives did not earn the money that was paid to them. He also had no facts to establish that there was any violation of the duties of loyalty or care in the directors' approval of the executives' compensation.

Ruling:

There is no credible evidence to find that the board of directors committed mismanagement in compensating the directors. Sinatra's demands were based on suspicion or curiosity.
Plaintiff Sinatra's motion for summary judgment is denied. Defendant's cross-motion is granted.

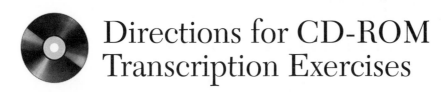

Directions for CD-ROM Transcription Exercises

In audio format are:

1. Terms for the unit with pronunciations from the thesaurus/dictionary feature.

2. Self-Test that appears in the book at mid-unit.*

3. Case that appears at the unit end.*

*speeds are 80 wpm/120 wpm for differing skill levels

CD-ROM icons appear where the three above are located within each unit.

Readers may practice transcription by listening to the CD-ROM where prompted by the icons in the book. However, for high success in testing your transcription skills, mastering all the terms and English skills in the unit is recommended before attempting the CD-ROM.

For Keyboard Transcriptionists: Listen to the CD-ROM audio file for this unit at 80 wpm or 120 wpm and transcribe from the dictation on your computer. Edit and proofread your work against the printed copy in the book.

For Reporting Writers: Listen to the CD-ROM audio file at 80 wpm or 120 wpm and take down the dictation on your writer. Either transcribe from your notes and proofread your work or edit and proofread your CAT (computer-aided transcription) transcript. Always check your work against the printed copy in the book.

 Student CD-ROM
For additional materials,
please go to the CD in this book.

 Online Companion™
For additional resources, please go to
http://www.paralegal.delmar.cengage.com

Unit 10 | Criminal Law and Procedure

The **Mistakes** That Court Reporters Make and *How to Avoid* Them

The Mistake:

Gerry Kowalski, an experienced reporter, was looking to work for a new deposition agency. He called around and was sent on a job by AAA Reporters. The job was a heavy technical that was videotaped. The owner of AAA told Gerry that she would have Gerry's first few jobs proofread.

A week later, the attorney called and wanted the job as soon as possible. Gerry had not even begun to work on the job. He sent it to his scopist, got it back a few days later, glanced at it, and sent it off to AAA Reporters. The proofreader for AAA found many, many errors including proper names that had not been researched, sentences that did not make sense, absolutely wrong words, and punctuation errors. Needless to say, the agency was very hesitant to give Gerry further work.

How to Avoid It:

Never send a job without proofreading it—never! Presumably Gerry would have caught several of the errors had he carefully proofread the job. Though everyone misses catching errors at times, "glancing" at a transcript in lieu of carefully proofreading is never going to be acceptable under any circumstances. When trying to impress a new agency owner, it goes without saying that proofreading is of the utmost importance.

Introduction

American society has defined the conduct expected from its members so that all may coexist peacefully. Criminal laws were created to describe prohibited acts. In criminal law the government brings a case on behalf of its people against the accused. The government is represented by an attorney called a district attorney or prosecutor. In civil law a citizen brings an action against another citizen and both parties have private attorneys.

There are different classes of crimes. As in the case at the end of the unit, the most serious crimes are called felonies, generally punishable by one year or more in prison. Less serious crimes are misdemeanors, usually punishable by fine and/or imprisonment for less than one year. The least serious crimes are ordinance violations, which are punishable by a fine or probation.

In order to charge a person with a crime it must be proven that the person performed a prohibited act with criminal intent. Proof beyond a reasonable doubt is required of a prosecutor for a conviction.

Criminal procedure is the process by which an arrest is made, charges are brought against the accused, as well as the stages up to and including the trial. The majority of cases are resolved prior to trial. In plea bargaining the prosecutor and the defense attorney reach agreement whereby the accused will generally plead guilty to lesser charges in lieu of trial on the more serious charges.

Criminal law and procedure are closely associated with the rights guaranteed by the United States Constitution and are constantly undergoing change by the state courts and legislature, the Congress, and the United States Supreme Court. In the case herein, the defendant's rights were violated.

Unit Objectives

- ■ Work with a legal dictionary/thesaurus.
- ■ Learn about criminal law and procedure.
- ■ Master the similarities and differences in definitions of key terms in this unit.
- ■ Master the pronunciations and spellings of legal terms in this unit.
- ■ Recognize the synonyms used for legal terminology in criminal law and procedure.
- ■ Practice usage of terms, definitions, and synonyms for criminal law and procedure.
- ■ Complete unit exercises in the forms of missing words, matching, multiple choice, true/false, synonyms, self-test, defining words, and also:
  - ● Punctuation/capitalization
  - ● Word pairs
  - ● Transcription of terms, self-test, and case
  - ● Proofreading

💿 Dictionary/Thesaurus

Note: All Dictionary/Thesaurus terms appear on the CD-ROM with audio pronunciations.

Term
[phonetic pronunciation]

---

accessory
[ak.*sess*.e.ree]

1. A person who is involved with the commission of a crime but who is not present at the time it is committed. *See also* aiding and abetting. 2. Anything that is a lesser part of a larger undertaking or thing.
• *n.* accomplice, abettor, conspirator, collaborator, consort, assistant ("accessory after the fact"); supplement, attachment, addition, extension

---

actus reus
[*ahk*.tus *ree*.us]

(*Latin*) An "answerable act," i.e., an act for which one is answerable; a guilty act. In combination with mens rea (a guilty or criminal intent), actus reus is an essential element of any crime. Thus, for EXAMPLE, the act of killing is the actus reus of murder.

---

aiding and abetting
[*ay*.ding and a.*bet*.ing]

Helping or encouraging a person to commit a crime.

---

alibi
[*al*.i.by]

The defense that the accused was elsewhere at the time the crime was committed.
• *n.* defense, excuse, explanation, proof, avowal

---

arraignment
[a.*rain*.ment]

The act of bringing an accused before a court to answer a criminal charge made against him and calling upon him to enter a plea of guilty or not guilty. *Compare* preliminary hearing.
• *n.* accusation, incrimination, formal accusal, judicial charge

---

arrest
[a.*rest*]

1. Detention of a person on a criminal charge. 2. Any detention of a person, with or without the intent to take him into custody.
• *v.* apprehend, catch, capture, block, seize ("the thief was arrested"); stop, block, foil, obstruct, hinder ("arrested development")
• *n.* apprehension, captivity, capture, confinement, detention, incarceration; stoppage, suspension, halt, cessation ("his arrest was of indefinite duration")

---

arson
[*ar*.sen]

The willful and malicious burning of a building. In some jurisdictions, arson includes the deliberate burning of any structure.
• *n.* pyromania, setting a fire, torching

assault
[a.*salt*]

An act of force or threat of force intended to inflict harm upon a person or to put the person in fear that such harm is imminent; an attempt to commit a battery. The perpetrator must have, or appear to have, the present ability to carry out the act.
• *v.* abuse, advance, assail, jump, set upon, bash, violate, storm ("the pedestrian assaulted the child")
• *n.* attack, advance, strike, violation ("the assault was aggressive")

assault and battery
[a.*salt* and *bat*.er.ee]

An achieved assault; an assault carried out by hitting or by other physical contact. *See also* battery.

attempt
[a.temt]

An act done with the intent to commit a crime, which would have resulted in the crime being committed except that something happened to prevent it.

bail
[bayul]

n. 1. The customary means of securing the release from custody of a person charged with a criminal offense, by assuring his appearance in court and compelling him to remain within the jurisdiction. 2. The security given for a defendant's appearance in court in the form of cash, real property, or a bail bond. 3. The person who is the surety on a bail bond.
v. To secure the release from custody of a person charged with a crime, pending trial, by posting a bail bond.
• *n.* bond, guarantee, security, warrant, collateral

battery
[*bat*.ter.ee]

The unconsented-to touching or striking of one person by another, or by an object put in motion by him, with the intention of doing harm or giving offense. Battery is both a crime and a tort. *Compare* assault.
See also assault and battery.
• *n.* beating, mugging, flogging, hitting, assault, thrashing, injury ("commit a battery"); batch, cluster, array ("a battery of elements")

beyond a reasonable doubt
[be.*yond* a *ree*.zen.ebl dout]

The degree of proof required to convict a person of a crime. A reasonable doubt is a fair doubt based upon reason and common sense, not an arbitrary or possible doubt. To convict a criminal defendant, a jury must be persuaded of his guilt to a level beyond "apparently" or "probably." Proof beyond a reasonable doubt is the highest level of proof the law requires.

bigamy
[*big*.e.mee]

The crime of marrying while married.

bribery
[*bry*.be.ree]

The crime of giving something of value with the intention of influencing the action of a public official, witness, juror, etc.
• *n.* corruption, perfidy, allurement, cajolery, inveiglement, connivance, venality, opportunism

burglary
[*ber*.gler.ee]

At common law, the offense of breaking and entering a dwelling at night with the intent to commit a felony (EXAMPLES: theft; murder). The crime of burglary has been broadened by statute to include entering buildings other than dwellings, with or without a breaking, and regardless of the time of day or night.
• *v.* robbery, larceny, breaking and entering, housebreaking, looting, crime, forcible entry, raiding

capital crime
[*ka*.pi.tel krime]

A crime punishable by death.

capital punishment
[*ka*.pi.tel *pun*.ish.ment]

The death penalty as a punishment for crime.

commutation of sentence
[kom.yoo.*tay*.shun ov *sen*.tense]

The substitution of a less severe punishment for a harsher punishment.

consecutive sentences
[ken.*sek*.yoo.tiv *sen*.ten.sez]

Sentences of imprisonment for crimes in which the time of each is to run one after the other without a break.

conspiracy
[ken.*spi*.re.see]

An agreement between two or more persons to engage in a criminal act or to accomplish a legal objective by criminal or unlawful means. Conspiracy is a criminal offense (a criminal conspiracy); it is also a wrong that is grounds for a civil action if damage is suffered.
• *n.* connivance, counterplot, frame, plot, scheme, trickery

crime
[kryme]

An offense against the authority of the state; a public wrong, as distinguished from a private wrong; an act in violation of the penal code; a felony or a misdemeanor. *See also* criminal statute.
• *n.* felony, misdemeanor, criminal act, misconduct, delinquency, corruption, offense, lawlessness

crime scene investigation
[*kryme* seen in.ves.ti.*gay*.shen]

An inquiry in a criminal matter by law enforcement investigators for the discovery and collection of facts and evidence.

criminal
[*krim*.i.nel]

adj. 1. Pertaining to crime or punishment. 2. Involving crime; guilty of crime.
n. A person who has been convicted of committing a crime.
• *n.* felon, culprit, violator, offender, delinquent, transgressor
• *adj.* unlawful, felonious, illegal, notorious, blameworthy, noncivil ("criminal intent")

criminal act
[*krim*.i.nel akt]

Any act punishable as a crime.

criminal action
[*krim*.i.nel *ak*.shen]

A criminal prosecution.

criminal capacity
[*krim*.i.nel ke.*pass*.i.tee]

A person can be guilty of a crime only if he has the capacity to appreciate the criminal nature of his act. In the eyes of the law, certain persons are conclusively presumed to lack criminal capacity. EXAMPLES: insane persons; persons who have not reached the age of reason.

criminal charge
[*krim*.i.nel charj]

An indictment, information, complaint, or other formal charge of the commission of a crime.

criminal law
[*krim*.i.nel law]

Branch of the law that specifies what conduct constitutes crime and establishes appropriate punishments for such conduct.

criminal offense
[*krim*.i.nel o.*fense*]

A crime.

criminal procedure
[*krim*.i.nel pro.*see*.jer]

The rules of procedure that govern criminal prosecutions.

criminal prosecution
[*krim*.i.nel pross.e.*kyoo*.shen]

The process of arresting, charging, trying, and sentencing a person for the commission of a crime. A criminal sentence generally involves the imposition of a fine, imprisonment, or death. A criminal prosecution is brought by the state, as opposed to a civil action, which is brought by a private party.

criminal statute
[*krim*.i.nel *stat*.shoot]

A statute that declares the conduct that it describes to be a crime, and establishes punishment for engaging in it.

critical stage
[*krit*.i.kel stayj]

The point in a criminal proceeding at which a defendant's constitutional right to counsel is violated unless she has counsel or has been advised of her right to counsel.

cruel and unusual punishment
[*kroo*.el and un.*yoo*.zhoo.el *pun*.ish.ment]

Forms of punishment for crime prohibited by the Eighth Amendment. The Supreme Court has determined that corporal punishment inflicted by the state is cruel within the meaning of the Constitution, but that capital punishment is not.

death penalty
[deth *pen*.el.tee]

Another term for capital punishment.

degrees of crime
[di.*greez* ov kryme]

The grades of crime ranked according to seriousness. EXAMPLES: first degree murder; second degree murder.

double jeopardy
[duh.bull *jep*.er.dee]

A rule originating in the Fifth Amendment that prohibits a second punishment or trial for the same offense.

embezzlement
[em.*bezl*.ment]

The fraudulent conversion of property, including but not limited to money, with which a person (EXAMPLES: an employee; a bailee; a trustee) has been entrusted.
• *n.* abstraction, misappropriation, misuse, theft, larceny, defalcation, peculation, pilferage

exclusionary rule
[eks.*kloo*.zhen.air.ree rule]

The rule of constitutional law that evidence secured by the police by means of an unreasonable search and seizure, in violation of the Fourth Amendment, cannot be used as evidence in a criminal prosecution.

extortion
[eks.*tor*.shen]

The criminal offense of obtaining money or other things of value by duress, force, threat of force, fear, or under color of office.
• *n.* coercion, intimidation, fraud, stealing, oppression ("the criminal extortion of funds")

felony
[*fel*.a.nee]

A general term for more serious crimes (EXAMPLES: murder; robbery; larceny), as distinguished from lesser offenses, which are known as misdemeanors. In many jurisdictions, felonies are crimes for which the punishment is death or more than one year of imprisonment. Persons convicted of felonies are generally incarcerated in prisons or penitentiaries, as opposed to local jails.
• *n.* gross offense, serious offense, transgression, wrongdoing, crime

felony murder rule
[*fel*.a.nee *mer*.der rule]

The rule that a death that occurs by accident or chance during the course of the commission of a felony is first degree murder. (EXAMPLE: If, during the course of an armed robbery by Robbers A and B, Robber A accidentally shoots and kills the storeowner, Robber B as well as Robber A is guilty of murder.) The felony murder rule, which is a common law doctrine, has been modified by statute in most states. *See also* murder.

forensic
[fo.*ren*.sik]

Pertaining to or belonging to the courts.

forensic pathology
[fo.*ren*.sik path.*aw*.le.jee]

Branch of medicine that pertains to the causes of disease and death.

forgery
[*for*.jer.ee]

The false making, material alteration, or uttering, with intent to defraud or injure, of any writing that, if genuine, might appear to be legally effective or the basis for legal liability. Forgery is a crime.
• *n.* falsification, fraudulence, misrepresentation, manipulation

grand jury
[grand *joo*.ree]

A body whose number varies with the jurisdiction, never less than six nor more than 23, whose duty it is to determine whether probable cause exists to return indictments against persons accused of committing crimes. The right to indictment by grand jury is guaranteed by the Fifth Amendment.

homicide
[*hom*.i.side]

The killing of a human being. Homicide may be noncriminal (excusable homicide or justifiable homicide) or criminal (felonious homicide). Excusable or justifiable homicide includes killing by accident or in self-defense. A felonious homicide is either murder or manslaughter. Manslaughter homicide includes negligent homicide and vehicular homicide.
• *n.* murder, manslaughter, slaying, assassination, killing, slaughter, felony, elimination, termination of life, extermination

incest [*in*.sest]	Sexual intercourse between persons so closely related that the law prohibits their marriage to each other.
indictment [in.*dite*.ment]	1. A charge made in writing by a grand jury, based upon evidence presented to it, accusing a person of having committed a criminal act, generally a felony. It is the function of the prosecution to bring a case before the grand jury. If the grand jury indicts the defendant, a trial follows. 2. The formal, written accusation itself brought before the grand jury by the prosecutor. *Compare* information.
information [in.fer.*may*.shen]	1. An accusation of the commission of a crime, sworn to by a district attorney or other prosecutor, on the basis of which a criminal defendant is brought to trial for a misdemeanor and, in some states, for a felony. 2. In some jurisdictions, which prosecute felonies only on the basis of indictment by a grand jury, an affidavit alleging probable cause to bind the defendant over to await action by the grand jury. • *n.* knowledge, facts, material, news; wisdom, enlightenment; charge, accusation, complaint, allegation ("felony information")
insane [in.*sane*]	Of unsound mind. *See also* insanity. • *adj.* unsound, deranged, demented, absurd, bizarre, mad
insanity [in.*san*.i.tee]	A term for a condition of the mind, which has no medical or scientific meaning and whose legal meaning depends upon the context in which it is used. Insanity as a criminal defense. Different states use different tests or standards for determining whether a criminal defendant was insane (that is, whether he had the capacity to form criminal intent) at the time he committed the crime. The most important of these tests are the M'Naghten rule, irresistible impulse, and, most frequently used, the Model Penal Code's standard, lack of capacity "as a result of mental disease or defect" to appreciate the criminality of one's conduct or to conform one's conduct to the requirements of law. The law also requires that a criminal defendant be sane at the time of trial, and permits imposition of the death penalty only if the person convicted is sane at the time of execution.
larceny [*lar*.sen.ee]	The crime of taking personal property, without consent, with the intent to convert it to the use of someone other than the owner or to deprive the owner of it permanently. Larceny does not involve the use of force or the threat of force. *Compare* robbery. *Also compare* burglary. • *n.* theft, embezzlement, burglary, pilferage, misappropriation, stealing
lesser included offense [*less*.er in.*kloo*.ded o.*fense*]	A criminal offense included within the crime for which a defendant has been indicted, and for which he may be convicted under the indictment so long as he is not convicted of the more serious offense; a crime that cannot be committed without at the same time committing one or more other crimes. EXAMPLE: It is impossible to commit first degree murder without also committing both second degree murder, voluntary manslaughter, and battery.

malice
[*mal*.iss]

State of mind that causes the intentional doing of a wrongful act without legal excuse or justification; a condition of mind prompting a person to the commission of a dangerous or deadly act in deliberate disregard of the lives or safety of others. The term does not necessarily connote personal ill will. It can and frequently does mean general malice.

As an element of murder, all those states of mind that prompt a person to kill another person without legal excuse or justification; an intent to do the deceased great bodily harm.

In the law of defamation, to be actionable, malice must be actual malice or express malice.

manslaughter
[*man*.slaw.ter]

The killing of a human being, without premeditation or malice and without legal excuse or justification. Voluntary manslaughter occurs when a homicide is intentional but the result of sudden passion or great provocation. Involuntary manslaughter is an unintentional killing in the course of doing an unlawful act not amounting to a felony or while doing a lawful act in a reckless manner. There are various degrees of manslaughter, which are not consistent from jurisdiction to jurisdiction. *Compare* murder.

mens rea
[menz *ray*.ah]

An "answerable intent," i.e., an intent for which one is answerable; an evil intent; a guilty mind; a criminal intent. In combination with actus reus (a guilty or criminal act), mens rea is an essential element of any crime except regulatory crimes or strict liability crimes and some petty offenses and infractions. Mens rea may be inferred or presumed.

Miranda rule
[mi.*ran*.da rule]

The Fifth Amendment and the Fourteenth Amendment to the Constitution require that, before a suspect who is in custody may be questioned, she must be informed that she has the right to remain silent and that anything she says may be used against her in court, be given the right to have an attorney present during questioning, and be advised that if she cannot afford an attorney one will be provided for her. If an interrogation occurs in the absence of these warnings, or in the absence of the suspect's attorney, any confession obtained is inadmissible unless the defendant has intelligently and knowingly waived her "Miranda rights," established by the case *Miranda v. Arizona*.

misdemeanor
[mis.de.*meen*.er]

A crime not amounting to a felony. In many jurisdictions, misdemeanors are offenses for which the punishment is incarceration for less than a year (generally in a jail, rather than in a prison or the penitentiary) or the payment of a fine. EXAMPLE: traffic violation.
• *n.* offense, transgression, wrong, misdeed, violation, trespass, impropriety

M'Naghten rule
[me.*naw*.ten rule]

An accused is not criminally responsible if, by defect of reason from disease of the mind, the accused did not know the nature of the act, or, if so, did not know it was wrong. *See also* insanity.

Model Penal Code
[*mod*.l *pee*.nel kode]

A proposed criminal code prepared jointly by the Commission on Uniform State Laws and the American Law Institute.

motive
[*moh*.tiv]

The reason that leads the mind to desire a result; that which leads the mind to engage in a criminal act; that which causes the mind to form criminal intent.

murder
[*mer*.der]

The intentional and premeditated killing of a human being (first degree murder); the intentional killing of a human being, without premeditation, but with malice aforethought, express or implied (second degree murder). Under most state statutes, a homicide that occurs during the commission of a felony is first degree murder, as are homicides perpetrated by lying in wait, torture, poison, and other criminal acts from which premeditation or deliberation can be inferred. Similarly, a homicide that results from deliberately doing a dangerous or deadly act with disregard for the safety of others is second degree murder, malice being inferred from the act itself. *Compare* manslaughter. *See also* felony murder rule.
• *n.* liquidation, slaughter, killing, slaying, homicide, execution, unlawful killing

nolo contendere
[*no*.lo kon.*ten*.de.ray]

(*Latin*) "I do not wish to contend." A plea in a criminal case, also referred to as no contest, which, although it is essentially the same as a guilty plea, and carries the same consequences with respect to punishment, can be entered only with leave of court, because it is not an admission of responsibility and cannot be used against the defendant in a civil action based upon the same facts.

parole
[pa.*role*]

The release of a person from imprisonment after serving a portion of her sentence, provided she complies with certain conditions. Such conditions vary, depending upon the case, but they generally include stipulations such as not associating with known criminals, not possessing firearms, and not leaving the jurisdiction without the permission of the parole officer. Parole is not an act of clemency; it does not set aside the sentence. The parolee remains in the legal custody of the state and under the control of her parole officer. She may be returned to prison if she breaches the specified conditions. However, due process requires that parole cannot be revoked without a hearing.
• *n.* release, freedom, emancipation, conditional release
• *v.* discharge, release, liberate, let out, disimprison, unchain, unfetter

plea bargain
[plee *barg*.in]

An agreement between the prosecutor and a criminal defendant under which the accused agrees to plead guilty, usually to a lesser offense, in exchange for receiving a lighter sentence than he would likely have received had he been found guilty after trial on the original charge.

preliminary hearing
[pre.*lim*.i.ner.ee *heer*.ing]

A hearing to determine whether there is probable cause to formally accuse a person of a crime; that is, whether there is a reasonable basis for believing that a crime has been committed and for thinking the defendant committed it. If the judge concludes that the evidence is sufficient to hold the defendant for trial, and if the offense is a bailable offense, the court sets bail. If the judge concludes that the evidence is insufficient to bind the defendant over for trial, the defendant is discharged from custody. *See also* probable cause.

prison
[*priz*.en]

A place of confinement for persons convicted of felonies, as opposed to jail, which is customarily a place of confinement for persons convicted of misdemeanors; a penitentiary.
• *n.* penitentiary, confinement, jail, house of detention, reformatory, guardhouse, pen, cell, facility

probable cause
[*prob*.ebl cawz]

A reasonable amount of suspicion, supported by circumstances sufficiently strong to justify a prudent and cautious person's belief that certain alleged facts are probably true. A judge may not issue a search warrant unless she is shown probable cause to believe there is evidence of crime on the premises. A police officer may not make an arrest without a warrant unless he has reasonable cause, based upon reliable information, to believe a crime has been or is being committed.

probation
[pro.*bay*.shen]

A sentence that allows a person convicted of a crime to continue to live and work in the community while being supervised by a probation officer instead of being sent to prison. A person may also be sentenced to a term of probation to commence after the expiration of his prison term.
• *n.* conditional release, test period, trial period, parole, furlough, exemption

prosecution
[*pross*.e.kyoo.shen]

A criminal action brought by the government.

prosecutor
[pross.e.*kyoo*.ter]

A public official, elected or appointed, who conducts criminal prosecutions on behalf of her jurisdiction. EXAMPLES: the district attorney of a county; the attorney general of a state; a United States attorney.

rape
[rayp]

Sexual intercourse with a woman by force or by putting her in fear or in circumstances in which she is unable to control her conduct or to resist (EXAMPLES: intoxication; unconsciousness). Under the common law definition of the crime, only a female can be raped and only a male can perpetrate the crime. In recent years, however, courts in several states have held that the rape statutes of their jurisdictions are gender-neutral and apply equally to perpetrators of either sex.
• *v.* molest, sexually assault, debauch, defile, ravish ("the woman was raped")
• *n.* violation, assault, sexual assault, nonconsensual sex, defilement, seduction, abuse

robbery
[*rob*.e.ree]

The felonious taking of money or any thing of value from the person of another or from his presence, against his will, by force or by putting him in fear. *Compare* larceny.
• *n.* theft, hold-up, piracy, commandeering, embezzlement, expropriation, abduction

scienter
[see.*en*.ter]

Knowledge, particularly guilty knowledge, that will result in one's own liability or guilt.

self-defense
[self-de.*fense*]

The use of force to protect oneself from death or imminent bodily harm at the hands of an aggressor. A person may use only that amount of force reasonably necessary to protect himself against the peril with which he is threatened; thus, deadly force may be used in self-defense only against an aggressor who himself uses deadly force.

sentence
[*sen*.tense]

n. The judgment of the court in a criminal case. A criminal sentence constitutes the court's action with respect to the consequences to the defendant of having committed the crime of which she has been convicted. Generally, criminal sentences impose a punishment of imprisonment, probation, fine, or forfeiture, or some combination of these penalties. In some jurisdictions, capital punishment may be imposed in cases involving the commission of a felony of extreme gravity. In some states, depending upon the crime, the jury, rather than the judge, establishes the sentence.

separate counts
[*sep*.ret kounts]

Two or more counts, charging separate offenses, contained in one indictment or information.

stop
[stop]

n. An arrest; a police officer's action in halting a person's freedom of action, even briefly.

stop and frisk
[stop and frisk]

The detaining of a person briefly by a police officer and "patting him down" with the purpose of ascertaining if he is carrying a concealed weapon.

violation
[vy.o.*lay*.shen]

1. The act of breaking the law; an infringement of the law; a violation of the law. 2. Sometimes used as a synonym for an infraction.
• *n.* abuse, contravention, illegality, misdemeanor, transgression
("a violation of the law")

Missing Words

Fill in the blanks below.

1. _____ is the detention of a person on criminal charges.

2. The grades of crime ranked according to seriousness are the _____ of crime.

3. A(n) _____ is the point in a criminal proceeding at which a defendant's constitutional right to counsel is violated unless she has counsel or has been advised of the right to counsel.

4. When a person is released from imprisonment after serving a portion of the sentence provided certain conditions are complied with, this is called _____.

5. A(n) _____ is an agreement between the prosecutor and a criminal defendant where the accused agrees to plead guilty to a lesser offense in exchange for receiving a lighter sentence.

6. _____ is a plea in a criminal case that means, "I don't wish to contend."

7. _____ are forms of punishment such as torture and banishment that are prohibited by the Eighth Amendment to the Constitution.

8. Branch of medicine that pertains to the causes of death is _____.

9. When you help a person to commit a crime, this is _____.

10. A(n) _____ is an offense against the authority of the state, known as a public wrong.

11. The _____ is a proposed criminal code prepared jointly by the Commission on Uniform State Laws and the American Law Institute.

12. _____ is a sentence that allows a person convicted of a crime to continue to live and work in the community instead of being sent to jail.

13. _____ is claimed when one uses force to protect oneself from death or imminent bodily harm at the hands of an aggressor.

14. _____ is an agreement between two or more persons to engage in a criminal act.

15. _____ is used as a criminal defense to show that the accused lacked the capacity to form criminal intent.

16. The crime of marrying while already married is _____.

17. Sexual intercourse with a woman by force is called _____.

18. The criminal offense of obtaining money or other things of value by duress, force, threat of force, fear, or under color of office is _____.

Matching

Match the letter of the definition to the term below.

_____ 19. Conspiracy

    A. An agreement between two or more persons to engage in a criminal act or accomplish a legal objective by criminal or unlawful means

_____ 20. Stop and frisk

    B. An act in violation of the penal code

_____ 21. Information

    C. Accusation of the commission of a crime sworn to by a district attorney or other prosecutor

_____ 22. Miranda rule

    D. State of mind that causes the intentional doing of a wrongful act without legal excuse or justification

_____ 23. Violation

    E. Crime not amounting to a felony

_____ 24. Exclusionary rule

    F. Before a suspect in custody may be questioned he or she must be informed of the right to remain silent

_____ 25. Parole

    G. Judgment of the court in a criminal case

_____ 26. Capital punishment

    H. Detaining of a person by police to see if a concealed weapon is being carried

_____ 27. Misdemeanor

    I. Sexual intercourse with a woman by force

_____ 28. Degree of crime

    J. Synonym for an infraction

_____ 29. Crime

    K. Grade of crime ranked according to seriousness

_____ 30. Sentence

    L. Evidence secured by police during an unreasonable search and seizure; cannot be used at trial

_____ 31. Malice

    M. Hearing to determine whether there is probable cause to formally accuse a person of a crime

_____ 32. Rape

N. Conditional release from prison after serving a portion of a sentence

_____ 33. Preliminary hearing

O. The death penalty as a punishment for a crime

_____ 34. Motive

P. Pertaining to the courts

_____ 35. Forensic

Q. Criminal intent

Multiple Choice

Select the best choice.

_____ 36. The security given for a defendant's appearance in court is known as:
   a. incest
   b. bail
   c. malice
   d. extortion

_____ 37. The crime of giving something of value with the intent of influencing a public official is called:
   a. robbery
   b. larceny
   c. embezzlement
   d. bribery

_____ 38. A general term for more serious crimes such as murder and robbery is:
   a. violation
   b. misdemeanor
   c. felony
   d. lesser included offense

_____ 39. The degree of proof needed to convict a person of a crime is:
   a. proof beyond a reasonable doubt
   b. preponderance of the evidence
   c. clear and convincing proof
   d. a scintilla of evidence

_____ 40. The willful and malicious burning of a building is called:
   a. larceny
   b. embezzlement
   c. arson
   d. forgery

_____ 41. The breaking and entering of a dwelling at night with the intent to commit a felony is called:
   a. robbery
   b. larceny
   c. extortion
   d. burglary

_____ 42. Sexual intercourse between persons so closely related that the law prohibits their marriage to each other is:
   a. incest
   b. bigamy
   c. sodomy
   d. rape

_____ 43. When a bank teller has been entrusted with money and converts the property for his own benefit, this is:
   a. larceny
   b. embezzlement
   c. aiding and abetting
   d. extortion

_____ 44. The intentional and premeditated killing of a human being is:
   a. murder
   b. manslaughter
   c. misdemeanor
   d. mens rea

_____ 45. The rule of constitutional law that evidence secured by the police by means of an unreasonable search and seizure cannot be used as evidence in a criminal prosecution is:
  a. strict liability crimes
  b. lesser included offense
  c. exclusionary rule
  d. beyond a reasonable doubt

_____ 46. The charge made in writing by a grand jury based upon evidence presented to it, accusing a person of having committed a criminal act, is the:
  a. preliminary hearing
  b. arrest
  c. stop
  d. indictment

_____ 47. The act of bringing an accused before a court to answer a criminal charge, and to enter a plea of guilty or not guilty is:
  a. arraignment
  b. plea bargain
  c. grand jury
  d. trial

_____ 48. A crime that cannot be committed without at the same time committing one or more other crimes is:
  a. double jeopardy
  b. extortion
  c. exclusionary rule
  d. lesser included offense

True/False

Mark the following T or F.

_____ 49. An accessory is a person who is involved with the commission of a crime but who is not present at the time it is committed.

_____ 50. A misdemeanor is an offense punishable by one year or more in prison.

_____ 51. The defense that the accused was elsewhere at the time the crime was committed is called an alibi.

_____ 52. Extortion is the willful and malicious burning of a building.

_____ 53. Malice is a state of mind that causes the intentional doing of a wrongful act without legal excuse or justification.

_____ 54. The unconsented-to touching or striking of one person by another is an assault.

_____ 55. When the death penalty is a punishment for a crime, this is called capital punishment.

_____ 56. A detention of a person on a criminal charge is called an indictment.

_____ 57. The arraignment is when the accused is brought into court to answer a criminal charge and asked to enter a plea.

_____ 58. A robbery is the breaking and entering of a dwelling at night with the intent to commit a felony.

____ **59.** The standard of evidence needed for the prosecutor to convict a defendant of a crime is by a preponderance of the evidence.

____ **60.** An attempt occurs where the accused has committed a crime but has not yet been arrested for the crime.

____ **61.** M'Naghten rule states that an accused isn't criminally responsible if found to be insane.

Synonyms

Select the correct synonym in parentheses for each numbered item.

62. ALIBI
    (arrest, confession, excuse)

63. BRIBE
    (kickback, present, request)

64. ATTEMPT
    (ponder, try, finish)

65. BATTERY
    (beating, frighten, tease)

66. LARCENY
    (forgery, lying, pickpocketing)

67. ACCESSORY
    (accomplice, violation, sodomy)

68. MURDER
    (torturing, killing, tormenting)

69. ARREST
    (detention, questioning, arraignment)

70. MALICE
    (willfulness, alibi, arson)

71. ASSAULT
    (threaten, attack, extortion)

72. FORGERY
    (bribery, alteration, bigamy)

73. HOMICIDE
    (burglary, robbery, killing)

74. CRIME
    (offense, defense, occasion)

75. CONSPIRACY
    (doubt, agreement, dispute)

76. CRIMINAL CHARGE
    (complaint, answer, demurrer)

77. MENS REA
    (crime, charge, intent)

78. ARSON
    (torching, incest, insane)

79. BAIL
    (attack, security, criminal)

80. PROSECUTION
    (persecution, criminal action, alibi)

Self-Test

Place the number of the correct term in the appropriate space.

81. Probation

82. Misdemeanors

83. Arrest

84. Degrees

85. Indictment

86. Parole

87. Plea bargain

88. Violations

89. Crime

90. Criminal procedure

91. Felonies

92. Preliminary hearing

93. Arraigned

94. Murder

A(n) _____ is an act in violation of the penal code. There are different _____ of

crime, meaning the grades of crime ranked by seriousness. The most serious are the _____ such as _____. Less serious are the _____, which are punishable by incarceration for less than a year, or the payment of a fine. _____ are the least serious, usually punishable by fine and/or probation.

_____ is the rules of procedure by which criminal actions are governed. Generally, some illegal activity occurs. Then, a(n) _____ is made, usually based on a warrant.

In some cases, there might be a(n) _____ to see if there is probable cause to formally accuse a person of a crime. Depending on the state, the grand jury then issues a(n) _____ for the more serious crimes. Thereafter, the accused is _____, and a plea is entered by the accused.

Not all cases go on to trial. In some instances, a(n) _____ is made, where the accused agrees to plead guilty to a lesser offense in exchange for a lighter sentence. Not all guilty defendants are imprisoned. Some defendants might be placed on _____ instead of being sent to prison. Even if a defendant is imprisoned, they might be released early on _____, provided certain conditions are complied with.

Defining Words

Complete the definition.

95. Misdemeanor _____

_____

96. Mens rea _____

_____

97. Accessory _____

_____

98. Alibi _____

_____

99. Assault _____

_____

100. Murder _____

_____

101. Bail _____

_____

102. Malice _____

_____

103. Burglary _____

_____

104. Felony _____

_____

105. Battery _____

_____

106. Larceny _____

_____

107. Violation _____

_____

108. Arson _____

_____

109. Aiding and abetting _____

_____

110. Crime scene investigation _____

_____

Punctuation/Capitalization

Punctuation in relationship to quotes.

Rule 1: Periods and commas always go inside of quotation marks with no exceptions in the language.

As asked for by the attorney, he inserted the word "alleged."
When she heard the word "illegal," she was very skeptical.
That's where I was told to put the "X."

Rule 2: Colons and semicolons always go outside of quotation marks with no exceptions in the language.

She turned to him and said, "You need to hurry up"; is that correct?
It is a quote from "The Measure of a Man": "Reggie Poitier knew what his legacy would be."
He used the word "crime"; right.

Rule 3: The question mark (called **"interrog"** in court reporting) goes inside of quotation marks when the quoted material is asking a question.

He asked, "Have you seen her since the fiasco at the meeting?"
"How far away are we?" she asked.
She asked him, "Are we doing this as a team or individually?"

Note that, if there is a question asked inside the quoted material, the question mark goes inside no matter what is going on outside the quotes.

Did he say to her, "Are you or are you not pregnant?"
Was the question "Where are you working right now?"
Did he ask, "What do you charge for this service?"

Rule 4: The question mark goes outside the quotation mark when the quoted material is making a statement and something else in the sentence is asking the question.

Did she say, "I want you to be here by 5:00"?
Is it true that he said, "Be here no later than 3:00"?
Did she repeat, "He is not welcome in this house"?

Rule 5: Capitalize the first word of a quote when the quoted material is a complete sentence or stands for a complete thought.

He said to me, "Out of my way."
Did she respond, "You will have to prove that to me"?
I replied, "The boss did."

Directions: Correct the punctuation in these sentences.

1. Did you say to her, "How long are you going to wait"?

2. "When is he going to leave," I asked her?

3. He said, "she is very slow but very accurate in her work."

4. Every day she said to him, "Is the report going to be finished today?

5. "I am actively supporting her cause", he said.

Word Pairs

aid/aide

aid = help, assist, support.
I cannot believe that he will be of any aid to me in this situation.
It is said he worked to aid and abet a felon.
Is there any way that you can aid me in lifting this off the floor?

aide = a person who assists or helps or supports.

She is working as a nurse's aide right now.
I will need an aide to assist with this.
How many aides were with him at the time?

arraignment/arrangement

arraignment = act of bringing an accused before a court. The verb form is *arraign*.

There was to be an arraignment of the suspect within 72 hours.
The arraignment was to take place on Friday, June 17.
He was arraigned on murder charges after the arrest.

arrangement = agreement, adaptation, organization. The verb form is *arrange*.

They had an arrangement about the tasks to be accomplished.
I did not agree with the arrangement they had made.
There was a pleasing arrangement of the flowers we were seeking.

bail/bale

bail = customary means of securing the release from custody of a person charged with a criminal offense, clear water from a boat, bar on typewriter that holds paper against the platen.

He posted bail of $25,000.
We could not bail the water fast enough to keep the boat from sinking.
The paper bail on the typewriter was broken.

bale = bundle, put into bundles.

There were hay bales covering the field.
He helped bale the paper to take to the recycle location.
The cardboard was transported in bales.

indictment/inditement

indictment = charge made in writing by a grand jury, accusing a person of having committed a criminal act. The verb form is *indict*.

The indictment returned was expected by everyone.
The grand jury returned an indictment on four different offenses.
He was indicted on all charges against him and will stand trial.

inditement = writing or composition. The verb form is *indite*.

She was very touched by the inditement he composed.
He indited a lovely poem to her.
The inditement was totally unexpected as he had never written anything before.

model/mottle

model = pattern, copy, form.

He modeled his behavior after his hero.
It is a perfect model of the complex.
He talked often of his father as his role model.

mottle = splotchy, irregular pattern of color.

Her skin was mottled in the intense heat.
The horse was a mottled gray.
The rug was a mottle of bright colors.

parol/parole

parol = spoken or oral rather than written.

He felt he had entered into a parol contract.
It is parol evidence.
It is suspected that they had only parol testimony.

parole = release of a person from imprisonment after serving a portion of her sentence.

He was paroled about a year after he first applied.
She was set for parole in September.
Do you think he will appear at the parole hearing?

persecute/prosecute

persecute = oppress, discriminate against, bully. The noun form is *persecution*.

He was persecuted for his religious views.
I don't think I would regard it as persecution.
She always claimed she was being persecuted by the administration.

prosecute = bring criminal proceedings against, take legal action. The noun form is *prosecution*.

He was being prosecuted for his acts of May 21.
The prosecution argued for the death penalty.
They decided they did not have enough evidence to prosecute.

Directions: Choose the correct word.

1. I talked to his aid/aide about the amount of work he was doing.

2. They had an arraignment/arrangement that seemed to work for them.

3. I knew he was going to bail/bale out on me before it ended.

4. The indictment/inditement included several lesser offenses.

5. I don't know when she is coming up for parol/parole.

6. He had been persecuted/prosecuted by his peers for his unusual physical appearance.

7. She appreciated that he indicted/indited so many lovely communications to her.

8. The bails/bales were stacked in groups of ten near the door.

9. The aid/aide he received was too little too late.

10. That was the argument of the persecution/prosecution in closing.

11. Her modeled/mottled skin was an indication of the disease.

12. It served as a model/mottle home for the development.

13. The jury heard parol/parole evidence without any written backup.

14. She was arraigned/arranged in a late-afternoon proceeding.

15. The bail/bale amount was too high for him to be able to meet it.

16. The nurses aid/aide was responsible for reporting that information.

17. He was bailing/baling it into 100-pound bundles.

18. Did you use that as a model/mottle for the design?

19. Was he let out on bail/bale before his wife was out on parol/parole?

20. The indictment/inditement was not unexpected, but she did expect to be offered bail/bale.

Is It One Word or Two? An Apostrophe? A Hyphen?

who's/whose

who's = contraction for "who is."

Who's calling her when we leave here?
Who's going to serve as president?
I know the man who's coming to assume the role.

whose = possessive form.

Whose car are you driving?
I don't know whose parents were chaperoning.
Do you have any idea whose purse this is?

Directions: Choose the correct form of the word.

1. Who's/Whose house is being used for the meeting?

2. Who's/Whose coming to work for us this next week?

3. I am not aware who's/whose living with him.

4. She doesn't know who's/whose been assigned to her.

5. He saw the woman who's/whose car was damaged in the accident.

Proofreading

Directions: Make necessary corrections, based on the material presented in the unit. If the sentence has no errors, write the word *correct* after the sentence.

1. The doctor asked, "Did you note any signs of modeling on the skin of her hands and feet"? _____

2. "How long will it be before he is arraigned for that offense," she asked? _____

3. The attorney stated, "my client is asking for bale", and said that he wanted it to be effective immediately. _____

4. Did he ask, "Was the aid responsible for taking his vital signs"? _____

5. Whose responsible for moving the bales into the shipping area? _____

6. I said, "Do you know the man who's in charge of that?" _____

7. "I have an arrangement with her", she said to me. _____

8. Did she say, "The persecution of my case is unfair because I have been wrongly accused". _____

9. He was accused of aiding and abetting the crime and was denied bail. _____

10. You said, "whose company did I negotiate with?" _____

An Adaptation from a Criminal Law Case

Facts:

Acting on an anonymous telephone tip that a "Joe Smith" was in possession of a large amount of crack that he had brought back to his home, detectives came to Smith's home. Before entering, they verified with Smith's girlfriend, who was leaving the house, that Smith lived there. The investigators confronted Smith and advised they had an anonymous tip and wanted to search the house. When Smith retreated down the hallway, one of the detectives pulled a gun and pointed it at him and said, "If you go down the hallway, it will be an officer safety issue," and then he put the gun away. When the officers asked again if they could search the place, Smith said, "Go ahead and search." They then entered and conducted a warrantless search. Crack cocaine was found at Smith's home during the search. While Smith consented, he claims that, since he was illegally detained in the entry to the house, that the consent was not voluntary. Joe Smith was convicted of possession with intent to distribute crack cocaine.

Procedural History:

Smith moved to suppress the drug evidence, arguing that his consent was involuntary. The District Court denied the motion. Smith appealed. The case was remanded for further factual findings. The court concluded that the detectives did not have reasonable suspicion to justify detaining Smith.

Issue:

Did the detectives have reasonable suspicion to detain Smith? Could the conviction stand if the cocaine evidence were suppressed?

Rationale:

Consent during an illegal detention is presumed invalid. Therefore, any evidence from a subsequent search is inadmissible unless there is some intervening act or long passage of time that may have changed the consent to an act of free will. If police approach a person in a confined space, the person does not feel free to decline the officers' request. Smith was seized in a confined space when the detective drew a gun. He had no voluntary choice. The anonymous tip did not lead to enough of a suspicion or reasonable suspicion to conclude that a crime was going to be committed and permit a warrantless search and seizure.

Ruling:

Smith's conviction was reversed.

Directions for CD-ROM Transcription Exercises

In audio format are:

1. Terms for the unit with pronunciations from the thesaurus/dictionary feature.

2. Self-Test that appears in the book at mid-unit.°

3. Case that appears at the unit end.°

°speeds are 80 wpm/120 wpm for differing skill levels

CD-ROM icons appear where the three above are located within each unit.

Readers may practice transcription by listening to the CD-ROM where prompted by the icons in the book. However, for high success in testing your transcription skills, mastering all the terms and English skills in the unit is recommended before attempting the CD-ROM.

For Keyboard Transcriptionists: Listen to the CD-ROM audio file for this unit at 80 wpm or 120 wpm and transcribe from the dictation on your computer. Edit and proofread your work against the printed copy in the book.

For Reporting Writers: Listen to the CD-ROM audio file at 80 wpm or 120 wpm and take down the dictation on your writer. Either transcribe from your notes and proofread your work or edit and proofread your CAT (computer-aided transcription) transcript. Always check your work against the printed copy in the book.

Student CD-ROM
For additional materials,
please go to the CD in this book.

Online Companion™
For additional resources, please go to
http://www.paralegal.delmar.cengage.com

The **Mistakes** That Court Reporters Make and *How to Avoid* Them

The Mistake:

Janet Walker stopped by XYZ Deposition Agency that she worked with to drop off some exhibits. While she was there, the office staff asked her to cover a job for the next day. Janet agreed. The next morning, she got a "better" offer and called XYZ and backed out of the job, leaving XYZ without a reporter to cover the job. Through a fortuitous set of circumstances, XYZ found out that Janet had taken the other job. They were reluctant to call her for jobs in the future.

How to Avoid It:

In the freelance world of reporting, it is going to happen that "better" jobs come along. Once your word is given, it is important to honor the commitment. It will all even out over the months and years of your career.

Introduction

Statistics show 50 percent of all marriages will end in divorce. Couples today enter marriage with less certainty than ever. In order to protect themselves, some couples are drafting prenuptial agreements setting forth the consequences of a possible divorce.

Most states follow principles of community property or equitable distribution in dividing property during a divorce. Issues of custody and support of the children may be addressed before, during, and after divorce proceedings, as in the case at the end of the unit.

Whether or not a man is the true father of a child is an issue that is raised in a paternity proceeding where blood or genetic tests are key evidence.

Sometimes problems arise in the care and raising of children. In some states, parents might find themselves in family court responding to civil charges of failure to properly supervise or support their children. However, charges of abuse, battering, or neglect in a family are usually criminal matters.

Unit Objectives

- ▩ Work with a legal dictionary/thesaurus.
- ▩ Learn about family law.
- ▩ Master the similarities and differences in definitions of key terms regarding family law.
- ▩ Master the pronunciations and spellings of legal terms in this unit.
- ▩ Recognize the synonyms used for legal terminology in this unit.
- ▩ Practice usage of terms, definitions, and synonyms for family law.
- ▩ Complete unit exercises in the forms of missing words, matching, multiple choice, true/false, synonyms, self-test, defining words, and also:
  - • Punctuation/capitalization
  - • Word pairs
  - • Transcription of terms, self-test, and case
  - • Proofreading

⊙ **Dictionary/Thesaurus**

Note: All Dictionary/Thesaurus terms appear on the CD-ROM with audio pronunciations.

Term
[phonetic pronunciation]

---

adoption
[a.*dop*.shen]

1. Approving; taking as one's own; ratifying. 2. The act of creating the relationship of parent and child between persons who do not naturally share that relationship.
• *n.* acceptance, embracement, approval, assumption ("their adoption of a hostile stance"); fostering, fosterage, raising ("adoption of the homeless child")

---

adultery
[a.*dul*.ter.ee]

Sexual intercourse by a married person with a person who is not his or her spouse.
• *n.* infidelity, affair, unfaithfulness, cuckoldry

---

affiliation proceeding
[a.*fil*.ee.ay.shun pro.*see*.ding]

A judicial proceeding to establish the paternity of an illegitimate child and to compel the father to contribute to its support. *See also* paternity suit.

---

alimony
[*al*.i.moh.nee]

Ongoing support payments by a divorced spouse, usually payments made for maintenance of the former spouse. Alimony is not child support. *See also* palimony.
• *n.* support, maintenance, sustenance, allowance, settlement

---

annulment of marriage
[a.*nul*.ment ov *mar*.ej]

The act of a court in voiding a marriage for causes existing at the time the marriage was entered into (EXAMPLE: the existing marriage of one of the parties). Annulment differs from divorce in that it is not a dissolution of the marriage but a declaration that no marriage ever existed.

---

antenuptial
[an.te.*nup*.shel]

Before marriage.
• *adj.* prenuptial, premarital

---

antenuptial agreement
[an.te.*nup*.shel a.*gree*.ment]

See prenuptial agreement.

---

arrears
[a.reerz]

Payments past due. Thus, for EXAMPLE, a person may be in arrears in alimony payments or in arrears on a mortgage.
• *n.* unpaid debts, obligations, delinquency, overdue payments ("arrears in alimony")

---

bigamy
[*big*.e.mee]

The crime of marrying while already married to another.

ceremonial marriage
[sehr.e.*mone*.ee.el *mehr*.ej]

A marriage performed by an appropriate religious or civil official, after the parties have met all legal requirements (EXAMPLE: securing a marriage license). *See also* solemnization of marriage. *Compare* common law marriage.

child
[child]

1. A very young person. 2. Offspring; progeny; descendent. "Child" is not a technical legal term with a definite meaning. Its meaning is always subject to construction in the context in which it is used.
• *n.* kid, adolescent, minor, youth, juvenile, youngster

child abuse
[child a.*byooss*]

The physical, sexual, verbal, or emotional abuse of a young person. Child abuse includes the neglect of a child. It is a crime in every state. *See also* child abuse reporting acts.

child abuse reporting acts
[child a.*byooss* re.port.ing aktz]

State statutes that make specified persons (EXAMPLES: physicians, teachers) responsible for reporting suspected child abuse.

child stealing
[child *steel*.ing]

The taking or removal of a child from a parent or from a person awarded custody. This is also the crime committed when a child is abducted from the custody of one parent by the other, although it is commonly called parental kidnapping.

child support
[child se.*port*]

1. Money paid, pending divorce and after divorce, by one parent to the other for the support of their children. *See also* support.
2. The obligation of parents to provide their children with the necessities of life.

civil union
[*sih*.vil *yoon*.yen]

An alternative to full marriage for gay couples. The state confers the rights of inheritance, joint ownership of property, health benefits, and other civil rights to same-sex couples.

cohabitation
[ko.ha.bi.*tay*.shen]

1. Living together as man and wife, although not married to each other.
2. Living together. 3. Having sexual intercourse.
• *n.* living together, common law marriage, alliance, union, residing together
• *ant.* separation

common law marriage
[*kom*.en law *mar*.ej]

A marriage entered into without ceremony, the parties agreeing between themselves to be husband and wife, followed by a period of cohabitation where the parties hold themselves out as actually married. Common law marriages are valid in some states but invalid in most. *Compare* ceremonial marriage.

community property
[ke.*myu*.ni.tee *prop*.er.tee]

A system of law under which the earnings of either spouse are the property of both the husband and the wife, and property acquired by either spouse during the marriage (other than by gift, under a will, or through inheritance) is the property of both. States that have adopted this system are called community property states. *Compare* equitable distribution.

condonation
[kon.do.*nay*.shen]

1. The forgiveness by one spouse of the other's conduct that constitutes grounds for divorce. Condonation is a defense to a divorce action based upon the conduct that has been condoned. 2. The act of overlooking or pardoning.
• *n.* forgiveness, pardon, overlooking, clemency, discharge, acquittal

connivance
[ke.nie.vense]

1. A secret cooperation in an illegal act. 2. As a defense in an action for divorce, fraudulent consent by one spouse to the other spouse's engaging in conduct that constitutes grounds for divorce. *Compare* no-fault divorce.
• *n.* secret, conspiracy, concert, collusion, consent, overlooking, condoning, contrivance

consortium
[kon.*sore*.shum]

The rights and duties of both husband and wife, resulting from marriage. They include companionship, love, affection, assistance, comfort, cooperation, and sexual relations. *See also* loss of consortium.

cruelty
[*kroo*.el.tee]

The infliction of physical or mental pain or distress. As a ground for divorce, "cruelty" means physical violence or threats of physical violence, or mental distress willfully caused.
• *n.* brutality, harshness, spitefulness, viciousness, torture, violence
• *ant.* sympathy, kindness

curtesy
[*ker*.te.see]

The rights a husband had under the common law with respect to his wife's property. Today these rights have been modified in every state in various ways, but all states that retain curtesy in some form extend the same rights to both spouses. *Note* that "curtesy" is not "courtesy."

custody
[*kuss*.te.dee]

As applied to persons, physical contact. (EXAMPLES: parents customarily "have physical custody" of their children; although, in the event of divorce, one parent may have sole custody, or both parents have joint custody or divided custody.) Custody carries with it the obligation on the part of the custodian to maintain and care for the person in his charge for the duration of their relationship.
• *n.* care, control, protection, possession, management, preservation, restraint

decree
[de.*kree*]

n. The final order of a court. For all practical purposes, the distinction between decrees and judgments no longer exists, and all relief in all civil actions, whether legal or equitable, is obtained by means of judgment.
v. To order, to dictate, to ordain, to enact, to command.
• *n.* mandate, commandment, directive, ordinance, statute, decision, ruling

desertion
[de.*zer*.shen]

1. As a ground for divorce, a voluntary separation of one of the parties to a marriage from the other without the consent of or without having been wronged by the second party, with the intention to live apart and without any intention to return to the cohabitation. 2. The criminal abandonment of a child in neglect of the parental duty of support.

dissolution of marriage
[dis.e.*loo*.shen ov *mar*.ej]

1. The termination of a marriage, whether by annulment, divorce a vinculo matrimonii, or no-fault divorce. 2. A term for divorce in some no-fault states.

divided custody
[di.vy.ded kuss.te.dee]

An arrangement under which the child of divorced parents lives a portion of the time with one parent and a portion of the time with the other. Legal custody, however, remains at all times with one of the parents. *Compare* joint custody. *See also* custody.

divorce
[di.*vorss*]

A dissolution of the marital relationship between husband and wife. *Compare* alimony. *See also* no-fault divorce.
• *n.* separation, division, break, break-up, parting, rupture, disunion
• *v.* rescind, dismiss, annul, cease, dissolve

divorce a vinculo matrimonii
[di.*vorss* ah *vin*.kyoo.loh mat.ri.*moh*.ni.eye]

A decree that dissolves the marriage because of matrimonial misconduct. Also called absolute divorce. *Compare* no-fault divorce.

divorce from bed and board
[di.*vorss* from bed and bord]

A decree that terminates the right of cohabitation, and adjudicates matters such as custody and support, but does not dissolve the marriage itself. *Compare* divorce a vinculo matrimonii; no-fault divorce.

domestic relations
[de.*mes*.tick re.*lay*.shenz]

The field of law relating to domestic matters, such as marriage, divorce, support, custody, and adoption; family law.

equitable adoption
[*ek*.wi.tebl e.*dop*.shen]

The principle that a child may enforce in equity a promise to adopt him, at least to the extent that he will be given rights of inheritance with respect to the property of the person who made the promise.

equitable distribution
[*ek*.wi.tebl dis.tri.*byoo*.shen]

Some jurisdictions permit their courts, in a divorce case, to distribute all property obtained during the marriage on an "equitable" basis. In deciding what is equitable, the court takes into consideration factors such as the length of the marriage and the contributions of each party, including homemaking. *Compare* community property.

family
[*fam*.i.lee]

A word of great flexibility, the meaning of which varies according to the context in which it appears. In its most common usage, it means the persons who live under one roof and under one head or management. A family is not necessarily limited to a father and mother (or a father or mother) and children.
In another of its common uses "family" refers to persons who are of the same bloodline, or are descended from a common ancestor.
• *n.* classification, progeny, descendants, paternity, genealogy, brood, household, family unit, issue

family court
[*fam*.i.lee kort]

A court whose jurisdiction varies from state to state. It may hear domestic relations cases; it may hear juvenile court matters; it may also try child abuse cases and oversee paternity suits.

family law
[*fam*.i.lee law]

Area of the law concerned with domestic relations.

foreign divorce
[forr.en di.*vorss*]

A divorce granted in a state or country other than the couple's state of residence.

foster child
[foss.ter child]

A child brought up by a person who is not her biological parent. *Compare* adoption.

foster parent
[foss.ter pair.ent]

A person who rears a foster child.

gay marriage
[gay *mehr*.ej]

The relationship of two men or women united as spouses, legalized in Massachusetts and California and recognized in New York if legal where the marriage is performed, including foreign jurisdictions like neighboring Canada. *See also* civil union.

guardian ad litem
[gar.dee.en ad *ly*.tem]

A person appointed by the court to represent and protect the interests of a minor or an incompetent person during litigation.
• *n.* attorney ad litem

HLA testing
[HLA *test*.ing]

Abbreviation of human leukocyte antigen testing. An HLA blood test is a paternity test.

incompatibility
[in.kum.pat.e.*bil*.e.tee]

Conflict in personality and temperament. As a requirement for no-fault divorce, a conflict so deep it cannot be altered or adjusted, rendering it impossible for the parties to continue to live together in a normal marital relationship.

irreconcilable differences
[ir.rek.en.*sy*.lebl *dif*.ren.sez]

A requirement for divorce or dissolution of marriage in some states with no-fault divorce laws. The term itself means that because of dissension and personality conflicts, the marriage relationship has been destroyed and there is no reasonable expectation of reconciliation. *See also* irremedial breakdown of marriage.

irremedial breakdown of marriage
[ir.re.*mee*.dee.el *brake*.down of *mehr*.ej]

A requirement for no-fault divorce in some states. *See also* irreconcilable differences.
• *n.* irretrievable breakdown of marriage

joint custody
[joynt *kuss*.te.dee]

An arrangement whereby both parties to a divorce retain legal custody of their child and jointly participate in reaching major decisions concerning the child's welfare.

juvenile
[*joo*.ve.nile]

adj. Young, youthful, immature.
• *n.* infant, youth, youngster, minor, teenager, stripling, kid, ward, teen
• *adj.* childish, inexperienced, puerile, sophomore, irresponsible, infantile, unwise, adolescent
• *ant.* adult

juvenile court
[*joo*.ve.nile kort]

A court having special jurisdiction over juvenile offenders, as well as abused and neglected children.

juvenile offender
[*joo*.ve.nile o.*fen*.der]

A minor who breaks the law. A juvenile offender is sometimes referred to as a delinquent child or a youthful offender.

legitimacy
[le.*jit*.i.mes.ee]

The state of having been born to parents who are married to each other.

loss of consortium
[los ov kun.*sore*.shem]

The loss of a spouse's assistance or companionship, or the loss of a spouse's ability or willingness to have sexual relations. If such loss results from a tort, it gives rise to a cause of action in favor of the partner of the spouse injured by the tort. *See also* consortium.

maintenance
[*main*.ten.ense]

The support of a person.
• *n.* upkeep, conservation, preservation, care, repair, protection, help, aid, finances, alimony, subsistence, livelihood ("maintenance for her health")

marital agreement
[mehr.i.tel a.*gree*.ment]

An agreement between two people who are married to each other (a postnuptial agreement), or two people who are about to marry (a prenuptial agreement), with respect to the disposition of the marital property or property owned by either spouse before the marriage, with respect to the rights of either in the property of the other, or with respect to support.

marriage
[*mehr*.ej]

1. The relationship of a man and a woman legally united as husband and wife. Marriage is a contract binding the parties until one dies or until a divorce or annulment occurs. 2. The act of becoming married; the marriage ceremony. *See also* common law marriage, gay marriage, and civil union.
• *n.* matrimony, wedlock, nuptial state, nuptials, sacrament, espousal ("to be joined in marriage")
• *ant.* divorce

marriage certificate
[*mehr*.ej ser.*tif*.i.ket]

A certificate that evidences a marriage, prepared by the person officiating at the ceremony and usually required by state law. *Compare* marriage license.

marriage license
[mehr.ej *ly*.sense]

Authorization to marry issued by the state in which the ceremony is to occur. It is a condition precedent to a ceremonial marriage. *Compare* marriage certificate.

merger in judgment
[mer.jer in *juj*.ment]

The extinguishment of a cause of action by entry of a judgment. EXAMPLE: The obligation to pay money under a separation agreement is superseded by a judgment for alimony.

no-fault divorce
[no-fawlt di.*vorss*]

A term for the requirements for divorce in jurisdictions in which the party seeking the divorce need not demonstrate that the other party is at fault. The requirements differ from state to state. EXAMPLES include irreconcilable differences, irremedial breakdown of marriage, and irretrievable breakdown of marriage.

palimony
[pal.i.moh.nee]

Alimony paid upon the break-up of a live-in relationship between two people who were not married to each other. In some states, such payment may be ordered by a court if the parties entered into an express contract or if the court finds the existence of an implied contract. In others, court-ordered palimony is based upon quantum meruit. In still others, palimony is considered to be contrary to public policy and is not recognized by the law.

partition
[par.tish.en]

A division made between two or more persons of land or other property belonging to them as co-owners, usually pursuant to a divorce action.

paternity
[pa.*ter*.ni.tee]

The status of being a father.
• *n.* fatherhood, derivation, ancestry, lineage, descent

paternity suit
[pa.*ter*.ni.tee sute]

A proceeding to establish the paternity of a child born out of wedlock, usually for the purpose of compelling the father to support the child. *See also* affiliation proceeding.

prenuptial agreement
[pree.*nup*.shel a.*gree*.ment]

An agreement between a man and a woman who are about to be married, governing the financial and property arrangements between them in the event of divorce, death, or even during the marriage. Prenuptial agreements are also called antenuptial agreements, antenuptial settlements, or premarital agreements. *See also* marital agreement.

reconciliation
[rek.en.sil.ee.*ay*.shen]

The act of resolving differences. In domestic relations law, a resumption of cohabitation by spouses who have been living apart.
• *n.* restoration, conciliation, rapprochement, concordance, rapport

recrimination
[re.krim.i.*nay*.shen]

A defense in an action for divorce based upon the misconduct by the plaintiff that would itself be grounds for divorce if the defendant had brought an action against the plaintiff.
• *n.* countercharge, retort, rejoinder, counterattack, reprisal, blame, retribution

same-sex marriage
[same-sex *mehr*.ej]

See gay marriage and civil union.

separation
[sep.e.*ray*.shen]

1. The status of a husband and wife who live separately. The state of being apart or coming apart.
• *n.* detachment, embarkation, disrelation, disassociation, partition, parting, sorting, rupture, uncompiling, disunion, alienation, cleavage

separation agreement
[sep.e.*ray*.shen a.*gree*.ment]

An agreement between husband and wife who are about to divorce or to enter into a legal separation, settling property rights and other matters (EXAMPLES: custody, child support, visitation, alimony) between them. Separation agreements are subject to court approval. *See also* marital agreement.

solemnization of marriage
[saw.lem.neh.*zay*.shen ov *mehr*.ej]

The performance of the marriage ceremony.

solemnize
[*saw*.lem.nize]

The performance of a formal ceremony; to act with formality.
See also solemnization of marriage.

spouse
[spouse]

A husband or wife, a marriage partner.
• *n.* wife, husband, mate, companion, partner

step-parent
[step-pair.ent]

A wife, in her relationship to her spouse's child by a former marriage;
a husband, in his relationship to his spouse's child by a former marriage.

support
[sup.ort]

To provide funds or other means of maintenance of a person.

surrogate
[*ser*.e.get]

A person who acts for another.
• *n.* alternate, substitute, agent, vicarious, actor, delegate, recourse, proxy,
stand-in ("surrogate mother")

surrogate motherhood
[*ser*.e.get *muth*.er.hood]

The status of a woman who "hosts" the fertilized egg of another woman in
her womb or who is artificially inseminated with the sperm of a man who is
married to someone else and to whom (with his wife) she has agreed to
assign her parental rights if the child is delivered.

tenancy by the entirety
[ten.en.see by the en.*ty*.re.tee]

A form of joint tenancy in an estate in land or in personal property that
exists between husband and wife by virtue of the fact that they are husband
and wife. As with a conventional joint tenancy, a tenancy by the entirety is
a tenancy with right of survivorship. "Tenancy," in this context, means
ownership of the jointly held estate or interest, whether, for EXAMPLE,
it is a fee simple estate, a life estate, a savings account, or the like.

visitation
[viz.i.*tay*.shen]

Short for visitation rights, i.e., the right of a divorced parent who does not
have custody of his child to visit the child at such times and places as the
court may order.

void marriage
[voyd *mehr*.ej]

A marriage absolutely prohibited by law. EXAMPLE: Marriage with
a person who is not of age.

wedlock
[*wed*.lok]

The state of being married; marriage.
• *n.* marriage, matrimony, connubiality, union

Missing Words

Fill in the blanks below.

1. The relationship of a man and woman legally united as husband and wife is called _____.

2. When a spouse loses assistance, companionship, or sexual relations of the other spouse this is called _____.

3. The status of a husband and wife who live separately is called _____.

4. A minor who breaks the law is known as a(n)_____.

5. The performance of the marriage ceremony is the _____ of marriage.

6. _____ is when people live together as man and wife although not married to each other.

7. The crime of marrying while already married to another is _____.

8. The support of a person is called _____.

9. The infliction of physical or mental pain is _____.

10. _____ is the ongoing court-ordered support payments by a divorced spouse.

11. _____ is an arrangement where both parties to a divorce action retain legal custody of their child and jointly participate in major decisions concerning the child's welfare.

12. _____ is an agreement between husband and wife who are about to divorce or enter into a legal separation, settling property rights and other matters.

13. _____ are any past due payments such as alimony or child support.

14. The _____ test is a blood test used to test for paternity.

15. A conflict in personality so deep that it cannot be altered, where it is impossible for the parties to continue to live together is _____.

16. _____ is the dissolution of the marital relationship between husband and wife.

17. A husband or wife is called a(n) _____.

Matching

Match the letter of the definition to the term below.

_____ 18. Alimony

_____ 19. Condonation

_____ 20. Support

_____ 21. Separation agreement

_____ 22. Bigamy

_____ 23. Consortium

_____ 24. Step-parent

_____ 25. Equitable adoption

_____ 26. Recrimination

_____ 27. Surrogate motherhood

_____ 28. Curtesy

_____ 29. Husband

A. Principle in equity that a child can enforce a promise to adopt him, at least to the extent that he will be given rights of inheritance

B. Court-ordered support payments by a divorced spouse to his or her former spouse

C. The crime of marrying while married

D. The rights a husband has under common law with respect to his wife's property

E. Rights and duties of both husband and wife resulting from marriage

F. A defense in an action for divorce based upon misconduct by the plaintiff that itself would be grounds for divorce if the defendant had brought an action against the plaintiff

G. To provide funds or other means of maintenance of a person

H. Status of a woman who "hosts" the fertilized egg of another woman in her womb, or who is artificially inseminated

I. A wife, in her relationship to her spouse's child by a former marriage; or a husband in his relationship to his spouse's child by a former marriage

J. Forgiveness by one spouse of the other's conduct that constitutes grounds for divorce

K. An agreement between husband and wife who are about to divorce or to enter into a legal separation, settling property rights and other matters

L. Infliction of physical or mental pain or distress

_____ 30. Cruelty   **M.** Spouse

_____ 31. Civil union   **N.** Alternative "marriage" for same-sex couples

_____ 32. Legitimacy   **O.** The state of one born to a married couple

Multiple Choice

Select the best choice.

_____ 33. A court whose jurisdiction varies from state to state. It may hear domestic relations cases, juvenile court matters, child abuse cases, or even paternity suits:
- **a.** U.S. Supreme Court
- **b.** Small Claims Court
- **c.** U.S. District Court
- **d.** Family Court

_____ 34. Ongoing court-ordered support payments by a divorced spouse, usually made by an ex-husband to his former wife:
- **a.** alimony
- **b.** child support
- **c.** palimony
- **d.** curtesy

_____ 35. A judicial proceeding to establish the paternity of an illegitimate child to compel the father to contribute to its support:
- **a.** equitable distribution
- **b.** cohabitation agreement
- **c.** affiliation proceeding
- **d.** partition

_____ 36. Physical, sexual, verbal, or emotional abuse of a young person is called:
- **a.** child abuse
- **b.** condonation
- **c.** connivance
- **d.** collusion

_____ 37. The act of a court in voiding a marriage for causes existing at the time the marriage was entered into:
- **a.** divorce
- **b.** annulment
- **c.** separation
- **d.** modification

_____ 38. A person who acts for another:
- **a.** consortium
- **b.** connivance
- **c.** wedlock
- **d.** surrogate

_____ 39. Sexual intercourse by a married person with a person not his or her spouse is:
- **a.** marriage by estoppel
- **b.** bigamy
- **c.** incest
- **d.** adultery

_____ 40. The right of a divorced parent who does not have custody of his child to visit the child at such times and places as the court may order:
- **a.** merger
- **b.** equitable distribution
- **c.** emancipation
- **d.** visitation rights

_____ 41. A person appointed by the court to represent and protect the interests of a minor or an incompetent person during litigation:
- **a.** guardian ad litem
- **b.** guardian
- **c.** foster parent
- **d.** step-parent

_____ 42. The act of creating the relationship of parent and child between persons who do not naturally share that relationship:
- **a.** custody
- **b.** paternity
- **c.** adoption
- **d.** maintenance

_____ 43. A conflict so deep it cannot be altered or adjusted, rendering it impossible for the parties to continue to live together in a normal mutual relationship:
- a. collusion
- b. incompatibility
- c. recrimination
- d. cohabitation

_____ 44. First legalized in the United States by Massachusetts, same-sex couples wed by:
- a. gay marriage
- b. civil union
- c. legitimacy
- d. partnership act

True/False

Mark the following T or F.

_____ 45. The field of law relating to domestic matters, such as marriage, divorce, support, custody, and adoption, is known as domestic relations.

_____ 46. When property acquired during the marriage is distributed without regard to whose name the property is in, this is known as community property.

_____ 47. Money paid by one parent to the other for the support of children is known as alimony.

_____ 48. When a party seeking a divorce need not demonstrate that the other party is at fault, this is known as a no-fault divorce.

_____ 49. A marriage entered into without a ceremony where the parties agree between themselves to be husband and wife, which is followed by cohabitation, is called common law marriage.

_____ 50. The right of a divorced parent who does not have custody of his child to visit the child is known as arrears.

_____ 51. Generally a husband and wife take property as tenants by the entirety.

_____ 52. Palimony is alimony that is paid upon the break-up of a live-in relationship between two people who were not married.

_____ 53. Adopting a child is the same thing as being a foster parent.

_____ 54. Annulment of a marriage is when a court declares that a marriage is void, and that it never existed.

_____ 55. Solemnization of marriage is the performance of the marriage ceremony.

Synonyms

Select the correct synonym in parentheses for each numbered item.

---

56. MERGER
(modification, consolidation, dower)

57. DECREE
(order, paternity, necessaries)

58. ARREARS
(separate property, laches, unpaid debts)

59. CUSTODY
(visitation, public policy, control)

60. AFFILIATION PROCEEDING
(paternity suit, alienation of affections, solemnization of marriage)

61. CONDONATION
(heart balm, recrimination, forgiveness)

62. ADULTERY
(bigamy, infidelity, marital rape)

63. JOINT CUSTODY
(consortium, shared custody, curtesy)

64. COMMUNITY PROPERTY
(shared, divided, sold)

65. DISSOLUTION OF MARRIAGE
(divorce, consensual union, interspousal immunity)

66. DOMESTIC RELATIONS
(corporations, agency, family law)

67. ANTENUPTIAL AGREEMENT
(prenuptial agreement, separation agreement, legal separation)

68. PATERNITY
(mother, sister, father)

69. MAINTENANCE
(addition, support, subtraction)

70. WEDLOCK
(marriage, divorce, separation)

71. SEPARATION
(divorced, together, apart)

72. JUVENILE OFFENDER
(juvenile delinquent, juvenile player, juvenile tackler)

73. DESERTION
(forced separation, voluntary separation, support)

74. LEGITIMACY
(child of married couple, dower, bigamy, paternity)

Self-Test

Place the number of the correct term in the appropriate space.

75. Divorce

76. Cohabitation

77. Family

78. Solemnization

79. Common law marriage

80. Marriage

81. No-fault

82. Separation

83. Prenuptial agreement

84. Irreconcilable differences

85. Recrimination

86. Separation agreement

87. Connivance

88. Annulment

89. Custody

90. Family law

A(n) _____ is commonly referred to mean the persons who live under one roof and under one head or management. A family is not necessarily limited to a father and mother and their children. Generally, a family starts with the _____ of a marriage. In some states, a marriage can be entered into without ceremony, with the parties agreeing between themselves to be husband and wife, followed by a period of _____. This is known as a(n) _____. With dissolution of the marriage arrangement, commonly referred to as divorce, becoming more prevalent in society, some couples will choose to execute a(n) _____ before marriage, regarding financial and property arrangements.

In the event a couple finds an irremedial breakdown of the marriage to exist, _____ become a requirement for _____ in some states, with _____ divorce laws. The parties might choose to try a(n) _____, and live apart for a while before making a final decision.

Should the parties decide that a divorce is necessary, they will have to make many decisions. A(n) _____ can be used to settle property rights and other matters, such as _____ of the children. There are certain defenses that can be raised in opposing a divorce action, such as _____, a spouse's consent to the other spouse's activities that constituted grounds for a divorce, or _____, the misconduct by the plaintiff.

Occasionally, the court will agree to void a marriage for causes that existed at the time the marriage was entered into. This is called a(n) _____. This is different from divorce, in that it is not a dissolution of the _____, but a declaration that none ever existed. _____ is the area of law concerned with these domestic relations issues.

Defining Words

Complete the definition.

_____

91. Family _____

_____

92. Annulment _____

_____

93. Void marriage _____

_____

94. Partition _____

_____

95. Prenuptial agreement _____

_____

96. Separation agreement _____

_____

97. Alimony _____

_____

98. Separation _____

_____

99. Spouse _____

_____

100. Child support _____

_____

101. Divorce _____

_____

102. Palimony _____

_____

103. Adoption _____

_____

104. Gay marriage _____

_____

Punctuation/Capitalization

Punctuation for appositives.

Definition: An appositive is a noun or pronoun that renames another noun or pronoun. Often the appositive immediately follows the word it renames.

I spoke with my husband, William, before I signed the contract.
My cousin Roz had traveled out of state to visit another cousin of mine.
We next marked Exhibit 3, a three-page letter.

Rule 1: When an appositive that comes right after the word it renames is needed to define the word it renames, it is called an essential appositive, and it does not take any punctuation. To distinguish this, try to decide whether the appositive can be removed from the sentence without any loss of communication. Look at this sentence.

My friend Susan lives in New Jersey.

We can assume that most people have more than one friend; thus we need the name *Susan* to define which friend. Without the name *Susan,* we do not know which friend. Therefore, the name *Susan* is essential to define the word *friend,* and there are no commas around it.

The dog Spot was found running free in the park.
The company Rayco was not involved in the negotiation.
The pilot Spenser received the training on the simulator that week.

Rule 2: When an appositive that comes right after the word it renames is not needed to define the word it renames, it is called a nonessential appositive, and it is surrounded by punctuation. Surrounding it by punctuation means it can be removed from the sentence without losing communication. When the appositive just adds extra information and, even without it, we already know whom or what the word it renames represents, the appositive is not needed in the sentence.

I spent a lot of time with my mother, Minnie, during that period.
Her only brother, James, represented the family in that matter.
She was driving with Marianne, her sister, when the accident occurred.

When the appositive does not immediately follow the word it renames, different rules apply, which we are not going to cover here.

Directions: Make necessary punctuation changes.

1. His wife Maria accompanied him to the court session.

2. He met with the CEO, Frank Oliver after he was hired.

3. She brought her classmate, Diana, with her.

4. I have eight brothers. My brother, Dan, is an attorney.

5. He was fired from his company, Verizon, just two weeks later.

Word Pairs

adapt/adept/adopt

adapt = modify to fit one's own needs, adjust. The noun form is *adaptation.*
He is going to adapt the floor plan to meet the needs of his office.
The play was adapted from a novel she wrote in her youth.
She was able to adapt to her surroundings.

adept = skillful. This form is an adjective and usually describes a person.
She was adept in handling the press corps.
It is the perception that he is not adept at public speaking.
She is an adept performer.

adopt = take as one's own, assume, agree to. The noun form is *adoption*.

The family has adopted three special-needs children.
We are going to adopt new ways to handle that.
The adoption of the new laws will make a difference.

born/borne

born = referring to the event of the birth. This form is one of the past participles of the verb *to bear*, meaning "to carry."

He was born on a Friday.
The twins will be born with specialists in attendance.
Where were you born?

borne = carried, endured. This form is one of the past participles of the verb *to bear*, meaning "to carry."

She has borne great difficulty since the death of her husband.
He has borne the full responsibility for the project.
It is an airborne disease.

courtesy/curtesy

courtesy = politeness, civility.

She extended several courtesies to us during our stay.
It is a matter of courtesy to be available to the newcomers.
His courtesy is very much appreciated.

curtesy = rights the husband had under the common law to his wife's property.

He tried to exercise his curtesy rights under the laws.
Curtesy has now been extended to both husband and wife.
The original curtesy laws were very unfair to women.

marital/marshal/martial

marital = pertaining to a marriage. This form is an adjective.

The marital discord was evident to everyone who was around them.
They reached agreement on the marital issues.
She did not see it as a marital problem.

marshal = garner, assemble, gather, law enforcement officer. The spelling with two *l*'s applies only to the proper name, as in "His name is Andres Marshall."

The marshal arrived at the door to serve the subpoena.
He intended to marshal his forces for the fight ahead.
She had marshaled her supporters before the meeting occurred.

martial = military, aggressive, warlike, hostile.

He was trained in martial arts.
Martial law was imposed after the riots.
His martial style of running things put people off.

partition/petition

partition = division made between two or more persons of land or other property belonging to them as co-owners.

There was an amicable partition of the property.
She fought the partition as it was decided by the court.
The partition was fair, but he didn't seem to think so.

petition = formally request, plead, lobby.

The petition was filed with the lower court.
She petitioned for admission into the university.
He claimed no knowledge of the petition filed on his behalf.

Directions: Choose the correct word.

1. The couple felt they had put that specific marital/marshal/martial problem behind them.

2. I sent him a copy simply as a courtesy/curtesy to him.

3. The partition/petition of the proceeds did not seem fair to the two of them.

4. His story was not born/borne out by the facts.

5. She did not seem particularly adapt/adept/adopt at that.

6. Marshal/Martial law was declared to keep order and peace.

7. Did they file the partition/petition for permission to use the facility?

8. Was he born/borne anywhere near the city where you lived?

9. We need to adapt/adopt a new plan as we do not have one in place.

10. The marital/marshal/martial came to the door before the sun came up.

11. It was identified as a waterborn/waterborne bacteria.

12. He tried to exercise his courtesy/curtesy rights under some ancient law.

13. She had a great deal of difficulty adapting/adopting to the new environment.

14. The partition/petition had more than 50,000 signatures.

15. She has born/borne most of the burden of rearing the children.

16. He was not really adapt/adept/adopt at resolving difficulties.

17. I need to marshal/martial the resources I have available.

18. I believe he was born/borne in a very small town.

19. He was not easily able to adapt/adept/adopt to a new situation.

20. She did not feel that the partition/petition was equitable.

Is It One Word or Two? An Apostrophe? A Hyphen?

altogether/all together

altogether = totally, completely, thoroughly, on the whole. This word is an adverb.

I was altogether too distraught to notice any details.
That remark was altogether uncalled for.
Altogether, it was a totally forgettable movie.

all together = everything or everybody in one place.
We were all together for Thanksgiving.
When they were all together, there were 22 of them.
I put them all together in one stack on the table.

Directions: Choose the correct word.

1. It was altogether/all together too soon for me to know.

2. They were altogether/all together in one stack on the table.

3. Will your family be altogether/all together at any time this week?

4. Is he altogether/all together too overly qualified for the job?

5. It is too soon, in her mind, for us to be altogether/all together.

Proofreading

Directions: Make necessary corrections, based on the material presented in the unit. If the sentence has no errors, write the word *correct* after the sentence.

1. Did you see his oldest sister Avanka who was borne just a year before he was? _____

2. The petition of the marital property was all together unfair to both parties. _____

3. Did she adapt the children before she was appointed to the post? _____

4. When marshal law was imposed, there was a 6:00 P.M. curfew. _____

5. The truth of what Meredith my sister said was born out in further testimony. _____

6. The plan would need to be adapted to fit with our company. _____

7. I intend to martial everything I have to get signatures on this partition. _____

8. My co-worker Jamison thought we would be altogether to make the decision. _____

9. They tried to get him to agree about how adopt she is with her hands. _____

10. I did not regard her as adept in human resource management. _____

An Adaptation from a Family Law Case

Facts:

The marriage of Nathan Robinson and Jeri Robinson was dissolved. There was one child, Richard, born of the marriage, and the parties agreed to a parenting plan sharing the child equally. Two years later, Jeri, the mother, remarried; was planning to move out of state to Illinois; and was petitioning the court to modify the parenting plan. Nathan sought the exact opposite situation, one in which he would have the child during the school year. The District Court ultimately agreed to a plan where the child would move and be with the mother except for spring break, summer break, and alternate holidays.

Procedural History:

Nathan appealed this decision.

Issue:

Must the District Court's finding be reversed because the court did not enter findings of fact and conclusions of law when entering their final decision?

Rationale:

The standard of review for custody modifications is to see whether those findings are "clearly erroneous." Findings are clearly erroneous if they are not supported by substantial evidence. The court will reverse a court's decision to modify custody or visitations only where an abuse of discretion is clearly demonstrated. The District Court is authorized to modify a parenting plan where a child's circumstances have clearly changed since the prior plan was entered and where the modification will best serve the interests of the child. Both parties agree the mother's move constitutes a change in circumstances. However, the amended parenting plan did not include any finding of the court upon which its conclusions rest.

Ruling:

Reversed and remanded for entry of findings of fact and conclusions of law.

Directions for CD-ROM Transcription Exercises

In audio format are:

1. Terms for the unit with pronunciations from the thesaurus/dictionary feature.

2. Self-Test that appears in the book at mid-unit.°

3. Case that appears at the unit end.°

°speeds are 80 wpm/120 wpm for differing skill levels

CD-ROM icons appear where the three above are located within each unit.

Readers may practice transcription by listening to the CD-ROM where prompted by the icons in the book. However, for high success in testing your transcription skills, mastering all the terms and English skills in the unit is recommended before attempting the CD-ROM.

For Keyboard Transcriptionists: Listen to the CD-ROM audio file for this unit at 80 wpm or 120 wpm and transcribe from the dictation on your computer. Edit and proofread your work against the printed copy in the book.

For Reporting Writers: Listen to the CD-ROM audio file at 80 wpm or 120 wpm and take down the dictation on your writer. Either transcribe from your notes and proofread your work or edit and proofread your CAT (computer-aided transcription) transcript. Always check your work against the printed copy in the book.

 Student CD-ROM
For additional materials,
please go to the CD in this book.

 Online Companion™
For additional resources, please go to
http://www.paralegal.delmar.cengage.com

Area of Law

Insurance

The **Mistakes** That Court Reporters Make and *How to Avoid* Them

The Mistake:

Allan McKnight was told there would be three attorneys to hook up to realtime for his afternoon deposition. When he arrived, the power cord for his machine would not reach as far as the electrical outlet. He asked the attorneys whether they had an extension cord and, of course, pointed out that it needed to be a surge protector extension cord. When he checked in his bag, he had only two cables to hook up the attorneys and again asked to "borrow" an extra cable. The attorneys did not have such a cable, making it impossible for one of the attorneys to be hooked up live for a realtime feed for the deposition. Needless to say, the attorneys were not pleased with Mr. McKnight.

How to Avoid It:

The reporter must always be prepared with more than enough cables for whatever he may need. Extension cords and cables are just a standard part of the equipment that every reporter must carry with him. Always have a full complement of what you might need.

Introduction

A couple buys a home with their life savings. Should the house catch on fire, it would take years to save enough money to buy another home. Insurance is a method of providing against known possible losses. A sum of money is paid to another who agrees to cover your loss in the event of a catastrophe or certain conditions occurring.

There are many different kinds of insurance: fire, automobile, theft, home, title, professional liability, flood, mortgage, and health insurance. The list is almost endless.

There are some professional models whose work depends on their beautiful hands or legs. The agencies for whom they work have obtained insurance covering their specific body parts in the event of injury or damage. A person with a fear of flying might obtain flight insurance prior to boarding a plane.

This unit explores the kinds of insurance and the ways insurance safeguards persons and property. In the case herein, the plaintiff appellant learns when an insurance policy doesn't safeguard anything.

Unit Objectives

- Work with a legal dictionary/thesaurus.
- Learn about the law of insurance.
- Master the similarities and differences in definitions of key terms regarding insurance.
- Master the pronunciations and spellings of legal terms in this unit.
- Recognize the synonyms used for terminology in this unit.
- Practice usage of terms, definitions, and synonyms for insurance.
- Complete unit exercises in the forms of missing words, matching, multiple choice, true/false, synonyms, self-test, defining words, and also:
  - Punctuation/capitalization
  - Word pairs
  - Transcription of terms, self-test, and case
  - Proofreading

 Dictionary/Thesaurus

Note: All Dictionary/Thesaurus terms appear on the CD-ROM with audio pronunciations.

Term
[phonetic pronunciation]

---

adjuster
[a.*just*.er]

A person who makes a determination of the value of a claim against an insurance company for the purpose of arriving at an amount for which the claim will be settled. An adjuster may be an agent for the insurance company or an independent adjuster.
• *n.* reconciler, arbitrator, intermediary, intervenor, mediator

annuity
[a.*nyoo*.i.tee]

1. A yearly payment of a fixed sum of money for life or for a stated number of years. 2. A right to receive fixed periodic payments (yearly or otherwise), either for life or for a stated period of time.
Most annuities are in the form of insurance policies. When payments are made until the death of the annuitant, the annuity is a life annuity. When payments will be terminated if the annuitant acts in a specified way (EXAMPLE: accepting full-time employment), the annuity is a term annuity. A contingent annuity is payable upon the occurrence of some stated event beyond the control of the annuitant (EXAMPLE: the death of the annuitant's father). A joint and survivorship annuity is paid to two annuitants and, after one of them dies, to the survivor. (EXAMPLE: Continued payment to a widow of an annuity that, prior to her husband's death, was paid to her and her husband jointly.) A retirement annuity is generally payable upon retirement from employment.
• *n.* payment, income, pension, subsidy, stipend, allotment

annuity policy
[a.*nyoo*.i.tee *pol*.i.see]

An insurance policy that provides for or pays an annuity.

bad faith
[bad fayth]

A devious or deceitful intent, motivated by self-interest, ill will, or a concealed purpose. The opposite of good faith. Bad faith is stronger than negligence, but may or may not involve fraud. EXAMPLE: An insurance company engages in bad faith when it refuses, with no basis for its action, to pay a claim.

beneficiary
[ben.e.*fish*.ee.air.ee]

A person who receives a benefit.

benefit
[*ben*.e.fit]

A payment made under an insurance policy, pension, annuity, or the like.
• *n.* aid, asset, exhibition ("a benefit for the homeless"); advantage, profit, gain, utility, return ("the benefit of success")
• *v.* help, build, aid, assist ("the concert benefited the children's home")

binder
[*bine*.der]

1. An interim memorandum, used when an insurance policy cannot be issued immediately, evidencing either that insurance coverage is effective at a specified time and continues until the policy issued, or that the risk is declined and giving notice of that fact. 2. An earnest money deposit that preserves a buyer's right to purchase real estate.
• *n.* deposit, pledge, stake, collateral, escrow, security ("a binder on the deal")

business interruption insurance
[biz.ness in.ter.*up*.shen in.*shoor*.ense]

Insurance protecting against loss from the interruption of business, as distinguished from coverage upon merchandise or other property used in the business. *See also* insurance.

cancellation
[kan.sel.*ay*.shen]

1. An erasure, blotting out, striking out, or crossing out of some portion of a written document or instrument. 2. The act of a party to a contract ending the contract after the other party has been guilty of breach of contract. Cancellation should be contrasted with termination, which provides the party ending the contract with fewer remedies.
• *n.* abandonment, reversal, recall, nullification, erasure, revocation, termination, withdrawal, rescission ("cancellation of the ethics committee meetings")

cancellation clause
[kan.sel.*ay*.shen kloz]

A provision in a contract that allows the parties to cancel the contract without obligation. Also known as an escape clause.
• *n.* escape clause

coinsurance
[*ko*.in.shoor.ense]

With respect to insurance, a division of the risk between the insurer and the insured. EXAMPLE: A health insurance policy under which the insurance company is obligated to pay 80 percent of every claim and the insured pays 20 percent.

collision insurance
[ke.*lizh*.en in.*shoor*.ense]

Automobile insurance that protects the owner or operator of a motor vehicle from loss due to damage done to his property by another.

comprehensive coverage
[kom.pre.*hen*.siv *kuv*.e.rej]

A package of coverage provided by a policy of comprehensive insurance that protects against a myriad of perils (collision, theft, etc.).

comprehensive insurance
[kom.pre.*hen*.siv in.*shoor*.ense]

Insurance that provides coverage for various risks (EXAMPLES: fire; theft; flood; wind; hail), each of which could also be covered under separate policies.

contribution between insurers
[kon.tra.byoo.shen be.*tween* in.*shoor*.erz]

The obligation of an insurance company that has issued a policy covering the same loss as that insured by another insurance company to contribute proportionally to the other insurer who has paid the entire loss.

deductible
[de.*duk*.tibl]

In insurance, portion of a loss that the insured must pay from his own pocket before the insurance company will begin to make payment. USAGE: "Because my policy has a $500 deductible, my insurance company will pay only $2,000 of the $2,500 damage to my car."

disability clause [dis.e.bil.i.tee kloz]	A clause in an insurance policy providing for a waiver of premiums in the event of the insured's disability.
disability insurance [dis.e.bil.i.tee in.*shoor*.ense]	Insurance that provides income in the event of disability.
double indemnity [dubl in.*dem*.ni.tee]	A benefit payable under an insurance policy at twice face value if loss occurs under certain conditions. EXAMPLE: Under a life insurance policy, the death of the insured by accidental, as opposed to natural, causes.
double insurance [dubl in.*shoor*.ense]	Coverage of the same risk and the same interest by different insurance companies. *See also* contribution between insurers.
exclusion [eks.*kloo*.zhen]	1. The action of a judge in ruling evidence to be inadmissible. 2. The amount of money a person can give away without paying a gift tax. 3. A provision in an insurance policy that removes a specified risk, person, or circumstance from coverage. 4. The act of keeping out or apart. • *n.* rejection, omission, dismissal, elimination, disallowance, nonacceptance, repudiation
fire insurance [fyer in.*shoor*.ense]	Insurance that indemnifies the insured against loss to property (EXAMPLES: a house, the contents of a house; a commercial building) due to fire.
group insurance [groop in.*shoor*.ense]	1. A contract providing life, accident, or health insurance for a group of employees. The terms of the contract are contained in a master policy; the individual employee's participation is demonstrated by a certificate of insurance that she holds. 2. A contract providing life, accident, or health insurance for any defined group of people. The contract is a master policy and is entered into between the group policyholder (for EXAMPLE, the American Automobile Association; the American Bar Association) and the insurance company for the benefit of the policyholder's members.
health insurance [helth in.*shoor*.ense]	Insurance that indemnifies the insured for medical expenses incurred as a result of sickness or accident.
homeowners policy [*home*.ohn.erz *pah*.li.see]	An insurance policy that insures homeowners against most common risks, including fire, burglary, and civil liability.
indemnification [in.dem.ni.fi.*kay*.shen]	1. The act of indemnifying or being indemnified. *See also* indemnify. 2. Payment made by way of compensation for a loss. *See also* indemnity insurance. • *n.* restitution, amends, compensation, insurance, payment, reparation
indemnify [in.*dem*.ni.fy]	1. To compensate or reimburse a person for loss or damage. 2. To promise to compensate or reimburse in the event of future loss or damage. *See also* indemnity insurance. • *v.* compensate, reimburse, secure, make amends, guarantee, restore, repay, redeem

indemnity insurance
[in.dem.ni.tee in.*shoor*.ense]

Insurance providing indemnification for actual loss or damage, as distinguished from liability insurance, which provides for payment of a specified sum upon the occurrence of a specific event regardless of what the actual loss or damage may be.

indemnity policy
[in.dem.ni.tee *paw*.li.see]

See indemnity insurance.

insurability
[in.shoor.e.*bil*.i.tee]

Having the qualities needed to be insurable: no preexisting health conditions, nonsmoker, under certain ages, etc.

insurable
[in.*shoor*.ebl]

Capable of being insured. EXAMPLE: As a condition of purchasing life insurance, being in sound health at the time the policy is issued.

insurable interest
[in.*shoor*.ebl in.trest]

An interest from whose existence the owner derives a benefit and whose nonexistence will cause her to suffer a loss. The presence of an insurable interest is essential to the validity and enforceability of an insurance policy because it removes it from the category of a gambling contract. An insurable interest in life insurance, for EXAMPLE, is: (a) one's interest in his own life; (b) one's natural interest in the continued life of a blood relative; (c) any reasonable expectation of financial benefit from the continued life of another (one's debtor, business partner, etc.).

insurance
[in.*shoor*.ense]

A contract (the policy) by which one party (the insurer), in return for a specified consideration (the premium) agrees to compensate or indemnify another (the insured) on account of loss, damage, or liability arising from an unknown or contingent event (the risk). There are almost as many kinds of coverage as there are risks. EXAMPLES of some of the most common types of insurance are accident insurance, automobile insurance, credit life insurance, disability insurance, fire insurance, flood insurance, health insurance, homeowners insurance, liability insurance, life insurance, major medical insurance, malpractice insurance, mortgage insurance, and title insurance.
The law does not permit a person to insure against the consequences of acts or transactions that violate public policy, for EXAMPLE, gambling losses. Most importantly, the law requires a person to have an insurable interest in whatever she wishes to insure.
• *n.* indemnification, assurance, coverage, policy, warranty, covenant, security, guarantee, indemnity against contingencies, safeguard

insurance adjuster
[in.*shoor*.ense a.*just*.er]

See adjuster.

insurance agent
[in.*shoor*.ense *ay*.jent]

A person authorized by an insurance company to represent it when dealing with third persons in matters relating to insurance. *Compare* insurance broker.

insurance binder
[in.*shoor*.ense *bine*.der]

See binder.

insurance broker
[in.*shoor*.ense *broh*.ker]

A person who acts as an intermediary between the insured and the insurer, who is not employed by any insurance company. The broker solicits insurance business from the public, and having obtained an order, either places the insurance with a company selected by the insured, or, if the insured does not select a carrier, then with a company of the broker's choice. Depending upon the circumstances, an insurance broker may represent either the insured, or the insurer, or both. *Compare* insurance agent.

insurance carrier
[in.*shoor*.ense *kehr*.ee.er]

A company engaged in the business of issuing insurance policies; an insurance company.

insurance company
[in.*shoor*.ense *kum*.pe.nee]

A company engaged in the business of issuing insurance policies.

insurance contract
[in.*shoor*.ense *kon*.trakt]

The formal name for an insurance policy.

insurance policy
[in.*shoor*.ense *pah*.li.see]

A contract to compensate or indemnify a person for loss arising from a contingent occurrence.

insurance premium
[in.*shoor*.ense *pree*.mee.um]

Money paid to an insurer for an insurance policy.

insure
[in.*shoor*]

1. To enter into a contract of insurance as an insurer; to issue an insurance policy. 2. To guarantee. 3. To make sure.
• *v.* obtain insurance, secure against loss, underwrite, guard, safeguard, shield, back, check, warrant, arrange, provide, assure, reassure

insured
[in.*shoord*]

A person protected by an insurance policy; a person whose property is protected by an insurance policy. One need not be the named insured (i.e., named in the policy) to be covered. A standard automobile insurance policy, for EXAMPLE, usually covers any person operating the insured vehicle with the permission of the named insured.

insurer
[in.*shoor*.er]

1. Generally, an insurance company, that is, the party who assumes the risk under an insurance policy and agrees to compensate or indemnify the insured. 2. One who guarantees something.
• *n.* indemnitor, indemnifier, guarantor, assurer, surety, underwriter

life insurance
[life in.*shoor*.ense]

A contract (the policy) in which the insurer, in exchange for the payment of a premium, agrees to pay a specified sum to a named beneficiary upon the death of the insured. *See also* straight life insurance; term life insurance; whole life insurance.

malpractice insurance
[mal.*prak*.tiss in.*shoor*.ense]

A type of liability insurance that protects professional persons (EXAMPLES: attorneys; physicians; psychotherapists) from liability for negligence and other forms of malpractice. It is also called professional liability insurance.

marine insurance
[ma.reen in.*shoor*.ense]

An insurance policy covering the risk of loss to a ship or its cargo from the perils of the sea.

material misrepresentation
[mah.teer.e.al mis.rep.re.zen.*tay*.shen]

A fraudulent or deliberately inaccurate statement that is intended to cause, or causes, a person to act in reliance. Also called a fraudulent misrepresentation.

no-fault insurance
[no-fawlt in.*shoor*.ense]

A type of automobile insurance required by law in many states, under which the insured is entitled to indemnification regardless of who was responsible for the injury or damage. Proof of negligence is not a condition of liability under such a policy. *See also* insurance.

personal liability
[per.sen.el ly.a.*bil*.i.tee]

Liability to satisfy a judgment, debt, or other obligation from one's personal assets.

preexisting condition clause
[pree.eg.*zis*.ting ken.*dish*.en kloz]

A provision in a health insurance policy that excludes from coverage, for a specified period of time, medical conditions that existed when the insured purchased the policy.

premium
[pree.mee.yum]

Money paid to an insurance company for coverage by an insurance policy.

proof of loss
[proof ov loss]

A written statement of the dollar amount of a loss sustained, submitted by an insured. Proof of loss is a standard requirement of casualty insurance policies.

reinsurance
[ree.in.*shoor*.ense]

A contract between two insurance companies under which the second company (the reinsurer) insures the first company (the insurer) against loss due to policyholders' claims.

reinsurer
[ree.in.*shoor*.er]

An insurance company's insurance company. *See also* reinsurance.

replacement value
[ree.plaiss.ment *val*.yoo]

In the context of an insurance loss, the cost of replacing insured property at its current value, as opposed to its original cost; that is, at what it costs now, not what it cost then.

rider
[*ry*.der]

1. A sheet or sheets of paper, written or printed, attached to a document, that refer to the document in a manner that leaves no doubt of the parties' intention to incorporate it into the document. Riders are most frequently used with insurance policies. 2. A new and often unrelated provision or measure added to a bill late in the legislative process, with the intention that it "ride" through.
• *n.* attachment, extension, insertion, supplement, addendum, codicil ("a rider to the bill")

self-insurance [self-in.*shoor*.ense]	Protecting one's property or business by establishing a fund out of which to pay for losses instead of purchasing insurance. Self-insurance is a means through which employers may provide workers' compensation and health coverage to their employees as an alternative to securing workers' compensation insurance and health insurance.
straight life insurance [strate life in.*shoor*.ense]	Life insurance in which the cash surrender value of the policy increases as the insured makes premium payments throughout her lifetime. Straight life insurance is also referred to as whole life insurance or ordinary life insurance. *Compare* term life insurance.
subrogation [sub.ro.*gay*.shen]	The substitution of one person for another with respect to a claim or right against a third person; the principle that when a person has been required to pay a debt that should have been paid by another person, she becomes entitled to all of the remedies that the creditor originally possessed with respect to the debtor. (EXAMPLE: After the insurance company that insures Lloyd's car indemnifies him for the damage done to his car by Mary's negligence, the insurance company has the same cause of action against Mary as Lloyd originally had.) Subrogation is sometimes referred to as substitution. • *n.* displacement, substitution, transfer, transference, exchange, switch, supplanting
term life insurance [term life in.*shoor*.ense]	Life insurance that provides protection only for a stated number of years and has no cash surrender value. *Compare* life insurance; straight life insurance; whole life insurance.
title insurance [ty.tel in.*shoor*.ense]	An insurance policy in which the insurer agrees to indemnify the purchaser of realty, or the mortgagee, against loss due to defective title.
umbrella policy [um.*brel*.a *pah*.li.see]	An insurance policy that provides coverage over and above the liability limitations of the insured's basic liability insurance policies.
waiver [*way*.ver]	The intentional relinquishment or renunciation of a right, claim, or privilege a person knows he has. • *n.* abandonment, abdication, forgoing, refusal, relinquishment, renunciation
whole life insurance [hole life in.*shoor*.ense]	Straight life insurance or ordinary life insurance, as opposed to term life insurance or group insurance.
workers' compensation insurance [*wer*.kerz kom.pen.*say*.shen in.*shoor*.ense]	State statutes provide for the payment by the employer of compensation to employees injured in their employment or, in case of death, to their dependents.

Missing Words

Fill in the blanks below.

1. A yearly payment of a fixed sum of money for life or a stated number of years is a(n) _____.

2. A payment made under an insurance policy, pension, or annuity is known as a(n) _____.

3. Money paid to an insurance company for an insurance policy is known as a(n) _____.

4. Insurance that indemnifies the insured for medical expenses incurred as a result of sickness or accident is _____.

5. An interim memorandum, used when an insurance policy cannot be issued immediately, is known as a(n) _____.

6. A division of the risk between the insurer and the insured is known as _____.

7. A(n) _____ is an insurance company's insurance company.

8. A person who makes a determination of the value of a claim against an insurance company for which the claim will be settled is _____.

9. _____ is the written statement of the dollar amount of a loss sustained that is submitted by the insured.

10. A contract by which one party, in return for a specified consideration, agrees to compensate or indemnify another on account of loss, damage, or liability arising from an unknown event is called _____.

11. A type of liability insurance that protects professional persons like attorneys and physicians is known as _____.

12. The _____ is a person protected by an insurance policy.

13. _____ provides benefits to an employee by an employer for injuries as a result of employment, regardless of whether or not the employer was negligent.

14. A person who receives a benefit is known as a(n) _____.

15. The portion of the loss the insured must pay out of pocket is the _____.

16. A provision in an insurance policy that removes a specified risk, person, or circumstance from coverage is _____.

17. The escape clause in an insurance contract is called the _____.

18. _____ is a benefit payable under an insurance policy at twice the face value.

Matching

Match the letter of the definition to the term below.

_____ 19. Business interruption insurance

_____ 20. Annuity

_____ 21. Whole life insurance

_____ 22. Homeowners insurance

_____ 23. Collision insurance

_____ 24. Workers' compensation

_____ 25. Comprehensive insurance

_____ 26. Malpractice insurance

_____ 27. No-fault insurance

_____ 28. Title insurance

_____ 29. Personal liability insurance

_____ 30. Straight life insurance

_____ 31. Term life insurance

A. Payment of compensation to employees who are injured on the job

B. Insurance that provides coverage for various risks that could be covered under separate policies

C. Protection against loss from interruption of a business

D. Policy that insures homeowners against most common risks

E. Insurance that protects owner or operator of a motor vehicle from loss due to damage done to his property by another

F. Insured is entitled to indemnification regardless of who is responsible for injury or damage

G. Yearly payment of a fixed sum of money

H. Straight life insurance

I. Protection against loss due to defective title of real property

J. Protects professional people from liability for negligence and other forms of malpractice

K. Whole life insurance

L. Provides income in event of disability

M. Liability to satisfy a judgment from one's personal assets

____ 32. Disability insurance

____ 33. Bad faith

____ 34. Beneficiary

____ 35. Coinsurance

N. Life insurance that provides protection for a stated number of years and has no cash surrender value

O. A person who receives a payment from a policy

P. A division of risk between the insurer and insured

Q. A devious or deceitful intent, motivated by self-interest

Multiple Choice

Select the best choice.

____ 36. An insurer's right to end an insurance contract when the insured breaches the terms of the contract is known as:
   a. exclusion
   b. endorsement
   c. cancellation
   d. waiver

____ 37. Insurance that indemnifies the insured against loss to property due to fire is known as:
   a. health insurance
   b. term life
   c. whole life
   d. fire insurance

____ 38. The portion of a loss that the insured must pay is known as a:
   a. deductible
   b. waiver
   c. benefit
   d. rider

____ 39. Self-insurance is where:
   a. a person purchases insurance from another
   b. you establish a fund out of which to pay your losses
   c. an employer purchases insurance for a group of employees
   d. none of the above

____ 40. A written statement of the dollar amount of a loss sustained, submitted by an insured, is known as a(n):
   a. proof of loss
   b. certificate
   c. policy
   d. insurable interest

____ 41. The person who is entitled to the proceeds of a life insurance policy when the insured dies is a(n):
   a. insurance agent
   b. insurance carrier
   c. beneficiary
   d. insurance broker

____ 42. An insurance agent is:
   a. the same as an insurance binder
   b. the same as an insurance carrier
   c. the same as an insurance adjuster
   d. a person who acts as an intermediary between the insured and the insurer who is not employed by any insurance company

_____ 43. After the insurance company that insures Mary Smith's car indemnifies her for damage done to her car by John Wheat's negligence, the insurance company has the same cause of action against John as Mary originally had. This is known as:
   a. subrogation
   b. self-insurance
   c. contribution between insurers
   d. comprehensive insurance

_____ 44. A type of automobile insurance where the insured is entitled to indemnification regardless of who was responsible for the injury or damage is known as:
   a. collision insurance
   b. title insurance
   c. no-fault insurance
   d. comprehensive insurance

_____ 45. A person who makes a determination of the value of a claim against an insurance company for the purpose of arriving at an amount for which the claim can be settled is an insurance:
   a. agent
   b. broker
   c. carrier
   d. adjuster

_____ 46. When an insurance company refuses without any basis to pay a claim, it is considered:
   a. bad faith
   b. exclusion
   c. subrogation
   d. rider

True/False

Mark the following T or F.

_____ 47. An umbrella policy provides coverage over and above the liability limitations of the insured's basic liability policies.

_____ 48. Subrogation is when you voluntarily relinquish or renounce a right one has.

_____ 49. A fraudulent or deliberately inaccurate statement intended to cause a person to act in reliance is a material misrepresentation.

_____ 50. Contribution between insurers is when insurers with policies covering the same loss must contribute proportionately to the insurer who has paid for the entire loss.

_____ 51. Reinsurance is where there is a contract between two insurance companies where the second company agrees to insure the first company against loss due to policyholders' claims.

_____ 52. The insured is the insurance company who assures the risk under an insurance policy.

_____ 53. Marine insurance is a policy covering the risk of loss to a ship or its cargo from the perils of the sea.

_____ 54. Coinsurance is where the risk is divided between the insurer and the insured.

____ **55.** A rider is used to make additions or changes to the original insurance policy.

____ **56.** The cost of replacing insured property at its current value, as opposed to its original cost, is known as a double indemnity clause.

____ **57.** Fire insurance indemnifies the insured against loss to property due to fire.

Synonyms

Select the correct synonym in parentheses for each numbered item.

58. WHOLE LIFE
(straight life, term life, group insurance)

59. DISABILITY
(incapacity, death, competency)

60. EXCLUSION
(inclusion, privilege, exception)

61. BENEFICIARY
(donor, recipient, insurer)

62. INSURANCE POLICY
(contract, release, waiver)

63. INSURED
(agent, buyer, covered person)

64. SUBROGATION
(exclusion, substitution, endorsement)

65. UMBRELLA POLICY
(basic coverage, excess coverage, duplicate coverage)

66. COLLISION INSURANCE
(personal injury insurance, theft insurance, property damage insurance)

67. INDEMNIFICATION
(loss, compensation, revocation)

68. INSURANCE CARRIER
(insurance company, insurance broker, insurance agent)

69. MALPRACTICE INSURANCE
(self-insurance, collision insurance, professional liability insurance)

70. BENEFIT
(return, loss, contribution)

71. INSURE
(cancel, waive, guarantee)

Self-Test

Place the number of the correct term in the appropriate space.

72. Insurance agent

73. Self-insurance

74. Broker

75. Policy

76. Insurable interest

77. Life

78. Beneficiary

79. Flood

80. Homeowners

81. Carriers

82. Insurer

83. Premium

84. Insured

85. Title insurance

There are many risks a person faces throughout the day. If a person has sufficient resources and foresight they might put aside money to cover all possible eventualities. When a person or organization sets aside money to cover their own risks, this is known as _____. Other people seek the services of a(n) _____ to obtain insurance for them through a variety of companies. Insurance is a contract (or _____) by which one party (the _____), in return for a specified _____, agrees to compensate another (the _____) for a loss.

There are many different kinds of coverage. The list is almost endless. You need a(n) _____ in whatever you wish to insure. If you are worried about providing for your family after you die, you might obtain _____ insurance. If you live in an area prone to flooding, you might obtain _____ insurance. If you wish to get a mortgage to buy a home, the bank will most likely require you to get _____ insurance and _____, to protect against defective title. Insurance is provided by various companies known as _____. The insurance company might authorize a person known as a(n) _____ to represent it when dealing with third persons. Once a person becomes a(n) _____ to an insurance policy, they will truly appreciate the necessity of insurance.

Defining Words

Complete the definition.

86. Policy _____

_____

87. Premium _____

_____

88. Insured _____

_____

89. Insurer _____

_____

90. Beneficiary _____

_____

91. Exclusion _____

_____

92. Deductible _____

_____

93. Rider _____

_____

94. Comprehensive coverage _____

_____

95. Waiver _____

_____

96. Group insurance _____

_____

97. Coinsurance _____

_____

98. Preexisting condition _____

_____

99. Whole life _____

_____

100. Umbrella policy _____

_____

Punctuation/Capitalization

Punctuation for impartial commentary.

It is common to see these kinds of phrases in transcripts:

in my opinion
to his knowledge
as you see it

These might be termed "impartial commentary" as they do not directly reflect on the content of a sentence.

Rule 1: Impartial commentary, no matter what grammatical construction it is, is surrounded by punctuation.
He said that, in his judgment, there was no question about the guilt of the defendant.
And are you, sitting here today, absolutely certain of your identification of this man?
Please tell us, to the best of your recollection, the time the accident took place.

Directions: Make necessary punctuation changes.

1. Were you to your knowledge ever considered to be a suspect in the case?

2. I believed in my heart of hearts, that he was not the one.

3. He was, in her opinion, addicted to drugs.

4. As I see it he is destined to do great things.

5. They were in my mind very scary people to be around.

Word Pairs

breach/breech

breach = several meanings.

- failure to observe the law or regulation, as in *breach of protocol*.
- break the surface, as in *breach the waves*.
- estrangement, as in *breach in the relationship*.
- fail to keep something, as in *breach of promise*.

The whales breached the ocean surface.
The breach in their relationship cannot be mended.
There has been a serious breach in the talks.

breech = several meanings.

- part of a firearm, as in *breech of a gun*.
- buttock, as in *breech birth*.
- thick end of anything, as in *breech portion*.

It was a difficult breech birth.
There were strange markings on the breech of the gun.
He inserted the ammunition into the breech of the cannon.

coated/coded

coated = covered, layered. Another conflict form is *coating*.

The wires were coated with a light covering of plastic.
His hands were coated with mud.
There was a fine coating of smoke on all the mirrors in the house.

coded = veiled, hidden, put into a secret language. Another conflict form is *coding*.

It was coded so that it could not be read by anyone.
The wires were color coded to indicate their purpose.
The coding was hard to decipher.

collision/collusion

collision = accident, conflict, crash. The verb form is *collide*.

It is sad that the collision took the lives of the entire family of four.
There was a collision at the intersection right at the beginning of rush hour.
I am not sure how the collision happened.

collusion = complicity, agreement, conspiracy. The verb form is *collude*.

The two companies were in collusion on the merger.
They were charged with collusion in the matter.
He colluded with her on the plan for the murder.

leased/least

leased = rented. This form is the past tense of the verb *lease.*

It had been leased for over a year in his name.
We leased it in order to use it for storage.
I think they leased several properties in that city.

least = slightest, smallest amount, minimum.

There were at least five that I did not recognize.
I felt it was the least I could do for him.
Her moods are the least of my worries.

wafer/waiver/waver

wafer = thin crisp cookie, medicinal encasing.

The fabric was wafer thin.
The wafers she tried to make broke easily.
They used rice paper as the wafer for the powdered medicine.

waiver = intentional relinquishment or renunciation of a right, claim, or privilege.
The verb form is *waive.*

Please do not interpret this as a waiver of his rights.
He would not agree to the waiver.
She stated emphatically that she would not support the waiver.

waver = fluctuate, hesitate, vacillate. The verb form is *wave.*

He did not waver in his commitment to the project.
She began to waver after an arduous five hours.
I know he wavered in his dedication from time to time.

Directions: Choose the correct word.

1. The breach/breech birth went very well.

2. The plate was coated/coded with a thin layer of gold.

3. The waiver/waver had been filed with the court.

4. It is the leased/least we could do for her.

5. Everyone thought they were in collision/collusion about that matter.

6. The whale breached/breeched the waves very near the shore.

7. The coating/coding could not be cracked by our expert staff.

8. There was a breach/breech of protocol on the part of the consul.

9. I believe the collision/collusion was just a fender-bender.

10. We had never leased/least a unit like this one.

11. The collision/collusion came to light during the trial.

12. There was a problem with the breach/breech of the cannon.

13. He knew little about the wafer/waiver/waver technology in the industry.

14. She did not waiver/waver in her dedication to him.

15. The dog was coated/coded with mud when he was found.

16. He was holding tightly to the breach/breech of the gun.

17. She was being sued for breach/breech of contract.

18. He was wafer/waiver/waver thin when he left the hospital.

19. It was coated/coded, and we could not read it.

20. At the very leased/least, he needs to apologize.

Is It One Word or Two? An Apostrophe? A Hyphen?

almost/all most

almost = nearly, just about, not quite. This form is an adverb.

We are almost ready to file the case.
He was almost to the corner when the accident happened.
There was an almost imperceptible crack in the bone.

all most = everyone or everything very. . . . *All* is a pronoun; *most* is an adverb.

We were all most happy to hear the news.
They were all most sad to have to leave.
We were all most gratified with the results.

already/all ready

already = prior to now, earlier. This form is an adverb.

He has already been appointed to the position.
Those regulations are already in place.
He has already seen several just like that.

all ready = everyone or everything prepared. *All* is a pronoun; *ready* is an adjective.

They were all ready to go when I got there.
It was all ready to be sold.
We were all ready for the holiday.

Directions: Choose the correct word.

1. We were almost/all most elated at the outcome of the race.

2. The books were already/all ready to be purchased by the students.

3. He had almost/all most fallen several times on that sidewalk.

4. There were already/all ready many errors in the transcript.

5. How far had almost/all most everyone in the contest walked?

Proofreading

Directions: Make necessary corrections, based on the material presented in the unit. If the sentence has no errors, write the word *correct* after the sentence.

1. We were almost happy to hear that the baby would not be breach.   _____

2. The coated message to my knowledge was easy to read.   _____

3. They were already, in their minds, to convict him.   _____

4. The collision was at leased very minor.   _____

5. The breach of contract in the opinion of the court is an open-and-shut case.   _____

6. He did not waiver about the fact that the marriage was over.   _____

7. The light coating gave a certain sheen to the already shiny fabric.   _____

8. As we understood it we had leased the apartment for six months only.   _____

9. They were already when I arrived to transport them from the scene of the collision.   _____

10. He was, in my mind, in collision with the others in the office.   _____

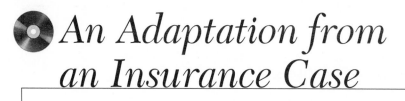

An Adaptation from an Insurance Case

Facts:

Martinez was issued an insurance policy and was named the insured under an insurance policy issued by United National Insurance Company, United, to provide coverage for a commercial building. During the policy period the building was destroyed by arson. The arsonist, a friend of Martinez's, died in the fire. United, in its opinion after an investigation, discovered several misrepresentations in Martinez's application for insurance. United rescinded the policy and offered to give Martinez the premium back. Martinez refused to accept the premium and filed this action. In his application for insurance, Martinez had claimed he was going to use the building for video production that included a studio and offices and that it was for a successful and ongoing business. In reality, the building was only used for two days to film a music video and then was leased to a garment business and then remained vacant thereafter when the garment business could not get a certificate of occupancy from the City. The building had multiple code violations. Martinez claimed that, to his knowledge, his friend who died in the fire was supposed to be showing the building to interested parties. Thereafter, the friend set the building on fire.

Procedural History:

The defendant insurance company was granted summary judgment on the issue of breach of contract. The court, in the opinion it handed down, concluded that there was no breach of contract on United's part nor a breach of the covenant of fair dealing and good faith.

Issue:

Had Martinez made material misrepresentations on his application to entitle United to rescind the policy of insurance?

Rationale:

Any misrepresentation, whether intentional or unintentional, may be grounds for rescinding a policy of insurance. A party to an insurance contract must disclose in good faith all facts within his knowledge which are or which he knows to be material to the contract. An entire policy is void if a party has willfully concealed or misrepresented any material fact or circumstance concerning the insurance with the intent to deceive.

Ruling:

Under the Insurance Code, an insurance company may rescind a fire insurance policy based on an insured's negligent or unintentional misrepresentation of a material fact in an insurance application.

Ruling:

Summary judgment affirmed for United.

Directions for CD-ROM Transcription Exercises

In audio format are:

1. Terms for the unit with pronunciations from the thesaurus/dictionary feature.

2. Self-Test that appears in the book at mid-unit.*

3. Case that appears at the unit end.*

*speeds are 80 wpm/120 wpm for differing skill levels

CD-ROM icons appear where the three above are located within each unit.

Readers may practice transcription by listening to the CD-ROM where prompted by the icons in the book. However, for high success in testing your transcription skills, mastering all the terms and English skills in the unit is recommended before attempting the CD-ROM.

For Keyboard Transcriptionists: Listen to the CD-ROM audio file for this unit at 80 wpm or 120 wpm and transcribe from the dictation on your computer. Edit and proofread your work against the printed copy in the book.

For Reporting Writers: Listen to the CD-ROM audio file at 80 wpm or 120 wpm and take down the dictation on your writer. Either transcribe from your notes and proofread your work or edit and proofread your CAT (computer-aided transcription) transcript. Always check your work against the printed copy in the book.

Student CD-ROM
For additional materials,
please go to the CD in this book.

Online Companion™
For additional resources, please go to
http://www.paralegal.delmar.cengage.com

Area of Law
Intellectual Property

The **Mistakes** That Court Reporters Make and *How to Avoid* Them

The Mistake:

Josephine Sanchez worked in the deposition field; therefore, transcripts were the bread and butter of her job. She decided she wanted more free time. She hired a scopist to do her work and already had a proofreader. Her thinking was that, if her jobs could be both scoped and proofread, then she would have more free time. She began to receive complaints about the quality of her transcripts. The agency owners were pointing out errors in her transcripts. Since she was not looking at the transcripts at all before they were made final, she had no way of knowing what these errors were.

How to Avoid It:

In giving over both the scoping and the proofreading, the reporter never sees the finished product before it goes out. There is a real advantage in having a second set of eyes look at the transcript. However, the reporter must look at it at some stage. The reporter is the one who was present at the proceedings. She can have a scopist and then proofread it herself or do the scoping and have the work proofread. There must be some reporter control over the final product.

Introduction

A field of law has developed to protect certain property produced as the result of original thoughts. The broad categories of protected property are known as patents, copyrights, trademarks, and trade secrets. The success of many businesses depends on their ability to protect and use intellectual property to their profitable advantage. When protected property is used without consent this is known as infringement.

When devices or processes that are both new and useful are invented, a patent application can be made by the inventor to gain the exclusive right to manufacture, sell, and use the invention for a period of time. A copyright is the right of an author to exclusively control the reproduction, distribution, and sale of literary and artistic works. Some of the items that may be protected by copyright are written works, music, films, sound recordings, photographs, painting, sculptures, and even some computer programs and chips. Use of a trademark is a method whereby a mark design, title, logo, or motto can be used to sell or advertise products of a particular company and distinguish them from other brands or products. Trade secrets are confidential information and property of a business that describe an industrial process or the way in which the business is conducted.

In the case herein, patent infringement is in the eye of the beholder.

Unit Objectives

- Work with a legal dictionary/thesaurus.
- Learn about the law of intellectual property.
- Master the similarities and differences in definitions of key terms in the unit.
- Master the pronunciations and spellings of legal terms in this unit.
- Practice usage of terms, definitions, and synonyms for intellectual property.
- Complete unit exercises in the forms of missing words, matching, multiple choice, true/false, synonyms, self-test, defining words, and also:
  - Punctuation/capitalization
  - Word pairs
  - Transcription of terms, self-test, and case
  - Proofreading

Dictionary/Thesaurus

Note: All Dictionary/Thesaurus terms appear on the CD-ROM with audio pronunciations.

Term [phonetic pronunciation]	
abandonment of trademark [a.ban.den.ment ov trade.mark]	Loss of trademark rights resulting from nonuse of the mark; demonstrated by sufficient evidence that the owner intends to discontinue use of the mark. May also occur when a mark has lost its distinctiveness or through the owner's misuse of trademark rights.
abstract [ab.strakt]	Summary of the invention that enables the reader to determine the character of the patentable subject matter.
access [ak.sess]	The reasonable opportunity of the defendant to view or hear the copyrighted work.
amendment to allege use [a.mend.ment to a.lej yoose]	Amendment to an intent-to-use application indicating use of a mark on commerce; the amendment can only be filed before approval of the mark for publication (or, if there is a rejection, within six months of the response period).
arbitrary mark [ar.bi.trare.ee mark]	Word or image that has a common meaning that does not describe or suggest the goods or services with which it is associated.
architectural work [ar.ka.tek.cha.ral werk]	The design of a building as embodied in any tangible medium of expression, including a building, architectural plans, or drawings; it includes the overall form as well as the arrangement and composition of spaces and elements in the design, but does not include individual standard features.
audiovisual works [aw.dee.o.vizh.u.al werkz]	Works that consist of a series of related images that are intrinsically intended to be shown by the use of machines or devices, such as projectors, viewers, or electronic equipment, together with accompanying sounds, if any, regardless of the nature of the material objects, such as films or tapes, in which the works are embodied.
author [*aw*.ther]	1. A person who produces a written work. 2. A person who originates something; a maker. In copyright law, a person can be an author without producing any original material, provided she does something beyond copying, such as compiling or editing. • *n.* producer, maker, originator, biographer, inventor, creator, planner
authorization of agent [aw.ther.i.zay.shen ov ay.jent]	Inventor's or patent owner's authorization of representation by a patent agent.

automated database
[awt.toh.may.ted day.tah.base]

A body of facts, data, or other information assembled into an organized format suitable for use in a computer and comprising one or more files.

basic registration
[*ba*.sik rej.is.*tray*.shen]

The primary copyright record made for each version of a particular work.

collective mark
[ku.*lek*.tiv mark]

A trademark or service mark used to identify a trade association, fraternal society, or union.

copyright
[*kop*.ee.rite]

n. The right of an author, granted by federal statute, to exclusively control the reproduction, distribution, and sale of her literary, artistic, or intellectual productions for the period of the copyright's existence. Copyright protection extends to written work, music, films, sound recordings, photographs, paintings, sculpture, and some computer programs and chips. The symbol © is used to show copyright protection. *See also* intellectual property; literary property.
v. To acquire a copyright.
• *n.* authority, grant, license, permit, privilege, authorization

derivative work
[*de*.riv.e.tiv werk]

n. A work based upon one or more preexisting works, such as a translation, musical arrangement, dramatization, fictionalization, motion picture version, sound recording, art reproduction, abridgment, condensation, or any other form in which a work may be recast, transformed, or adapted. A work consisting of editorial revisions, annotations, elaborations, or other modifications that, as a whole, represent an original work of authorship is also a derivative work.

design patent
[de.zine *pat*.ent]

A patent of a design that gives an original and pleasing appearance to an article.

device
[de.*vice*]

1. In patent law, an invention. 2. An emblem such as a business logo or a union label. 3. An apparatus; machine, appliance, or contrivance.
• *n.* instrument, mechanism, contraption, invention, construction, apparatus ("an eating device")

dilution
[dil.loo.shen]

The adverse effect of use of a similar mark on the reputation of a distinctive mark, even though the use may not confuse consumers as to the source of the goods or services; occurs when the defendant's use weakens or reduces the distinctive quality of the mark. A claim of dilution is available only under state laws, sometimes known as antidilution statutes.

disclaimer
[dis.klame.er]

Statement that a trademark owner asserts no exclusive right in a specific portion of a mark, apart from its use within the mark.

disparagement
[dis.*pa*.rej.ment]

Discredit; detraction; dishonor; denunciation; disrespect.

disparagement of goods
[dis.*pa*.rej.ment ov goodz]

Criticism that discredits the quality of merchandise or other property offered for sale.

display publicly [dis.play pub.lik.lee]	To show a copy of a copyrighted work, either directly or by means of a film, slide, television image, or any other device or process where the public is gathered or the work is transmitted or otherwise communicated to the public.
distinctive [dis.*tink*.tiv]	• *adj.* characteristic, distinguishing, particular, uncommon, idiosyncratic, salient
divisional application [da.vizh.an.el ap.li.kay.shen]	Application made for an independent invention that has grown out of an earlier application; a method of dividing an original application that contains two or more inventions. Trademark applications may also be divided.
doctrine of equivalents [dok.trin ov ee.kwiv.e.lentz]	Right of patent owner to prevent sale, use, or manufacture of a discovery or invention if it employs substantially the same means to achieve substantially the same results in substantially the same way as that claimed.
dramatic works [dra.mat.ik werkz]	Narrative presentations (and any accompanying music) that generally use dialogue and stage directions as the basis for a theatrical exhibition.
drawing (trademark) [draw.ing trayd.mark]	A substantially exact representation of the mark as used (or, in the case of intent-to-use applications, as intended to be used). A drawing is required for all federal trademark applications and for many state trademark applications.
evaluation agreement [i.val.yoo.ay.shen a.gree.ment]	Contract by which one party promises to submit an idea and the other party promises to evaluate the idea. After the evaluation, the evaluator will either enter into an agreement to exploit the idea or promise not to use or disclose the idea.
exclusive jurisdiction [eks.kloo.siv joo.ris.dik.shen]	A court's sole authority to hear a certain type of case.
exclusive license [eks.kloo.siv *ly.sense*]	Agreement to restrict the grant of proprietary rights to one person.
exhaustion doctrine [eg.zaws.chen *dok*.trin]	When a patented product (or product resulting from a patented process) is sold or licensed, the patent owner loses some or all patent rights as to the resale of that particular article.
fair use doctrine [fayr yoos *dok*.trin]	The principle that entitles a person to use copyrighted material in a reasonable manner, including a work's theme or idea, without the consent of the copyright owner. EXAMPLE: teachers photocopying one page of a magazine for students.
generic [jen.*err*.ik]	1. Pertaining to a kind, class, or group. 2. General; inclusive.
idea [eye.*dee*.uh]	• *n.* concept, thought, belief, proposal

infringement [in.*frinj*.ment]	A violation of a right or privilege. • *n.* violation, misfeasance, invasion, encroachment, interference, breach ("infringement of patent")
infringement of copyright [in.*frinj*.ment ov *kop*.ee.rite]	Using any portion of copyrighted material without the consent of the copyright owner. *Compare* fair use doctrine. *See also* copyright.
infringement of patent [in.*frinj*.ment ov *pat*.ent]	The manufacture, use, or sale of a patent or process patent without the authorization of the owner of the patent.
infringement of trademark [in.*frinj*.ment ov trayd.mark]	A use or imitation of a trademark in such manner that a purchaser of goods is likely to be deceived into believing that they are the goods of the owner of the trademark.
intangible [in.*tan*.jibl]	*adj.* Without physical substance; nonmaterial. *Compare* tangible property. *n.* A thing that may or may not have value, but has no physical substance; an intangible asset or intangible property. EXAMPLES: a copyright; goodwill. *Compare* tangible property. • *adj.* nonphysical, abstract, imperceptible, impalpable
intangible asset [in.*tan*.jibl *ass*.et]	Intangible property that has value. *Compare* tangible property.
intangible property [in.*tan*.jibl *prop*.er.tee]	1. An incorporeal right unrelated to a physical thing. EXAMPLES: a right to sue (i.e., a cause of action); a right to inherit property. 2. Property that has no intrinsic value, but evidences something of value. EXAMPLE: a stock certificate (which evidences a share in the ownership of the corporation that issued it). *Compare* tangible property.
intellectual property [in.te.*lek*.choo.el *prop*.er.tee]	Property (EXAMPLES: copyrights; patents; trade secrets) that is the physical or tangible result of original thought. Modern technology has brought about widespread infringement of intellectual property rights. EXAMPLE: the unauthorized reproduction and sale of videotapes, audiotapes, and computer software. *See also* infringement of copyright, infringement of patent, literary property, piracy.
invention [in.*ven*.shen]	1. The act of creating something patentable. *See also* patent, device. 2. The thing that has been invented. 3. The act of creating something new. • *n.* finding, discovery, creation, improvisation
inventor [in.*ven*.ter]	A person who creates an invention. • *n.* author, maker, creator, devisor, pioneer, improviser
license [*ly*.sense]	1. A special privilege, not a right common to everyone. 2. Authorization by the owner of a patent to make, use, or sell the patented article; permission by the owner of a trademark or copyright to use the trademark or to make use of the copyrighted material.
licensee [ly.sen.*see*]	A person to whom the owner of a patent, copyright, or trademark grants a right to use.

literary property
[lit.e.re.ree *prop*.er.tee]

The interest of an author, or anyone to whom she has transferred her interest, in her own work; the exclusive right of an author to use and profit from her own written or printed intellectual production. *See also* intellectual property; literary work; infringement of copyright.

literary work
[lit.e.re.ree werk]

In copyright law, "works, other than audiovisual works, expressed in words, numbers, or other verbal or numerical symbols or induced, regardless of the nature of the material objects, such as books, periodicals, manuscripts, phone records, film, tapes, disks, or cards, in which they are embodied."

logo
[*loh*.go]

Graphic symbols that function as a mark. *See also* trademark.

misappropriation of trade secret
[mis.a.pro.pree.ay.shen ov trayd see.kret]

Improper acquisition of a trade secret by a person who has reason to know that the trade secret was obtained by improper means, or the disclosure or use of a trade secret without consent by a person who either had a duty to maintain secrecy or who used improper means to acquire the secret.

moral rights
[mor.el rytz]

Rights that protect the professional honor and reputation of an artist by guaranteeing the right to claim or disclaim authorship of a work and the right to prevent, in certain cases, distortion, mutilation, or other modification of the work.

motion picture
[moh.shen pik.chur]

Audiovisual works consisting of a series of related images that, when shown in succession, impart an impression of motion with sound, if any.

patent
[*pat*.ent]

n. 1. The exclusive right of manufacture, sale, or use granted by the federal government to a person who invents or discovers a device or process that is new and useful. *See also* device, invention. 2. The grant of a right, privilege, or authority by the government. The abbreviation "Pat." is often used.
v. To obtain a patent upon an invention.
• *n.* permit, license, certificate, trademark, right, legal right

Patent and Trademark Office
[*pat*.ent and trayd.mark *off*.iss]

Authorized by the Constitution and established by Congress, this office of the federal government registers all trademarks and grants all patents issued in the United States. Its duties also include examining patents, hearing and deciding appeals from inventors and trademark applicants, and publishing the *Official Gazette*.

patent infringement
[*pat*.ent in.*frinj*.ment]

See infringement of patent.

patent medicine
[*pat*.ent *med*.i.sin]

An over-the-counter medication; a medication concocted by a manufacturer, often according to a secret formula. Note that a patent medicine is generally not patented; however, it is often protected by trademark.

patent rights
[*pat*.ent rytz]

The rights a patentee receives with respect to her invention as a result of having been granted a patent for it.

patentability [*pat*.ent.a.bil.a.tee]	The quality of being patentable.
patentable [*pat*.ent.ebl]	Entitled to receive a patent. To be patentable, an idea must include every essential characteristic of the complete and practical invention.
patentee [pat.en.*tee*]	A person who receives a patent.
pioneer patent [*py*.e.neer *pat*.ent]	A patent in a new field; a totally new device; a basis patent.
piracy [*py*.re.see]	A term for infringement of copyright or for using literary property without permission, plagiarism. • *n.* plagiarism, infringement, appropriation ("printing an article without the author's permission is piracy")
public use [*pub*.lik yoos]	In patent law, any use of an invention other than a secret or experimental use.
registration [rej.is.*tray*.shen]	The act of registering. • *n.* recording, reservation, inscription, enrollment, filing, listing
service mark [*ser*.viss mark]	A mark design, title, or motto used in the sale or advertising of services to identify the services and distinguish them from the services of others. A service mark is the property of its owner and, when registered under the Trademark Act, is reserved for the exclusive use of its owner. *Compare* trademark.
tangible property [tan.jibl *prop*.er.tee]	Property, real or personal, that has physical substance; property that can be physically possessed. EXAMPLES: real estate; automobiles; jewelry.
trade dress [trayd dres]	The size, shape, texture, color, graphics, and other distinct features of a product that constitute its total appearance used to promote the sale of the product.
trade libel [trayd *ly*.bel]	A libel that defames the goods or products a person produces in her business or occupation, as opposed to a libel against the person herself.
trade name [trayd naym]	The name under which a company does business. The goodwill of a company includes its trade name. *Compare* trademark.
trade secret [trayd *see*.kret]	Confidential information concerning an industrial process or the way in which a business is conducted. Trade secrets are of special value to a business and are the property of the business.

trademark
[trayd.mark]

A mark, design, title, logo, or motto used in the sale or advertising of products to identify them and distinguish them from the products of others. A trademark is the property of its owner and, when registered under the Trademark Act, is reserved for the exclusive use of its owner. The symbol ® is used to indicate a registered trademark. *Compare* service mark, trade name. *See also* collective mark.
• *n.* logo, brand, identification, mark, design, initials, logotype, stamp

trademark infringement
[trayd.mark in.*frinj*.ment]

Use of a substantially similar mark by a junior user that creates a likelihood of consumer confusion. *See also* infringement of trademark.

trademark license
[trayd.mark *ly*.sense]

Agreement granting limited trademark rights.

transfer of copyright ownership
[tranz.fer ov kop.ee.rite oh.ner.ship]

An assignment, mortgage, exclusive license, transfer by will or intestate succession, or any other change in the ownership of any or all of the exclusive rights in a copyright, whether or not it is limited in time or place of effect, but not including a nonexclusive license.

transmit
[tranz.mit]

To communicate a copyrighted work by any device or process whereby images or sounds are received beyond the place from which they are sent.

tying
[tye.ing]

(Also called tie-in.) Business practice in which the purchase of a patented item is tied to a second, nonpatented item. An unjustified tying arrangement is patent misuse.

unfair competition
[un.fare kom.pe.tish.en]

A collection of common law principles that protect against unfair business practices.

use in commerce
[yoos in kom.urs]

Use of a trademark by placing it on goods or containers, tags or labels, displays associated with the goods (or, if otherwise impracticable, on documents associated with the goods), and selling or transporting the goods in commerce regulated by the United States.

useful article
[yoos.ful ar.tikl]

An article having an intrinsic utilitarian function that is not merely to portray the appearance of the article or to convey information. An article that is normally a part of a useful article is considered a useful article.

usefulness
[yoos.ful.ness]

An invention must have a use or purpose and must work (i.e., be capable of performing its intended purpose).

utility patents
[yoo.til.i.tee pat.entz]

Legal protection granted for inventions or discoveries that are categorized as machines, processes, compositions, articles of manufacture, or new uses of any of these.

visually perceptible copy
[vizh.yoo.e.lee per.sep.ta.ble kop.ee]

A copy that can be visually observed when it is embodied in a material object, either directly or with the aid of a machine or device.

work made for hire
[werk mayd for hyer]

1. A work prepared by an employee within the scope of his or her employment. 2. A work specially ordered or commissioned for use as a contribution to a collective work, as a part of a motion picture or other audiovisual work, as a translation, as a supplementary work, as a compilation, as an instructional text, as a test, as answer material for a test, or as an atlas, if the parties expressly agree in a written instrument signed by them that the work shall be considered a work made for hire.

work of authorship
[werk ov aw.ther.ship]

Creation of intellectual or artistic effort fixed or embodied in a perceptible form and meeting the statutory standards of copyright protection.

work of visual art
[werk ov vizh.yoo.ul art]

Under the Copyright Act of 1976, either (1) a painting, drawing, print, or sculpture, existing in a single copy, in a limited edition of 200 copies or fewer that are signed and consecutively numbered by the author, or, in the case of a sculpture, in multiple cast, carved, or fabricated sculptures of 200 or fewer that are consecutively numbered by the author and bear the signature or other identifying mark of the author; or (2) a still photographic image produced for exhibition purposes only, existing in a single copy that is signed by the author.

writ of seizure
[rit ov seez.yer]

Order of the court directing the federal marshal to seize and hold infringing merchandise; granted only upon payment of a bond.

writing
[*write*.ing]

1. Anything that is written. The Uniform Commercial Code defines "written" or "writing" to include "printing, typewriting, or any other intentional reduction (or words) to tangible form." 2. The expression of ideas by visible letters, numbers, or other symbols.

Missing Words

Fill in the blanks below.

1. A(n) _____ is a summary of the invention that enables the reader to determine the character of the patentable subject matter.

2. Confidential information concerning an industrial process or the way in which a business is conducted is known as a(n) _____.

3. The _____ doctrine is the principle that entitles a person to use copyrighted material without consent of the copyright owner.

4. The right of an author to control the reproduction, sale, and distribution of literary, artistic, or intellectual productions is known as _____.

5. When any portion of a copyrighted material is used without the consent of the owner, this is called _____ of copyright.

6. A(n) _____ is the name under which a company does business.

7. _____ are the expression of ideas by visible letters, numbers, or other symbols.

8. A person who makes a written work is a(n) _____.

9. The act of creating something patentable is known as a(n) _____.

10. Authorization by the owner of a patent to make, use, or sell the patented article is known as a(n) _____.

11. A mark, design, title, or motto used in the sale or advertising of services is known as a(n) _____.

12. A graphic symbol that functions as a mark is a(n) _____.

13. A work based upon one or more preexisting works such as a translation or musical arrangement is known as a(n) _____.

14. In patent law, another word for an invention is a(n) _____.

15. A trademark used to identify a trade association is a(n) _____.

16. _____ pertains to a kind, class, or group.

17. In patent law _____ is any use of an invention other than a secret or experimental use.

18. _____ is the distinct features of a product used to promote its sale.

Matching

Match the letter of the definition to the term below.

_____ 19. Writing

_____ 20. Trademark

_____ 21. Inventor

_____ 22. Collective mark

_____ 23. Disparagement of goods

_____ 24. Intellectual property

_____ 25. Dilution

_____ 26. Author

_____ 27. Distinctive

_____ 28. Tying

_____ 29. Pioneer patent

_____ 30. Access

_____ 31. Abstract

_____ 32. Trade dress

A. A trademark or service mark used to identify a trade association, fraternal society, or union

B. The adverse effect of use of a similar mark on the reputation of a distinctive mark

C. The expression of ideas by visible letters, numbers, or other symbols

D. Business practice where the purchase of a patented item is tied to a second, nonpatented item

E. A mark, design, title, logo, or motto used in the sale or advertising of products

F. A person who produces a written work

G. Criticism that discredits the quality of merchandise or other property offered for sale

H. Uncommon or distinguishing

I. A person who creates an invention

J. Property that is the physical or tangible result of original thought

K. Reasonable opportunity to view or hear copyrighted work

L. Summary of an invention

M. Patent in a new field

N. Size, shape, texture, color, and graphics of a product

Multiple Choice

Select the best choice.

_____ 33. The exclusive right to manufacture a new and useful device is known as:
   a. copyright
   b. service mark
   c. trademark
   d. patent

_____ 34. The symbol used to show that a writing is copyrighted is:
   a. ⓐ
   b. ⓑ
   c. ⓒ
   d. ⓓ

_____ 35. In order to protect an original writing an author might obtain a:
   a. patent
   b. copyright
   c. generic name
   d. collective mark

_____ 36. The fair use doctrine:
   a. entitles a person to use patented materials
   b. entitles a person to use copyrighted material
   c. prohibits a person from using patented material
   d. prohibits a person from using copyrighted material

_____ 37. The following abbreviation is used to show an invention has been patented:
   a. Pate
   b. Paten
   c. Pa
   d. Pat

_____ 38. Graphic symbols that function as a mark:
   a. logo
   b. license
   c. patent
   d. patentee

_____ 39. When a business uses a mark in the sale of advertising products and distinguishes them, that is known as:
   a. palming off
   b. misappropriation
   c. trademark
   d. invention

_____ 40. Confidential information concerning an industrial process or the way in which a business is conducted is known as a:
   a. service mark
   b. trade secret
   c. generic name
   d. secondary meaning

_____ 41. Copyright protection covers the following:
   a. written works
   b. music and film
   c. photographs and paintings
   d. all of the above

_____ 42. Client lists and secret recipes are examples of:
   a. generic name
   b. service mark
   c. copyright
   d. trade secrets

_____ 43. The owner of a registered trademark is entitled to use which of the following symbols?
   a. T
   b. TM
   c. S
   d. R

_____ 44. The primary copyright record made for a work:
   a. tying
   b. dilution
   c. basic registration
   d. disclaimer

True/False

Mark the following T or F.

_____ 45. The fair use doctrine permits teachers to photocopy portions of copyrighted works for use in the classroom.

_____ 46. A trademark is used in the sale or advertising of a service.

_____ 47. A musician should obtain a patent to protect a new song.

_____ 48. Copyright protection is needed to protect an inventor's interest in a new invention.

_____ 49. An artist who paints a portrait should obtain a service mark to protect her creation.

_____ 50. A trade secret is of little value to a business.

_____ 51. When an author has an idea for a new novel, this is an example of a tangible writing.

_____ 52. Misappropriation of trade secrets is when the seller of goods misrepresents himself as someone else to induce a buyer to purchase something.

_____ 53. Disparagement of goods occurs when someone criticizes the quality of merchandise or other property for sale.

_____ 54. The office of the federal government that registers all trademarks and grants all patents is known as the Patent and Trademark Office.

_____ 55. Intellectual property is that property which is the physical or tangible result of original thought.

Synonyms

Select the correct synonym in parentheses for each numbered item.

56. TANGIBLE
    (touchable, imaginary, fake)

57. DISTINCTIVE
    (usual, common, distinguishing)

58. ORIGINAL
    (unique, copy, irregular)

59. MISAPPROPRIATE
    (take, give, review)

60. DISPARAGEMENT
    (praise, criticize, demonstrate)

61. PIRACY
    (infringement, sale, barter)

62. ABSTRACT
    (revelation, secret, summary)

63. PUBLIC USE
    (secret, experimental, nonprivate)

64. INVENTION
    (edition, distraction, discovery)

65. WRITING
    (print, oral, action)

66. INFRINGEMENT
    (inflation, breach, admission)

67. REGISTRATION OF TRADEMARK
    (filing, typing, copying)

68. COLLECTIVE MARK
    (trade association, individual, government)

69. TRADE NAME
    (trademark, patent, goodwill)

70. INVENTOR
    (piracy, creator, purchaser)

71. LICENSE
    (privilege, fair use, logo)

Self-Test

Place the number of the correct term in the appropriate space.

72. Patent infringement

73. Trade secrets

74. Author

75. Fair use doctrine

76. Trademark

77. Infringement

78. Unfair competition

79. Misappropriation of trade secrets

80. Copyright

81. Service mark

82. Intellectual property

83. Patent

84. Trademark infringement

85. Piracy

Property that is the physical or tangible result of original thought is called _____. Should a(n) _____ produce a written work such as a song or book, and desire exclusive control of the reproduction and sale of the work, he or she should obtain _____ protection. A person who creates an invention and seeks the exclusive right to manufacture and sell the invention should apply for a(n) _____ through the Patent and Trademark Office. In the event a mark, design, title, logo, or motto is used in the sale or advertising of a product, a(n) _____ should be registered. Another property of a business that is of special value and needs to be protected is _____, the confidential information concerning an industrial process or the way in which a business is conducted. Should a business use a mark, design, title, or motto in the sale or advertising of services, a(n) _____ should be registered.

Much to the surprise of many authors, copyright protection does not guarantee that the public won't be allowed to use copyrighted material. The _____ entitles a person to use copyrighted material in a reasonable manner, without the consent of the copyright owner.

When intellectual property rights are violated, this is called _____. When trade secrets are improperly acquired, this is called _____. _____ occurs when a patent is used without authorization of the owner. _____ refers to the infringement of copyright protection. There is _____ when a similar mark is used to create consumer confusion. Many unfair business practices are called _____.

Defining Words

Complete the definition.

86. Patent _____

_____

87. Trademark _____

_____

88. Copyright _____

_____

89. Intellectual property _____

_____

90. Original work _____

_____

91. Generic name _____

_____

92. Public use doctrine _____

_____

93. Service mark _____

_____

94. Trade secret _____

_____

95. Dramatic works _____

_____

96. Literary property _____

_____

97. Pioneer patent _____

_____

98. Tying _____

_____

99. Dilution _____

_____

100. Trade dress _____

_____

Punctuation/Capitalization

Punctuating repeating words.

Rule 1: When a word repeats and has exactly the same meaning each time, there is a comma between the repeated words.

He had many, many chances to remedy the situation.
All he had time to do was work, work, work.
It was a hard, hard decision for him.

Rule 2: When a word repeats and has a different function or different meaning, there is no comma between the repeated words.

We had had a good time there.
She is sure that that is the truth.
He called in in time to stop the order.

Directions: Make necessary punctuation changes.

1. All I wanted to do was sleep sleep sleep.

2. He found out, out of sheer determination.

3. I know that that is a statement I do not agree with.

4. We had, had to listen to all five hours of the tapes.

5. He sped up up the hill.

Word Pairs

affect/effect

Rule 1: When the *a* of *affect* is pronounced as a short *a* (as it is in the word *sat*), it is the psychiatric term that refers to the overall look and demeanor of the patient, and it is spelled with the *a* just as it sounds. The reporter hears the *a* sound clearly pronounced and writes it correctly on the machine.

The doctor noted that she had a very flat affect.

Her overly animated affect alarmed him.

It is important to pay attention to the affect.

The problem occurs when both words are identically pronounced with the schwa sound, that is, the *"uh"* sound the letter *e* has in the word *category*. We say *uh/fect* for both words. The dictionary definitions are not of much help because both definitions contain the word *influence*, and *affect* is defined as "to have an effect on."

To be sure to get the right form, ask these questions (putting aside the psychiatric use of the word):

Rule 2: Is the part of speech a noun? (One clue might be whether it has the word *a* or *the* in front of it.) If the answer is yes, then the word you want is *effect*.

Her response had no effect on my decision.

It is a simple matter of cause and effect.

His body was ravaged by the effects of the disease.

Rule 3: If it is not a noun, can "bring about" or "make happen" be substituted directly for the word? If the answer is yes, then the word you want is *effect*.

The changes will be effected the first part of May.

This regulation was effected to protect the workers.

The laws to be effected were all encompassing.

Rule 4: If it is not a noun, can "bring about" or "make happen" be substituted directly for the word? If the answer is no, then the word you want is *affect*.

This regulation does not affect anyone in our division.

I was unaffected by his emotional plea.

She was deeply affected by his death.

cite/sight/site

cite = refer to. The noun form of the word is *citation*. When you get a traffic ticket, a citation, the officer is making reference to your violation of a specific law in the Vehicle Code. When the attorney cites a case, he is referring to a specific case in the body of case law. When a person cites an author, he is making reference to something the author said.

He cited four different cases that set the precedent for this type of case.

The cite can be found in the California Appellate series.

The citation he gave us does not really apply.

sight = several meanings.

- vision, as in *his eyesight.*
- alignment device, as in *the sight on a gun.*
- something seen, as in *the sights of the city.*
- range for perceiving something, as in *out of sight.*
- to see, as in *to sight him in the crowd.*

She was a sight when she got off that bus.
The sight was off; so he missed the target.
She set out to see the sights of the city.

site = location. This word should be used as a noun, but it is increasingly used as a verb in a sentence like "The new building will be sited at the corner of Main and Elm."

There was no signal at the intersection at the site of the accident.
The construction site was littered with debris.
The new site is not really big enough.

incite/insight/in sight

incite = stir up, arouse. A common legal expression is *incite to riot,* meaning "to stir people up and encourage them to riot."

He incited the crowd with his wild rhetoric.
His very presence tended to incite them.
She was charged by the police with inciting to riot.

insight = perceptiveness.

Her keen insight aided her attempts to help him.
I have no insight into his work mentality.
It is imperative to have more insight into the problem.

in sight = within the range of vision.

She kept the kids in sight at all times.
We were in sight of the building when it happened.
The police had him in sight when he fired on them.

Directions: Choose the correct word.

1. The death of her mother had a profound affect/effect on this child.

2. The death of her mother affected/effected a change in the personality of this child.

3. The death of her mother affected/effected this child deeply.

4. The new law will have no affect/effect on the department.

5. The new law will affect/effect everyone in the department.

6. The new law will be affected/effected on January 1.

7. The officers went in to affect/effect the arrest.

8. His illegal activities affected/effected his wife and children the most.

9. We had to affect/effect changes in the policy, and it resulted that everyone was affected/effected.

10. What had no affect/effect on him seemed to affect/effect her deeply.

11. He decided to cite/sight/site her at the scene of the accident.

12. The cite/sight/site of the tragedy was closed to the public.

13. A citing/sighting/siting of the suspect alarmed the neighbors.

14. The attorney cited/sighted/sited a case that is very obscure.

15. She was a real cite/sight/site when she got off the bus.

16. The defense tried to prove that the cite/sight/site of the gun was off.

17. I did not make the trip to the cite/sight/site.

18. We tried to keep the car incite/insight/in sight, but the speed was excessive.

19. His very presence seemed to incite/insight/in sight everyone.

20. She has no special incite/insight/in sight into this problem.

Is It One Word or Two? An Apostrophe? A Hyphen?

Rule 1: When two or more words in front of a noun act as a single unit, there is a hyphen between the two words. One test is to check to see whether the words work individually in front of the noun. If they do not, there is a hyphen. So if it is a four-year college, check to see whether *four college* and *year college* work. Since they do not, the combination is hyphenated.

His long-range plan is to finish college and spend a year in Europe.
The old-fashioned dress was not appropriate in the business setting.
He has a two-month commitment to the program.

There are some other aspects to this rule that are not covered here.

Rule 2: When two words in front of a noun do not act as a unit, they are not hyphenated.
She has a colorful red necklace that she wears on nights like this.
It was a different computer issue that I had not encountered before.
He is interested in the rich baseball history of this team.

Directions: Correct the hyphenation.

1. His testimony is that it was a light colored Chevrolet.

2. It is a U shaped curve and is very dangerous.

3. She wrote to her long-time friend in the East.

4. The prizes went to the first-three students in line.

5. The old VW bus was unique.

Proofreading

Directions: Make necessary corrections, based on the material presented in the unit. If the sentence has no errors, write the word *correct* after the sentence.

1. The three older women affect sympathy and compassion wherever they go.   _____

2. Our intention to effect the new provisions was now insight and would become a reality.   _____

3. The issues will affect everyone with any measure of in sight in the large, large company.   _____

4. She remained uneffected even though there were many many reasons to be concerned.   _____

5. We did not plan to affect this plan before the site on Broadway was purchased.   _____

6. The effects of the disease have affected her fragile-mental stability.   _____

7. There were reasons to test the affects of the heavy, heavy medication frequently.   _____

8. I wanted to affect the new orders but had had trouble getting the approval.   _____

9. What she said affected everyone in the close knit family.   _____

10. He sighted the old law because he was unaware a new law was effected this year.   _____

An Adaptation from an Intellectual Property Case

Facts:

Appellant Marquez Razinski owns both of the cell phone patents in the suit—U.S. Design Patent No. 567, 571—referred to as the "571" patent, which looks like a clam shell when closed—and U.S. Design Patent No. 567, 598—referred to as the "598" patent, which looks like a lawn chair when folded and which has a thicker hinge than the 571. Defendant Yoshida owns a design patent on a cell phone, which patent will be referred to here as the "581" patent.

Procedural History:

The District Court reviewed the defendant's cell phone, 581, and compared it to both the 571 and the 598 of plaintiff and granted summary judgment for Yoshida. The District Court held that Yoshida's telephone design does not infringe either of the plaintiff's two design patents in this suit.

Issue:

Does defendant's design patent 581 infringe on the design patents of 571 or 598 granted to plaintiff for his telephone?

Rationale:

Design patents are granted for "any new, original, and ornamental design for an article of manufacture." If, from the eye of an ordinary purchaser, two designs are substantially the same and if the effect is that he is induced to buy one product supposing it is the other product, then the first product patented has been infringed by the other. The District Court could find no substantial similarities and cited many, many differences between the phones: One, the top half of the phone in the 598 patent is longer than the bottom half, and the two halves of the Yoshida phone are the same; Two, the phone of the 598 has circular-shaped buttons arranged in rows and columns in the top half, and the Yoshida phone has teardrop-shaped buttons in the bottom half, and not all are prearranged in rows and columns; And, lastly, the 598 has an oval-shaped speaker area, and the Yoshida has a shell-shaped speaker area.

Ruling:

The judgment of the district court for defendant was affirmed.

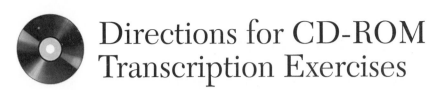

Directions for CD-ROM Transcription Exercises

In audio format are:

1. Terms for the unit with pronunciations from the thesaurus/dictionary feature.

2. Self-Test that appears in the book at mid-unit.°

3. Case that appears at the unit end.°

°speeds are 80 wpm/120 wpm for differing skill levels

CD-ROM icons appear where the three above are located within each unit.

Readers may practice transcription by listening to the CD-ROM where prompted by the icons in the book. However, for high success in testing your transcription skills, mastering all the terms and English skills in the unit is recommended before attempting the CD-ROM.

For Keyboard Transcriptionists: Listen to the CD-ROM audio file for this unit at 80 wpm or 120 wpm and transcribe from the dictation on your computer. Edit and proofread your work against the printed copy in the book.

For Reporting Writers: Listen to the CD-ROM audio file at 80 wpm or 120 wpm and take down the dictation on your writer. Either transcribe from your notes and proofread your work or edit and proofread your CAT (computer-aided transcription) transcript. Always check your work against the printed copy in the book.

Student CD-ROM
For additional materials,
please go to the CD in this book.

Online Companion™
For additional resources, please go to
http://www.paralegal.delmar.cengage.com

Area of Law
Labor and Employment

The **Mistakes** That Court Reporters Make and *How to Avoid* Them

The Mistake:

Laurie Lilly, a relatively new reporter, was driving to her morning deposition, when her car began to sputter and lose power. She managed to pull to the side of the road before it completely died. She called AAA and then her husband to talk to him about what exactly to do. They decided to have their car towed to their mechanic, who was just 20 minutes or so from where Laurie was. She rode with AAA to the mechanic, where her husband met her to take her home. When she got home, she called her agency to tell them what had happened and why she did not go to the deposition. Of course, it was too late. The attorney for whom she was to work that morning had already called the agency and was very irate that a reporter had not shown up.

How to Avoid It:

There are certainly going to be emergency situations that arise. Laurie's first call should have been to the agency to make them aware of the situation and give them an opportunity to get a replacement reporter. An option might even be to catch a cab to the job and worry about the car later. Whatever you do, it is not going to be okay to just call when the emergency has been resolved and apologize. Laurie's actions placed her agency in jeopardy with the attorney firm—something you never want to be responsible for.

Introduction

The very core of the American economy is its work force. Historically, employers and employees were free to bargain at will, setting up any sort of employment relationship that was desired. With the increase in factories at the start of the Industrial Revolution, the U.S. government could no longer maintain a laissez-faire attitude toward business.

The policy of leaving big businesses completely unregulated and workers unprotected led to labor strife. The need for government intervention became evident. Frequent complaints were made of dangerous working conditions, unsafe machinery, abuse of child labor, discrimination, long hours of work at unfair wages, and frequent on-the-job injuries. Laws at the state and federal levels were enacted to better control the workplace, making it safer for employees. Some of these laws include the Fair Labor Standards Act, workers' compensation acts, Occupational Safety and Health Act, Employee Retirement Income Security Act, Social Security Unemployment Compensation, the Equal Pay Act, the Americans with Disabilities Act, and the Civil Rights Act.

In 1935, the National Labor Relations Act was passed, giving employees the right to form and join unions. Now, individual workers had bargaining power with large corporations. The National Labor Relations Board is a federal agency that oversees unions and monitors labor practices by both unions and employers, the subjects of this area of law.

In the case ending this unit, mining dangers illustrate why workplace safety is a protected activity.

Unit Objectives

■ Work with a legal dictionary/thesaurus.

■ Learn about labor law.

■ Master the similarities and differences in definitions of key terms regarding labor law.

■ Master the spellings and pronunciations of legal terms in this unit.

■ Recognize the synonyms used in this unit.

■ Practice usage of terms, definitions, and synonyms for labor law.

■ Complete unit exercises in the forms of missing words, matching, multiple choice, true/false, synonyms, self-test, defining words, and also:

   ● Punctuation/capitalization
   ● Word pairs
   ● Transcription of terms, self-test, and case
   ● Proofreading

● Dictionary/Thesaurus

Note: All Dictionary/Thesaurus terms appear on the CD-ROM with audio pronunciations.

Term
[phonetic pronunciation]

---

affirmative action
[a.*fer*.me.tiv *ak*.shen]

1. Positive or constructive action rather than inaction or negative or punitive action. 2. When used in conjunction with "plan," "program," or "guidelines," a term applied to the obligation to remedy discrimination based on sex, race, color, creed, or age with respect to, for EXAMPLE, employment, union, membership, or college admission. *See also* Civil Rights Act.

---

agency shop
[ay.jen.see shop]

A collective bargaining agreement states that union membership is optional but that nonmembers must pay the union as much as members pay in dues. Agency shops are prohibited in states with right to work laws.

Americans with Disabilities Act (ADA)
[a.*mare*.i.kenz with dis.e.*bil*.i.tees akt]

A federal statute that prohibits discrimination against disabled persons in employment, public services, and public accommodation.

---

arbitration
[ar.bi.*tray*.shen]

A method of settling disputes by submitting a disagreement to a person (an arbitrator) or a group of individuals (an arbitration panel) for decision instead of going to court. If the parties are required to comply with the decision of the arbitrator, the process is called binding arbitration; if there is no such obligation, the arbitration is referred to as nonbinding arbitration. Compulsory arbitration is required by law, most notably in labor disputes.
• *n.* adjustment, compromise, mediation, determination ("compulsory arbitration is the name for arbitration required by law")

---

arbitration clause
[ar.bi.*tray*.shen kloz]

A clause in a contract providing for arbitration of controversies that arise out of performance of the contract.

---

arbitration panel
[ar.bi.*tray*.shen *pan*.el]

A number of arbitrators who hear and decide a case together.

---

arbitrator
[*ar*.bi.tray.ter]

A person who conducts an arbitration. Generally, the primary consideration in choosing an arbitrator is impartiality and familiarity with the type of matter in dispute.
• *n.* judge, umpire, mediator, intervenor, adjudicator

---

at will employment
[at will em.*ploy*.ment]

Termination of employment for any cause; may be initiated by employer or employee.

back pay
[bak pay]

Unpaid wages to which an employee is entitled.

back pay order
[bak pay *or*.der]

The order of a court, arbitrator, or administrative agency that employees be given their back pay. Such orders are most common in cases involving the reinstatement of employees who were improperly discharged.

boycott
[*boy*.kot]

A joining together in a refusal to do business with a company, unless it changes practices felt to be injurious to those who are joining together, or to some of them, in an attempt to bring about modification of the practice. EXAMPLE of practices that might be the subject of a boycott of a company's service or product: a manufacturer's policy of having most of its labor performed abroad.

certification (of bargaining agent)
[ser.ti.fi.*kay*.shen ov *bar*.gen.ing *ay*.jent]

A formal pronouncement by the National Labor Relations Board, or a similar state agency, that it has determined that a union seeking to represent an employer's employees represents a majority of those employees in an appropriate collective bargaining unit and is therefore their collective bargaining agent. *See also* representation election.

Civil Rights Act
[*sih*.vil rytz akt]

A term that may refer to any or all of the various statutes enacted by Congress relating to civil rights. The Civil Rights Act of 1964 assured access to places of public accommodation, public facilities, and education, without regard to religion, color, race, national origin, or sex; Title VII of that act prohibited discrimination in employment. The Civil Rights Act of 1991 provided for both compensatory damages and punitive damages for intentional discrimination or unlawful harassment in the workplace on the basis of sex, race, religion, or disability. Additionally, the Age Discrimination in Employment Act and the Americans with Disabilities Act are often classified as civil rights acts. States, as well as the federal government, have legislated extensively in the area of civil rights. *See also* Equal Employment Opportunity Commission.

closed shop
[klozed shop]

A place of employment in which all employees are required by a collective bargaining agreement to be members of the union in order to be employed. *Compare* agency shop.

collective bargaining
[ko.*lek*.tiv *bahr*.gen.ing]

The negotiation of terms and conditions of employment between a union, acting on behalf of employees, and an employer or an association of employers. *See also* collective bargaining agreement.

collective bargaining agent
[ko.*lek*.tiv *bahr*.gen.ing *ay*.jent]

A union that engages in collective bargaining on behalf of an employer's employees.

collective bargaining agreement
[ko.*lek*.tiv *bahr*.gen.ing a.*gree*.ment]

An agreement covering wages, hours, and working conditions, entered into between an employer and the union that is the collective bargaining agent for the employer's employees. *See also* collective bargaining.

collective bargaining contract [ko.*lek*.tiv *bahr*.gen.ing *kon*.trakt]	*See* collective bargaining agreement.
collective bargaining unit [ko.*lek*.tiv *bahr*.gen.ing *yoo*.nit]	An employee group permitted by law to be represented by a collective bargaining agent. EXAMPLES: all of an employer's maintenance employees, all of its drivers, or all employees in the finishing department.
company union [*kum*.pe.nee *yoo*.nyen]	A labor union whose total membership consists of the employees of a single company and is controlled by the company.
comparable worth [*kom*.per.ebl werth]	The concept that men and women are entitled to equal pay when their work requires equal skills or duties and is therefore of "comparable worth." Several states have adopted legislation putting this concept into practice in varying degrees. *See also* Equal Pay Act.
concerted activity [ken.*ser*.ted ak.*tiv*.i.tee]	In labor law, conduct engaged in by an employer's employees, a union, or others for the purpose of supporting collective bargaining demands. Concerted activity that constitutes an unfair labor practice (EXAMPLE: a secondary boycott) is prohibited by the National Labor Relations Act. *Compare* concerted protected activity.
concerted protected activity [ken.*ser*.ted pro.*tek*.ted ak.*tiv*.i.tee]	In labor law, conduct engaged in by two or more employees acting together for the purpose of influencing the terms and conditions of their employment, including but not limited to wages and hours. Such activity is protected by the National Labor Relations Act if it falls within the terms of that statute. EXAMPLES: joining a union; striking; picketing.
condition of employment [kon.*dish*.en ov em.*ploy*.ment]	A matter with respect to which the National Labor Relations Act requires an employer to bargain collectively. EXAMPLES: wages; hours; vacation pay; seniority. *See also* collective bargaining.
deferred compensation [de.*ferd* kom.pen.*say*.shen]	Compensation paid after the services are rendered (pension and payments made for profit sharing).
discharge [dis.*charj*]	1. To terminate an employee from employment. 2. To fire an employee. USAGE: "He was discharged from his job."
discrimination [dis.krim.in.*ay*.shen]	Violations of the Fourteenth Amendment's equal protection clause distinguishing between classes of people in voting, education, employment, and other areas of human activity.
dues [dooz]	Annual or other regular payments made by a member of a club, union, or association to retain membership.
employ [em.ploy]	To enter into a contract of employment; to hire.

employee
[em.*ploy*.ee]

A person who works for another for pay in a relationship that allows the other person to control the work and direct the manner in which it is done. The earlier legal term for employee was servant.
Note that statutory definitions of "employee" may differ, depending upon the purpose of the statute. For EXAMPLE, although the distinctions between the definitions of employee in the Social Security Act, the Fair Labor Standards Act, and the National Labor Relations Act may seem insignificant, they may, in any given instance, be critical.

employee assistance program
[em.*ploy*.ee e.*sis*.tense *proh*.gram]

An employer-sponsored program, often in conjunction with an insurance company or a health maintenance organization, that provides treatment referrals for employees impaired or disabled by chemical dependency or other problems requiring counseling services. It is often referred to by its abbreviation, EAP.

Employee Retirement Income Security Act
[em.*ploy*.ee re.*tire*.ment *in*.kum see.*kyoo*.re.tee akt]

Better known by its acronym ERISA; a federal statute that protects employee pensions by regulating pension plans maintained by private employers, the way in which such plans are funded, and their vesting requirements. ERISA has important tax implications for both employers and employees. *See also* vested pension.

employer
[em.*ploy*.er]

A person who hires another to work for her for pay in a relationship that allows her to control the work and direct the manner in which it is done. The earlier legal term for employer was master.

employers' liability acts
[em.*ploy*.erz ly.e.*bil*.i.tee aktz]

Now called workers' compensation acts. Employers' liability acts abolished or substantially restricted the defenses previously available to an employer (EXAMPLES: contributory negligence; assumption of risk) when an employee brought suit for an injury incurred on the job pursuant to the Federal Employees' Liability Act (FELA).

employment
[em.*ploy*.ment]

1. The relationship between an employee and an employer. 2. That which occupies a person's time.
• *n.* livelihood, service, business, trade, vocation, occupation, job, profession, work

employment at will
[em.*ploy*.ment at will]

A hiring for an indefinite period of time. In the absence of an agreement to the contrary, all employment is at will and either the employer or the employee may terminate it at any time.

Equal Employment Opportunity Commission
[ee.kwel em.ploy.ment op.er.tew.ni.tee kuh.mish.en]

A federal agency whose purpose is to prevent and remedy discrimination based on race, color, religion, national origin, age, or sex with respect to most aspects of employment, including hiring, firing, promotions, and wages. The commission, which is known as the EEOC, enforces many federal civil rights acts and antidiscrimination statutes.

Equal Pay Act
[*ee*.kwel pay akt]

A federal statute that requires men and women to be paid equally for the same work. *See also* comparable worth.

Fair Labor Standards Act
[fayr *lay*.ber *stan*.derdz akt]

A federal statute that establishes a maximum work week for certain employees, sets a minimum hourly wage, and imposes restrictions on child labor. The act covers employers in interstate commerce and other employers, including state and local government. Additionally, all states have statutes governing hours; most also have minimum wage requirements. *See also* wage and hour acts.

green card
[green kard]

A document that evidences an alien's status as a resident alien. It permits the alien to seek and gain employment within the United States.

grievance
[*gree*.venss]

1. A formal complaint filed by an employee or by an employees' union claiming that the employer has violated the collective bargaining agreement. 2. A similar complaint filed against a union by an employer.

hostile environment
[*hoss*.tel en.*vi*.ron.ment]

A situation in which offensive conduct is permitted to infect the workplace, making it difficult or impossible for an employee to work.

labor
[*ley*.ber]

1. In common usage, physical work, although the word refers with equal accuracy to work involving the application of professional or intellectual skills. 2. Work performed for a wage or salary, as opposed to work performed in order to realize a profit. 3. The body or group of persons who work for wages, as a class and as distinguished from management. *See also* labor dispute; unfair labor practice.
• *n.* work, occupation, undertaking, toil, enterprise, task, responsibility, energy, exertion, effort
• *v.* work, agonize, struggle, toil, slave, travail, strain

labor agreement
[*lay*.ber a.*gree*.ment]

See collective bargaining agreement.

labor contract
[*lay*.ber *kon*.trakt]

See collective bargaining agreement.

labor dispute
[*lay*.ber dis.*pyoot*]

A controversy between an employer and its employees or their collective bargaining agent concerning wages, hours, or other working conditions, or concerning union representation.

labor laws
[*lay*.ber lawz]

Federal and state statutes and administrative regulations that govern such matters as hours of work, minimum wages, unemployment insurance, safety, and collective bargaining. EXAMPLES: the National Labor Relations Act; the Fair Labor Standards Act; the Occupational Safety and Health Act.

labor organization
[*lay*.ber or.gan.i.*zay*.shen]

See labor union.

Labor Relations Act
[*lay*.ber re.*lay*.shenz akt]

See National Labor Relations Act.

labor relations acts [*lay*.ber re.*lay*.shenz aktz]	Federal and state statutes that regulate relations between management and labor. EXAMPLE: the National Labor Relations Act.
Labor Relations Board [*lay*.ber re.*lay*.shenz bord]	*See* National Labor Relations Act.
Labor Standards Act [*lay*.ber *stan*.derdz akt]	*See* Fair Labor Standards Act (FLSA).
labor union [*lay*.ber *yoo*.nyen]	An association of workers formed for the purpose of engaging in collective bargaining with employers on behalf of workers concerning wages, hours, and other terms and conditions of their employment. *See also* collective bargaining agent.
laborer [*lay*.ber.er]	A person who performs labor for compensation. • *n.* worker, employee, help, toiler
lockout [*lok*.out]	The closing of the workplace by the employer, or to withhold work, to enhance the employer's bargaining position in labor negotiations.
mediation [mee.dee.*ay*.shen]	The voluntary resolution of a dispute in a nonadversarial manner.
merit [*mehr*.it]	Worth; quality; value.
merit increase [*mehr*.it *in*.kreess]	In labor law, an increase in pay given in recognition of the quality of an employee's work, as opposed to a pay raise granted on the basis of length of service or seniority.
minimum wage [*min*.i.mum wayj]	*See* minimum wage laws.
minimum wage laws [*min*.i.mum wayj lawz]	State and federal statutes establishing a minimum rate of wages to be paid employees. The Fair Labor Standards Act is the federal minimum wage statute. *See also* wage and hour acts.
National Labor Relations Act [*nash*.en.el *lay*.ber re.*lay*.shenz akt]	Actually several Acts of Congress, including the Wagner Act and the Taft-Hartley Act, which, collectively, regulate relations between management and labor by, among other things, prohibiting certain activities (unfair labor practices) that unreasonably hamper employers in the conduct of their business or that interfere with the right of employees to be effectively represented by unions of their choice.
National Labor Relations Board (NLRB) [*nash*.en.el *lay*.ber re.*lay*.shenz bord]	A federal administrative agency created by the National Labor Relations Act for the purpose of enforcing the Act. Commonly referred to as the NLRB.

pension
[*pen*.shen]

1. A retirement benefit in the form of a periodic payment, usually monthly, made to a retired employee from a fund created by the employer's contributions, or by the joint contributions of the employer and employee, over the period the employee worked for the employer. *See also* pension plan. 2. With respect to a former government employee or a retired member of the military, a regular allowance paid in consideration of the prior service.
• *n.* benefits, annuity, compensation, Social Security, support, reward ("a vested pension")

Pension Benefit Guaranty Corporation
[*pen*.shen *ben*.e.fit gehr.en.tee kore.per.*ay*.shen]

A public corporation of the United States government, that, under certain circumstances and within certain limits, guarantees the payment of employer pension plans that terminate without sufficient assets to pay the promised benefits. *See also* Employee Retirement Income Security Act (ERISA).

pension fund
[*pen*.shen fund]

A fund from which a pension is paid.

pension plan
[*pen*.shen plan]

A plan through which an employer provides a pension for its employees' retirement. There are many types of pension plans. Some are funded solely by employer contributions; some are funded jointly by the employer and the employee. Most are regulated by the federal government under the Employee Retirement Insurance Security Act. All pension plans involve significant tax implications. Tax-deferred pension plans are also available to self-employed persons under certain circumstances.

picket
[*pik*.et]

n. A person who engages in picketing.
v. To engage in picketing.
• *v.* patrol, march, protest, rally ("we picketed the erring employer's plant")
• *n.* demonstrator, protester, striker, signholder, guard ("Mary was a picket in last week's strike")

picketing
[*pik*.e.ting]

1. In connection with a labor dispute, the presence of employees or others at an employer's place of business for the purpose of influencing other employees or prospective employees to refrain from working, or for the purpose of informing the public, customers, or suppliers of the dispute and inducing them not to do business with the employer. 2. Similar activity by any group of people at any location for the purpose of protesting anything.

polygraph
[*pol*.i.graf]

Commonly called a lie detector, a machine for recording impulses caused by changes in a person's blood pressure, pulse, respiration, and perspiration while under questioning. The results, which are interpreted to indicate the truth or falsity of the answers given, are not admissible as evidence in many states, and in others may be admitted only in limited circumstances for limited purposes. Federal law prohibits employers from administering polygraph tests to employees or applicants for employment except in very restricted circumstances.
• *n.* examination, inspection, lie detector machine

reasonable accommodation [*ree*.zen.ebl a.kom.o.*day*.shen]	Any change or adjustment to a job or work environment that permits a qualified applicant or employee with a disability to enjoy benefits and privileges of employment equal to those enjoyed by employees without disabilities.
reinstatement [ree.in.*state*.ment]	The act of restoring a person or thing to a position or condition from which she or it has been removed. EXAMPLES: rehiring an employee who has previously been fired; restoring coverage under an insurance policy that has lapsed for nonpayment. • *n.* restoration, rehiring, readmittance
representation election [rep.re.zen.*tay*.shen e.*lek*.shez]	An election conducted by the National Labor Relations Board for the purpose of determining whether a majority of an employer's employees wish to be represented by the union or unions named on the ballot for the purpose of collective bargaining. *See also* certification of bargaining agent.
secondary boycott [*sek*.en.dare.ee *boy*.kott]	A boycott applied by a union to third persons to cause them, against their will, not to patronize or otherwise deal with a company with whom the union has a dispute. A secondary boycott is one form of secondary activity.
self-employment [self-em.*ploy*.ment]	Working for oneself.
self-employment tax [self-em.*ploy*.ment takz]	The Social Security tax paid by people who are self-employed.
seniority [see.nyor.i.tee]	1. In labor law, the principle that length of employment determines the order of layoffs, recall to work, promotions, and frequently, rate of pay. 2. The status or state of being senior. • *n.* tenure, longevity, longer service, station, rank, standing
sexual harassment [*sek*.shoo.el ha.*rass*.ment]	A form of sex discrimination. Sexual harassment includes unwanted sexual attention from a supervisor. It also includes the toleration by an employer of sexual coercion or "hassling" in the workplace. *See also* Civil Rights Act; Equal Employment Opportunity Commission (EEOC).
strike [strike]	*n.* A concerted stoppage of work by a group of employees for the purpose of attempting to compel their employer to comply with a demand or demands they have made. *v.* To act together with other employees in refusing to work; to engage in a strike. *See also* strike (*noun*). • *v.* mediate, mutiny, resist, revolt, slow down ("to strike from work") • *n.* boycott, revolt, walkout, dispute, boycott
strike breaker [strike *brake*.er]	A person who takes the job of an employee who is on strike. • *n.* scab
Title VII [*ty*.tel *sev*.en]	The section of the Civil Rights Act of 1964 dealing with the prohibition of discrimination in employment.

unemployment [un.em.*ploy*.ment]	A term usually applied to the state or status of being involuntarily unemployed.
unemployment compensation [un.em.*ploy*.ment kom.pen.*say*.shen]	Short for unemployment compensation benefits or unemployment insurance.
unemployment compensation acts [un.em.*ploy*.ment kom.pen.*say*.shen aktz]	State statutes that provide for the payment of benefits to persons who are unemployed through no fault of their own. An employee who, for EXAMPLE, has voluntarily left her employment, or has been discharged for willful misconduct, is ineligible to received unemployment compensation benefits. Unemployment compensation is a form of social insurance.
unemployment compensation benefits [un.em.*ploy*.ment kom.pen.*say*.shen *ben*.e.fits]	*See* unemployment compensation acts.
unemployment insurance [un.em.*ploy*.ment in.*shoor*.ense]	*See* unemployment compensation acts.
unfair labor practice [un.*fare lay*.ber *prak*.tiss]	An action by either a union or an employer in violation of the National Labor Relations Act or similar state statutes. EXAMPLES: firing an employee because she joins a union; secondary picketing.
unfair labor practice strike [un.*fare lay*.ber *prak*.tiss strike]	A strike for the purpose of protesting or of inducing an employer to refrain from unfair labor practices.
vested pension [*vest*.ed *pen*.shen]	A pension that cannot be taken away, regardless of what the employer or the employee does. Note, however, that a pension may vest either fully or partially. *See also* Employee Retirement Income Security Act (ERISA).
wage [wayj]	Compensation paid to employees, whether by the hour or by some other period of time, or by the job or piece. Wages include all remuneration paid for personal services, including commissions, bonuses, and gratuities, and, under the Fair Labor Standards Act, include board and lodging as well. In one sense, the term "wage" includes salary; in other uses, the term "salary" is reserved for the remuneration paid to executives, professionals, or supervisors, usually on a weekly, biweekly, monthly, or semimonthly basis. *See also* minimum wage laws. • *n.* allowance, compensation, emolument, payment, salary, stipend ("daily wage") • *v.* carry out, conduct, do, fulfill, make, prosecute, pursue ("to wage a war")
wage and hour acts [wayj and ower aktz]	Federal and state statutes establishing the minimum wage that may be paid to employees and the number of hours they may work. The Fair Labor Standards Act is the federal wage and hour act. *See also* minimum wage laws.

wage and hour laws
[wayj and ower lawz]

See wage and hour acts.

wildcat strike
[*wild*.kat strike]

A strike that is not authorized by the union representing the strikers.

worker
[*wer*.ker]

1. A person who does work. 2. A person who is employed.
• *n.* artisan, breadwinner, employee, laborer, toiler, trader

workers' compensation
[*wer*.kerz kom.pen.*say*.shen]

Short for workers' compensation acts or workers' compensation insurance.

workers' compensation acts
[*wer*.kerz kom.pen.*say*.shen aktz]

State statutes that provide for the payment of compensation to employees injured in their employment or, in case of death, to their dependents. Benefits are paid under such acts whether or not the employer was negligent; payment is made in accordance with predetermined schedules based generally upon the loss or impairment of earning capacity. Workers' compensation laws eliminate defenses such as assumption of risk, contributory negligence and fellow servant. Workers' compensation systems are funded through employer contributions to a common fund, through commercially purchased insurance, or both. Occupational diseases are compensable under these acts as well pursuant to Federal Employee's Liability Act (FELA).

workers' compensation insurance
[*wer*.kerz kom.pen.*say*.shen
in.*shoor*.ense]

See workers' compensation acts.

Missing Words

Fill in the blanks below.

1. Unpaid wages to which an employee is entitled are known as _____.

2. The _____ is a federal statute that requires men and women to be paid equally for the same work.

3. The FICA deduction appears on an employee's pay stub. A(n) _____ is required by federal statute to deduct money from an employee's salary to fund Social Security and Medicare.

4. A(n) _____ is a labor union whose total membership consists of employees of a single company and is controlled by the company.

5. A federal statute that protects employee pensions is known as _____.

6. A concerted stoppage of work by a group of employees for the purpose of compelling their employer to comply with labor demands is _____.

7. A(n) _____ is the compensation paid to employees, either hourly or by another time period, by the job, or by the piece.

8. Benefits payable according to state statutes to employees injured in their employment is _____.

9. The presence of employees or others at an employer's place of business to influence employees to refrain from working is known as _____.

10. A strike that is not authorized by the union representing the strikers is known as a(n) _____.

11. _____ is the negotiation of terms and conditions of employment between a union and an employer.

12. Benefits paid to employees who are unemployed through no fault of their own are known as _____.

13. When an employer fires an employee for joining a union, this is a(n) _____ in violation of the National Labor Relations Act.

14. A(n) _____ is a place of employment where all employees are required to be members of a union.

15. When a state has _____, the termination of employment may be for any reason and be initiated by employer or employee.

16. A(n) _____ is a joining together in a refusal to do business with a company unless it changes its practices.

Matching

Match the letter of the definition to the term below.

_____ 17. Affirmative action

_____ 18. Certification

_____ 19. Green card

_____ 20. Polygraph

_____ 21. EEOC

_____ 22. Arbitration

_____ 23. Discharge

_____ 24. Dues

_____ 25. Strike breaker

_____ 26. OSHA

_____ 27. Wage and hour laws

_____ 28. Comparable work

_____ 29. Reinstatement

_____ 30. Sexual harassment

_____ 31. Title VII

_____ 32. ADA

_____ 33. Lockout

A. Method of settling disputes by submitting an agreement to a person or group of individuals instead of to a court

B. Regular payments made to a union

C. To fire an employee

D. Person who takes the job of an employee who is on strike

E. Obligation to remedy discrimination based on sex, race, color, creed, or age

F. Federal agency that prevents and remedies discrimination

G. Act of Congress to eliminate dangerous provisions in the workplace

H. Document that establishes an alien's status as a resident alien and permits him to work in the United States

I. Commonly called a lie detector

J. NLRB determines that a union seeking to represent employees represents a majority of the employees in an appropriate collective bargaining unit

K. Form of sex discrimination

L. Equal pay for equal skills or duties

M. Rehire an employee who was fired

N. Wage and hour acts

O. Prohibits discrimination against disabled persons

P. The closing of the workplace by the employer

Q. Prohibits discrimination in employment per Civil Rights Act

Multiple Choice

Select the best choice.

_____ 34. In the absence of an agreement to the contrary that all employment is at will, this means:
   a. only the employer may terminate employment
   b. only the employee may terminate employment
   c. neither the employee nor employer may terminate employment
   d. either the employee or employer may terminate employment at any time

_____ 35. Collective bargaining is when:
   a. an employee tries to negotiate for numerous benefits in his employment contract
   b. several employers offer work to one employee
   c. a union negotiates a contract with an employer on behalf of employees
   d. an employee directly negotiates an employment contract with an employer

_____ 36. In a closed shop situation all employees:
   a. must belong to a union
   b. are barred from joining a union
   c. can only join a union after one year of employment
   d. none of the above

_____ 37. When a supervisor asks an employee to rub his back, this is an example of:
   a. sex discrimination
   b. religious discrimination
   c. age discrimination
   d. sexual harassment

_____ 38. A secondary boycott is an action:
   a. applied by a union against the employer
   b. applied by the union to the third persons
   c. resulting in a factory slowdown
   d. by teachers

_____ 39. A concerted stoppage of work by a group of employees for the purpose of attempting to compel their employer to comply with their demands is known as:
   a. product picketing
   b. hot cargo contract
   c. union solicitation
   d. a strike

_____ 40. Under the doctrine of comparable worth, men and women are entitled to equal pay:
   a. if they are the same age
   b. if they start working on the same day
   c. when their work requires equal skills or duties
   d. all of the above

_____ 41. Under an agency shop agreement, union membership is:
   a. optional
   b. required
   c. illegal
   d. none of the above

_____ 42. An employer may hire an employee on the basis of gender when:
   a. clients voice a preference
   b. when a business is dominated by one gender
   c. an employer is a sole proprietor of a business
   d. if sexual characteristics are essential to performance of the job

_____ **43.** Firing an employee for joining a union is an example of:
  a. an unfair labor practice
  b. a strike
  c. a boycott
  d. an employer lockout

_____ **44.** Concerted activity is conducted by employees for the purpose of:
  a. supporting collective bargaining demands
  b. opposing collective bargaining demands
  c. closing a shop
  d. employee discharge

True/False

Mark the following T or F.

_____ **45.** Conduct engaged in by an employer's employees for the purpose of supporting collective bargaining demands is known as a concerted activity.

_____ **46.** A method of settling disputes by submitting a disagreement to a person or a group of individuals rather than resorting to the courts is known as arbitration.

_____ **47.** Right to work laws prohibit clauses in employment contracts that compel employees to join a union.

_____ **48.** When a labor union's total membership consists of employees of a single company and is controlled by the company, this is known as a hiring hall.

_____ **49.** A strike to bring about changes in wages, hours, or other conditions of employment is known as a wildcat strike.

_____ **50.** When employees are injured on the job, benefits are paid to the employee whether or not the employer was negligent. This is known as workers' compensation.

_____ **51.** The National Labor Relations Act prohibits employment discrimination against qualified individuals with disabilities in regard to job application procedures, hiring, compensation, training, promotion, and termination.

_____ **52.** The National Labor Relations Board is a labor organization composed of skilled craft workers.

_____ **53.** An employee assistance program (EAP) is an employer-sponsored program that provides treatment referrals for employees with problems.

_____ **54.** A wildcat strike is defined as a strike to bring about changes in wages, hours, or other conditions of employment.

_____ **55.** Reasonable accommodation is a method of testing food safety.

_____ **56.** Hostile work environment is exemplified by posters of nude women in an office of female and male employees.

Synonyms

Select the correct synonym in parentheses for each numbered item.

57. VESTED
    (fixed, variable, undermined)

58. MERIT
    (friendship, feelings, worth)

59. DUES
    (collection, payment, account)

60. PICKET
    (protest, agree, discharge)

61. SCAB
    (strike starter, strike breaker, illegal striker)

62. BOYCOTT
    (join, avoid, crossover worker)

63. REINSTATEMENT
    (rehire, fire, polling)

64. CERTIFICATION
    (lottery, debate, election)

65. SENIORITY
    (status, wealth, education)

66. CIVIL RIGHT
    (constitutional right, bargaining right, protected activity)

67. GRIEVANCE
    (shutdown, relocation, complaint)

68. ARBITRATION
    (interrogation, compromise, discharge)

69. AFFIRMATIVE ACTION
(positive action, inaction, punitive action)

70. DISCHARGE
(fire, hire, sell)

71. EMPLOYER
(servant, master, laborer)

72. WAGE
(discharge, compensation, merit)

73. MEDIATION
(resolution, labor dispute, grievance)

74. WORKERS' COMPENSATION ACTS
(federal law, state statutes, local ordinances)

Self-Test

Place the number of the correct term in the appropriate space.

75. Conditions of employment	**83.** Employer
76. Labor unions	**84.** Strike
77. Collective bargaining	**85.** Collective bargaining agreement
78. At will	**86.** Employer's
79. Company union	**87.** Picketing
80. Boycotting	**88.** Arbitration
81. Closed shop	**89.** Arbitrator
82. Employees	

In the United States, employers and _____ may terminate employment at any time. This is called _____ employment. When workers join together for the purposes of engaging in _____ with employers on behalf of workers concerning wages, hours, and other terms and _____, these associations of workers are known as _____.

There are all different types of unions. A(n) _____ is a labor union whose total membership consists of employees of a single company. In contrast, a(n) _____ is a place of employment where all employees are required by a(n) _____ to be members of a union in order to be employed. Sometimes, even though employees have formed a union, this is no guarantee that employers will comply with all their demands.

A(n) _____ is a stoppage of work by a group of employees to compel an employer to comply with their demands. When there is a labor dispute, employees might be present at the place of business of a(n) _____ to inform the public and induce them not to do business with the _____; this is called _____. Should the general public be unhappy with a business or its practices, persons might join together and refuse to do business with a company unless it changes practices felt to be injurious; this is known as _____.

In the event an employer cannot resolve a dispute with its employees, a(n) _____ might be hired to settle the dispute by conducting a(n) _____. If the parties are required to follow the decision of the arbitrator, this is called binding arbitration.

Defining Words

Complete the definition.

90. Minimum wage _____

91. Polygraph _____

92. Boycott _____

93. Pension _____

94. Self-employment _____

95. Unemployment compensation _____

96. Merit _____

_____

97. Seniority _____

_____

98. Strike breaker _____

_____

99. Strike _____

_____

100. Wage and hour acts _____

_____

101. Sexual harassment _____

_____

102. National Labor Relations Board _____

_____

103. Americans with Disabilities Act _____

_____

Punctuation/Capitalization

Punctuating numbers.

There are differences of opinion over the transcription of numbers; however, the over ten/under ten rule is observed by most reporters.

Rule 1: General numbers from one to ten are written out in words.

There were five people injured in the crash.
I observed no more than three people going in and out of the house.
The board comprised seven members.

Rule 2: General numbers 11 and over are put into figures.

I know of 12 people that were affected by it.
The firm sent 24 to the convention.
I felt that 50 was the limit.

Rule 3: Numbers that measure "like" amounts are transcribed the same way. This is called the consistency rule, and it overrides the two rules above. Note that the numbers must measure the same kinds of things. In the sentence "There are 15 people in three offices," there is no rule to make the numbers match as they are not describing like things. In considering the form for one number that is under ten and one that is over, if it is a consideration of writing the number out or putting it in figures, it usually goes into figures.

My understanding is that there were 14 people in one van and 7 in the other.
One committee had 6 members and the other 12.
We put 9 in one batch and 22 in the other.

Rule 4: All dates are in figures.
We decided to meet and confer on the 7th.
She mentioned that May 5 was the actual date.
I believe we paid it on September 2.

Rule 5: All numbers that represent times are in figures and have the ciphers added for those on the hour.
We left the hotel at 5:00 in the morning.
She showed up a little after 11:00.
I had a 4:15 appointment with the new dentist.

It is not the intention here to cover the entire gambit of how to transcribe all numbers. There are many other rules concerning numbers that are not covered here.

Directions: Correct any number forms.

1. I saw 12 movies in seven days when I was sick.

2. She was assigned to a group of seven; he was in a group of 11.

3. They said they arrived at five on the seventh of June.

4. We sent at least 8 letters and 12 e-mails to them.

5. The meeting began at 8 sharp with 9 men and 11 women in attendance.

Word Pairs

brake/break

brake = stop, restrain, slow, halt. This form is both the noun and the verb. The principal parts of the verb are *brake, braked, braked.*

We need to put the brakes on this operation.
I believe it was discovered that the brakes were faulty.
Did he brake to a complete stop at the time?

break = rest, shatter, crack, destroy. This form is both the noun and the verb. The principal parts of the verb are *break, broke, broken.*

We will take a five-minute break at 2:30.
I was praying that the vase did not break during shipment.
They tried hard not to break anything that was fragile.

final/finale

final = last, ending, concluding.

It is the final notice a person receives.
He had the task of choosing her final resting place.
It was the final exam that he did not pass.

finale = final event in a series, closing number.

He did not appear in the finale.
It was the finale that kind of left me flat.
She did not stay for the finale as she had an appointment.

loose/lose/loss/lost

loose = relaxed, not tight, imprecise, slack. This word is an adjective.

The prisoner was loose in the woods.
The loose screw in the engine was a contributory factor.
The office was fairly loose with enforcement of the rules.

lose = fail to win, unable to find something or control something. This form is a verb.

Will he lose his position with the firm?
Did your company lose the competition?
He did lose control of his emotions on a regular basis.

loss = death, reduction, someone or something lost. This form is a noun.

Her death is a huge loss for everyone who knew her.
The monetary loss for the company was monumental.
We looked at the profit and loss statement for the firm.

lost = someone or something unable to be found.

She was lost when we installed the new computer program.
We had lost so much money by then.
I was lost in thought when he entered the room.

meat/meet/mete

meat = edible animal part, material for thought, core.

She does not eat red meat.
He gets to the meat of the matter.
I love the meat of the coconut.

meet = convene, get together.

The attorneys agreed to meet and confer.
I will meet you on Friday at 4:00.
He refused to meet to talk to her.

mete = dole out, give out in measured amounts.

The leader meted out the meager supplies.
She tends to mete out the rewards of the job.
He metes out compliments to a very few.

right/rite/write/wright

right = several meanings.

- politically conservative, as in *right wing*.
- correct, as in *have right answers*.
- direction, as in *turned right at the corner*.
- healthy, as in *doesn't feel right*.
- proper, as in *doing it the right way*.

He took a left instead of a right.
She is part of the right-wing conservative movement.
I do not think it is right that he has done that.

rite = ceremony, ritual, sacrament.

He was administered last rites.
It is simply part of the rite of being a teenager.
She believes strongly in the rite of marriage.

write = put to paper, mark, inscribe.

Did you write down the amount you were expecting?
She did not write even a postcard the entire time she was away.
He intends to write the great American novel.

wright = an old word that means someone who constructs things, usually from wood. The word is no longer acceptable as a stand-alone word but does occur in words such as *playwright* (a person who builds plays) and *shipwright* (a person who builds ships).

role/roll

role = part in a production, function, responsibility.

He intends to take a major role in this project.
Do you know what the role of the administrator consists of?
Hers is a lesser role in the production.

roll = several meanings.

- list, as in *the voter rolls*.
- bread, as in *dinner roll*.
- turn over, as in *car rolled several times*.

- move, as in *roll along.*
- elapse, as in *time rolls by.*
- get started, as in *the project is rolling.*
- sound, as in *a drum roll.*
- throw dice, as in *a roll of seven.*

She felt he was trying to roll over everyone with his strong-arm tactics.
He always rolled in a few minutes late.
I discovered that my name was not on the roll.

Directions: Choose the correct form of the word.

1. I think the problem is that the fastener was loose/lose/loss.

2. It was a real loss/lost for everyone involved.

3. He roled/rolled in to meet/meat/mete with the directors.

4. I didn't really like the final/finale to the musical.

5. He needs to put the brakes/breaks on his use of drugs.

6. Is it possible that we can take a break/brake in the next few minutes?

7. Did he take part in the right/rite/write that honored her memory?

8. I hate to see her loose/lose her benefits over this.

9. We are going to have to meat/meet/mete out the meager supplies.

10. Did he play a role/roll in the demise of the company?

11. He would not agree to a meet/meat/mete and confer with opposing counsel.

12. It was reported that the loose/lose/loss/lost is going to be in the millions.

13. He was to the right/rite/write of center on most issues.

14. After the brake/break in the proceedings, I had trouble concentrating.

15. It is time to get to the meat/meet/mete of the matter.

16. He just continues to role/roll along in that position.

17. She is an up-and-coming playright/playwrite/playwright.

18. I think it will probably be too lose/loose/loss/lost for him to fix.

19. The brake/break is just above the knee at the end of the femur.

20. This is the final/finale warning you will receive about this matter.

Is It One Word or Two? An Apostrophe? A Hyphen?

Rule 1: When the word *self* is a prefix, it is always hyphenated to the word it is combining with. Sometimes the word *self* is the root of the word. When that is the case, it forms one word with its prefix or suffix.

His self-confidence served him well as he negotiated for the job.
It was thought that he was involved with a group that practiced self-flagellation.
That is a self-serving comment.

Directions: Correct any hyphenation errors.

1. He made selfincriminating comments during the proceedings.

2. I believe that he left the selfsame day.

3. She was lacking in self-esteem.

4. He said the statue of the human was intended to be self-imitating.

5. The only thing she was interested in was self enrichment.

Proofreading

Directions: Make necessary corrections, based on the material presented in the unit. If the sentence has no errors, write the word *correct* after the sentence.

1. His selfrighteous attitude was evident to the 8 of us on the roles of the organization. _____

2. On the tenth of June, he began to meet out the punishment for the offenses. _____

3. He roled into town to help write the final for the screen version of the musical. _____

4. She braked the car to a stop just before it would have rolled over the hill. _____

5. The right on August third was very solemn and self reflective. _____

6. He finally got to the meet of the matter with his teammates after the lost in the championship game by 2 points. _____

7. As we entered the zoo, we discovered that a tiger was lose and had to be caught. _____

8. We left a little before 8 but didn't mete with them until the afternoon. _____

9. We were loss after we made a wrong right-hand turn. _____

10. There were 15 when we started, and we needed to loose 7 along the way. _____

An Adaptation from a Labor and Employment Law Case

Facts:

Pierre Rock and Stone is a small mining company owned by Peter Pierre. Bonsall, an employee, started working for the company in March. Six months later he decided to meet with a government official and file a confidential safety complaint with the Mine Safety Health Administration, MSHA. On November 17 and 18, the MSHA investigators came to the company to investigate the complaint. The investigators gave Pierre a copy of the complaint with Bonsall's name deleted. Pierre asked who filed it but then said he knew who filed it and would see that the complainant lost his job. When Pierre saw Bonsall, he handed him the complaint and said he believed he had had a role in filing it. The inspectors warned Pierre that he had no right to fire someone for complaining and that he could be charged with discrimination for doing this. After the investigation, the investigators issued 15 safety citations against the company. On November 30 Pierre told Bonsall to look for another job. Thereafter, Bonsall was repeatedly told that he needed to take a break from the job and that there was no work for him. On December 6 Pierre told Bonsall to turn in his uniform and pick up his final check the next day. Later that month Pierre told the investigators that Bonsall had quit.

Procedural History:

This is a petition for review of a final order of the Federal Mine Safety and Health Review Commission finding that the company discriminated against Barry Bonsall by discharging him for engaging in a protected activity, filing a safety complaint.

Issue:

Was Bonsall fired for poor performance, or was this just a pretext, the real reason being because he had complained of workplace safety issues?

Rationale:

Substantial evidence supports the ALJ's findings of pretext and discrimination. Pierre said he would fire the complainant, and Pierre believed the complainant to be Bonsall. Additionally, there was no documented evidence that Bonsall had ever been a poor performer or that any disciplinary action had even been taken against him or that Bonsall had said he quit.

Ruling:

The Commission's order was affirmed.

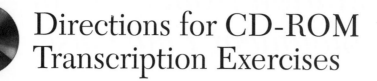

Directions for CD-ROM Transcription Exercises

In audio format are:

1. Terms for the unit with pronunciations from the thesaurus/dictionary feature.

2. Self-Test that appears in the book at mid-unit.*

3. Case that appears at the unit end.*

*speeds are 80 wpm/120 wpm for differing skill levels

CD-ROM icons appear where the three above are located within each unit.

Readers may practice transcription by listening to the CD-ROM where prompted by the icons in the book. However, for high success in testing your transcription skills, mastering all the terms and English skills in the unit is recommended before attempting the CD-ROM.

For Keyboard Transcriptionists: Listen to the CD-ROM audio file for this unit at 80 wpm or 120 wpm and transcribe from the dictation on your computer. Edit and proofread your work against the printed copy in the book.

For Reporting Writers: Listen to the CD-ROM audio file at 80 wpm or 120 wpm and take down the dictation on your writer. Either transcribe from your notes and proofread your work or edit and proofread your CAT (computer-aided transcription) transcript. Always check your work against the printed copy in the book.

Student CD-ROM
For additional materials,
please go to the CD in this book.

Online Companion™
For additional resources, please go to
http://www.paralegal.delmar.cengage.com

Area of Law

Legal Ethics

The **Mistakes** That Court Reporters Make and *How to Avoid* Them

The Mistake:

Howard Stephanopoulos was a reporter in court, but since he did not yet have a permanent assignment, he floated to cover for illness and vacations. On Thursday afternoon he was sent to cover for a reporter who had gone home ill. The trial was wrapping up, and Howard took the end of the closing argument of the prosecution with no problem. When the defense counsel began his closing argument, Howard could not believe his ears. The argument seemed very flawed and senseless to Howard; and as he listened, he grimaced, shook his head, raised his eyebrows, and just generally showed his total lack of belief in what the defense counsel was saying. Because Howard sat directly in front of the witness box, he was directly facing the jury. The judge noticed Howard's antics and called a recess in the proceedings to speak with Howard.

How to Avoid It:

No matter what you think about what you are hearing, you must not react in any way that gives anyone the idea that you agree or disagree with what is being said. It is always the role of the reporter to be the disinterested party, that is, not showing any sign of allegiance to one side or the other.

Introduction

The attorney-client relationship is a very special one where a high degree of trust is involved. Clients might be placing their life savings or even their very lives in a lawyer's hands. It is important that the client completely trust the attorney and feel free to share confidences so that the attorney might adequately represent the client's interests. The couple in the case at the end of the unit could not trust their "attorney."

The American Bar Association (ABA), an organization representing attorneys, has formulated model rules to guide attorneys in their professional conduct. The ABA is interested in protecting the image portrayed by attorneys so that the practice of law continues to be a respected and trusted profession. Each state has adopted portions of the ABA's model rules. Some states follow the ABA's Model Code of Professional Responsibility, while other states have adopted the more recent Model Rules of Professional Conduct, or a combination of the two. The ultimate sanction for lawyers is disbarment.

Unit Objectives

■ Work with a legal dictionary/thesaurus.

■ Learn about legal ethics and professional responsibility.

■ Master the similarities and differences in key terms concerning ethics.

■ Master the pronunciations and spellings of the terms in this unit.

■ Recognize the synonyms used for terminology in this unit.

■ Practice usage of terms, definitions, and synonyms for legal ethics.

■ Complete unit exercises in the forms of missing words, matching, multiple choice, true/false, synonyms, self-test, defining words, and also:

- Punctuation/capitalization
- Word pairs
- Transcription of terms, self-test, and case
- Proofreading

💿 **Dictionary/Thesaurus**

Note: All Dictionary/Thesaurus terms appear on the CD-ROM with audio pronunciations.

Term
[phonetic pronunciation]

---

abuse of process
[a.byoos ov *pross*.ess]

The use of legal process in a manner not contemplated by the law to achieve a purpose not intended by the law. EXAMPLE: causing an ex-husband to be arrested for nonsupport of his child in order to secure his agreement with respect to custody. *Compare* malicious use of process.

American Association for Paralegal Education (AAPE)
[a.*mare*.i.ken a.so.see.*ay*.shen for pa.re.*lee*.gal ed.yoo.*kay*.shen]

A national organization of paralegal teachers and educational institutions, which provides technical assistance and supports research in the paralegal field, promotes standards for paralegal instruction, and cooperates with the American Bar Association and others in developing an approval process for paralegal education.

American Bar Association
[a.*mare*.i.ken bar a.so.see.*ay*.shen]

The country's largest voluntary professional association of attorneys, commonly referred to as the ABA. Its purposes include enhancing professionalism and advancing the administration of justice.

---

attorney
[a.*tern*.ee]

An attorney at law or an attorney in fact. Unless otherwise indicated, generally means attorney at law.
• *n.* lawyer, counselor, advocate, legal advisor, barrister, counsel, legal eagle

---

attorney at law
[a.*tern*.ee at law]

A person who is licensed to practice law; a lawyer.

---

attorney fees
[a.*tern*.ee feez]

Compensation to which an attorney is entitled for her services. This is usually a matter of contract between the attorney and the client. *See also* retainer. However, where authorized by statute, a court may enter an order in a lawsuit directing the payment of a party's attorney fees by the opposite party. In some types of cases, attorney fees are set by a statute that also requires that the fees be paid by the defendant if the plaintiff or claimant prevails in the action. EXAMPLE: under many workers' compensation acts, the claimant's attorney is entitled to a specified percentage of the claimant's award. *See also* contingent fee.

---

attorney in fact
[a.*tern*.ee in fakt]

An agent or representative authorized by his principal, by virtue of a power of attorney, to act for her in certain matters.

---

attorney of record
[a.*tern*.ee ov *rek*.erd]

The attorney who has made an appearance on behalf of a party to a lawsuit and is in charge of that party's interests in the action.

attorney-client privilege
[a.tern.ee-klie.ent priv.i.lej]

Nothing a client tells his attorney in connection with his case can be disclosed by the attorney, or anyone employed by him or his firm, without the client's permission. *See also* privileged; privileged communication.

attorney's lien
[a.*tern*.eez leen]

A lien that an attorney has upon money or property of her client (including papers and documents) for compensation due her from the client for professional services rendered. It is a possessory lien.

attorney's work product
[a.*tern*.eez werk pro.dukt]

See work product; work product rule.

canon
[*kan*.on]

A law or rule.
• *n.* law, rule, statute, act, code, order, standard, criterion, measure, ethic, norm, test

censure
[*sen*.shoor]

Severe criticism; condemnation.
• *n.* disapproval, rebuke, reproach, reprimand, criticism, condemnation, denunciation, disapproval, castigation
• *v.* condemn, criticize, scold, reprimand, admonish, reprove, decry, assail, chastise, denigrate

certified legal assistant (CLA)
[*ser*.ti.fide *lee*.gul uh.sis.tent]

A legal assistant who has been certified by the National Association of Legal Assistants after passing NALA's examination.

client
[*klie*.ent]

1. A person who employs an attorney. 2. A person who discusses with an attorney the possibility of hiring the attorney.
• *n.* customer, consumer, patron
• *ant.* seller

Code of Judicial Conduct
[kohd ov joo.*dish*.el *kon*.dukt]

A set of principles and ethical standards promulgated by the American Bar Association, and subsequently adopted by a majority of states, which establish ethical standards, both personal and professional, for judges. *See also* ethics.

commingling of funds
[ko.*ming*.ling ov fundz]

The act of an agent, broker, attorney, or trustee in mingling his own funds with those of his client, customer, or beneficiary. Such conduct is unethical and often illegal as well.

competent
[*kom*.pe.tent]

1. Having legal capacity. 2. Capable; qualified. 3. Sufficient; acceptable.

confidential communication
[kon.fi.*den*.shel
kum.yoo.ni.*kay*.shen]

See privileged communication.

confidential relationship [kon.fi.*den*.shel re.*lay*.shen.ship]	A fiduciary relationship, and any informal relationship between parties in which one of them is duty-bound to act with the utmost good faith for the benefit of the other. Although the terms "confidential relationship" and "fiduciary relationship" are often used interchangeably, there is a distinction between them. "Fiduciary relationship" is a term correctly applicable to legal relationships (EXAMPLES: guardian and ward; trustee and beneficiary; attorney and client), while "confidential relationship" includes these as well as every other relationship in which one's ability to place confidence is important, such as, for EXAMPLE, business transactions in which one party relies upon the superior knowledge of the other.
confidentiality [kon.fi.den.shee.*al*.i.tee]	*See* privileged; privileged communication.
conflict of interest [*kon*.flikt ov *in*.trest]	1. The existence of a variance between the interests of the parties in a fiduciary relationship. EXAMPLE: the conduct of an attorney who acts both for her client and for another person whose interests conflict with those of her client. 2. The condition of a public official or public employee whose personal or financial interests are at variance or appear to be at variance with his public responsibility. EXAMPLE: ownership, by the secretary of defense, of stock in a company that contracts with the Department of Defense for the manufacture of military equipment.
contingent fee [kon.*tin*.jint fee]	A fee for legal services, calculated on the basis of an agreed-upon percentage of the amount of money recovered for the client by his attorney. *See also* attorney fees; fee.
disbarment [dis.*bahr*.ment]	The revocation of an attorney's right to practice law. *See also* Rules of Professional Conduct. • *n.* banishment, debarment, discharge, dismissal, ejection, eviction, removal
disciplinary rules [*dis*.i.plin.eh.ree rulz]	Rules and procedures for sanctioning attorneys guilty of professional misconduct. All jurisdictions have adopted such rules. Sanctions may include disbarment, suspension, probation, or reprimand. *See also* Rules of Professional Conduct.
disqualified judge [dis.kwal.i.fide juj]	A judge who is disqualified to act in a particular case because of personal interest in the subject matter of the suit or because of his preconceived mental attitude. *See also* recusation.
escrow [*es*.kroh]	A written instrument (EXAMPLES: stock, bonds, a deed), money, or other property deposited by the grantor with a third party (the escrow holder) until the performance of a condition or the happening of a certain event, upon the occurrence of which the property is to be delivered to the grantee. • *adj.* separate, designated, specified ("keep the money in an escrow account")

escrow account
[es.kroh e.*kount*]

A bank account in the name of the depositor and a second person, the deposited funds being returnable to the depositor or paid to a third person upon the happening of a specified event (EXAMPLE: money for the payment of property taxes that a mortgagor pays into the escrow account of the mortgage company or bank).

escrow contract
[es.kroh *kon*.trakt]

A contract that describes the rights of the parties to an escrow.

escrow holder
[es.kroh *hole*.der]

The third party to an escrow.

ethics
[*eth*.iks]

1. A code of moral principles and standards of behavior for people in professions such as law or medicine (EXAMPLES: the Code of Judicial Conduct; the Rules of Professional Conduct). 2. A body of moral principles generally.
• *n.* principles, values, morals, mores, criteria, canon, rules

fee
[fee]

1. A charge made for the services of a professional person, such as a lawyer or physician. *See also* attorney fees; contingent fee. 2. A statutory charge for the services of a public officer. EXAMPLE: court fees.

fiduciary duty
[fi.*doo*.shee.air.ee *dew*.tee]

The duty to act loyally and honestly with respect to the interests of another; the duty the law imposes upon a fiduciary.

frivolous pleading
[friv.e.les *plee*.ding]

A pleading that is good in form but false in fact and not pleaded in good faith.

frivolous suit
[friv.e.les soot]

A lawsuit brought with no intention of determining an actual controversy. EXAMPLE: an action initiated for purposes of harassment.

grievance
[*gree*.venss]

1. Any complaint about a wrong or an injustice. 2. Formal complaint filed by a client who is unhappy with an attorney's work.
• *n.* complaint, protest, allegation, accusation, objection

IOLTA
[eye.*ol*.ta]

Acronym for Interest on Lawyers' Trust Accounts. In states with IOLTA programs, lawyers who hold funds belonging to clients deposit such money into a common fund, the interest on which is used for charitable, law-related purposes such as legal services to the poor. Some states' IOLTA programs are voluntary, some are mandatory.

Juris Doctor
[*joor*.is *dok*.ter]

The primary degree given by most law schools. It is commonly expressed in its abbreviated form, JD or J.D.

legal assistant
[*lee*.gl e.sis.tant]

One who, although not an attorney, performs many of the functions of an attorney under the supervision of an attorney. *See also* paralegal.
• *n.* paralegal, lawyer's assistant

loyalty
[*loy*.el.tee]

Adherence to law or to the government; faithfulness to a person or to a principle.
• *n.* allegiance, fealty, devotion, bond, faith, support ("he has shown great loyalty to his country")

malicious prosecution
[ma.lish.us pross.e.*kyoo*.shen]

A criminal prosecution or civil suit commenced maliciously and without probable cause. After the termination of such a prosecution or suit in the defendant's favor, the defendant has the right to bring an action against the original plaintiff for the tort of "malicious prosecution."

malicious use of process
[ma.lish.us use ov *pross*.ess]

The use of process for a purpose for which it was intended, but out of personal malice or some other unjustifiable motive (EXAMPLE: to extort money) and without probable cause. It is, in effect, a form of malicious prosecution.

meritorious defense
[mehr.i.toh.ree.us de.*fense*]

A defense that goes to the merits of the case; a defense warranting a hearing, although it may not be a perfect defense or a defense assured of succeeding.

National Association of Legal Assistants (NALA)
[*nash*.en.el a.so.see.*ay*.shen ov *leeg*.el a.*sis*.tents]

A national organization of legal assistants and paralegals whose purpose is to enhance professionalism and the interests of those in the profession, as well as to advance the administration of justice generally. Among its other undertakings, NALA has established a "Code of Professional Responsibility" for paralegals and legal assistants and provides professional certifications, continuing education, and assistance in job placement. A person who receives certification through NALA is entitled to so indicate by the use of "CLA" (Certified Legal Assistant) after his or her name.

National Association of Legal Secretaries (NALS)
[*nash*.en.el a.so.see.*ay*.shen ov *leeg*.el *sek*.re.tare.eez]

A national organization of legal secretaries whose purpose is continuing legal education and professionalism. Membership in NALS provides publications, seminars and workshops, and other educational tools. NALS also grants professional legal secretary certification to qualified applicants.

National Federation of Paralegal Associations (NFPA)
[*nash*.en.el fed.e.*ray*.shen ov pehr.e.*leeg*.el a.so.see.*ay*.shenz]

An association of paralegal and legal assistant organizations nationwide whose purpose is to enhance professionalism and the interests of those in the profession, as well as to advance the administration of justice. Among its other undertakings, NFPA has established the "Affirmation of Responsibility," a code of professional conduct for paralegals and legal assistants, and provides continuing education and assistance in job placement.

paralegal
[*pehr*.e.leeg.el]

A person who, although not an attorney, performs many of the functions of an attorney under an attorney's supervision. The American Bar Association defines a paralegal as a "person, qualified through education, training, or work experience, who is employed or retained by a lawyer, law office, governmental agency, or other entity in a capacity or function which involves the performance, under the ultimate direction and supervision of an attorney, of specifically designated substantive legal work, which work, for the most part, requires a sufficient knowledge of legal concepts that, absent such assistant, the attorney would perform the task."
• *n.* legal assistant, paraprofessional, aide, lay advocate, legal technician, lawyer's assistant

privileged
[*priv*.i.lejd]

Entitled to a privilege; possessing a privilege.
• *adj.* protected, excused, immune, exempt, elite ("a privileged class"); confidential, secret, exceptional, top-secret ("privileged records")

privileged communication
[*priv*.i.lejd kem.yoon.i.*kay*.shen]

A communication between persons in a confidential relationship or other privileged relationship (EXAMPLES: husband and wife; physician and patient; attorney and client). The contents of such communications may not be testified to in court unless the person possessing the privilege waives it.

privileged relationship
[*priv*.i.lejd re.*lay*.shen.ship]

A relationship of a type such that communications between the parties to the relationship are protected by law against disclosure (i.e., are "privileged") unless the party whom the law protects waives the right to protection. *See also* privileged communication.

pro bono publico
[pro *bone*.oh *poob*.li.koh]

(Latin) Means "for the public good." An attorney who represents an indigent client free of charge is said to be representing her client pro bono.

pro hac vice
[pro hak *vy*.see]

(Latin) Meaning "for this occasion," an attorney who is not a member of the bar of a particular state may be admitted for one particular case.

pro se
[pro say]

(Latin) Means "for one's self." Refers to appearing on one's own behalf in either a civil action or a criminal prosecution, rather than being represented by an attorney.

probation
[pro.*bay*.shen]

A sentence that allows a person convicted of a crime to continue to live and work in the community while being supervised by a probation officer, instead of being sent to prison.

professional corporation
[pro.*fesh*.en.el kore.per.*ay*.shen]

A corporation formed for the purpose of practicing a profession (EXAMPLES: law; medicine; psychotherapy; dentistry) and to secure certain tax advantages. The members of a professional corporation remain personally liable for professional misconduct. Professional corporations often identify themselves by the abbreviation PC. Thus, for EXAMPLE, a professional corporation composed of attorneys Jessica Smith and Sam Smith might be named "Smith and Smith, Esqs., PC."

professional ethics
[pro.*fesh*.en.el *eth*.iks]

See ethics. *See also* Code of Judicial Conduct; Rules of Professional Conduct.

professional legal secretary
[pro.*fesh*.en.el *leeg*.el *sek*.re.teh.ree]

A person who has met the requirements for certification by the National Association of Legal Secretaries.

professional misconduct
[pro.*fesh*.en.el mis.*kon*.dukt]

1. Malpractice. 2. In the case of an attorney, violating the disciplinary rules of a jurisdiction in which he practices. *See also* Rules of Professional Conduct.

recusation [rek.yoo.*zay*.shun]	The act of challenging a judge or a juror for prejudice or bias. *See also* disqualified judge.
reprimand [*rep*.ri.mand]	A severe and solemn rebuke or censure for disobedience or wrongdoing. • *n.* admonishment, castigation, censure, reprehension, chiding, lecture, warning, reproval • *v.* chastise, rebuke, reprove, admonish, castigate, deprecate
retainer [re.*tane*.er]	1. The act of hiring an attorney. 2. A preliminary fee paid to an attorney at the time she is retained, in order to secure her services. 3. In certain circumstances, the right of a person (EXAMPLE: an executor) who is rightfully in possession of funds belonging to a person who owes him money (EXAMPLE: money belonging to the decedent's estate that he is administering) to retain an amount sufficient to satisfy the obligation. • *n.* fee, contract, engagement fee, compensation, remuneration
retaining lien [re.*tane*.ing leen]	An attorney's lien.
Rules of Professional Conduct [rulz ov pro.*fesh*.en.el *kon*.dukt]	Rules promulgated by the American Bar Association that detail an attorney's ethical obligations to her client, the courts, and opposing counsel. With variations, these rules have been adopted by most states and incorporated into their statutory codes of ethics. *See also* ethics.
sanction [*sank*.shen]	*n.* 1. Action taken by a tribunal, for EXAMPLE, a court or an administrative board or commission, by way of enforcing its judgment, decision, or order. EXAMPLES of sanctions include the imposition of a fine or a penalty, the seizure of property, and the revocation or suspension of a license. *v.* 1. To punish; to penalize. • *v.* punish, ban, boycott ("the bar sanctioned the erring attorney") • *n.* ban, boycott, decree, injunction, penalty, sentence, punishment ("unimposed sanctions")
solicitation [so.liss.i.*tay*.shen]	1. The act of an attorney in seeking clients. 2. Inviting a business transaction. • *n.* petition, requisition
special counsel [*spesh*.el *koun*.sel]	An attorney, employed by the attorney general of the United States or a state, to assist in a particular case as a prosecutor.
suspend [sus.*pend*]	1. To temporarily remove from office or from employment. USAGE: "The mayor has the right to suspend the chief of police for good cause." 2. To temporarily withdraw a privilege. USAGE: "If I am arrested for speeding once more, the state will suspend my driver's license." *See also* suspended. • *v.* withdraw, revoke ("suspend his license")
suspended [sus.*pen*.ded]	Temporarily inactive or temporarily not effective.

unauthorized practice of law
[un.aw.ther.ized prak.tiss ov law]

Engaging in the practice of law without the license required by law.

work product
[werk *prod*.ukt]

Material prepared by counsel in preparing for the trial of a case.
EXAMPLES: notes; memoranda; sketches.

work product rule
[werk *prod*.ukt rool]

The rule that an attorney's work product is not subject to discovery.
This includes the materials produced by persons working for the attorney.

Missing Words

Fill in the blanks below.

1. A person who employs an attorney is known as a(n) _____.

2. Until a real estate closing is completed, all documents and funds are held in _____ by the attorneys for the parties.

3. _____ can use the abbreviation CLA after their names.

4. An association of paralegal and legal assistant organizations nationwide, known by the abbreviation NFPA, is called _____.

5. A sanction against an unethical attorney can be the revocation or _____ of the attorney's license to practice.

6. When an attorney represents both the plaintiff and the defendant in an action this is considered a(n) _____ and is generally prohibited.

7. A(n) _____ is a preliminary fee paid to an attorney to secure his services.

8. When an attorney invites a business transaction this is called _____.

9. The country's largest voluntary professional association is the _____.

10. Anything clients tell their attorney in confidence regarding their case is considered a(n) _____ that cannot be introduced at the time of trial.

11. Where defendants choose to represent themselves in a legal matter, rather than being represented by an attorney, this is called _____.

12. Material such as pleading prepared by an attorney in preparation for the trial is called _____ and is not subject to discovery by the opposing party.

13. When an attorney mixes a client's settlement funds with the general bank account of the law office this is known as the _____.

14. _____ is a code of moral principles.

15. When an attorney represents a client free of charge this is called _____.

16. A(n) _____ is a law or rule.

17. When an attorney's license is revoked this is known as a(n) _____ by the court.

18. The duty to act loyally and honestly with respect to another's interest is _____ .

Matching

Match the letter of the definition to the term below.

_____ 19. Retainer

_____ 20. Disbarment

_____ 21. Professional misconduct

_____ 22. Rules of Professional Conduct

_____ 23. IOLTA

_____ 24. Certified legal assistant

_____ 25. Grievance

_____ 26. Privileged relationship

_____ 27. Censure

_____ 28. Licensing

_____ 29. Contingent fee

_____ 30. Attorney at law

_____ 31. Confidentiality

_____ 32. Malicious prosecution

_____ 33. Probation

A. Preliminary fee paid to attorney

B. Severe criticism

C. Act or process of granting a license

D. Relationship of a type such that communications between the parties are protected

E. Complaint by client regarding attorney's work

F. Fund for depositing client monies

G. Revocation of an attorney's right to practice law

H. Rules made by ABA that detail an attorney's ethical obligation to his client, court, and opposing counsel

I. Legal assistant certified by NALA

J. Malpractice

K. Fee based upon amount of money collected for client

L. Privileged communication

M. A suit commenced without probable cause

N. Person who is licensed to practice law

O. A process that allows an attorney to be admitted to the bar for one particular case

____ **34.** Special counsel

____ **35.** Pro hac vice

P. Assists in the prosecution of a particular case at the request of the attorney general

Q. A sentence that allows a person convicted of a crime not to go to prison

Multiple Choice

Select the best choice.

____ **36.** Professional misconduct occurs when:
   a. the attorney is rude to clients
   b. the attorney practices medicine without a license
   c. the attorney fails to exercise the degree of care and skill usually used by members of the legal profession
   d. none of the above

____ **37.** When an attorney represents a client free of charge this is called:
   a. pro se
   b. pro bono publico
   c. pro choice
   d. pro temporare

____ **38.** An attorney must deposit client funds in:
   a. a trust account
   b. a safe deposit box
   c. the case file
   d. a Chinese wall

____ **39.** When an attorney represents both the husband and wife with differing interests in a divorce proceeding this is known as a:
   a. privileged document
   b. confidential relationship
   c. malicious use of process
   d. conflict of interest

____ **40.** The country's largest professional association of attorneys is known as the:
   a. Federal Bar Association
   b. National Bar Association
   c. United States Bar Association
   d. American Bar Association

____ **41.** The preliminary fee paid to an attorney is known as:
   a. a retainer
   b. a censure
   c. work product
   d. escrow

____ **42.** A flat fee is where:
   a. an attorney works without compensation
   b. an attorney collects a fee only if successful in the matter
   c. an attorney is paid a set amount for all services rendered
   d. an attorney bills the client a specific amount for each hour of work completed

____ **43.** A grievance is:
   a. a client's psychological problems
   b. the loss of a family member
   c. a constitutional question of law
   d. a complaint made by a client against his attorneys

____ **44.** The primary degree given by most law schools:
   a. is a Juris Doctor
   b. is an IOLTA
   c. is the same as certification
   d. can never be revoked

_____ **45.** The attorney-client privilege:
   a. prohibits a client from being truthful with his attorney
   b. requires that anything said to any attorney must be revealed in a court of law
   c. provides that only judges may hear such privileged communications
   d. prevents disclosure of a client's private conversations with his attorney

_____ **46.** The set of principles and ethical standards set by the American Bar Association and adopted by the majority of states to establish ethical standards for judges is known as:
   a. the Constitution
   b. privileged communication
   c. Code of Judicial Conduct
   d. work product rule

True/False

Mark the following T or F.

_____ **47.** A confidential communication is the same as a privileged communication.

_____ **48.** The National Association of Legal Assistants provides certification for paralegals and legal assistants.

_____ **49.** A reprimand is the act of challenging a judge or juror for prejudice or bias.

_____ **50.** Engaging in the practice of law without the license required by law is the unauthorized practice of law.

_____ **51.** When one appears on one's own behalf in a legal matter this is known as pro se.

_____ **52.** A censure is severe criticism.

_____ **53.** A paralegal is a person who, although not an attorney, performs many of the functions of an attorney, under an attorney's supervision.

_____ **54.** A privileged communication is a communication between persons in a confidential relationship, such as attorney and client.

_____ **55.** The Code of Judicial Conduct is a set of principles and ethical standards for judges.

_____ **56.** The country's largest voluntary professional association of attorneys is the American Bar Association.

_____ **57.** An attorney's notes are part of her work product and protected from disclosure.

Synonyms

Select the correct synonym in parentheses for each numbered item.

---

58. COMMINGLING OF FUNDS
    (mixing, separating, controlling)

59. CONTINGENT FEE
    (flat fee, hourly fee, percentage fee)

60. PRIVILEGED DOCUMENT
    (public, protected, useless)

61. MERITORIOUS DEFENSE
    (worthy, worthless, false)

62. CONFIDENTIAL RELATIONSHIP
    (fiduciary relationship, estranged relationship, proud relationship)

63. SANCTION
    (award, penalty, copy)

64. GRIEVANCE
    (complaint, praise, theory)

65. CENSURE
    (commend, review, criticize)

66. FRIVOLOUS PLEADING
    (truthful, clear, false)

67. COMPETENT
    (qualified, loyal, malicious)

68. CLIENT
    (canon, customer, expert)

Self-Test ◉

Place the number of the correct term in the appropriate space.

---

69. Conflict of interest

70. Attorneys

71. Disciplinary rules

72. Disbarment

73. Grievance

74. American Bar Association

75. Disqualified

76. Code of Judicial Conduct

77. Suspension

78. Frivolous

79. Solicitation

80. Commingling of funds

81. Rules of Professional Conduct

82. Recusation

The _____, the code of conduct for lawyers that governs their moral and professional duties, is an issue of great public concern. The media has been calling attention to a variety of cases where _____ have failed to follow specific _____, resulting in reprimands, sanctions, _____ of license, or even permanent _____ from the practice of law.

When an attorney actively seeks business this is known as _____ and may be prohibited where direct client contact is made. Another practice that is frowned upon is when a client wishes to leave money or other property to an attorney; that attorney should not prepare the will under which the attorney would benefit. This situation is known as a(n) _____. The attorney cannot zealously represent the client's interests where the attorney may stand to benefit from the matter. It is prohibited as well for attorneys to bring lawsuits for the purpose of harassment, where there is no true actual controversy between parties. These _____ suits are unethical and should be avoided.

A client could have a(n) _____ where his attorney fails to put client funds into a trust account, resulting in a(n) _____ with those of the attorney.

The largest professional association of attorneys, known as the _____, has enacted a(n) _____ establishing standards for judges. A judge might be _____ to act in a case because of personal interest. When a judge is challenged for bias this is called _____.

Defining Words

Complete the definition.

83. Client _____

_____

84. Competent _____

_____

85. Loyalty _____

_____

86. Ethics _____

_____

87. Confidential relationship _____

_____

88. Sanction _____

_____

89. Grievance _____

_____

90. Escrow _____

_____

91. Disbarment _____

_____

92. Suspend _____

_____

93. Code of Judicial Conduct _____

_____

94. Work product _____

_____

95. Certified legal assistant _____

_____

96. National Association of Legal Assistants _____

_____

97. Work product rule _____

_____

98. Probation _____

_____

99. Special counsel _____

_____

100. Pro hac vice _____

_____

Punctuation/Capitalization

Run-on sentences.

_____

Definition: A *run-on sentence* is defined as two sentences that have no conjunction between them and have been put together with no punctuation or with a comma instead of a period or semicolon. These are run-on sentences that have been created by bad punctuation.

He was walking alone on the walkway, that's what I heard.
There were 15 of them that I know of, that's all.
He turned left the car began to skid.

Rule 1: Two sentences that have no conjunction between them must be separated by a period, not a comma. It is never okay to create a run-on sentence by using bad punctuation.

He was walking alone on the walkway. That's what I heard.
There were 15 of them that I know of. That's all.
He turned left. The car began to skid.

Rule 2: When two sentences have no conjunction between them and the grammar is very parallel, the period is best replaced by a semicolon.

He works at Sears; I work at Penney's.
He made $40,000 on the project; she made $60,000 on the project.
My mother is French; my father is Italian.

Directions: Make necessary punctuation changes.

1. I called later in the day, no one answered.

2. She was the head of human resources he was head of finance.

3. He said he was from the southern part of the state, I believed him.

4. The helicopter had been serviced the week prior to the accident. That's in the report.

5. She left at 5:00; he left at 6:00.

Word Pairs

cannon/canon/canyon

cannon = field gun.

They fired the cannon in salute.
Cannons were used in bygone wars.
He has a nonworking cannon in his backyard.

canon = law, rule, statute, act, code, criterion, ethic.

This is not according to the canon, as I understand it.
It is assumed to be a canon of investing.
He follows the canon of the Catholic Church.

canyon = gorge, valley, chasm.

It was felt that the coyote came up from the canyon.
The accident happened on a winding canyon road.
The fire burned up the wall of the canyon.

censer/censor/censure/sensor

censer = vessel in which incense in burned.

It is thought that the fire came from the censer on the table.
She had censers in various rooms in the house.
He objected to the censer she had.

censor = remove objectionable material. This form is both a noun and a verb.

He tried to censor his own remarks so as not to be offensive.
The censors removed the violent scenes from the children's movie.
She resisted all attempts to censor her work.

censure = severe criticism, condemnation.

It is thought that he should be censured on the floor of the Senate.
The censure proceedings seemed a little harsh.
It is my feeling that the censure should take place immediately.

sensor = detecting device, antenna.

The sensors were not effective for that test.
One of the sensors had pulled out.
The sensors picked up every sound in the room.

consul/council/counsel

consul = ambassador, diplomat. The location is called the *consulate*.

We went to the office of the consul from Germany.
A worker from the consulate helped me with the passport.
The consul from Japan is a personal friend of ours.

council = governing body.

He is a member of the city council.
The council will take up the subject later this evening.
I think this is beyond the bailiwick of the council.

counsel = attorney, aid, advise, advocate. The plural is also *counsel*.

I spoke with counsel regarding the papers.
The argument between counsel was not resolved.
He counseled her about her financial situation.

emigrant/immigrant

emigrant = person who leaves from a country. This word is often used with the word *from*.
The verb form is *emigrate*.

We emigrated from the United States in the 1960s.
She is an emigrant from France.
They wanted to emigrate from China but were not allowed to.

immigrant = person who comes into a country. This word is often used with the word *to*.
The verb form is *immigrate*.

He immigrated into this country as a child.
The immigrants settled in an area just outside of town.
She is an immigrant of just two years and has learned English.

ethic/ethnic

ethic = code of moral principles. This is often used in the plural.

This is a matter of the ethics that he espouses.
I believe that it is an ethics consideration.
I do not agree with his ethics as he practices them.

ethnic = racial, cultural.

It was an ethnic minority that was taking the heat.
She wore ethnic clothing to church.
It is a part of the ethnic origins of my people.

Directions: Choose the correct word.

1. He was consul/council/counsel for the defense.

2. Did you think it was an ethics/ethnics question?

3. Once he emigrated/immigrated from his country, he never went back.

4. He followed the cannon/canon/canyon of ancient law.

5. Before the article goes out, it has to be run by the censer/censor/censure/sensor.

6. It was the opinion of most that he should be censered/censored/censured/sensored on the floor of the House.

7. I believe that it is part of his ethic/ethnic origins.

8. He was elected to the consul/council/counsel for the small city.

9. The emigrants/immigrants to this country were treated well.

10. He set up censers/censors/censures/sensors all around his apartment for security.

11. They emigrated/immigrated to this area of the country several years ago.

12. The ethics/ethnics committee will meet to discuss this issue.

13. Our house sat on the edge of the canon/cannon/canyon where the fire started.

14. The old cannon/canon/canyon is from the era of the Civil War.

15. The consul/council/counsel from Turkey was involved in the accident.

16. She tried to consul/council/counsel the young couple before they married.

17. The censer/censor/censure/sensor was criticized for his overly zealous approach.

18. It is thought that the car went over the edge of the cannon/canon/canyon.

19. The consul/council/counsel needs to vote to restore the law.

20. He emigrated/immigrated from his country when the civil war broke out.

Is It One Word or Two? An Apostrophe? A Hyphen?

sometimes/some times

sometimes = occasionally. This form is an adverb.

I sometimes saw him outside his house.
Sometimes we failed to act accordingly.
He is sometimes ill when we need him at work.

some times = certain occasions. This is the word *some* as an adjective that modifies the noun *times*.

There were some times I couldn't stand the pain.
I know he had some times that he didn't like the treatment he got.
There are some times that I ignore him.

sometime/some time

sometime = occasional ("here one day, gone the next"). This is the meaning when the word *sometime* is acting as an adjective right directly in front of a noun.

He was a sometime friend.
She is a sometime advocate of the environment.
I am a sometime enthusiast of his works.

sometime = indefinite point in time. This form is an adverb.

I will be there sometime in the morning.
She promised it to us sometime early in January.
I always wondered whether he would call me sometime.

some time = indefinite period of time. This is the word *some* used as an adjective to modify the noun *time*. With this meaning, often the word *some* can be omitted, and the sentence will make sense.

I will have some time tomorrow afternoon.
We spent some time in an attempt to help her with the forms.
There is some time set aside for that during the weekend.

Some time has to be two words when it is the object of the preposition and when it is used with the words *ago* and *back*.

I haven't seen her in some time.
Some time back, he called me late in the evening and talked for some time.
She saw him some time ago.

Directions: Choose the correct form of the words.

1. I saw him for sometime later that month.

2. She had an appointment sometime next week.

3. I have sometime to discuss it next week.

4. Some time ago there was an audit of the books.

5. I have spent sometime on this.

Proofreading

Directions: Make necessary corrections, based on the material presented in the unit. If the sentence has no errors, write the word *correct* after the sentence.

1. It was sometime in February that he legally emigrated into this country.   _____

2. For sometime he feared censer on the floor of the Senate.   _____

3. I saw counsel for the plaintiff before the trial started, we spoke briefly.   _____

4. Sometimes we hike into the canyon, he goes with us.   _____

5. The office of consul for Austria is handling the tragedy.   _____

6. Sometime back, he spoke of his belief in the cannon of the church.   _____

7. I intend to meet with counsel for the defense at sometime in the future.   _____

8. He is an emigrant from his native France, she is an immigrant from her native Spain.   _____

9. As far as council are concerned, it is a matter of the ethnics of the participants in the case.   _____

10. I attended the counsel meeting in the city hall she was not there.   _____

An Adaptation from an Ethics Case

Facts:

Lola Arizaga, a paralegal, formed a corporate entity called Access, Inc., to provide legal services to people with immigration issues, who were trying to enter the country. Rafael Moya, Esq., worked as an attorney for the company and did "piecemeal" legal work for the company at the rate of $200 for each item of work. Nadia Petrova and Kareem Kuzetzka, a husband and wife, traveling on tourist visas, sought assistance in obtaining further legal status. The wife was an accomplished gymnast, and the husband had suffered persecution and torture in his native land. It was Arizaga who counseled the couple to apply for visas based on the wife's skills as a gymnast rather than seeking political asylum because the husband had been persecuted. The couple's application for an extension was denied, and their visas expired. Thereafter, the couple consulted with an immigration attorney in California, who told them their time to apply for asylum had expired.

Procedural History:

The couple later brought an action and was granted asylum. Normally the time limit would have been one year, but based on the "ineffective representative of counsel" exception, they were allowed to bring the action.

Issue:

Did attorney Moya provide competent representation to the couple concerning their immigration concerns? Was Moya involved in acts of fraud or misrepresentation?

Rationale:

The referee found that the couple was harmed because Moya never informed them of the status of their claim or that their lawful status would lapse. In fact, he didn't even have a file on them. He never met with the couple. He had no notes concerning them. Instead of the paralegal being employed by and working for the attorney, it was the other way around.

Ruling:

Rafael Moya was suspended from the practice of law for one year. The suspension became effective 30 days after the filing of this opinion so that he had time to close out his practice and protect the interests of existing clients. Moya was ordered to pay restitution to the couple in the sum of $2,400, and judgment was entered for the Florida Bar Association for the costs of this action in the sum of $2,618.10.

Directions for CD-ROM Transcription Exercises

In audio format are:

1. Terms for the unit with pronunciations from the thesaurus/dictionary feature.

2. Self-Test that appears in the book at mid-unit.*

3. Case that appears at the unit end.*

*speeds are 80 wpm/120 wpm for differing skill levels

CD-ROM icons appear where the three above are located within each unit.

Readers may practice transcription by listening to the CD-ROM where prompted by the icons in the book. However, for high success in testing your transcription skills, mastering all the terms and English skills in the unit is recommended before attempting the CD-ROM.

For Keyboard Transcriptionists: Listen to the CD-ROM audio file for this unit at 80 wpm or 120 wpm and transcribe from the dictation on your computer. Edit and proofread your work against the printed copy in the book.

For Reporting Writers: Listen to the CD-ROM audio file at 80 wpm or 120 wpm and take down the dictation on your writer. Either transcribe from your notes and proofread your work or edit and proofread your CAT (computer-aided transcription) transcript. Always check your work against the printed copy in the book.

Student CD-ROM
For additional materials,
please go to the CD in this book.

Online Companion™
For additional resources, please go to
http://www.paralegal.delmar.cengage.com

Area of Law

Real Property and Landlord/Tenant

The **Mistakes** That Court Reporters Make and *How to Avoid* Them

The Mistake:

Gena Hasbro was running late. A single mom, she had trouble getting the kids out of the house that morning and left late for her 9:00 A.M. deposition and, to make matters worse, hit bumper-to-bumper traffic on her way. She arrived at the deposition at 9:10. As luck would have it, the attorneys and the witness were all sitting there, ready to go. She hurriedly set up her equipment with everyone watching her every move. At 9:20 she was settled in to write. Later in the day, her agency called and said that the attorney had called to complain about her tardiness and had asked that she never be sent back.

How to Avoid It:

This is a "whatever it takes" situation. There is just no excuse for being late. If there is a chance that you are not going to be able to be on time, do not agree to take the job. Murphy's Law will have it that, on the day that you are late, everyone else will be on time! You know what it takes to get yourself out of the house and to the job. You must honor that time span and be on time to the job.

Introduction

The law treats property as either personal or real. Real property is land or whatever is permanently attached to it. For instance, houses, barns, and wells are attached to the land while automobiles are not. Personal property is defined as anything not attached to the land, such as an automobile, chair, or even a tree that has been chopped down.

Rules governing the ownership of property compose the law of real property. Everyone owns property in different ways. Some own it alone while others own property jointly with others, perhaps family members.

A person might not enjoy the right of ownership at all, just the right to possess property that belongs to others. This arrangement is descriptive of a landlord/tenant relationship where one rents a house, apartment, or condominium from another for a period of time at a set amount of money, the terms of which are usually written in a lease, such as in the case at the end of the unit.

Other issues in property law include the searching of title to property, financing, mortgages, and transfers, as well as the manner in which people hold title to property. All are discussed in this unit.

Unit Objectives

- Work with a dictionary/thesaurus.
- Learn about real property and landlord/tenant law.
- Master the similarities and differences in definitions of key terms.
- Master the pronunciations and spellings of legal terms in this unit.
- Practice usage of terms, definitions, and synonyms for terms used in landlord/tenant law.
- Complete unit exercises in the forms of missing words, matching, multiple choice, true/false, synonyms, self-test, defining words, and also:
  - Punctuation/capitalization
  - Word pairs
  - Transcription of terms, self-test, and case
  - Proofreading

Dictionary/Thesaurus

Note: All Dictionary/Thesaurus terms appear on the CD-ROM with audio pronunciations.

Term [phonetic pronunciation]	
abstract of title [*ab*.strakt ov *ty*.tel]	A short account of the state of the title to real estate, reflecting all past ownership and any interests or rights, such as a mortgage or other liens, which any person might currently have with respect to the property. An abstract of title is necessary to verify title before purchasing real property. *See also* chain of title; search.
adverse possession [*ad*.verse po.*zesh*.en]	The act of occupying real property in an open, continuous, and notorious manner, under a claim of right, hostile to the interests of the true owner for a period of years. *See also* tacking.
broker [*broh*.ker]	A person whose business is to bring buyer and seller together; an agent who, for a commission, negotiates on behalf of his principal in connection with entering into contracts or buying and selling any kind of property. A broker does not generally take possession of the property with respect to which he deals. • *n.* agent, middleman, proxy, representative, emissary, mediator, intermediary
chain of title [chayn ov *ty*.tel]	The succession of transactions through which title to a given piece of land was passed from person to person from its origins to the present day. *See also* abstract of title; search.
color of title [*kull*.er ov *ty*.tel]	That which gives the appearance of title, but is not title in fact; that which, on its face, appears to pass title but fails to do so. EXAMPLE: a deed to land executed by a person who does not own the land.
condominium [kon.de.*min*.ee.um]	A multi-unit dwelling, each of whose residents owns her individual apartment absolutely while holding a tenancy in common in the areas of the building and grounds used by all the residents. *Compare* cooperative apartment house. • *n.* home, multi-unit dwelling, separate ownership
contract for sale of land [con.trakt for sale ov land]	A contract in which one party agrees to sell and the other to purchase real estate. *Note* that a contract for the sale of land is not a deed, but merely an agreement to transfer title.
convey [kon.*vay*]	1. To transfer title to property from one person to another by deed, bill of sale, or other conveyance. 2. To transfer, to transmit.

conveyance [kon.*vay*.ense]	1. The transferring of title to real property from one person to another. 2. Any document that creates a lien on real property or a debt or duty arising out of real estate. EXAMPLES: a lease; a mortgage; an assignment. 3. Any transfer of title to either real property or personal property.
conveyancing [kon.*vay*.ense.ing]	The act of transferring title to or creating a lien on real estate by deed, mortgage, or other instrument.
cooperative apartment house [koh.*op*.er.a.tive a.*part*.ment hows]	A multi-unit dwelling in which each tenant has an interest in the corporation or other entity that owns the building as well as a lease entitling her to occupy a particular apartment within the building. *Compare* condominium.
co-ownership [koh-*ohn*.er.ship]	Ownership of property by more than one person. *See also* joint tenancy; tenancy in common.
covenant [*kov*.e.nent]	*n.* In a deed, a promise to do or not to do a particular thing, or an assurance that a particular fact or circumstance exists or does not exist. *See also*, for EXAMPLE, covenant for quiet enjoyment; covenant appurtenant. *v.* To contract; to pledge; to make a binding promise. • *n.* agreement, promise, pledge, vow, bond, compact, commitment ("covenant not to sue")
covenant appurtenant [*kov*.e.nent a.*per*.te.nent]	*See* covenant running with the land.
covenant for quiet enjoyment [*kov*.e.nent for *kwy*.et en.*joy*.ment]	A covenant that title is good and that therefore the grantee will be undisturbed in her possession and use of the property.
covenant running with the land [*kov*.e.nent *run*.ing with the land]	A covenant that passes with the land when the land is conveyed. Such a covenant imposes upon the next purchaser, and all subsequent purchasers, both the liability for performance and the right to demand performance.
deed [deed]	*n.* 1. Document by which real property, or an interest in real property, is conveyed from one person to another. 2. An act or action; something done or completed. *v.* To transfer or convey by deed. • *v.* transfer, convey, grant • *n.* instrument, release, assignment, conveyance, contact ("warranty deed"); achievement, action, accomplishment, performance ("good deed")
deed of covenant [deed ov *kov*.e.nent]	*See* deed of warranty.
deed of gift [deed ov gift]	A deed conveying property without consideration.

deed of quitclaim
[deed ov *kwit*.klame]

See quitclaim deed.

deed of release
[deed ov re.*leess*]

See quitclaim deed.

deed of trust
[deed ov trust]

A deed that creates a trust in real estate and is given as security for a debt. A deed of trust is in the nature of a mortgage, but differs from a mortgage in that it is executed in favor of a disinterested third person as trustee, while a mortgage is executed directly to the creditor to be secured.

deed of warranty
[deed ov *war*.en.tee]

1. A deed that contains title covenants. 2. A deed that contains covenants concerning the property conveyed and is a separate document from the deed that actually conveys the property.

demise
[de.*mize*]

n. 1. A deed. 2. The transfer of property by will.
v. To convey; to pass on by will or inheritance.
• *v.* bequeath, transmit, confer, endow
• *n.* conveyance, transfer ("the demise of an estate"); decease, passing, fall, collapse

dominant tenement
[dom.i.nant *ten*.e.ment]

Real property that benefits from an easement that burdens another piece of property, known as the servient tenement. *Compare* servient tenement.

dower
[*dow*.er]

The legal right or interest that a wife acquires by marriage in the property of her husband. Dower, which was very important under the common law, ensured that a widow was able to live upon and make use of a portion of her husband's land, usually a third, as long as she lived. Dower, as such, no longer exists or has been substantially modified in most states, but every state retains aspects of the concept for the protection of both spouses (EXAMPLES: elective share; election by spouse; election under the will). *Note* that "dower" is not "dowry."

easement
[*eez*.ment]

1. A right to use the land of another for a specific purpose. EXAMPLE: a right of way given by a landowner to a utility company to erect and maintain power lines. 2. A right to use water, light, or air. *See also* easement of light and air.
• *n.* privilege, liberty, servitude, advantage, right of way

easement in gross
[*eez*.ment in grose]

An easement in gross does not exist so that the owner of adjoining property may better enjoy his property; rather, it is a personal interest in the use of another's land, unrelated to his own. (EXAMPLE: a right to take water from the property of another.) As easement in gross may be a right in either real property or personal property, depending upon its intended duration. *See also and compare* dominant tenement; servient tenement.

easement of access
[*eez*.ment ov *ak*.sess]

The right of an owner of real property bordering a public road to come from and go to the highway without being obstructed.

easement of light and air [*eez*.ment ov lite and air]	An easement for the enjoyment of light and air unobstructed by structures on the adjoining premises.
eminent domain [*em*.i.nent doh.*main*]	The power of the government to take private property for a public use or public purpose without the owner's consent, if it pays just compensation. The process by which this is done is called condemnation. • *n.* condemnation, expropriation, compulsory acquisition
estate [es.*tate*]	1. The property left by a decedent; i.e., a decedent's estate. 2. The right, title, and interest a person has in real or personal property, either tangible or intangible. Estates in real property (estates in land or landed estates) include both freehold estates (EXAMPLES: a fee simple; a fee tail; a life estate) and estates less than freehold (EXAMPLES: estates for years; estates at will). 3. The property itself. • *n.* assets, wealth, property, fortune, personality, effects
eviction [ee.*vik*.shen]	The act of putting a tenant out of possession of premises that she has leased. • *n.* expulsion, ouster, ejection, dislodgement, removal, dispossession
Fair Housing Act [fayr *how*.zing akt]	Another name for the Civil Rights Act of 1968, which prohibits practices that deny housing to anyone because of race, color, religion, or national origin.
fair market value [*fayr mar*.ket *val*.yoo]	Actual value; value in money. The amount a buyer will pay and a seller will accept when neither is under pressure to buy or sell and both have a reasonable degree of knowledge of the relevant facts. Fair market value is virtually synonymous with actual cash value, fair cash value, and fair value. When there is no market, it is sometimes necessary for a court to construct a fair market value, relying upon expert testimony with respect to a hypothetical buyer and seller in the same circumstances.
Fannie Mae [*fan*.ee may]	From the initials FNMA, Federal National Mortgage Association, it is the agency that supplies a market for mortgages insured by the Federal Housing Administration.
Federal Housing Administration [*fed*.er.el *how*.zing ad.min.is.*tray*.shen]	Commonly referred to as the FHA; an agency of the United States that supports the availability of housing and of a sound mortgage market by insuring bank mortgages granted to borrowers who meet its standards.
fee [fee]	An estate in real property that may be inherited. When "fee" is used without words of limitation (for EXAMPLE, base fee, conditional fee, determinable fee, or qualified fee), it always means fee simple. • *n.* estate, property, inheritance, holding ("absolute fee")
fee estate [fee es.*tate*]	A fee in land; an estate in fee.

fee simple [fee *sim*.pl]	Also known as a fee simple absolute; the most complete estate in land known to the law. It signifies total ownership and control. It may be sold or inherited free of any condition, limitation, or restriction by particular heirs. *Compare* fee tail.
fee simple absolute [fee *sim*.pl *ab*.so.loot]	*See* fee simple.
fee simple estate [fee *sim*.pl es.*tate*]	*See* fee simple.
fee tail [fee tayl]	An estate in land that is given to a person and her lineal descendants only, the heirs in general being deprived of any interest in the estate. In the absence of lineal descendants, the estate reverts to the donor. A fee tail estate given only to the donor's female lineal descendants is called a fee tail female; a fee tail estate limited to the donor's male lineal descendants is called a fee tail male. *See also* reversion. *Compare* fee simple.
fee tail female [fee tayl *fee*.male]	*See* fee tail.
fee tail male [fee tayl male]	*See* fee tail.
fixture [*fiks*.cher]	An article, previously personal property, that, by being physically affixed to real estate, has become part of the real property; something so connected to a structure for use in connection with it that it cannot be removed without doing injury to the structure. EXAMPLES: a chandelier; an outdoor television antenna; a furnace. • *n.* attachment, permanent addition, immovable object
foreclosure [for.*kloh*.zher]	1. A legal action by which a mortgagee terminates a mortgagor's interest in mortgaged premises. *See also* mortgage. 2. The enforcement of a lien, deed of trust, or mortgage on real estate, or a security interest in personal property, by any method provided by law. • *n.* blockage, obstruction, confiscation, prohibition, removal, dispossession, removal, eviction
foreclosure decree [for.*kloh*.zher de.*kree*]	A decree that orders the sale of mortgaged real estate, the proceeds to be applied in satisfaction of the debt.
foreclosure sale [for.*kloh*.zher sayl]	A sale of mortgaged premises in accordance with a foreclosure decree.
future interest [fyu.cher *in*.trest]	An estate or interest in land or personal property, including money, whether vested or contingent, that is to come into existence at a future time. EXAMPLES: a remainder; a reversion; payments or income to be received in the future.

grant [grant]	*n.* 1. A word used in conveying real property; a term of conveyance. 2. The conveyance or transfer itself. 3. That which is conveyed, conferred, or given. EXAMPLE: land. *v.* 1. To convey; to bequeath; to devise. USAGE (in a deed): "grant, bargain and sell." 2. To bestow; to confer; to give; to give away. 3. To concede; to acknowledge; to admit. • *v.* authorize, allow, relinquish; award, donate, assign, allot; consent, yield, agree, acknowledge • *n.* allocation, gift, contribution, privilege, endowment, donation
grantee [gran.*tee*]	The person to whom a grant is made; the party in a deed to whom the conveyance is made. *Compare* grantor.
grantee-grantor indexes [gran.*tee*-gran.*tor in*.dek.sez]	*See* grantor-grantee indexes.
grantor [gran.*tor*]	The person who makes a grant; the party in a deed who makes the conveyance. *Compare* grantee.
grantor-grantee indexes [gran.*tor*-gran.*tee in*.dek.sez]	Volumes maintained in most county courthouses that list every deed, mortgage, secured transaction, and lien of every type ever recorded in the county. All transactions are alphabetically indexed, both by grantor (the grantor-grantee index) and by grantee (the grantee-grantor index).
home [home]	A word whose legal significance may be either "house," "residence," or "domicile," depending upon the context in which it appears. • *n.* residence, domicile, house, abode, domain; native land, birthplace, motherland, fatherland
joint tenancy [joynt *ten*.en.see]	An estate in land (EXAMPLES: a fee simple estate; a life estate; an estate for years) or in personal property (EXAMPLE: a savings account) held by two or more persons jointly, with equal rights to share in its enjoyment. The most important feature of a joint tenancy is the right of survivorship, which means that upon the death of a joint tenant the entire estate goes to the survivor (or, in the case of more than two joint tenants, to the survivors, and so on to the last survivor). *See also* tenancy by the entirety. *Compare* tenancy in common.
land [land]	1. As used in the law, the soil and everything attached to it, whether naturally (EXAMPLES: trees; water; rocks) or by man (EXAMPLES: buildings; fixtures; fences), extending from the surface downward to the center of the earth and upward endlessly to the skies. "Land" is properly used interchangeably with "real estate," "real property," and "realty." "Property" is often used by itself to mean "land." *See also* covenant running with the land. 2. An interest in land or an estate in land. EXAMPLES: a fee simple; a life estate. • *n.* real estate, property, earth, terrain, soil, ground, nation, realty, territory, acreage

land contract [land *kon*.trakt]	A contract for sale of land; installment land contract.
land sale contract [land sale *kon*.trakt]	A contract for sale of land; installment land contract.
land use regulation [land yoos reg.yoo.*lay*.shen]	Government regulation of the way in which land is used. Zoning statutes and ordinances are EXAMPLES of land use regulation. *See also* zoning.
landlord [*land*.lord]	An owner of real property who leases all or a portion of the premises to a tenant. A landlord is also called a lessor; a tenant is called a lessee. • *n.* lessor, landowner, possessor, proprietor • *ant.* lessee
landlord's lien [*land*.lordz leen]	A lien for rent that is in arrears, which a landlord has on a tenant's personal property located on the leased premises.
landowner [*land*.oh.ner]	A person who owns real property. • *n.* landlord, owner, proprietor, possessor, title holder
lands, tenements, and hereditaments [landz, ten.e.mentz, and he.red.i.ta.mentz]	A term found in deeds and other documents relating to land, which expresses the most inclusive interest a person can own in real property, i.e., an inheritable interest in the land and everything on it or under it (EXAMPLES: structures, minerals), and all rights arising out of it (EXAMPLES: the right to collect rent; the right to harvest timber).
lease [lees]	*n.* 1. A contract for the possession of real estate in consideration of payment of rent, ordinarily for a term of years or months, but sometimes at will. The person making the conveyance is the landlord or lessor; the person receiving the right of possession is the tenant or lessee. 2. Under the Uniform Commercial Code, a contract transferring the right to possession and use of personal property ("goods") for a term in return for consideration.
lease with option to purchase [lees with *op*.shen to *per*.chess]	A lease that provides the lessee with the option, at the end of the term (or, under some leases, at any time during the term), to purchase the property for a specified sum.
legal description [le.gl des.*krip*.shen]	In deeds and mortgages, a description of the real estate that is the subject of the conveyance, by boundaries, distances, and size, or by reference to maps, surveys, or plats. *See also* metes and bounds.
life estate [life es.*tate*]	An estate that exists as long as the person who owns or holds it is alive. Its duration may also be the lifetime of another person (EXAMPLE: "To Sarah so long as Sam shall live").
listing agreement [lis.ting a.*gree*.ment]	A contract between an owner of real property and a real estate agent under which the agent is retained to secure a purchaser for the property at a specified price, for a commission.

lot [lot]	A tract or parcel into which land has been divided.
lot book [lot book]	*See* plat book.
mechanic's lien [me.*kan*.iks *lee*.en]	A lien created by law for the purpose of securing payment for work performed or materials furnished in constructing or repairing a building or other structure.
metes and bounds [meets and bowndz]	A property description, commonly in a deed or mortgage, that is based upon the property's boundaries and the natural objects and other markers on the land. *See also* legal description.
mortgage [*more*.gej]	A written pledge of real property to secure a debt, usually to a bank.
mortgage insurance [*more*.gej in.*shoor*.ense]	1. Insurance purchased by a mortgagor that pays the mortgage if the mortgagor is unable to because of death or disability. 2. Insurance purchased by a mortgagee insuring him against loss resulting from the mortgagor's inability to make payment. Mortgage insurance is a form of credit insurance.
mortgage loan [*more*.gej lown]	A loan secured by a mortgage.
mortgage note [*more*.gej note]	A note that evidences a loan for which real estate has been mortgaged.
partition deed [par.tish.en deed]	A deed that achieves a partition or splitting of real estate.
perpetuity [per.pe.*tyoo*.i.tee]	1. Literally, something that lasts forever. 2. As used in the law of property, a limitation of a contingent future interest in violation of the rule against perpetuities. • *n.* eternity, continuation, indefiniteness, forever
plat [plat]	A map of a tract of land, showing the boundaries of the streets, blocks, and numbered lots. A plat is also referred to as a "plat map" or a "plot." • *n.* map, plan, chart, sketch, diagram ("we needed to see the plat of the city")
plat book [plat book]	An official book of plat maps. *See also* plat.
plot [plot]	1. A plan or scheme to achieve some purpose, particularly a dishonest purpose. 2. The story line of a novel or other literary work. • *n.* plat, field, land, area; plan, scheme, conspiracy, trick, deception; story, design, events, scene, scenario ("Agatha Christie's plots are fun to read") • *v.* design, prepare, plan, scheme, outline, conspire ("she plotted her actions very carefully")

possibility of reverter
[pos.i.*bil*.i.tee ov re.*ver*.ter]

A type of future interest that remains in a grantor when, by grant or devise, he has created an estate in fee simple determinable or fee simple conditional, the fee automatically reverting to him or his successors upon occurrence of the event by which the estate is limited. EXAMPLE: Sam conveys Blackacre to the school district with the condition that it should revert back to Sam or his assigns when the school district ceases to use the land for school purposes. In these circumstances, Sam owns a possibility of reverter. *See also* reversion.

property
[*prop*.er.tee]

1. The right of a person to possess, use, enjoy, and dispose of a thing without restriction, i.e., not the material object itself, but a person's rights with respect to the object. 2. Ownership or title, either legal or equitable. 3. In the more common sense, real property and personal property; tangible property and intangible property; corporeal property and incorporeal property. 4. As employed in the Fifth Amendment and the Fourteenth Amendment, the right to acquire, possess, and dispose of things and objects. 5. Anything that can be owned.
• *n.* possessions, investments, holdings, capital ("his property at death"); characteristic, quality, attribute, trait ("a property of water"); land, real estate, realty, territory, acreage ("a beautiful piece of property")

real property
[real *prop*.er.tee]

Land, including things located on it or attached to it directly (EXAMPLE: buildings) or indirectly (EXAMPLE: fixtures). *See also* property.
• *n.* real estate

recording
[ree.*kore*.ding]

1. The act of making a record. 2. A copy or a record of a transaction for the sale of land. *See also* recording acts.

recording acts
[ree.*kore*.ding aktz]

State statutes that provide for the recording of instruments, particularly those affecting title to real estate (EXAMPLES: a deed; a mortgage; a tax lien) and security interests in personal property (EXAMPLES: a conditional sale contract; a security agreement). There are several types of recording acts. In notice act states, an instrument that is not recorded is invalid with respect to a person who subsequently purchases the property who has no actual knowledge of the unrecorded transaction. In race act states, actual notice is immaterial because, in the event of conflicting claims of ownership, absolute priority is given to the first person who "wins the race to the courthouse" to record her instrument. Race-notice acts, which are in effect in some jurisdictions, combine various features of notice acts and race acts.
• *n.* recording laws, recording statutes

remainder
[ree.*mane*.der]

1. An estate in land to take effect immediately after the expiration of a prior estate (known as the particular estate), created at the same time and by the same instrument. EXAMPLE (in a will): "I will leave my land to Joe Jones for life, and after his death to Sarah Green and her heirs." The interest or estate of Sarah Green and her heirs is a remainder; Joe Jones's interest is a life estate. *Compare* reversion. 2. That which is left over; the residue.
• *n.* balance, residue, surplus, excess, remains; estate, interest, property

remainderman
[ree.*mane*.der.man]

A person entitled to receive a remainder.

restrictive covenant
[ree.*strik*.tiv *kov*.e.nent]

1. A covenant in a deed prohibiting or restricting the use of the property (EXAMPLE: the type, location, or size of buildings that can be constructed on it). A covenant prohibiting the sale of real property to persons of a particular race is unenforceable because it is an unconstitutional restraint on alienation. 2. A covenant not to sue.

reversion
[re.*ver*.zhen]

1. A future interest in land to take effect in favor of the grantor of the land or his heirs after the termination of a prior estate he has granted; in other words, the returning of the property to the grantor or his heirs when the grant is over. (EXAMPLE: "I leave Blackacre to Joe Jones for life, and after his death to my heirs." The grantor's heirs have a reversionary interest in Blackacre, which will vest when Joe Jones dies; Joe Jones's interest is a life estate.) A reversion arises by operation of law. *Compare* remainder. 2. The interest or estate of an owner of land during the period of time for which he has granted his possessory rights to someone else. Thus, in the above EXAMPLE, the grantor and his heirs may also be said to have a reversionary interest in Blackacre during Joe Jones's life. A landlord's interest in premises that she has leased to a tenant is another EXAMPLE of a reversionary interest.
• *n.* remainder, future interest, residue, estate, interest; return, throwback, retrogression, regression, turnaround

reversionary interest
[re.*ver*.zhen.a.ree *in*.trest]

A future interest, i.e., the right to the future enjoyment of a reversion.

revert
[re.*vert*]

1. With respect to an interest in land, to come back to a former owner or her heirs at a future time. USAGE: "After Bill dies, the life estate in Blackacre that Sam granted to Bill will revert to Sam, and if Sam is also dead, it will revert to Sam's heirs." *See also* reversion. 2. Turn backward.

riparian land
[ry.*pare*.ee.en land]

Land along the bank of a river or stream. Only land within the watershed of the river or stream is considered to be riparian.

search
[serch]

A title search or examination of all mortgages, liens, debts, etc., that affect ownership of land.

servient tenement
[*serv*.ee.ent *ten*.e.ment]

Real property that is subject to an easement that benefits another piece of property, known as the dominant tenement.

survey
[*ser*.vey]

n. 1. The method by which the boundaries of land are determined.
2. A map, plat, or other document reflecting a surveyor's determination of the boundary or boundaries of land.
v. 1. To determine the boundaries of land. 2. To examine or to look something over in detail.
• *v.* appraise, assay, canvass, measure, prospect, reconnoiter, scrutinize, superintend ("to survey the land")
• *n.* analysis, study, audit, outline, scan, review, précis, syllabus ("a survey of the history of western civilization")

tacking
[tack.ing]

With respect to acquiring title to land by adverse possession, a doctrine allowing an adverse possessor to add her period of possession to that of a previous possessor to establish continuous possession. *See also* adverse possession.

tenancy
[*ten*.en.see]

The right to hold and occupy realty or personalty by virtue of owning an interest in it.
• *n.* holding, leasing, occupancy, residence, rental

tenancy by the entirety
[*ten*.en.see by the en.*ty*.re.tee]

A form of joint tenancy in an estate in land or in personal property that exists between husband and wife by virtue of the fact that they are husband and wife. As with a conventional joint tenancy, a tenancy by the entirety is a tenancy with right of survivorship. "Tenancy," in this context, means ownership of the jointly held estate or interest, whether, for EXAMPLE, it is a fee simple estate, a life estate, a savings account, or the like. *Compare* tenancy in common.

tenancy for life
[*ten*.en.see for life]

A life estate.

tenancy for years
[*ten*.en.see for yeerz]

A tenancy under a lease or other contract for the period of a year or for a stated number of years.

tenancy from month to month
[*ten*.en.see from month to month]

1. A tenancy in which no definite term is agreed upon and the rate is so much per month; i.e., a tenancy under a month to month lease. 2. A tenancy at will. 3. The tenancy of a holdover tenant, i.e., a tenancy at sufferance. *Compare* tenancy from year to year.

tenancy from year to year
[*ten*.en.see from yeer to yeer]

A tenancy in which no definite term is agreed upon and the rate is so much per year. A tenancy from year to year may also be a tenancy at sufferance or a tenancy at will. *Compare* tenancy from month to month.

tenancy in common
[*ten*.en.see in *kahm*.en]

A tenancy in which two or more persons own an undivided interest in an estate in land, for EXAMPLE, in a fee simple estate or a life estate, or in personal property, for EXAMPLE, in a savings account. As opposed to joint tenants, tenants in common have no right of survivorship; when a tenant in common dies, her interest passes to her heirs rather than to her cotenant or cotenants. *Compare* tenancy by the entirety.

tenant
[*ten*.ent]

1. A person who holds or possesses realty or personalty by virtue of owning an interest in it. 2. A person who occupies realty under a lease with a landlord; a lessee. *See also* tenancy.
• *n.* lessee, occupier, renter, boarder, leaseholder, inhabitant, roomer

tenantable
[*ten*.nen.tebl]

Premises that are habitable or ready to live in because plumbing, electricity, heat, and water are all in working condition.

tenants in common
[*ten*.entz in *kahm*.en]

Two or more owners of property under a tenancy in common.

trespass
[*tress*.pas]

An unauthorized entry or intrusion by one (trespasser) onto the real property of another.

variable rate mortgage
[vair.ee.ebl rate *more*.gej]

Another term for an adjustable rate mortgage, one where the percentage rate changes annually, or in some stipulated period.

variance
[*var*.ee.ense]

In zoning law, an exception from the strict application of a zoning ordinance, granted to relieve a property owner of unnecessary hardship. A variance allows the landowner to use the land in a matter that the law would not otherwise permit.

warranty deed
[war.en.*tee* deed]

A deed that contains title covenants.

warranty of habitability
[war.en.*tee* ov hab.it.e.*bil*.i.tee]

A warranty implied by law that leased premises are fit to copy.

waste
[wayst]

1. The destruction, misuse, alteration, or neglect of premises by the person in possession, to the detriment of another's interest in the property. EXAMPLE: A tenant's polluting of a pond on leased land. 2. That which is left over, useless or even dangerous. EXAMPLES: hazardous waste; solid waste; toxic waste.
• *n.* decay, desolation, disuse, improvidence, misapplication, squandering; badlands, barrens, brush

zone
[zone]

n. 1. An area or district created by a zoning board in accordance with zoning regulations. 2. A distinct area that is unlike the surrounding areas.
v. To engage in zoning.
• *n.* area, belt, circuit, district, realm, territory, tract sector

zoning
[*zone*.ing]

The creation and application of structural, size, and use restrictions imposed upon the owners of real estate within districts or zones in accordance with zoning regulations or ordinances. Although authorized by state statutes, zoning is generally legislated and regulated by local government. Zoning is a form of land use regulation and is generally of two types: regulations having to do with structural and architectural design; and regulations specifying the use(s) to which designated districts may be put, for EXAMPLE, commercial, industrial, residential, or agricultural.

zoning board
[*zone*.ing bord]

An administrative agency of a municipality that administers zoning regulations or ordinances.

Missing Words

Fill in the blanks below.

1. _____ is the destruction of premises by the person in possession.

2. _____ is a multi-unit dwelling, where residents own individual apartments.

3. An exception to the strict application of a zoning ordinance is called a(n) _____.

4. A(n) _____ is the transferring of title to real property from one person to another.

5. A person whose business is to bring a buyer and seller together is _____.

6. _____ is the power of the government to take private property for a public use.

7. _____ is the most complete estate in land one can own.

8. _____ is an estate that exists as long as the person who owns or holds it is alive.

9. A(n) _____ is the transfer of property by a will.

10. When a tenant is put out of possession, it is called _____.

Matching

Match the letter of the definition to the term below.

_____ 11. Deed

_____ 12. Abstract of title

_____ 13. Estate

_____ 14. Real property

_____ 15. Easement

_____ 16. Foreclosure

_____ 17. Zoning

A. Land including things located on it or attached to it

B. A short account of the state of the title to real estate

C. Right, title, and interest a person has in real or personal property

D. Personal property that becomes part of real estate

E. The method by which the boundaries of land are determined

F. Right to use land of another for a specific purpose

G. Document by which real property is conveyed from one person to another

_____ 18. Mortgage

H. A pledge of real property to secure a debt

_____ 19. Recording

I. A contract for the possession of real estate in consideration of payment of rent

_____ 20. Lease

J. The act of making a record

_____ 21. Survey

K. A legal action by which a mortgagee terminates a mortgagor's interest in mortgaged premises

_____ 22. Co-ownership

L. The ownership of property by at least two persons

_____ 23. Fixture

M. Restrictions imposed upon owners of real estate within districts or zones

Multiple Choice

Select the best choice.

_____ 24. A document by which real property or an interest in real property is conveyed from one person to another is a(n):
   a. mortgage
   b. deed
   c. fixture
   d. easement

_____ 25. The creation and application of structural, size, and use restrictions imposed upon owners of real estate within districts or zones is called:
   a. recording
   b. partition
   c. zoning
   d. trespass

_____ 26. The method by which the boundaries of land are determined:
   a. mortgage
   b. clear title
   c. foreclosure
   d. survey

_____ 27. An estate or interest in land or personal property that is to come into existence at a future time is a:
   a. fee
   b. fee simple estate
   c. fee tail
   d. future interest

_____ 28. Ownership of property by more than one person:
   a. co-ownership
   b. fee
   c. covenant
   d. satisfaction

_____ 29. A short account of the state of the title to real estate, reflecting all past ownership and any interests or rights that a person might currently have with respect to the property is:
   a. an abstract of title
   b. satisfaction
   c. license
   d. clean title

_____ 30. An agreement to transfer title to land:
  a. deed
  b. mortgage
  c. contract for sale of land
  d. lease

_____ 31. Legal action by which a mortgagee terminates a mortgagor's interest in mortgaged premises:
  a. mortgage
  b. license
  c. recording
  d. foreclosure

_____ 32. The right to hold and occupy realty or personalty by virtue of owning an interest in it:
  a. tenancy
  b. partition
  c. covenant
  d. fee

_____ 33. In a deed, a promise to do or not do a particular thing, or an assurance that a particular fact or circumstance exists or does not exist:
  a. convey
  b. survey
  c. fixture
  d. covenant

_____ 34. An article, previously personal property, that becomes real property:
  a. fixture
  b. personal property
  c. real property
  d. abstract of title

_____ 35. The most complete estate in land known to law. It signifies total ownership and control:
  a. fee simple estate
  b. fee tail
  c. condominium
  d. cooperative

_____ 36. An unauthorized entry or intrusion onto real property:
  a. burglary
  b. trespass
  c. transgression
  d. fault

True/False

Mark the following T or F.

_____ 37. A fee is an estate in real property that may be inherited.

_____ 38. A tenant is the purchaser of real estate.

_____ 39. A fee tail is an estate in land that is given to a person and their lineal descendants only.

_____ 40. An abstract of title is a pledge of real property to secure a debt.

_____ 41. A joint tenancy is an estate in land or in personal property held by two or more persons jointly, with equal rights to share in its enjoyment, with rights of survivorship.

_____ 42. A cooperative is a multi-unit dwelling in which each tenant has an interest in the corporation or other entity that owns the building.

_____ **43.** An estate is the right, title, and interest a person has in real or personal property.

_____ **44.** The power of the government to take private property for a public use or purpose is called trespass.

_____ **45.** An article that was previously personal property that, by being physically affixed to real estate, has become part of the real property is called a fixture.

_____ **46.** A tenancy in common is a tenancy in which two or more persons own an undivided interest in an estate in land without rights of survivorship.

_____ **47.** An oven built into a wall becomes a fixture that cannot be removed at the time of sale.

Synonyms

Select the correct synonym in parentheses for each numbered item.

48. CONVEY
(transfer, edit, produce)

49. REAL PROPERTY
(land, goods, money)

50. DEED
(easement, conveyance, mortgage)

51. WASTE
(neglect, preservation, maintenance)

52. TRESPASS
(stroll, convey, intrusion)

53. SURVEY
(recording, easement, outline)

54. MORTGAGE
(sell, pledge, variance)

55. CO-OWNERSHIP
(joint, several, individual)

56. VARIANCE
(exception, conformity, estate)

57. COVENANT
    (failure, assurance, satisfaction)

58. ABSTRACT OF TITLE
    (chain of title, loss of title, adverse possession)

59. BROKER
    (owner, agent, seller)

Self-Test

Place the number of the correct term in the appropriate space.

60. Condominium	67. Abstract of title
61. Eminent domain	68. Eviction
62. Tenants	69. Fair Housing Act
63. Landlord	70. Broker
64. Lease with option to purchase	71. Tenancy from month to month
65. Tenancy for years	72. Warranty of habitability
66. Deed	73. Contract for sale of land

After the county government took their house by _____, for the new freeway construction, Sajaad and Kishori Rajan wanted to buy a new house. While their savings were not quite sufficient to build a new house, they began searching for a rental property with a(n) _____. While they wished to be owners instead of _____ they couldn't find a suitable place through an agent or real estate _____.

Now the Rajans decided to rent for the shortest period of time and began checking the classified advertisements. They wanted a(n) _____ that would not obligate them to a long-term lease.

The next day's newspaper had an advertisement for a short-term house rental that attracted the Rajans' attention and they telephoned the _____ of the house. She said it was not ready to be seen because the previous occupants left it a mess after they were ejected in a(n) _____ proceeding. The Rajans insisted on seeing the house that day and the owner reluctantly agreed. When the Rajans arrived at the house, the owner said, "I'll show it but it isn't fit to occupy and there is no _____. And if you take it

I'll insist on at least a 12-month lease making it a(n) _____." The Rajans were upset and wondered

if, because of their accents, they were being denied housing in violation of the _____.

Finally, the Rajans found a beautiful apartment that was part of a multi-unit dwelling called a

_____. They took all the papers pertaining to the sale for their attorney to review. The attorney

requested to see the _____, the _____, and the _____.

Defining Words

Complete the definition.

74. Estate _____

_____

75. Real property _____

_____

76. Deed _____

_____

77. Mortgage _____

_____

78. Eviction _____

_____

79. Lease _____

_____

80. Easement _____

_____

81. Convey _____

_____

82. Fee simple estate _____

_____

83. Abstract of title _____

_____

84. Waste _____

_____

85. Fixture _____

_____

86. Survey _____

_____

87. Tenancy by the entirety _____

_____

88. Reversionary interest _____

_____

89. Remainderman _____

_____

90. Fannie Mae _____

_____

Punctuation/Capitalization

Punctuation of the word okay.

_____

Depending upon where and how it is used, the word *okay* has different punctuation.

Rule 1: When the word *okay* is used alone at the beginning of a sentence, it usually is short for something like "That is okay" and is punctuated with a period. Attorneys frequently use *okay* in this way.

Okay. Now I want to move on to discuss the night of the incident.
Fine. Okay. Do you want to take a break now?
Okay. I anticipate we will be another few hours at least.

Rule 2: When the word *okay* is used at the end of a sentence, there is a period at the end of the sentence and a question mark after *okay* if it is being used to ask a question. Often it is possible to determine whether it should be a period or a question mark only by the intonation of the speaker.

I am going to call you later today. Okay?
He needs to come get this within the hour. Okay?
You have to let me know when you need to leave. Okay?

Rule 3: When the word *okay* is used at the end of a sentence, there is a period at the end of the sentence and a period after *okay* if it is being used to make a statement. Often it is possible to determine whether it should be a period or a question mark only by the intonation of the speaker.

You said there were 15 of them in line. Okay.
We have established that he was alone. Okay.
He had five people under his control. Okay.

Directions: Make necessary punctuation changes.

1. Okay, how far away were you standing at the time?

2. We are going to take a break around noon, okay.

3. You said he was there with his father, okay.

4. All right. Okay. Did you see him?

5. Okay he will go with us to examine the contents of the file.

Word Pairs

medal/meddle/metal/mettle

medal = award, honor, win in a competition.

He won the Medal of Honor in Vietnam.
She was just hoping to medal in the race.
The medal meant more to him than the money he won.

meddle = interfere, intrude.

She always meddled in everyone else's business.
His meddling got him into trouble with the boss.
I pleaded with her not to meddle in his affairs.

metal = chemical element, type of music with the word *heavy*.

I am not fond of heavy metal music.
It is made of a heavy metal.
The molten metal oozed from the fissure.

mettle = courage, heart, good spirit.

He is in fine mettle today.
She has the mettle to finish the marathon.
It took mettle to accomplish what she did.

plait/plat/plate

plait = ponytail, braid.

She wore her dark hair in a plait.
He is very adept at plaiting hair.
She cut her plaited hair to donate to cancer victims.

plat = map of a tract of land.

The geological plat was studied by the team of engineers.
We need to see the plat map before we proceed.
He was part of the team that drew up the plat map.

plate = shield, serving dish, coat.

I have too much on my plate right now.
It is part of the tectonic plate theory.
She broke the plate in anger.

real/reel

real = genuine, authentic, factual.

It is a real diamond in her necklace.
He is facing a real-life situation.
As far as I can tell, his story is real.

reel = roll, spool, stagger, stumble.

The news of her death left us reeling.
He reeled under the pressure of the announcement.
His story reeled her in.

reality/realty

reality = authenticity, truth, veracity.

Her reality turned out to be very different from her dreams.
In reality, we lived there only a very short time.
She does not seem to live in reality.

realty = land, synonym for *real estate*. When pronounced, this word is just two syllables: REAL/TEE.

He deals in realty in the coastal area.
Local realty is selling well.
She specializes in realty.

tack/tact

tack = nail, pin, direction, approach.

The ship tacked out of the harbor.
We need to take a new tack with them.
She stepped on the tack that he had dropped.

tact = skill, diplomacy, judgment.

He displays absolutely no tact in his dealing with her.
This situation requires real tact.
She always tries to be tactful when speaking with the boss.

tenant/tenement/tenet

tenant = person who holds or possesses or occupies realty.

The tenants were impeccable in keeping up the property.
We are looking for quiet tenants.
The current tenants are leaving the end of the month.

tenement = apartment building, usually with the implication of run-down and in bad condition.

The tenement living was depressing for the family.
The City demanded that the tenement be cleaned up.
He owned several tenement buildings in the poor section of town.

tenet = belief, theory, principle.

He practices the tenets of his faith.
She believes in the tenets of good business practices.
That is one of the tenets of her beliefs.

Directions: Choose the correct form of the word.

1. He does not have the medal/meddle/metal/mettle to conquer that fear.

2. If you do not take a new tack/tact, you will not win this battle.

3. His interest in reality/realty as a career is misguided.

4. His mother needs to real/reel him in a little.

5. We studied the plait/plat/plate map of the area.

6. It is one of the tenants/tenements/tenets by which he lives.

7. He will tack/tact up the note so that he doesn't forget.

8. The problem is that the tenant/tenement/tenet does not pay on time.

9. It is a real/reel problem in her life that she is going to have to solve.

10. She was allergic to the medal/meddle/metal/mettle in the earrings.

11. I do not understand why she has to medal/meddle/metal/mettle in everything he does.

12. He is responsible for the medal/meddle/metal/mettle plait/plat/plate on it.

13. The problem is that he totally lacks any measure of tack/tact.

14. Her intention is to medal/meddle/metal/mettle at the Olympics.

15. He is realing/reeling from the news about his father.

16. She makes money on the side from plaiting/plating hair.

17. We had to move from the tenant/tenement/tenet because of the conditions.

18. It is time to face reality/realty about the marriage.

19. Please do not medal/meddle/metal/mettle in their relationship.

20. A different tack/tact may work with them.

Is It One Word or Two? An Apostrophe? A Hyphen?

Little words make a difference in English. Look at these combinations.

take up	stand off
take over	stand out
take in	stand by

Depending on which little word follows *take* and *stand,* there is a difference in meaning. There are literally hundreds of these combinations in English. Further, the form of the word—whether it is one word, hyphenated, or two words—depends upon the part of speech.

Rule 1: When the word and the little word combination is used as a verb, the form is always two words.
They tried to break up the fight.
They will stake out the house to watch the activity.
She wants to give back to the people that were so good to her.

Rule 2: When the word and the little word combination is used as a noun, the form is either one word or hyphenated. The only way to be sure is to look up the word in a standard dictionary. All of the words in this section were researched in Merriam-Webster's Collegiate Dictionary, 11th Edition.
He is a standout on the college soccer team.
There were a number of break-ins in the neighborhood.
The cleanup of the oil spill will take months.

Directions: Make corrections in word forms.

1. The playoffs begin on Saturday.

2. They will markdown the prices after the season begins.

3. He was expecting a hand out when he went there.

4. She expected to wake up with a hangover.

5. I will print-out the directions for you.

Proofreading

Directions: Make necessary corrections, based on the material presented in the unit. If the sentence has no errors, write the word *correct* after the sentence.

1. Okay, there has been a break down in the talks, and you will need a new tact. _____

2. The stakeout near the tenement did not yield any results. _____

3. You are telling me he won the metal at the games that were organized by the school, okay. _____

4. Okay. The earthquake is attributed to the phenomenon of plat tectonics. _____

5. That is a tenant of the code. _____

6. In reality, he has the metal to accomplish anything he sets out to do. _____

7. The boats collided as they tried to tact out of the harbor. _____

8. There were two reals that showed the plat map with the build up of tenant buildings. _____

9. Her mettling is not what caused them to breakup. _____

10. The turn out at the ballgame included all the tenants of my building. _____

An Adaptation from a Real Property and Landlord Tenant Case

Facts:

Hillerman purchased commercial property and later sold it to Ray Commercial, a company that owns and operates commercial buildings. The closing of the property was set for November 30. Prior to the closing, Ray Commercial had a chance to view the premises and perform any inspections. Ray Commercial was purchasing the property "as is." Once purchased, Ray Commercial was leasing the premises back to Hillerman. It is noteworthy that Ray Commercial was fully aware that, in the past, metal plating operations that used hazardous chemicals such as cyanide had been conducted on the property. Ray Commercial knew that Hillerman was going to continue its metal plating operations on the premises as it had done in the past. The lease agreement was to end on June 21 of the next year. At that time, according to the terms of the lease, the tenant was to leave the premises in the same condition as existed at the commencement of the lease, reasonable wear and tear excepted, and remove any equipment or other property that may be contaminated or hazardous. At the end of the lease, Ray Commercial insisted that Hillerman remove the cement floor that it determined was contaminated with cyanide. Hillerman claimed it was not responsible for years of buildup that occurred prior to its lease. Hillerman ended up staying beyond its lease period to remove the concrete floor and sent a communication to Ray Commercial, saying, "Okay. We have removed the concrete floor. This has cost our company several hundred thousand dollars."

Procedural History:

Ray Commercial sued Hillerman, claiming that Hillerman stayed beyond the lease, and sought five months of additional rent. Ray Commercial sought summary judgment against Hillerman. Hillerman cross-moved for summary judgment against Ray Commercial. Hillerman's motion was granted.

Issue:

Did Hillerman have an obligation under the lease to remove the concrete floor and therefore was responsible to pay additional rent?

Rationale:

While the lease did not define all materials to be removed, a cyanide-contaminated floor does not constitute "materials or other property." The phrase clearly was only referring to movable materials and movable property. Since Hillerman fulfilled its obligation in this regard and cleared out all movable property, it clearly fulfilled all obligations under the lease and should not be responsible for additional rent.

Ruling:

Decision of District Court granting summary judgment to Hillerman is affirmed.

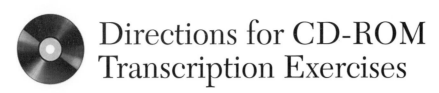

Directions for CD-ROM Transcription Exercises

In audio format are:

1. Terms for the unit with pronunciations from the thesaurus/dictionary feature.

2. Self-Test that appears in the book at mid-unit.°

3. Case that appears at the unit end.°

°speeds are 80 wpm/120 wpm for differing skill levels

CD-ROM icons appear where the three above are located within each unit.

Readers may practice transcription by listening to the CD-ROM where prompted by the icons in the book. However, for high success in testing your transcription skills, mastering all the terms and English skills in the unit is recommended before attempting the CD-ROM.

For Keyboard Transcriptionists: Listen to the CD-ROM audio file for this unit at 80 wpm or 120 wpm and transcribe from the dictation on your computer. Edit and proofread your work against the printed copy in the book.

For Reporting Writers: Listen to the CD-ROM audio file at 80 wpm or 120 wpm and take down the dictation on your writer. Either transcribe from your notes and proofread your work or edit and proofread your CAT (computer-aided transcription) transcript. Always check your work against the printed copy in the book.

Student CD-ROM
For additional materials,
please go to the CD in this book.

Online Companion™
For additional resources, please go to
http://www.paralegal.delmar.cengage.com

Area of Law

Tax Law

The **Mistakes** That Court Reporters Make and *How to Avoid* Them

The Mistake:

During an afternoon break the court reporter, Jeanne Renoir, found herself alone in the room with the deponent, who was the defendant in the case. The defendant struck up a conversation and was just chatting about random things with Jeanne. Soon the conversation turned to the case, and the defendant began asking Jeanne's opinion on how things were going and what she thought of the merits of the case, et cetera. Not wanting to be impolite, Jeanne responded to the questions.

How to Avoid It:

At no time is it okay to discuss a case with anyone involved—neither attorneys nor witnesses. Because they were alone in the room, the minute the defendant began to chat, Jeanne should have excused herself and left the room. If the circumstance makes that impossible, then the reporter must simply state that she cannot discuss anything regarding the case. It is best not to involve yourself one-on-one in any conversation with the litigants.

Introduction

The government uses taxes as a source of raising revenue and regulating the economy. Individuals and businesses are taxed by federal, state, and local levels of government. Taxpayers pay taxes on wages, earned income, gifts, real estate, purchases of goods, even on the receipt of services.

Some taxpayers prepare and file their own income tax returns with the Internal Revenue Service (IRS), while others require the services of an attorney, accountant, or other tax preparer. It is ironic that in the case herein the defendant cites legal terminology as the source of his problem.

Accurate and detailed records and receipts must be kept. One must be able to determine total income for each year. Not all income is taxable income; certain deductions and credits are allowed. Depending on one's tax bracket and the amount of taxes withheld from bonuses and commissions as well as salary, one may still owe the government additional taxes. Those who have overpaid by over-withholding taxes receive a refund from the IRS. Those who have falsely reported income, or underpaid taxes might be the subject of an IRS tax audit. All the taxpayer's books and records may be examined to determine the accuracy of the return. Tax evasion, also known as tax fraud, is very serious and could result in a felony charge, penalties, and fines. Should taxpayers fail to settle or disagree with the Internal Revenue Service's ruling, they can file an appeal and ultimately resort to the tax courts for relief.

Unit Objectives

- Work with a legal dictionary/thesaurus.
- Learn about the law of tax.
- Master the similarities and differences in definitions of key terms regarding tax.
- Master the pronunciations and spellings of legal terms in this unit.
- Practice usage of terms, definitions, and synonyms for terms used in tax law.
- Complete unit exercises in the forms of missing words, matching, multiple choice, true/false, synonyms, self-test, defining words, and also:
  - Punctuation/capitalization
  - Word pairs
  - Transcription of terms, self-test, and case
  - Proofreading

 Dictionary/Thesaurus

Note: All Dictionary/Thesaurus terms appear on the CD-ROM with audio pronunciations.

Term [phonetic pronunciation]	
accelerated depreciation [ak.*sel*.e.ray.ted de.pree.shee.*ay*.shen]	Rapid depreciation of the value of a capital asset in order to produce larger tax deductions during the early years of the life of the asset. *Compare* straight-line depreciation. *See also* depreciation.
accrued income [a.krewd *in*.kum]	Income that a person has earned but has not yet claimed. *See also* income; earned income.
accrued interest [a.krewd *in*.trest]	Interest that has been earned but has not yet been paid.
ad valorem tax [ad va.lore.em takz]	A tax established in proportion to the value of the property to be taxed. EXAMPLE: a tax of $3 on an antique worth $100 and $9 on an antique worth $300, the tax being 3 percent of the value, as distinguished from a $5 tax regardless of the value of the antique.
adjusted [a.*just*.ed]	1. Corrected; balanced. 2. Brought into line.
adjusted basis [a.*just*.ed *bay*.siss]	For the purpose of calculating the amount of income tax due, the original cost of property offset for such things as casualty losses and depreciation.
adjusted gross income [a.*just*.ed *grose in*.kum]	An income tax term for gross income less the deductions (generally, business expenses) permitted by law. *Compare* taxable income.
amended return [a.mend.ed re.*tern*]	Within the limitations prescribed by law, amended tax returns may be filed to correct inaccuracies and omissions in the original return. *See also* return.
amortization [am.er.ti.*zay*.shen]	The act of amortizing. *See also* amortize.
amortize [*am*.er.tize]	1. To gradually pay off a debt by regular payments in a fixed amount over a fixed period of time. 2. To depreciate an intangible asset (EXAMPLES: stock; bills).
appreciation [a.pree.she.*ay*.shen]	1. An increase in the value of something. *Compare* to depreciation. 2. Recognition of value.

assessment [a.*sess*.ment]	1. Imposing of tax on the basis of a listing and valuation of the property to be taxed. 2. Requiring a payment above and beyond that which is normal. EXAMPLE: the imposition of a 15 percent penalty on property taxes paid after a certain date.
assessor [a.*sess*.er]	A public official who makes an assessment of property, usually for purposes of taxation. • *n.* charger, estimator, collector
audit [*aw*.dit]	1. A formal or official examination and verification of accounts, vouchers, and other financial records as, for EXAMPLE, a tax audit or an independent audit of a company's books and records. 2. Any verification of figures by an accountant. • *n.* analysis, review, scrutiny, verification ("the audit is complete") • *v.* analyze, balance, investigate, examine, monitor, probe ("the accountant audited the books")
auditor [*aw*.dit.er]	1. A person who conducts an audit. 2. A civil servant whose duty it is to examine the accounts of state officials to determine whether they have spent public funds in accordance with the law. • *n.* accountant, bookkeeper, cashier, inspector
back taxes [back *tak*.sez]	1. Taxes that are owed from a prior date. 2. Taxes on which the ordinary processes for collection have been exhausted.
basis [*bay*.siss]	In tax law, the cost of property as of a certain date, upon which depreciation can be computed and gain or loss can be calculated when the property is sold or exchanged. • *n.* cost ("the tax basis of the property")
capital [*ka*.pi.tel]	*adj.* Relating to wealth. *n.* 1. Broadly, the total assets of a business. 2. Money or property used for the production of wealth. 3. An owner's equity in a business. • *n.* cash, stock, wealth, holdings, financial assets, funds, resources
capital assets [*ka*.pi.tel *ass*.ets]	All assets except those excluded from that category by the Internal Revenue Code.
capital gain [*ka*.pi.tel gayn]	Financial gain resulting from the sale or exchange of capital assets. *See also* gain.
capital gains tax [*ka*.pi.tel gaynz takz]	Income tax upon financial gain resulting from the sale or exchange of capital assets. *See also* gain.
death taxes [deth *tak*.sez]	Another term for inheritance taxes or estate taxes.

declaration of estimated tax
[dek.le.ray.shen ov *ess*.ti.may.ted takz]

A formal estimate of income anticipated during the forthcoming tax year, required under federal and state tax codes from corporations, trusts, and estates, and individuals who receive income that is not subject to withholding (generally, income other than wages). Such declarations must be accompanied by payment of the estimated tax.

deductible
[de.*duk*.tibl]

In tax law, expenses that a taxpayer is permitted to subtract, in whole or in part, in computing her taxable income. EXAMPLES: interest on the mortgage on one's home; casualty losses; charitable contributions.
See also deduction.
• *adj.* removable, allowable, discountable

deduction
[de.*duk*.shen]

1. The amount allowed a taxpayer in reduction of gross income for the purpose of determining adjusted gross income. 2. That which may be taken away or subtracted, particularly money.
• *n.* subtraction, withdrawal, removal, exemption, allowance ("the home office deduction"); conclusion, assumption, understanding

deferred
[de.*ferd*]

Put off to a future time; postponed.

deferred income
[de.*ferd in*.kum]

A tax law term for payments received before they are earned. (EXAMPLE: payment of $1,000 in 1994 to a tutor who is to provide 20 lessons in 1995.)

dependent
[dee.*pen*.dent]

In tax law, a person whose relationship to the taxpayer is such that the taxpayer is entitled to claim her as an exemption when filing his income tax return. EXAMPLE: A child of the taxpayer who is less than 19 years of age.
• *n.* minor, charge, ward

depreciation
[dee.pree.shee.*ay*.shen]

1. The lessening in worth of any property caused by wear, use, time, or obsolescence. *Compare* appreciation. 2. In computing income tax, a deduction allowed for the gradual loss of usefulness of a capital asset used in business or in the production of income.
• *n.* devaluation, reduction, deflation
• *ant.* appreciation

direct tax
[dye.rekt takz]

A tax (also called a property tax or an ad valorem tax) levied directly on real or personal property based upon value, or directly upon income (i.e., an income tax). Such a tax should be distinguished from an indirect tax, which is levied upon the importation, consumption, manufacture, or sale of articles and upon the privilege of doing business or engaging in a profession.

earn
[urn]

• *v.* gain, draw, win, acquire ("earn wages")

earned
[urnd]

1. Received as a result of labor or service. 2. Merited; deserved. 3. Gained; acquired.

earned income
[urnd *in*.kum]

Income received for work or for the performance of some service. Unearned income includes dividends, interest, etc.

earned income credit
[urnd *in*.kum *kred*.it]

A tax credit on earned income for low income workers with dependent children, as defined by the Internal Revenue Code.

equalization of taxes
[ee.kwe.li.zay.shen ov *tak*.sez]

Carried out by boards of equalization; the process of adjusting the total assessments on all real estate in a tax district to equalize them with the total assessments in other tax districts in the state, the goal being equality and uniformity in taxation.

estate tax
[es.*tate* takz]

A tax imposed by the federal government and most states upon the transmission of property by a deceased person. The tax is imposed upon the net estate of the decedent without reference to the recipients' relationship to the decedent or to the amount a recipient receives. An estate tax is a transfer tax.

exemption
[eg.*zemp*.shen]

1. An allowance granted by way of a deduction when computing one's taxable income. EXAMPLES: a tax exemption for a dependent; a personal exemption. 2. The person for whom an exemption may be claimed in an income tax return.

extension of time
[eks.ten.shen ov time]

1. Modification of an obligation by giving additional time for performance. 2. An enlargement of time. 3. Any lengthening of a previously set period of time.

fiscal year
[fis.kel yeer]

An accounting period of 12 consecutive months. Both businesses and individuals may choose any such 12-month period as their tax year. A fiscal year is often referred to by its abbreviation, FY.

gain
[gayn]

1. Earnings; profits; proceeds; return; yield; interest; increase; addition. 2. In tax law, excess of revenue over expense. *Compare* loss.
• *n.* acquisition, profit, appreciation, enhancement
• *v.* accomplish, attain, procure, consummate

gift tax
[gift takz]

A tax on the transfer by gift, by a living person, of money or other property. The federal government and most states impose gift taxes. By comparison, there are distinctly different tax consequences if the transfer of the gift occurs upon the death of the donor (*see also* estate tax). Additionally, special tax considerations apply to gifts made by living persons in contemplation of death. A gift tax is a transfer tax.

gross
[grose]

adj. Without deduction; as a whole; entire; total. EXAMPLES: gross earnings; gross income; gross pay. *Compare* net income.

gross estate
[grose es.*tate*]

1. The value of all property left by a decedent, before payment of taxes and expenses. 2. The value of all taxable property in a decedent's estate.

gross income
[grose *in*.kum]

1. Total income. 2. The whole or entire profit from a business. 3. Under the Internal Revenue Code, "all income from whatever source derived," before allowance for deductions or exemptions. *Compare* net income. *See also* adjusted gross income.

head of household
[hed ov *house*.hold]

In tax law, a single person, other than a surviving spouse, who provides a home for certain persons, generally dependents. Also, married persons who live apart are each a head of household. A head of household is entitled to pay federal income tax at a lower rate than other single persons.

income
[*in*.kum]

The gain derived from capital or from labor, including profit gained through a sale or conversion of capital assets. *See also* adjusted gross income; earned income; gross income; net income; taxable income.
• *n.* wages, salary, earning, profit, livelihood

income tax
[*in*.kum takz]

A tax based on income, personal or corporate. The Internal Revenue Code, which is the federal tax law, taxes income from "whatever source derived." Many states and municipalities tax income as well.

income tax return
[*in*.kum takz re.*tern*]

See tax return.

individual retirement account
[in.de.vid.joo.el re.*tire*.ment a.*kount*]

Under the Internal Revenue Code, individuals who are not included in an employer-maintained retirement plan may deposit money (up to an annual maximum amount set by the Code) in an account for the purchase of retirement annuities. No tax is paid on income deposited to an IRA, and the proceeds are taxable only when they are withdrawn.

Internal Revenue Code
[in.*tern*.el *rev*.e.new kode]

A compilation of all federal statutes that impose taxes (EXAMPLES: income tax, estate tax; gift tax; excise tax) or provide for the administration of such laws.

IRS

Abbreviation of Internal Revenue Service.

Internal Revenue Service
[in.*tern*.el *rev*.e.new *ser*.viss]

Popularly known as the IRS, the organization that administers and enforces the Internal Revenue Code. The Internal Revenue Service is an agency within the Department of the Treasury.

joint return
[joynt re.*tern*]

A single income tax return filed by a husband and wife reporting their combined incomes. Although married persons are entitled to file separately, their total tax liability is usually greater if they do.

loss
[loss]

The term is also applied extensively in tax law, where it is used in contradistinction to gain, and refers to transactions involving an excess of expense over revenue.

net income
[net *in*.kum]

Gross income less ordinary and necessary expenses; taxable income. *Compare* gross income.

penalty [*pen*.el.tee]	An additional charge because of a delinquency in making payment. The IRS imposes such a penalty on taxpayers who file late tax returns. *Note* that a penalty is not interest, and is usually assessed in addition to interest. • *n.* sanction, sentence, forfeiture, castigation, retribution, punishment
return [re.*tern*]	A formal accounting of a person's income, for EXAMPLE, a tax return.
straight-line depreciation [strayt-line de.pree.shee.*ay*.shen]	In income tax law, a method of depreciating an asset at an even pace by subtracting its estimated salvage value from its cost and dividing the remainder by the number of years of its estimated useful life. *Compare* accelerated depreciation. *See also* depreciation.
tax [takz]	An involuntary charge imposed by the government (whether national, state, or local, or any of their political subdivisions) upon individuals, corporations, or trusts, or their income or property, to provide revenue for the support of the government. Taxes may be imposed on, among other things, sales, gifts, and estates, and may be called, among other things, imposts, duties, excises, levies, and assessments. EXAMPLES of different types of taxes include: ad valorem tax, capital gains tax, estate tax, excise tax, export tax, franchise tax, gift tax, income tax, inheritance taxes, intangibles tax, luxury tax, occupation tax, payroll tax, privilege tax, property tax, sales tax, school taxes, and transfer tax. • *n.* levy, assessment, tribute, impost, exaction, imposition, capitulation, tithe ("a graduated tax") • *v.* assess, levy, exact, collect, require
tax audit [takz *aw*.dit]	An examination by the IRS of a taxpayer's books and records to determine the accuracy of his income tax return.
tax credit [takz *kred*.it]	A credit that reduces the amount of income tax owed by a taxpayer, as opposed to a deduction, which merely reduces a taxpayer's taxable income. *See also* exemption.
tax evasion [takz e.*vay*.zhen]	Willfully avoiding payment of taxes legally due, for EXAMPLE, fraudulently concealing or understating one's income. Tax evasion is also referred to as tax fraud and is a felony.
tax exemption [takz eg.*zemp*.shen]	1. Freedom from the obligation to pay taxes. 2. A personal exemption under the Internal Revenue Code. *See also* exemption.
tax return [takz re.*tern*]	1. A formal accounting that every person who has income is required to make to the government every tax year; the form on which a taxpayer reports his taxable income annually and on the basis of which he pays his income tax. 2. Independent of income, any formal accounting required by law to be made to any taxing authority with respect to property, gifts, estates, sales, or the like. *See also* return, amended return, declaration of estimated tax, joint return.

taxable [*tak*.sebl]	Subject to tax; liable to taxation. • *adj.* liable to taxation, assessable, chargeable, exactable ("a taxable gift")
taxable income [*tak*.sebl *in*.kum]	With respect to liability for federal income tax; in the case of an individual, adjusted gross income, less itemized deductions, or the standard deduction plus personal exemptions; in the case of a corporation, gross income less deductions.
taxation [tak.*say*.shen]	The act or process of levying, assessing, and collecting taxes; the act of taxing.
taxing [*tak*.sing]	The act or process of levying, assessing, and collecting a tax; taxation.
taxpayer [*taks*.pay.er]	A person who is under a legal obligation to pay a tax; a person who has paid a tax.
W-2 wage and tax statement [W-2 wayj and takz stayt.ment]	A form issued to a taxpayer annually showing earnings summary as well as withholding taxes.
W-4 form [W-4 form]	A document where taxpayers state the number of exemptions claimed for employer's payroll purposes per IRS regulations.
withholding tax [with.hole.ding takz]	Federal and state income tax and FICA contributions deducted by an employer from the pay of employees and remitted by the employer to the IRS.

Missing Words

Fill in the blanks below.

1. _____ is when you willfully avoid payment of taxes legally due.

2. _____ is the rapid depreciation of the value of a capital asset.

3. Gross income less the deductions permitted by law is called _____.

4. A(n) _____ is the tax imposed by the federal government and in most states upon the transmission of property by a deceased person.

5. _____ are taxes that are in arrears.

6. Excess of revenue over expense is called a(n) _____.

7. An allowance granted by way of a deduction when computing one's taxable income is a(n) _____.

8. The _____ is a compilation of all federal statutes that impose taxes or provide for the administration of such laws.

9. _____ is the income received for work or the performance of some service.

10. All income from whatever source derived is _____.

11. A transaction involving an excess of expense over revenue is called a(n) _____.

12. A(n) _____ is imposed upon taxpayers who file late tax returns.

13. A(n) _____ is a single income tax return filed by a husband and wife reporting their combined incomes.

14. A(n) _____ is an involuntary charge imposed by the government to provide revenue for the support of the government.

15. A(n) _____ is a person under a legal obligation to pay a tax.

16. _____ refers to payments before they are earned.

17. An accounting period of 12 consecutive months is a(n) _____.

18. The lessening in worth of any property caused by wear, use, time, or obsolescence is _____.

19. An examination of a taxpayer's books and records by the IRS to determine accuracy of an income tax return is _____.

20. A public figure who makes an assignment of property is _____.

Matching

Match the letter of the definition to the term below.

_____ 21. Accrued income

_____ 22. Internal Revenue Service

_____ 23. Exemption

_____ 24. Loss

_____ 25. Tax

_____ 26. Tax bracket

_____ 27. Form W-2

_____ 28. IRA

_____ 29. Appreciation

_____ 30. Itemized deduction

_____ 31. Penalty

_____ 32. Amended return

_____ 33. Extension

_____ 34. Fiscal year

A. An allowance granted by way of a deduction

B. Income that a person has earned but has not yet claimed

C. Charge imposed by government

D. Individual retirement account

E. Organization that administers and enforces the Internal Revenue Code upon individuals, corporations, or trusts, or their income or property

F. Deduction from adjusted gross income used instead of standard deduction

G. Withholding statement by employer of federal and state income taxes and FICA contribution deducted from pay

H. Transaction involving an excess of expense over revenue

I. An increase in the value of something

J. A taxpayer's tax rate category

K. Used to correct inaccuracies and omissions in a tax return

L. Accounting period of 12 consecutive months

M. An additional charge because of a delinquency in an original income tax return

N. An enlargement of time

Multiple Choice

Select the best choice.

____ 35. A person who is under a legal obligation to pay a tax is known as a:
- a. tax collector
- b. taxpayer
- c. dependent
- d. tax preparer

____ 36. A tax return is:
- a. a refund
- b. a rebate
- c. the form on which a taxpayer reports his income
- d. a deed evidencing the transfer of title

____ 37. A tax credit:
- a. reduces a taxpayer's taxable income
- b. increases a taxpayer's taxable income
- c. reduces the amount of income tax owed
- d. increases the amount of income tax owed

____ 38. A standard deduction is:
- a. when all taxpayers have the same amount added to their taxes
- b. when a specified standard sum is deducted from adjusted gross income
- c. the same as an itemized deduction
- d. the same as depreciation

____ 39. A capital gain is:
- a. a gain resulting from the sale or exchange of capital assets
- b. a gift
- c. a donation
- d. the lessening in worth of any property

____ 40. Appreciation is:
- a. the basis of property
- b. a loss
- c. an exemption
- d. an increase in the value of something

____ 41. Gross income is:
- a. tax evasion
- b. a capital gain
- c. appreciation
- d. total income

____ 42. Straight-line depreciation is:
- a. a method of depreciating an asset
- b. the same as accelerated depreciation
- c. a method to rapidly depreciate the value of a capital asset
- d. used to determine your earned income credit

____ 43. An exemption is:
- a. a contribution
- b. a dividend
- c. interest
- d. an allowance granted by way of a deduction in computing taxable income

____ 44. An amended return is:
- a. needed when you file your tax return early
- b. needed when you fail to file your tax return
- c. used to correct inaccuracies and omissions in the original return
- d. used when you lose your W-2 form

____ 45. The IRS imposes a penalty on taxpayers:
- a. who file late tax returns
- b. who take exemptions
- c. who take credits
- d. who take deductions

____ 46. A tax established in proportion to the value of property to be taxed is:
- a. back tax
- b. ad valorem tax
- c. death tax
- d. direct tax

True/False

Mark the following T or F.

_____ **47.** Tax-exempt income is all income that is taxable.

_____ **48.** A tax return is the formal document used by taxpayers to report income to the government.

_____ **49.** A tax credit increases the amount of tax owed by a taxpayer.

_____ **50.** A deduction is the amount allowed a taxpayer in reduction of gross income.

_____ **51.** Depreciation is when the worth of a property goes up in value.

_____ **52.** Withholding tax is the federal and state income tax and FICA contributions deducted by an employer from an employee's pay.

_____ **53.** A joint return is when a husband and wife file two separate tax returns to report their income.

_____ **54.** The compensation allowed by law, or fixed by the parties for the use or forbearance of borrowed money, is known as dividends.

_____ **55.** A dependent is a person whom the taxpayer can claim as an exemption when filing a tax return.

_____ **56.** A head of household is a single person, other than a surviving spouse, who provides a home for certain persons.

_____ **57.** Taxes that are in arrears are back taxes.

_____ **58.** A gift tax is a tax imposed by the federal government and most states upon transmission of property by a deceased person.

Synonyms

Select the correct synonym in parentheses for each numbered item.

59. AMORTIZE
(depreciate, round off, recapture)

60. GIFT
(interest, capital asset, donation)

61. EXEMPTION
    (offset, deduction, contribution)

62. GROSS INCOME
    (taxable income, adjusted income, total income)

63. BASIS
    (cost, gain, loss)

64. APPRECIATION
    (decrease, increase, appeal)

65. AUDIT
    (contribution, examination, standard deduction)

66. ESTATE TAX
    (transfer tax, withholding tax, inheritance tax)

67. FISCAL YEAR
    (tax year, calendar year, partial year)

68. GAIN
    (profits, distribution, cost)

69. INTERNAL REVENUE CODE
    (federal law, state law, local ordinance)

70. TAX EVASION
    (felony, misdemeanor, violation)

71. JOINT RETURN
    (filed by twins, filed by married couple, duplicate return)

72. DIRECT TAX
    (importation tax, consumption tax, ad valorem tax)

Self-Test

Place the number of the correct term in the appropriate space.

73. Dependents

74. Tax return

75. Gross income

76. Adjusted gross income

77. Internal Revenue Service

78. Exemptions

79. Taxpayers

80. Internal Revenue Code

81. Tax credit

82. Deductions

83. Amended return

84. Audit

Each year as the deadline of April 15th approaches, _____ are reminded of their obligation to the government by the _____. A formal accounting of a person's income, referred to as a(n) _____, must be filed. Under the _____, "all income from whatever source derived" is called _____ and must be listed. A taxpayer is allowed to reduce their gross income through the use of itemized and standard _____.

   Allowance is also granted by way of deductions called _____ when computing one's taxable income. A taxpayer is also allowed to claim _____, including one's self, spouse, and children as exemptions when filing a tax return.

   After taking all exemptions and credits, taxpayers will determine their _____. Then, instead of reducing taxable income, a(n) _____ may be used to reduce the amount of income tax owed by the taxpayer.

   In the event a taxpayer makes omissions in the original tax return that is filed, a(n) _____ should be filed. By filing an accurate and complete tax return, a taxpayer reduces the chances of a(n) _____.

Defining Words

Complete the definition.

85. Tax _____

_____

86. Internal Revenue Service _____

_____

87. W-4 form _____

_____

88. Extension _____

_____

89. Deduction _____

_____

90. Tax credit _____

_____

91. Dependent _____

_____

92. Income _____

_____

93. Joint return _____

_____

94. Loss _____

_____

95. Penalties _____

_____

96. Head of household _____

_____

97. Adjusted basis _____

_____

98. Straight-line depreciation _____

_____

99. Amortization _____

_____

100. Adjusted gross income _____

_____

Punctuation/Capitalization

Using the apostrophe with an adjective before a noun.

Look at these expressions.

a two-week vacation   two weeks' vacation

This is a construction in English in which we use an amount, a value, a time, a measurement as an adjective in front of a noun. Depending on the form used, there is an apostrophe or a hyphen.

Rule 1: When the adjective form does not have an *s* on it, a hyphen is used to show the words are a unit before the noun.

There was a 20-minute delay in the action.
I took a one-hour break each afternoon to answer e-mail.
He detected a three-inch gap in the foundation.

Rule 2: When the adjective form denotes an amount, a value, a time, a distance, a measurement and when it has an *s* on it, it will take an apostrophe. Note that this rule applies only to a very specific form: an adjective denoting a time, et cetera, with an *s* on it, modifying a noun.

When the adjective represents a singular measurement, it takes an apostrophe *s*.

There will be one hour's delay before we start.
He is taking one week's vacation at this time.
The sentence is of one month's duration.

When the adjective represents a plural measurement, it takes an *s* apostrophe.

There was 30 minutes' delay before the start of the match.
He has four weeks' vacation each year.
It was several thousand dollars' worth of merchandise.

Directions: Make necessary punctuation changes.

1. We intend to take several minute's break right now to deal with this.

2. I have an hours worth of work to do this evening.

3. He took a two week' leave of absence for his personal problems.

4. It was just a stone's throw from here.

5. There was a three inch difference in the elevation of the sidewalk there.

Word Pairs

accelerate/exhilarate

accelerate = speed up, hurry.

She said the accelerator stuck.
He is on an accelerated program to finish school.
I accelerated into the turn, and it is the last thing I remember.

exhilarate = excite, thrill, invigorate.

The wind in my face exhilarated me.
The exhilaration he felt at the news was overwhelming.
It was exhilarating to win the long race.

capital/capitol

capital = several meanings.

- money to invest, usually in larger sums, as in *the capital to invest.*
- involving punishment by death, as in *a capital case.*
- seat of government, as in *the state capital.*
- upper-case letter, as in *a capital T.*
- first rate, excellent, as in *a capital idea.*
- resource, as in *political capital.*

He does not believe in capital punishment.
I only wish I had the capital to do that.
We traveled to the capital for the meeting.

capitol = the building. If it is the building in Washington, D.C., the national site, it has an upper-case letter—*Capitol.* (If it is referred to as *Capitol Hill,* both words have upper-case letters.) If the building is for the state, it is a lower-case letter.

I walked up the steps of the capitol in Sacramento.
The Capitol in Washington, D.C., is an impressive structure.
I believe that shot was taken on the steps of the capitol in Denver.

defer/differ

defer = postpone, put off, concede. The noun forms are *deference* and *deferment.*

He wants to defer his period of service to the church.
I will defer to your judgment on the matter.
She could not defer it any longer.

differ = vary, change, diverge, disagree. The noun form is *difference.*

They always seem to differ politically.
They differed only in color.
There seems to be no possibility of differing with him.

evade/invade/inveighed

evade = escape, dodge, elude. The noun form is *evasion*.

He manages to continually evade his responsibility.
She evaded the police by hiding in a public restroom.
The procedures were effective in evading the usual complications.

invade = penetrate, attach, assault. The noun form is *invasion*.

The ants had invaded the kitchen.
His body was massively invaded by the deadly bacteria.
The army invaded the country from the north.

inveighed = protested, criticized, railed. This word is usually followed by the word *against*.

He inveighed against the oppressive regime.
She inveighed against the high rate of tax.
I inveighed against the rule but to no avail.

fiscal/physical

fiscal = having to do with money.

It is due at the end of the fiscal year.
I do not agree with their fiscal policies.
Do you think the company is fiscally responsible?

physical = having to do with the body, substantial.

The physical body cannot withstand that.
I believe that that exercise is very physically demanding.
The pain is mental as well as physical.

Directions: Choose the correct form of the word.

1. I was accelerated/exhilarated by the news from our corporate offices.

2. The company has shown no fiscal/physical responsibility.

3. We deferred/differed in our approach to the problem.

4. He evade/invade/inveighed against the constant oppression.

5. We walked up the steps of the capital/capitol of our state.

6. He feels he has political capital/capitol to spend.

7. Because of his fiscal/physical condition, he is no longer able to walk.

8. She has capital/capitol to invest in the project.

9. She claimed he was evading/invading her personal space.

10. I would defer/differ to your expertise in this field.

11. The report is that they continue to evade/invade/inveighed capture.

12. We need to accelerate/exhilarate the process if we are to finish in time.

13. The two packages defer/differ only in the size of the label on each one.

14. His fiscal/physical condition does not allow him to afford this investment.

15. It is a capital/capitol case that is being tried.

16. The bacteria seem to have evaded/invaded every area of the lungs.

17. I believe that the acceleration/exhilaration he felt was short lived.

18. She does not have the capital/capitol to invest right now.

19. It was done in deference/difference to her status.

20. I beg to defer/differ with that.

Is It One Word or Two? An Apostrophe? A Hyphen?

anytime/any time

anytime = whenever, an indefinite point in time. This form is an adverb.

Call me anytime.
She told me she could do it anytime.
He will be there to help anytime.

any time = indefinite period of time. Often, the word *any* can be omitted, and the sentence will make sense. This is always the form when the word *time* is the object of the preposition.

I do not have any time to discuss that right now.
She cannot wait at any time tomorrow.
Is there any time that you can see me today?

Directions: Choose the correct form of the word.

1. She does not have anytime/any time to look at this.

2. He can do it anytime/any time.

3. They will meet with you at anytime/any time it is convenient for you.

4. Does he spend anytime/any time with her?

5. I don't want to see her anytime/any time.

Proofreading

Directions: Make necessary corrections, based on the material presented in the unit. If the sentence has no errors, write the word *correct* after the sentence.

1. Did you at anytime differ to his higher ranking?   _____

2. He invaded against two month's delay in the rollout.   _____

3. The capital was invaded by ants in almost every room.   _____

4. There was several hundred dollars worth of expenses in his physical plan.   _____

5. I would defer to his expertise any time.   _____

6. Is there anytime to send a representative to the state capital?   _____

7. I have one hour's break before the reporters evade this office to get the details.   _____

8. She does not have any time to spend on the differences between the two.   _____

9. The acceleration she felt as they sped through the countryside overwhelmed her.   _____

10. There was a two hour' delay at the airport in the capitol.   _____

An Adaptation from a Tax Case

Facts:

Roddick was the sole owner of a business engaged in installing and repairing heating and air-conditioning systems. As a business owner, he had to file a Schedule C form showing the details of his business profits and losses. As of the current year, he had yet to file his tax forms for the three previous years. After being contacted by the IRS, Roddick contacted an accountant to fill out his tax forms. Roddick's business records were unorganized; so he created a one-page summary of his business profits and losses rather than giving the actual records to the accountant. The accountant prepared the forms, based on the summary, and sent Roddick the signature pages of the forms. Then the IRS contacted Roddick for a review. When Roddick turned over his actual records, it was determined that he had grossly underreported his gross receipts.

Procedural History:

A jury convicted Defendant Roddick of evading federal income taxes, and he was sentenced to 28 months of probation and 4 months of home detention. On appeal, Roddick contended there was not sufficient evidence to show he acted willfully.

Issue:

Was there sufficient evidence for a jury to find that Defendant Roddick acted willfully in evading federal income taxes?

Rationale:

To show Roddick acted willfully, there must be more than a showing that he just acted with careless disregard for the truth. A mere underreporting does not require a finding of willfulness; it could be caused by negligence or inadvertence. In his defense Roddick claims he confused the terminology of gross receipt and net receipt.

Ruling:

The decision is affirmed.

Directions for CD-ROM Transcription Exercises

In audio format are:

1. Terms for the unit with pronunciations from the thesaurus/dictionary feature.

2. Self-Test that appears in the book at mid-unit.*

3. Case that appears at the unit end.*

*speeds are 80 wpm/120 wpm for differing skill levels

CD-ROM icons appear where the three above are located within each unit.

Readers may practice transcription by listening to the CD-ROM where prompted by the icons in the book. However, for high success in testing your transcription skills, mastering all the terms and English skills in the unit is recommended before attempting the CD-ROM.

For Keyboard Transcriptionists: Listen to the CD-ROM audio file for this unit at 80 wpm or 120 wpm and transcribe from the dictation on your computer. Edit and proofread your work against the printed copy in the book.

For Reporting Writers: Listen to the CD-ROM audio file at 80 wpm or 120 wpm and take down the dictation on your writer. Either transcribe from your notes and proofread your work or edit and proofread your CAT (computer-aided transcription) transcript. Always check your work against the printed copy in the book.

Student CD-ROM
For additional materials,
please go to the CD in this book.

Online Companion™
For additional resources, please go to
http://www.paralegal.delmar.cengage.com

Area of Law

Torts and Personal Injury

The **Mistakes** That Court Reporters Make and *How to Avoid* Them

The Mistake:

Alana Smithson liked to look professional on the job. She always wore business suits. She had just purchased two new suits that had straight skirts that hit just above the knees when she was standing up. The first day wearing one of the suits, she realized that, when she sat with her machine between her legs, there was a problem. The skirt was too tight to allow for the machine and too short to be at all modest—and was not even close to "professional." She spent the day trying to pull down the short skirt.

How to Avoid It:

Always give thought to how you look on the job. Short straight skirts are probably never going to work. A business suit with pants might be more practical. To maintain a professional look, you might want to also avoid low-cut blouses, floppy sandals, "frilly" hair, et cetera.

Introduction

A tort involves a breach of duty and results in an injury to the person or property of another. A tort is a violation of a duty established by law. Some torts are intentional or deliberate acts.

Often, torts result from the failure of one to exercise reasonable care and avoid injuring others or their property. One might not intend any harm to anyone, but while drinking coffee and driving your car, you may become so distracted that you fail to notice pedestrians crossing the road. If your car strikes and injures them, you haven't committed a deliberate tort but may be found negligent for failing to see that which a reasonably prudent driver would have seen and avoided.

Sometimes liability is based upon the relationship people have to one another and the duty they owe based on their relationship. The case at the end of the unit addresses the owner/operator relationship as it relates to car accidents.

The victim of a tort may suffer personal injury. A tort is defined as injury to the body of a person. A person might have suffered a broken bone, swelling and stiffness, or emotional harm such as a nervous breakdown. If personal injury is found to result from the torts of another, the injured party might be entitled to sue for damages by law.

Another class of torts is caused by dangerous instrumentalities such as explosives and fumigation. These are services that society needs, but are extremely dangerous. Even when every possible precaution is taken, injuries to others might occur. If these dangerous instrumentalities cause injury, the law may impose liability even if there was no negligence. A dangerous instrumentality is the basis for absolute or strict liability.

Unit Objectives

■ Work with a legal dictionary/thesaurus.

■ Learn about the law of torts and personal injury.

■ Master the similarities and differences in definitions of key terms regarding torts and personal injury.

■ Master the pronunciations and spellings of legal terms in this unit.

■ Practice usage of terms, definitions, and synonyms for torts and personal injury.

■ Complete unit exercises in the forms of missing words, matching, multiple choice, true/false, synonyms, self-test, defining words, and also:

- Punctuation/capitalization
- Word pairs
- Transcription of terms, self-test, and case
- Proofreading

Dictionary/Thesaurus

Note: All Dictionary/Thesaurus terms appear on the CD-ROM with audio pronunciations.

Term [phonetic pronunciation]	

absolute liability
[ab.so.*loot* ly.e.*bil*.i.tee]

Liability for an injury whether or not there is fault or negligence. *See also* strict liability.

act
[akt]

n. That which is done voluntarily; putting one's will into action.
v. To put a conscious choice into effect; to do.
• *n.* performance
• *v.* perform, do, behave, enact, execute, transact

actual damages
[*ak*.chew.al *dam*.e.jez]

Monetary compensation for a loss or injury that a plaintiff has suffered rather than a sum of money awarded by way of punishing a defendant or to deter others. *Compare* punitive damages. *See also* damage.

ad damnum clause
[ad *dahm*.num clawz]

The clause in a complaint that sets forth the plaintiff's demand for damages and the amount of the claim.

assault
[a.*salt*]

An act of force or threat of force intended to inflict harm upon a person or to put the person in fear that such harm is imminent; an attempt to commit a battery. The perpetrator must have, or appear to have, the present ability to carry out the act.

assault and battery
[a.*salt* and *bat*.er.ee]

An achieved assault; an assault carried out by hitting or by other physical contact. *See also* battery.

assumption of risk
[a.*sump*.shen ov risk]

The legal principle that a person who knows and deliberately exposes herself to a danger assumes responsibility for the risk, rather than the person who actually created the danger. Assumption of risk is often referred to as voluntary assumption of risk.

attractive nuisance
[a.*trak*.tiv *nyoo*.sense]

An unusual mechanism, apparatus, or condition that is dangerous to young children but is so interesting and alluring as to attract them to the premises on which it is kept. EXAMPLES: an abandoned mine shaft; an abandoned house; a junked car. *See also* nuisance.

attractive nuisance doctrine
[a.*trak*.tiv *nyoo*.sense *dok*.trin]

The principle in the law of negligence that a person who maintains an attractive nuisance on his property must exercise reasonable care to protect young children against its dangers, or be held responsible for any injury that occurs, even though the injured child trespassed upon his property or was otherwise at fault.

battery [*bat*.ter.ee]	The unconsented-to touching or striking of one person by another, or by an object put in motion by him, with the intention of doing harm or giving offense. Battery is both a crime and a tort. *Compare* assault. *See also* assault and battery.
breach of duty [breech ov *dyoo*.tee]	The failure to do that which a person is bound by law to do, or the doing of it in an unlawful manner. *See also* duty.
breach of warranty [breech ov *war*.en.tee]	The violation of an express warranty or implied warranty.
care [kayr]	1. Custody; safekeeping. 2. Attention; awareness; caution. Care is a word of variable and relative meaning that must always be interpreted in the context in which it appears. It is extremely important as a standard for determining negligence, in which context it always relates to the level of care that the law requires in the circumstances. • *n.* custody, safekeeping, interest, regard, attention, awareness, caution • *v.* beware, be cautious, guard; foster, nurture, watch, support, supervise
causation [kaw.*zay*.shen]	A causing; the producing of a result. *See also* proximate cause. • *n.* production, origination, root, spawning, formation
comparative negligence [kem.*par*.i.tiv *neg*.li.jense]	The doctrine adopted by most states that requires a comparison of the negligence of the defendant with the negligence of the plaintiff: the greater the negligence of the defendant, the lesser the level of care required of the plaintiff to permit her to recover. In other words, the plaintiff's negligence does not defeat her cause of action, but it does reduce the damages she is entitled to recover. *Compare* contributory negligence.
compensatory damages [kem.*pen*.se.to.ree *dam*.e.jez]	Damages recoverable in a lawsuit for actual loss or injury suffered by the plaintiff as a result of the defendant's conduct. Also called actual damages, they may include expenses, loss of time, reduced earning capacity, bodily injury, and mental anguish.
consent [ken.*sent*]	Agreement; approval; acquiescence; being of one mind. Consent necessarily involves two or more persons because, without at least two persons, there cannot be a unity of opinion or the possibility of thinking alike. • *v.* agree, accept, allow, approve, concede, yield, comply, sanction, ratify • *n.* agreement, approval, acquiescence, concession, allowance, permission, accord, affirmance, concordance
contribution [kon.tri.*byoo*.shen]	1. A payment of his share of a debt or judgment by a person who is jointly liable. 2. The right of a person who has satisfied a shared indebtedness to have those with whom she shared it contribute in defraying its cost. • *n.* indemnification, restitution, reparation, repayment, satisfaction

contributory negligence
[kon.tri.*byoo*.tor.ee *neg*.li.jense]

In the law of negligence, a failure by the plaintiff to exercise reasonable care that, in part at least, is the cause of an injury. Contributory negligence defeats a plaintiff's cause of action for negligence in states that have not adopted the doctrine of comparative negligence. *Compare* comparative negligence.

conversion
[ken.*ver*.zhen]

Control over another person's personal property that is wrongfully exercised; control applied in a manner that violates that person's title to or rights in the property. Conversion is both a tort and a crime.
• *n.* theft, larceny, misappropriation, deprivation, embezzlement

culpable negligence
[kulp.abl *neg*.li.jense]

Both in the law of negligence and as used in criminal negligence and manslaughter statutes, a conscious and wanton disregard of the probability that death or injury will result from the willful creation of an unreasonable risk.

damage
[*dam*.ej]

The loss, hurt, or harm to person or property that results from injury that, in turn, is the negligent or deliberate invasion of a legal right. Although the words damage, damages, and injury are often treated as synonyms, there are important differences in their meanings. Injury is the illegal invasion of a legal right, i.e., a wrong; damage is the loss, hurt, or harm that results from the injury; and damages are the reparation awarded for that which has been suffered. Additional damages may be awarded if the damage resulted from an injury that was inflicted recklessly or with malice. *See also* punitive damages.
• *n.* loss, hurt, harm, destruction, impairment
• *ant.* benefit

dangerous instrumentality
[*dane*.jer.*ess* in.stroo.men.*tal*.i.tee]

A thing so dangerous (EXAMPLES: explosives; hazardous waste; a gun) that if it causes injury the law may impose liability even though there was no negligence. A dangerous instrumentality is a basis for absolute liability.

defamation
[def.e.*may*.shen]

Libel or slander; the written or oral publication, falsely and intentionally, of anything that is injurious to the good name or reputation of another person.
• *n.* libel, slander, defamatory statement, deprecation, belittlement, slur, vilification, traducement, opprobrium, calumny
• *ant.* praise

degree of care
[de.gree ov kayr]

A relative standard by which conduct is tested to determine whether it constitutes negligence. EXAMPLES: due care; extraordinary care; ordinary care; reasonable care.

duty
[*dew*.tee]

1. A legal obligation, whether imposed by the common law, statute, court order, or contract (USAGE: "When a right is invaded, a duty is violated.") A tort is committed only when there has been a breach of duty resulting in injury. 2. Any obligation or responsibility.
• *n.* responsibility, requirement, role, assignment, charge, mandatory act, pledge, obligation

fault
[fawlt]

A wrongful act or omission. Neglect or violation of a legal duty; lack of prudence; failure to exercise care. In the language of the law, "fault" indicates negligence. In ordinary language, however, fault is not committed to negligence; it includes simple blame and moral failure as well.
• *n.* negligence, blame, frailty, malfeasance, oversight, inadequacy, flaw, imperfection, weakness

Federal Tort Claims Act
[*fed*.er.el tort klaymz akt]

An Act of Congress that allows the federal government to be sued for most torts committed by its employees and agents. The Act largely nullifies the doctrine of sovereign immunity as it applies to the federal government, with some exceptions, including discretionary acts of public officials.

foreseeable
[for.*see*.ebl]

That which may be anticipated or known in advance; that which a person should have known. In the law of negligence, a person is responsible for the consequences of his acts only if they are foreseeable. *See also* proximate cause.
• *adj.* imminent, prospective, forthcoming

foreseeable injury
[for.*see*.ebl *in*.jer.ee]

An injury that a reasonably prudent person should reasonably have anticipated was a likely result of a given act or failure to act.

fraud
[frawd]

Deceit, deception, or trickery that is intended to induce, and does induce, another to part with anything of value or surrender some legal right. EXAMPLES: actual fraud; badges of fraud; constructive fraud; extrinsic fraud; false representation; intrinsic fraud; mail fraud; misrepresentation; tax fraud; wire fraud.

general damages
[*jen*.e.rel *dam*.e.jez]

Damages that are the natural and probable result of the wrongful acts complained of.

gross negligence
[grose *neg*.li.jenss]

Willfully and intentionally acting, or failing to act, with a deliberate indifference to how others may be affected. *See also* negligence.

hedonic damages
[hee.*don*.ik *dam*.e.jez]

Damages awarded by some courts for the loss of enjoyment of life's pleasures.

injunction
[in.*junk*.shen]

A court order that commands or prohibits some act or course of conduct. It is preventive in nature and designed to protect a plaintiff from irreparable injury to his property or property rights by prohibiting or commanding the doing of certain acts. (EXAMPLE: a court order prohibiting unlawful picketing.) An injunction is a form of equitable relief.

injury
[*in*.jer.ee]

The invasion of a legal right; an actionable wrong done to a person, her property, or her reputation. (*Compare* "damage," which is the loss, hurt, or harm resulting from "injury.") *Note* that an injury, as the law uses that term, is not limited to physical harm done to the body; *note too* that, in the language of the law, an injury to the body (that is, a personal injury) may mean death as well as mere physical harm.
• *n.* wrong, damage, loss, detriment, harm, offense
• *ant.* benefit

intent
[in.*tent*]

Purpose; the plan, course, or means a person conceives to achieve a certain result. Intent is an essential element of intentional torts but not negligence or strict liability crime or a regulatory offense, and some petty offenses and infractions. Intent is not, however, limited to conscious wrongdoing, and may be inferred or presumed. *See also* malice.
• *n.* determination, scheme, plan, resolve, view, goal, contemplation, will, leaning, premeditation

intentional injury
[in.*tent*.shen.al *in*.je.ree]

An injury inflicted by positive, willful, and aggressive conduct, or by design, as opposed to an injury caused by negligence or resulting from an accident. *See also* injury.

invasion of privacy
[in.*vay*.zhen ov *pry*.ve.see]

A violation of the right of privacy. *See also* privacy.

joint and several liability
[joynt and *sev*.rel ly.e.*bil*.i.tee]

The liability of two or more persons who jointly commit a tort (joint tortfeasors). They are responsible individually as well as together.

joint tortfeasors
[joynt *tort*.fee.zerz]

Two or more persons whose acts, together, contribute to producing a single injury to a third person or to property. Joint tortfeasors are jointly and severally liable. *See also* joint and several liability.

last clear chance doctrine
[last cleer chayns *dok*.trin]

A rule of negligence law by which a negligent defendant is held liable to a plaintiff who has negligently placed himself in peril, if the defendant had a later opportunity than the plaintiff to avoid the occurrence that resulted in injury. In some jurisdictions, the doctrine is referred to as the discovered peril doctrine and in others as the humanitarian doctrine.

liability
[ly.e.*bil*.i.tee]

Although broadly speaking "liability," as used in the law, means legal responsibility, it is a general term whose precise meaning depends upon the context in which it appears. A person's responsibility after she has committed a tort that causes injury.
See also absolute liability; joint and several liability; product liability; strict liability; vicarious liability.
• *n.* responsibility, debt, obligation, indebtedness

libel
[*lie*.bul]

A false and malicious publication, expressed either in printing, writing, or by signs and pictures, tending to harm a person's reputation and expose him to public hatred, contempt, or ridicule. *Note* that "libel" is not "liable." *Compare* slander. *See also* malice; defamation.
• *n.* defamation, slander, malice, denunciation, accusation, aspersion, calumny, vilification

loss of consortium
[loss ov ken.*sore*.shem]

The loss of a spouse's assistance, companionship, and a spouse's ability to have sexual relations. If such loss results from a tort, it gives rise to a cause of action.

malice
[*mal*.iss]

1. State of mind that causes the intentional doing of a wrongful act without legal excuse or justification; a condition of mind prompting a person to the commission of a dangerous or deadly act in deliberate disregard of the lives or safety of others. The term does not necessarily connote personal ill will. It can and frequently does mean general malice. *Compare* intent.
2. As an element of malicious prosecution, a prosecution motived either by personal malice (EXAMPLE: anger) or by an unjustifiable purpose (EXAMPLE: extortion).
3. In the law of defamation, to be actionable malice must be actual malice or express malice, as distinct from implied malice or constructive malice. A privileged communication is conditioned upon an absence of malice. *See also* libel; slander.
4. In the law of damages, additional damages may be awarded if the damage to the plaintiff resulted from an injury inflicted recklessly or with malice. *See also* punitive damages.

malicious prosecution
[mal.*iss*.us pross.e.*kyoo*.shen]

Civil suit commenced maliciously and without probable cause. After the termination of such a suit in the defendant's favor, the defendant has the right to bring an action against the original plaintiff for the tort of "malicious prosecution."

misrepresentation
[mis.rep.re.zen.*tay*.shen]

The statement of an untruth; a misstatement of fact designed to lead one to believe that something is other than it is; a false statement of fact designed to deceive.

necessity
[ne.*sess*.i.tee]

1. That which is necessary; that which must be done. 2. That which is compelled by natural forces and cannot be resisted.

negligence
[*neg*.li.jense]

The failure to do something that a reasonable person would do in the same circumstances, or the doing of something a reasonable person would not do. Negligence is a wrong generally characterized by carelessness, inattentiveness, and neglectfulness rather than by a positive intent to cause injury.
See also comparative negligence; contributory negligence; gross negligence.
• *n.* thoughtlessness, default, breach of duty, oversight, delinquency, irresponsibility, carelessness, dereliction, recklessness, inattentiveness ("the doctor's negligence caused the tumor to go undetected")

negligence in law
[*neg*.li.jense in law]

1. A breach of the duty to use care; the failure to observe a duty established by law that proximately causes injury to the plaintiff. *See also* proximate cause. 2. Negligence per se.

negligence per se
[*neg*.li.jense per say]

Negligence that is beyond debate because the law, usually a statute or ordinance, has established a duty or standard of care that the defendant has violated, as a result of which he has caused injury to the plaintiff.
EXAMPLE: Failure to stop at a stop sign, as required by law, which is the proximate cause of injury to another driver or a pedestrian.
See also absolute liability; negligence in law; strict liability.

negligent
[*neg*.li.jent]

1. Being responsible for an act of negligence. 2. Careless; heedless; inattentive; lax. 3. Reckless.
• *adj.* careless, heedless, inattentive, lax, reckless, irresponsible

negligent homicide
[*neg*.li.jent *hom*.i.side]

The crime of causing the death of a person by negligent or reckless conduct.

nominal damages
[*nom*.i.nel *dam*.e.jez]

Damages awarded to a plaintiff for a small or symbolic amount ($1.00) where no actual damages have been incurred, but the law recognizes the need to indicate the plaintiff.

nuisance
[*noo*.sense]

1. Anything a person does that annoys or disturbs another person in her use, possession, or enjoyment of her property, or which renders the ordinary use or possession of the property uncomfortable. (EXAMPLES: noise; smoke; a display of public indecency; an encroachment.) What constitutes a nuisance in a particular case depends upon numerous factors, including the type of neighborhood in which the property is located, the nature of the act or acts complained of, their proximity to the persons alleging injury or damage, their frequency or continuity, and the nature and extent of the resulting injury, damage, or annoyance. 2. An annoyance; an inconvenience; a bother.
• *n.* annoyance, inconvenience, bother, intrusion, aggravation, devilment, hindrance, problem
• *ant.* benefit

omission
[o.*mish*.en]

1. Not doing something required by the law. 2. A failure to act; a failure to do something that ought to be done.
• *n.* breach, neglect, cancellation, disregard, exclusion, oversight, repudiation

pain and suffering
[*payn* and *suf*.e.ring]

Mental anguish or physical plan. Damages may be recoverable if the pain and suffering is caused by a tort.

privacy
[*pry*.ve.see]

As used in the law, a reference to the right of privacy. The right of privacy is the right to be left alone. The right of privacy means, among other things, that a person's writings that are not intended for public consumption (EXAMPLES: a diary; personal letters) cannot be made public, that a person's photographs may not be publicly distributed, and that a person's private conversations may not be listened in on or recorded. It also means that personal information of the kind in the possession of, for EXAMPLE, the government, insurance companies, and credit bureaus may not be made public. The right to privacy, which is grounded in the Constitution, is supported, and to some extent enforced, by federal and state privacy acts.

product liability
[*pro*.dukt ly.e.*bil*.i.tee]

The liability of a manufacturer or seller of an article for an injury caused to a person or to property by a defect in the article sold. A product liability suit is a tort action in which strict liability is imposed. The manufacturer or seller of a defective product may be liable to third parties (EXAMPLE: bystanders) as well as to purchasers, as privity of contract is not a requirement in a product liability case.

proximate cause [prok.si.mit cawz]	As an element of liability in a tort case, that cause which, unbroken by any intervening cause, produced the injury, and without which the result would not have occurred; the primary cause; the efficient cause. *Note* that the proximate cause of an injury is not necessarily the final cause or the act or omission nearest in time to the injury.
prudent person [proo.dent per.sun]	A reasonable person, or ordinary prudent person. *See also* reasonable person test.
punitive damages [*pyoo*.ni.tiv *dam*.e.jez]	Damages that are awarded over and above compensatory damages or actual damages because of the wanton, reckless, or malicious nature of the wrong done by the plaintiff. Such damages bear no relation to the plaintiff's actual loss and are often called exemplary damages, because their purpose is to make an example of the plaintiff to discourage others from engaging in the same kind of conduct in the future.
reasonable care [ree.zen.ebl kayr]	Due care or ordinary care. The degree of care exercised by a reasonable person. *See also* reasonable person test.
reasonable person test [ree.zen.ebl per.sun test]	A standard for determining negligence, which asks: "What would a reasonable person have done in the same circumstances?" In short, it measures the failure to do that which a person of ordinary intelligence and judgment would have done in the same circumstances, or the doing of that which a person of ordinary intelligence and judgment would not have done.
res ipsa loquitur [race *ip*.sa *lo*.kwe.ter]	(*Latin*) Means "the thing speaks for itself." When an instrumentality (i.e., a thing) causes injury, an inference or rebuttable presumption arises that the injury was caused by the defendant's negligence, if the thing or instrumentality was under the exclusive control or management of the defendant and the occurrence was such as in the ordinary course of events would not have happened if the defendant had used reasonable care. EXAMPLE: The utility company may properly be held liable under the doctrine of res ipsa loquitur for a gas explosion that destroys a building in which its equipment is functioning imperfectly.
slander [*slan*.der]	A false and malicious oral statement tending to blacken a person's reputation or to damage her means of livelihood. *Compare* libel. *See also* malice; defamation. • *n.* defamation, slur, aspersion, calumny, vilification, denigration, vituperation ("slander of character")
special damages [*spesh*.el *dam*.e.jez]	Damages that may be added to the general damages in a case, and arise from particular (special) circumstances of the case.
strict liability [strikt ly.e.*bil*.i.tee]	Liability for an injury whether or not there is fault or negligence; absolute liability. The law imposes strict liability in product liability cases.

sudden emergency doctrine
[*sud*.en e.*mer*.jen.see *dok*.trin]

The principle that a person who is placed in a position of sudden emergency, not created by his own negligence, will not be held responsible if he fails to act with the degree of care that the law would have required of him had he had sufficient time for thought and reflection.

supervening cause
[soo.per.*veen*.ing cawz]

In the law of negligence, a new or additional event that occurs subsequent to the original negligence and becomes the proximate cause of injury.

supervening negligence
[soo.per.*veen*.ing *neg*.li.jense]

The negligence of a defendant who is held liable under the last clear chance doctrine; the negligence of a defendant whose conduct is the supervening cause of an injury.

tort
[tort]

A wrong involving a breach of duty and resulting in an injury to the person or property of another. A tort is distinguished from a breach of contract in that a tort is a violation of a duty established by law, whereas a breach of contract results from a failure to meet an obligation created by the agreement of the parties. Although the same act may be both a crime and a tort, the crime is an offense against the public that is prosecuted by the state in a criminal action; the tort is a private wrong that must be pursued by the injured party in a civil action. *See also* Federal Tort Claims Act; intentional injury; joint tortfeasors.
• *n.* wrong, civil wrong, violation, breach of duty

tortfeasor
[*tort*.fee.zer]

A person who commits a tort. *See also* joint tortfeasors.

tortious
[*tore*.shus]

1. Involving a tort; wrongful. 2. Pertaining to a tort.

trespass
[*tress*.pas]

1. An unauthorized entry or intrusion on the real property of another. 2. In the widest sense of the term, any offense against the laws of society or natural law; any wrong; any violation of law. 3. An action at common law for the recovery of damages for injury resulting from the use or application of force. 4. Any misdeed, act of wrongdoing, or sin.
• *n.* breach, contravention, entry, encroachment, iniquity, misdemeanor, obtrusion, poaching

unavoidable accident
[un.a.*voyd*.abl *ak*.si.dent]

An inevitable accident; an inescapable peril; an occurrence that could not reasonably have been foreseen or prevented.

unavoidable casualty
[un.a.*voyd*.abl *kazh*.you.al.tee]

An occurrence or accident that is beyond human foresight or control.

unavoidable cause
[un.a.*voyd*.abl cawz]

In the law of negligence, a cause that could not have been avoided by the exercise of due diligence and foresight; an accidental cause.

vicarious liability
[vy.*kehr*.ee.us ly.e.*bil*.i.tee]

Liability imposed upon a person because of the act or omission of another. EXAMPLES: the liability of an employer for the conduct of her employees; the liability of a principal for the conduct of her agent.

willful and malicious injury
[*will*.ful and ma.*lish*.ess *in*.jer.ee]

An injury to a person or property inflicted intentionally and deliberately, without cause and with no regard for the legal rights of the injured party.

willful and wanton act
[*will*.ful and *want*.en akt]

1. An act or conduct that the perpetrator knows or should know is likely to result in injury, but about which he is indifferent. **EXAMPLE**: reckless driving. 2. A deliberate and intentional wrong.

willful neglect
[*will*.ful neg.*lekt*]

The deliberate or intentional failure of a person to perform a duty to others as required by law. **EXAMPLES** of such duties include: the duty of a parent to care for a child in some circumstances; the duty of a spouse to provide care to his or her partner; the obligation of a public official to perform a duty required by virtue of her office.

willful negligence
[*will*.ful *neg*.li.jense]

Reckless disregard of a person's safety, evidenced by the failure to exercise ordinary care to prevent injury after discovering an imminent peril. *See also* negligence.

wrongful death
[*rong*.ful deth]

A death that results from a wrongful act, such as negligence by a doctor in surgery.

wrongful death action
[*rong*.ful deth *ak*.shen]

An action arising under a wrongful death statute.

wrongful death statutes
[*rong*.ful deth *stat*.shoots]

State statutes that allow the personal representative of the decedent to bring an action on behalf of the decedent's statutory beneficiaries (**EXAMPLES**: spouse; children) if the decedent's death was the result of the defendant's wrongful act.

Missing Words

Fill in the blanks below.

___

1. _____ occurs when a person who knows and deliberately exposes herself to a danger assumes responsibility for the risk, rather than the person who actually created the danger.

2. A(n) _____ is a court order that commends or prohibits some act or course of conduct.

3. A(n) _____ is anything a person does that annoys or disturbs another person in use, possession, or enjoyment of property.

4. A legal obligation is known as a(n) _____.

5. The standard for determining negligence is the _____.

6. _____ is a rule of negligence law where a negligent defendant is held liable to a plaintiff who has negligently placed himself in peril, if the defendant had a later opportunity than the plaintiff to avoid the occurrence that resulted in injury.

7. A(n) _____ is a wrong involving a breach of duty and resulting in an injury to the person or property of another.

8. A(n) _____ is the statement of an untruth.

9. A failure to act is called a(n) _____.

10. A state of mind that causes the intentional doing of a wrongful act without legal excuse is known as _____.

11. The doctrine followed in most states that requires a comparison of the negligence of the parties, where the plaintiff's negligence does not defeat the cause of action, is called _____.

12. _____ can be either libel or slander.

13. An element of liability in a tort case, that cause which, unbroken by an intervening cause, produced the injury, is called _____.

14. _____ is where liability is imposed upon a person because of the act or omission of another.

15. A(n) _____ is a person who commits a tort.

16. A new or additional event that occurs subsequent to the original negligence is a(n) _____ of injury.

17. An unauthorized entry is a(n) _____.

Matching

Match the letter of the definition to the term below.

_____ 18. Trespass

    A. The sum of money that may be recovered in the courts as financial reparation for an injury or wrong

_____ 19. Tortfeasor

    B. That which may be anticipated or known in advance; that which a person should have known

_____ 20. Battery

    C. A failure by the plaintiff to exercise reasonable care that, in part at least, is the cause of an injury

_____ 21. Malicious prosecution

    D. An unauthorized entry or intrusion on the real property of another

_____ 22. Conversion

    E. The unconsented-to touching or striking of one person by another

_____ 23. Damages

    F. Liability imposed upon a person because of the act or omission of another

_____ 24. Foreseeable

    G. The liability of a manufacturer or seller of an article for an injury caused by a defect in the article sold

_____ 25. Vicarious liability

    H. A person who commits a tort

_____ 26. Product liability

    I. A suit commenced maliciously without probable cause

_____ 27. Contributory negligence

    J. Control over another person's personal property that is wrongfully exercised

_____ 28. Tortious

    K. A reasonable person

_____ 29. Prudent person

    L. Damages awarded over and above compensatory damages because of wanton or reckless conduct

_____ 30. Punitive damages

    M. Pertaining to a tort

_____ 31. General damages

_____ 32. Hedonic damages

_____ 33. Nominal damages

_____ 34. Special damages

N. Loss of enjoyment of life's pleasures

O. Natural and probable result of a wrongful act

P. Small or symbolic damages

Q. Added damages that arise from a particular circumstance

Multiple Choice

Select the best choice.

_____ 35. The local newspaper deliberately wrote a false story about a shopkeeper, stating that he was a drunk. This is known as:
  a. libel
  b. slander
  c. conversion
  d. battery

_____ 36. Maria Johnson aimed her gun into a busy restaurant, firing three shots. Two people were killed. This is an example of:
  a. trespass to chattel
  b. transferred intent
  c. abuse of process
  d. foreseeability

_____ 37. Scott Hansen wants to get a lot of money for his 1989 car. He tells the purchaser the car only has 30,000 miles, when in reality it has 130,000 miles. This is an example of:
  a. necessity
  b. misrepresentation
  c. infliction of emotional distress
  d. contributory negligence

_____ 38. Fred Hunt approaches a Bromley elevator, which stops six inches higher than the floor. The elevator has not been serviced in over 10 years. Fred Hunt was in a hurry and ran into the elevator, not looking where he was going. Fred trips and was severely injured. Should the matter go to trial, the court will weigh the evidence comparing the negligence of the plaintiff with that of the defendant. This is known as:
  a. last clear chance
  b. assumption of risk
  c. comparative negligence
  d. invasion of privacy

_____ 39. A bank teller is counting up the money in his drawer at the end of the day. Not having enough money to go to the movies that evening, he slips $20 into his pocket, figuring he needs the money more than the bank does. This is an example of:
  a. a reasonable person
  b. conversion
  c. sovereign immunity
  d. attractive nuisance

_____ 40. An employee sets fire to one end of the factory where she was previously employed. Unknown to her, another employee sets fire to the other end of the factory at the very same time. The entire building burns down and the night custodian is killed. It is unclear which of the fires caused the death. The two employees are held responsible because of:
  a. joint liability
  b. reasonable care
  c. trespass to land
  d. slander

_____ 41. A teenager purchases a new car. He wants to show his friends how powerful the engine is. He floors the gas pedal and drives through town going 90 miles per hour in a 30 mile per hour zone. An entire family crossing the street is struck and instantly killed by the vehicle. This is an example of:
   a. assault
   b. joint liability
   c. gross negligence
   d. wrongful life

_____ 42. To save production costs, the manufacturer of a baby formula deliberately leaves out the iron that is advertised as a major feature of the formula. A baby is fed the formula for several weeks and suffers severe anemia. The baby's parents hire a lawyer to proceed against the manufacturer after they have the product tested at a lab. The lawyer will most likely recommend a suit based on:
   a. wrongful death
   b. necessity
   c. product liability
   d. contributory negligence

True/False

Mark the following T or F.

_____ 43. The violation of an express or implied warranty is called breach of warranty.

_____ 44. The principle that the U.S. government or any state is immune from suit except when it consents to be sued is known as zone of danger.

_____ 45. The Federal Tort Claims Act allows the federal government to be sued for most torts committed by its employees and agents.

_____ 46. A thing so dangerous that if it causes injury the law may impose absolute liability even though there was no negligence is a dangerous instrumentality.

_____ 47. A false and malicious statement that brings into question a person's right or title to property, causing him damage, is trespass.

_____ 48. The failure to do something that a reasonable person would do in the same circumstances is known as negligence.

_____ 49. The unconsented-to touching or striking of one person by another is an assault.

_____ 50. Deceit, deception, or trickery that is intended and induces another to part with something of value is known as invasion of privacy.

_____ **51.** A state statute that allows the personal representative of a decedent to bring an action on behalf of the decedent's wife and children where the death was the result of the defendant's wrongful act is known as a wrongful death statute.

_____ **52.** A failure to do something that ought to be done is an act.

Synonyms

Select the correct synonym in parentheses for each numbered item.

---

53. TORT
(a measurement, a wrong, a test)

54. DEFAMATION
(libel, fraud, conversion)

55. MALICE
(lunacy, evasiveness, willfulness)

56. TRESPASS
(entry, exit, negotiate)

57. OMISSION
(act, oversight, conversion)

58. FRAUD
(disclosure, honesty, misrepresentation)

59. NUISANCE
(annoyance, conversion, causation)

60. INJUNCTION
(permission, acceptance, prohibition)

61. CONSENT
(permission, refusal, appreciation)

62. DUTY
(obligation, negligence, causation)

63. LIABILITY
(illness, responsibility, forgetfulness)

64. DAMAGES
    (battery, assault, compensation)

65. REASONABLE CARE
    (little care, ordinary care, extraordinary care)

Self-Test

Place the number of the correct term in the appropriate space.

66. Compensatory damages

67. Omission

68. Reasonable person

69. Contributory negligence

70. Foreseeable

71. Intentional tort

72. Damages

73. Pain and suffering

74. Proximate

75. Strict liability

76. Negligence

77. Tortfeasor

78. Comparative negligence

79. Punitive damages

When a person fails to do something that the _____ would do in the same circumstances, that is known as _____. This is different than a(n) _____, where an act is done with intent or knowingly. In both negligence actions and intentional torts, the _____ is punished for wrongs against individuals.

For negligence actions, the court looks for the presence of certain elements. An act or _____ that is the _____ cause of injury is usually found. A person is responsible for the consequences of his acts only if they are _____.

In some jurisdictions, the plaintiff must not be even the slightest bit at fault for an incident or they can't recover. This is known as _____. In contrast, other jurisdictions prefer a system whereby a plaintiff's fault does not stop them from bringing an action, but merely reduces the amount of their total recovery in an action. This is known as the theory of _____.

Sometimes, no matter how much care or skill is used, an accident may occur. This is particularly true when explosives and other dangerous materials are handled. In these instances, a person might be injured where all possible precautions are taken. Because society recognizes the need for explosives in the building industry and for other needed services, a theory of _____ has developed where liability is imposed regardless of fault or negligence when using dangerous materials.

In the event an injured plaintiff wins her tort action, she might be awarded _____ for loss or harm to her person or property. Actual or _____ might be awarded for loss of time from work. If the defendant is found to be reckless, there might be an award of _____. If a plaintiff has suffered physical pain, damages might be awarded for _____.

Defining Words

Complete the definition.

_____

80. Necessity _____

_____

81. Res ipsa loquitur _____

_____

82. Omission _____

_____

83. Duty _____

_____

84. Intent _____

_____

85. Assumption of risk _____

_____

86. Injunction _____

_____

87. Battery _____

_____

88. Negligence _____

_____

89. Fraud _____
_____

90. Consent _____
_____

91. Attractive nuisance doctrine _____
_____

92. Foreseeable _____
_____

93. Contribution _____
_____

94. Contributory negligence _____
_____

95. Loss of consortium _____
_____

Punctuation/Capitalization

Punctuation/Capitalization for direct address.

Definition: *Direct address* is the use of a title or name to identify someone when speaking directly to him.

I want to know, Counsel, whether your client intends to answer these questions.

She spoke to him, Ms. Henley, about the time that you were also there.

Now, ladies and gentlemen of the jury, we want to turn to the issue of guilt or innocence.

Rule 1: Direct address is always surrounded by punctuation.

Come over here, gentlemen, and look at this gear assembly.

She is objecting, Mr. Suarez, based on the issue of self-incrimination.

Yes, sir, she is.

Rule 2: Direct address is capitalized if it is a proper name or a title.

Thank you, Detective, for your time here today.

Please let me finish, Counsel, before you begin speaking again.

I respectfully submit, Mr. Speaker, this bill for consideration.

Rule 3: Direct address is not capitalized if it is not a proper name or title.

No, ma'am, I am not.

Please listen now, members of the jury, to this admonition.

Come here, sir, and look at the exhibit.

Directions: Make necessary punctuation/capitalization changes.

1. Please let me know Ms. Leoni, when you will be arriving.

2. I spoke with him, Ma'am, just after 12:00.

3. We will, counsel take that into consideration.

4. How far away were you, Lieutenant, from the corner?

5. No sir, he cannot.

Word Pairs

apt/liable/libel/likely

apt = able, capable, skillful. It should not be used to mean *likely*.

He is apt in the arts.
She was apt in music.
She is apt in photography.

liable = responsible, probably (when the outcome is negative). The noun form is *liability*.

He is liable for the acts of his children.
She has been declared liable for the injuries in the accident.
His liability extends to the totality of the damages.

libel = a false and malicious publication, tending to harm a person's reputation. The adjective form is *libelous*.

It was a case of libel against the publisher of the paper.
His statements were deemed libel by the courts.
She accused him of libelous comments about her.

An interesting usage point in English is between *liable* and *likely*. Both mean "probably," and the difference has to do with the expected outcome. Though, as reporters, there is nothing we would do with the misuse of one of these words, it is always good to know what is really correct.

likely = probably (when the outcome is positive).

liable = probably (when the outcome is negative).

It is liable to rain in the flooded area.
It is likely to rain in the drought-stricken area.
He is liable to be injured on the job, where he is likely to be very well compensated.

bar/bare/bear

bar = tablet, block, ingot, tavern. The principal parts of the verb are *bar, barred, barred.*

We met at a bar near the campus.
He was barred from attending the events.
There were several gold bars.

bare = divulge, nude, sparse, uncovered, basic. The principal parts of the verb are *bare, bared, bared.*

They could afford no more than the bare essentials.
The room was bare with few signs of human occupation.
She bared her soul in the courtroom.

bear = carry, tolerate, stand, animal. The principal parts of the verb are *bear, bore, borne/born.*

I cannot bear to see what is happening to him.
She is bearing a heavy load of responsibility.
She stepped out of the tent only to be face to face with a small bear cub.

casual/causal

casual = not formal, relaxed, laid back.

The dress for the event was casual.
I do not like his casual attitude about that.
It is a casual relationship.

causal = making something happen, fundamental.

A causal agent in that disease is the airborne bacteria.
We believe that to be a causal development.
The most important causal factor is his lack of a job.

decree/degree

decree = proclamation, announcement, declaration.

He seems to think he can rule us by decree.
It was decreed by the powers that be.
The decree was all encompassing.

degree = quantity, level, extent, academic certificate.

To some degree, I want to believe his story.
He pled to a charge of a lesser degree.
She has a degree in astrophysics.

lesser/lessor

lesser = smaller, slighter, less important.

He was involved with her to a lesser degree.
He can get by with a lesser amount.
It really felt as if it were the lesser of two evils.

lessor = someone who grants a lease.

The lessor of the property is my brother.
I paid the full amount to the lessor.
My understanding is that the lessor is a corporation.

tortious/tortuous/torturous

tortious = involving a tort, wrongful.

It was a tortious act.
There is no doubt it was done with tortious intent.
Her actions were tortious, in my opinion.

tortuous = twisted, winding, convoluted.

The tortuous mountain road had everyone's nerves frayed.
It was a tortuous route to the top.
Her tortuous thoughts were just a manifestation of her illness.

torturous = causing pain and anguish.

The actions of his captors were torturous.
The dental procedure was torturous.
It was a torturous surgical procedure.

Directions: Choose the correct word.

1. He is liable/likely to profit greatly from this venture.

2. It is a tortious/tortuous/torturous action, in the court's opinion.

3. It is a lesser/lessor included offense.

4. To some decree/degree, he must assume responsibility in this.

5. It was a casual/causal factor in the accident.

6. I cannot bar/bare/bear to watch that again.

7. It is said that they will be liable/libel for the damages in the accident.

8. They tried to bar/bare/bear her entrance into the meeting.

9. Driving on that tortious/tortuous/torturous road was giving me a headache.

10. The decision was tortious/tortuous/torturous for him because it caused so much pain for so many people.

11. She is apt/likely to join us a little later.

12. I was not looking for a casual/causal relationship with him.

13. It was decreed/degreed for everyone throughout the plant.

14. She barred/bared intimate details of their relationship.

15. Parents are liable/libel for the actions of their minor children.

16. The newspaper columnist was accused of liable/libel in his interview.

17. Is it possible to prove that that was a casual/causal factor in the breakup of the company?

18. The lesser/lessor of the property does not live in the state.

19. His tortious/tortuous remarks about her job performance landed him in the middle of this lawsuit.

20. That has no baring/barring/bearing on this matter.

Is It One Word or Two? An Apostrophe? A Hyphen?

Rule 1: When *cross* is a prefix, it is most often hyphenated to the word it combines with. This includes the many words involved in counteractions in a lawsuit. When in doubt, it is best to look up the word in a standard dictionary. Note that *cross-examination* is hyphenated but *direct examination* is not.

The cross-examination was brutal.
He is one of the cross-complainants in the action.
I spoke with the cross-defendant before he was cross-examined.

Directions: Correct hyphenation errors.

1. She was set to cross examine the defendant this afternoon.

2. He cross-moved in the action to protect his interests.

3. I believe he is a crossdefendant in that case.

4. We were furious with his tactics during cross-examination.

5. It is my opinion that she won the case during the direct examination of the defendant.

Proofreading

Directions: Make necessary corrections, based on the material presented in the unit. If the sentence has no errors, write the word *correct* after the sentence.

1. The crossdefendant is the lesser of the property in question, judge.   _____

2. This is not ladies and gentlemen a casual factor in what happened here.   _____

3. He is libel for the degree to which she was injured in the accident.   _____

4. She is liable to bear a lot of grisly details that will be harmful to his side of the case.   _____

5. Is it your testimony officer that she was driving alone on that tortious road?   _____

6. The waiting, Sir, for the decision was just torturous.   _____

7. We will cross examine him on the validity of the degree he says he holds.   _____

8. She bars/bares/bears no resemblance to you ma'am.   _____

9. The cross-action will deal with the lessor and his partners.   _____

10. He is liable/likely to win if he continues to play.   _____

An Adaptation from a Torts and Personal Injury Case

Facts:

Sergio Castanez, a Portuguese diplomat, was driving in Chicago and rear-ended another vehicle. Castanez's passenger, the plaintiff here, was seriously injured and sued both Castanez and Subaru, the car's owner and lessor. The Portuguese embassy had a long-term lease with Subaru. The Supreme Court dismissed the suit against the diplomat, claiming Castanez had diplomatic immunity. Subaru claimed that, if the diplomat driver was not liable, then how could it be vicariously liable as the owner of the vehicle.

Procedural History:

Plaintiff moved for summary judgment against Subaru, which cross-moved to dismiss. The Supreme Court agreed with Subaru, concluding that the company could not be vicariously liable and that plaintiff could sue only in Federal court against the diplomat's insurance. The Appellate Division reversed and reinstated the complaint against Subaru.

Issue:

Can a driver's immunity from suit cancel out the vicarious liability of the owner of the vehicle?

Rationale:

Subaru claims that, because the diplomat has immunity from suit, that the plaintiff is barred from suing them in state court as well. However, there is nothing in the federal statutes to prohibit such an action. Plaintiff can bring an action against the diplomat's insurance carrier in federal court or bring a state court action against Subaru, the owner of the car, if desired.

Ruling:

We affirm.

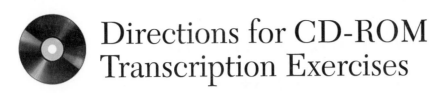

Directions for CD-ROM Transcription Exercises

In audio format are:

1. Terms for the unit with pronunciations from the thesaurus/dictionary feature.

2. Self-Test that appears in the book at mid-unit.°

3. Case that appears at the unit end.°

°speeds are 80 wpm/120 wpm for differing skill levels

CD-ROM icons appear where the three above are located within each unit.

Readers may practice transcription by listening to the CD-ROM where prompted by the icons in the book. However, for high success in testing your transcription skills, mastering all the terms and English skills in the unit is recommended before attempting the CD-ROM.

For Keyboard Transcriptionists: Listen to the CD-ROM audio file for this unit at 80 wpm or 120 wpm and transcribe from the dictation on your computer. Edit and proofread your work against the printed copy in the book.

For Reporting Writers: Listen to the CD-ROM audio file at 80 wpm or 120 wpm and take down the dictation on your writer. Either transcribe from your notes and proofread your work or edit and proofread your CAT (computer-aided transcription) transcript. Always check your work against the printed copy in the book.

Student CD-ROM
For additional materials,
please go to the CD in this book.

Online Companion™
For additional resources, please go to
http://www.paralegal.delmar.cengage.com

Area of Law

Wills, Trusts, and Estates

The **Mistakes** That Court Reporters Make and *How to Avoid* Them

The Mistake:

Ricardo Gomez took an all-day deposition of Volume 2 in an ongoing case. Volumes 3, 4, and 5 were to follow within the week. Ricardo did not get started on the job as life got very busy for him. Two weeks later, he was working on the job but had not completed it. The reporter who took Volume 3 called him for the beginning page number. Since he had not completed the job, he could not give it to her. That, of course, also held up the production of Volumes 4 and 5. Everyone had to wait for Ricardo to finish his volume, which took him three full weeks.

How to Avoid It:

It is more important than ever, when doing one in a series of volumes, to be sure you get your work out on time. Your timeliness affects every reporter who is doing the subsequent volumes. Since the outside turnaround is often in the neighborhood of two weeks, it was essential for this reporter to have the transcript completed.

Introduction

The area of wills, trusts, and estates is one of the most active "bread and butter" areas of practice for law firms, probate, and surrogate courts in the United States. The reason it creates interest is that it slices across nearly every other specialty in law, especially real property, corporations, partnerships, agency, contracts, administrative law, intellectual property, tax, insurance, ethics, and family law.

The terminology that is used by professionals working with wills, trusts, and estates may be recognized by professionals from these other areas of law. Terminology is an issue of concern because a variety of terms are used interchangeably in describing or defining how an estate is administered and who is administering the estate.

In the case at the end of the unit the surrogate court had a very difficult decision to make. On the one hand, they tried to follow the general principle that testamentary instruments should be strictly construed to give full effect to a testator's clear intent. On the other hand, equity clearly prevents a wrongdoer from profiting from a crime. See what you think.

The legal instruments, trusts, and wills that are developed and used in estate administration are the subject of this unit. Wills are testamentary instruments in which a testator disposes of personal or real property in a predetermined manner, while trusts are fiduciary relations involving a trustee who holds trust property for the benefit or use of a beneficiary. Both are used for the successful arrangement of a person's property, called estate planning. The entire idea is to design an estate in the manner best calculated to maintain and protect the family, both during the testator's lifetime and after the death of the testator.

Unit Objectives

- Work with a legal dictionary/thesaurus.
- Learn about the law of wills, trusts, and estates.
- Master the similarities and differences in definitions of key terms regarding wills, trusts, and estates.
- Master the pronunciations and spellings of legal terms in this unit.
- Recognize the synonyms used for legal terminology in this unit.
- Practice usage of terms, definitions, and synonyms for wills, trusts, and estates.
- Complete unit exercises in the forms of missing words, matching, multiple choice, true/false, synonyms, self-test, defining words, and also:
  - Punctuation/capitalization
  - Word pairs
  - Transcription of terms, self-test, and case
  - Proofreading

Dictionary/Thesaurus

*Note: All Dictionary/Thesaurus terms appear on the CD-ROM
with audio pronunciations.*

Term
[phonetic pronunciaton]

---

administrator
[ad.*min*.is.tray.ter]

1. A person who is appointed by the court to manage the estate of a person either who died without a will or whose will failed to name an executor or named an executor who declined or was ineligible to serve.
The administrator of an estate is also referred to as a personal representative. 2. A person who administers anything.
• *n.* representative, executor, trustee ("the estate's administrator"); manager, supervisor, director, facilitator, leader ("the administrator of the department")

---

administrator cum testamento annexo
[ad.*min*.is.tray.ter kum tes.ta.*men*.to an.*eks*.o]

The court-appointed administrator of the estate of a decedent whose will failed to name an executor or whose named executor cannot or refuses to serve. Cum testamento annexo, a Latin phrase meaning "with will attached," is often abbreviated CTA. *Compare* administrator DBN.

---

administrator de bonis non
[ad.*min*.is.tray.ter day *boh*.nis non]

The court-appointed administrator of the estate of a decedent whose executor has died or resigned. De bonis non, a Latin phrase meaning "goods not administered," is often abbreviated DBN. *Compare* administrator CTA.

---

attest
[a.*test*]

To swear to; to bear witness to; to affirm to be true or genuine. *See also* attestation.
• *v.* adjure, announce, assert, aver, certify, swear, support, sustain

---

attestation
[a.tes.*tay*.shen]

The act of witnessing the signing of a document, including signing one's name as a witness to that fact.
• *n.* endorsement, affirmation, certification, testimony, evidence ("an attestation clause")

---

attestation clause
[a.tes.*tay*.shen clawz]

A clause, usually at the end of a document such as a deed or a will, that provides evidence of attestation. EXAMPLES: "signed, sealed, and delivered in the presence of "; "witness my hand and seal."

---

attesting witness
[a.*test*.ing *wit*.nes]

A person who witnesses the signing of a document. *See also* attestation.

---

beneficiary
[ben.e.*fish*.ee.air.ee]

1. A person who receives a benefit. 2. A person who has inherited or is entitled to inherit under a will. 3. A person for whom property is held in trust. 4. A person who is entitled to the proceeds of a life insurance policy when the insured dies. 5. A person designated by statute as entitled to the proceeds of a legal action such as a wrongful death action.
• *n.* heir, recipient, successor, legatee, assignee

bequeath [be.*kweeth*]	To leave personal property or money by will; such a gift is called a bequest or a legacy. A gift of real property by will is properly called a devise, although the courts generally construe "bequeath" as synonymous with "devise" when it is used in connection with a testamentary gift of real estate. • *v.* grant, give, assign, remit, leave, provide
bequest [be.*kwest*]	Technically, a gift of personal property by will, i.e., a legacy, although the term is often loosely used in connection with a testamentary gift of real estate as well. *Compare* devise. *See also* bequeath. • *n.* gift, devise, endowment, heritage, legacy
codicil [*kod*.i.sil]	An addition or supplement to a will, which adds to or modifies the will without replacing or revoking it. A codicil does not have to be physically attached to the will. • *n.* addition, supplement, appendix, accessory, addendum, attachment, extension ("codicil to a will")
decedent [de.*see*.dent]	A legal term for a person who has died. *See also* decedent's estate. • *n.* deceased, testator, intestate, dead individual, departed
decedent's estate [de.*see*.dents es.*tate*]	The total property, real and personal, that a decedent owns at the time of her death.
devise [de.*vize*]	*n.* A gift of real property by will, although it is often loosely used to mean a testamentary gift of either real property or personal property. *Compare* bequest; legacy. *v.* 1. To dispose of real property by will. By comparison, "bequeath" is a word used in wills to transfer personal property. However, the term "devise and bequeath" applies to both real property and personal property. *Compare* bequest; legacy. 2. To invent; to originate; to make; to plan. • *v.* confer, bequeath, convey, endow ("she devised her business operation to her daughter") • *n.* inheritance, legacy, transfer, conveyance ("the devise of the family jewels")
devisee [de.vie.*zee*]	The beneficiary of a devise.
devisor [de.*vie*.zor]	A testator who makes a devise.
estate [es.*tate*]	1. The property left by a decedent; i.e., a decedent's estate. 2. The right, title, and interest a person has in real or personal property, either tangible or intangible. Estates in real property (estates in land or landed estates) include both freehold estates (EXAMPLES: a fee simple; a fee tail; a life estate) and estates less than freehold (EXAMPLES: estates for years; estates at will). 3. The property itself. • *n.* assets, wealth, property, fortune, personality, effects

estate of inheritance
[es.*tate* ov in.*herr*.i.tense]

Also known as a fee, a freehold interest in land that is inheritable; i.e., an interest that the tenant is not only entitled to enjoy for his own lifetime, but which, after his death, if he leaves no will, his heirs will inherit under the intestate laws.

estate per autre vie
[es.*tate* per *oh*.tre vee]

An estate that is to last for the life of a person other than the tenant. EXAMPLE: "I give Blackacre to my son-in-law, Samuel Jones, for as long as my daughter, Mary Brown Jones, shall live."

estate planning
[es.*tate plan*.ing]

Pre-death arrangement of a person's property and estate best calculated to maximize the estate for the beneficiaries during and after the person's life.

estate tax
[es.*tate* takz]

A tax imposed by the federal government and most states upon the transmission of property by a deceased person. The tax is imposed upon the net estate of the decedent without reference to the recipients' relationship to the decedent or to the amount a recipient receives. An estate tax is a transfer tax.

estate upon condition
[es.tate up.*on* ken.*dish*.en]

An estate whose existence, enlargement, or termination is conditioned upon the happening of a particular event. Such conditions are either expressed in the deed, will, or other instrument that creates the estate, or they are implied by law.

exculpate
[*eks*.kul.pate]

1. Absolve; exonerate; acquit. 2. Condone; excuse; forgive; pardon.
• *v.* vindicate, justify, dissolve, clear, pardon
• *ant.* convict

exculpatory
[eks.*kul*.pe.toh.ree]

Tending to free from blame or to acquit of a criminal charge. USAGE: "I think the defendant will be acquitted; virtually all of the evidence was exculpatory."

exculpatory clause
[eks.kul.pe.toh.ree clawz]

A clause in a contract or other legal document excusing a party from liability for his wrongful act. EXAMPLE: a provision in a lease relieving a landlord of liability for trespass.

excusable
[eks.*kyoo*.zebl]

That which may be forgiven or overlooked.
• *adj.* pardonable, forgivable, permissible ("excusable negligence")

excusable homicide
[eks.*kyoo*.zebl *hom*.i.side]

A homicide committed in the course of performing a lawful act, without any intention to hurt (for EXAMPLE, by accident) or committed in self-defense.

excusable neglect
[eks.*kyoo*.zebl neg.*lekt*]

Dilatory neglect that may be forgiven or overlooked by a court, upon a showing of good reason therefore. For EXAMPLE, a court may authorize the opening of a default judgment after expiration of the time normally allowed. The court may authorize belated action in some circumstances if the failure to act was due to excusable neglect.

excusable negligence
[eks.*kyoo*.zebl *neg*.li.jenss]

See excusable neglect.

excuse
[eks.*kyooss*]

n. A reason for being relieved from a duty or obligation.
v. 1. To relieve from liability. 2. To relieve from a duty or obligation.
• *v.* pardon, vindicate, exculpate, forbear; absolve, liberate ("excuse from duty")
• *n.* explanation, vindication, defense, rationalization ("a lame excuse")

execute
[*ek*.se.kyoot]

1. To sign a document. USAGE: "I will not rest until I execute my will."
2. To put a person to death in accordance with a sentence of death. *See also* capital punishment.
• *v.* accomplish, perform, achieve, administer, complete ("she was quick to execute her obligations under the contract"); eliminate, finish, liquidate, condemn, assassinate ("the prisoner was scheduled to be executed at 9 A.M.")

executed
[*ek*.se.kyoot.ed]

1. Completed, performed, or carried out. 2. Signed. 3. Put to death.
• *adj.* cut, signed, killed, terminated, destroyed

executor
[eg.*zek*.yoo.tor]

A person designated by a testator to carry out the directions and requests in the testator's will and to dispose of his property according to the provisions of his will. *Compare* administrator.
• *n.* administrator, fiduciary, custodian, personal representative

holographic will
[hol.o.*graf*.ik will]

A will that is entirely written and signed by the testator in his own handwriting. In many states, the requirement that the signing of a will be witnessed is not imposed in the case of a holographic will, because a successful counterfeit of another person's handwriting is very difficult; the requirement that the will be entirely in handwriting is therefore thought to be sufficient protection against forgery.

inter vivos trust
[in.ter vee.vo trust]

Living trust.

intestacy
[in.*tess*.ste.see]

The status of the estate or property of a person who dies without leaving a valid will. *See also* intestate. *Compare* testacy.

intestate
[in.*tess*.tate]

adj. Pertaining to a person, or to the property of a person, who dies without leaving a valid will. EXAMPLE: "John died without a will and left an intestate estate." *See also* intestacy. *Compare* testate.
n. 1. A person who dies without leaving a valid will. USAGE: "John is an intestate." 2. The status of a person who dies without leaving a valid will. USAGE: "John died intestate." *See also* intestacy. *Compare* testate.

intestate estate
[in.*tess*.tate es.*tate*]

The estate of a person who dies without leaving a valid will.

intestate laws
[in.*tess*.tate lawz]

State statutes that set forth the rules by which property passes when a person dies intestate. *See also* intestate succession.

intestate succession
[in.*tess*.tate suk.*sesh*.en]

Inheritance from a person who dies intestate. *Compare* testate succession.

legacy
[*leg*.e.see]

Accurately, a gift of personal property by will, although the term is often loosely used to mean any testamentary gift; a bequest. *Compare* devise.
• *n.* grant, bequest, endowment, present; tradition, history, meaning ("the legacy of River Phoenix")

legatee
[*leg*.e.*tee*]

A person who receives personal property as a beneficiary under a will, although the word is often loosely used to mean a person who receives a testamentary gift of either personal property or real property. *Compare* devisee, legator.
• *n.* recipient, devisee, beneficiary, donee, legal heir

legator
[*leg*.a.tor]

A person who makes a gift of property in a will to the legatee.

nuncupative will
[*nun*.kyoo.pay.tiv will]

A will declared orally by a testator during his last illness, before witnesses, and later reduced to writing by a person who was present during the declaration.
• *n.* oral will; deathbed will

pretermitted heir
[pree.ter.*mit*.ed air]

One born after a will is written or one who is unintentionally left out of a will and may inherit by intestate succession.

probate
[*proh*.bate]

n. 1. The judicial act whereby a will is adjudicated to be valid. 2. A term that describes the functions of the probate court, including the probate of wills and the supervision of the accounts and actions of administrators and executors of decedents' estates.
v. 1. To prove a will to be valid in probate court. 2. To submit to the jurisdiction of the probate court for any purpose.
• *v.* validate, authenticate, certify, establish, substantiate ("the court must probate this will")
• *n.* validation, adjudication, verification, confirmation

publication clause
[pub.li.*kay*.shen klawz]

Portion of a will that states that the instrument reflects the wishes of the testator.

testacy
[*tes*.te.see]

The status of the estate or property of a person who dies without leaving a valid will. *Compare* intestacy. *See also* testate.

testament
[*tes*.te.ment]

1. A will. The terms "testament," "will," "last will," and "last will and testament" are synonymous. 2. A declaration of faith, belief, or principle.
• *n.* attestation, colloquy, covenant, demonstration, statement, exemplification, testimonial, will, last will

testamentary
[tes.te.*men*.ter.ee]

Pertaining to a will; pertaining to a testament.

testamentary capacity
[tes.te.*men*.ter.ee ke.*pass*.i.tee]

The mental capacity of a testator, at the time of making her will, to be able to understand the nature of her act and, generally if not precisely, the nature and location of her property and the identity of those persons who are the natural objects of her bounty.

testamentary gift [tes.te.*men*.ter.ee gift]	1. A gift that is the subject of a testamentary disposition. 2. A generic term for a legacy, bequest, or devise.
testamentary instrument [tes.te.*men*.ter.ee *in*.stroo.ment]	An instrument whose language clearly indicates that its author intended to make a disposition of his property, or some of his property, to be effective upon his death. A will is an EXAMPLE of a testamentary instrument.
testamentary intent [tes.te.*men*.ter.ee in.*tent*]	For a court to admit a will to probate, it must determine that the testator intended the instrument to be her last will.
testamentary trust [tes.te.*men*.ter.ee trust]	A trust created by will.
testate [*tes*.tate]	*adj.* Pertaining to a person, or to the property of a person, who dies leaving a valid will. *Compare* intestate. *See also* testacy. *n.* 1. A person who dies leaving a valid will. 2. The status of a person who dies leaving a valid will. *Compare* intestate.
testate estate [*tes*.tate es.*tate*]	The estate of a person who dies leaving a valid will.
testate succession [*tes*.tate suk.*sesh*.en]	Taking property under a will rather than by inheritance. *Compare* intestate succession.
testator [*tes*.tay.ter]	A person who dies leaving a valid will.
trust [trust]	1. A fiduciary relationship involving a trustee who holds trust property for the benefit or use of a beneficiary. Property of any description or type (real, personal, tangible, intangible, etc.) may properly be the subject of a trust. The trustee holds legal title to the trust property (also called the res or corpus of the trust); the beneficiary holds equitable title. A trust is generally established through a trust instrument, such as a deed of trust or a will, by a person (known as the settlor) who wishes the beneficiary to receive the benefit of the property but not outright ownership. A trust may, however, also be created by operation of law (EXAMPLES: a constructive trust; a resulting trust; an implied trust). There are many types of trusts; EXAMPLES include spendthrift trusts, Claflin trusts, Totten trusts, inter vivos trusts, Massachusetts trusts, and revocable trusts. 2. Although not every fiduciary relationship is a trust in the technical sense of the term, every fiduciary relationship, and every confidential relationship, is a relationship "of trust," that is, a relationship in which one person has, or has a right to have, faith or trust in another's honesty or integrity. *See also* trust fund. • *n.* assurance, certainty, certitude, dependence, positiveness, reliance ("the trust you have in your parents"); account, charge, duty, guardianship, liability, obligation ("in trust for"); bunch, cartel, combine, conglomerate, crowd, multinational, outfit, syndicate ("a corporate trust") • *v.* advance, aid, command, consign, delegate, store, transfer

trust estate [trust es.*tate*]	Phrase sometimes used to mean the property held by the trustee for the benefit of the beneficiary, and sometimes used to mean the interest that the beneficiary has in the property.
trust fund [trust fund]	1. A fund held in trust by a trust company or other trustee. *See also* trust funds. 2. A fund that, although not held in trust in the technical sense, is held under a relationship "of trust" that gives one the legal right to impose certain obligations upon the holder of the funds.
trust funds [trust fundz]	Money held in a trust account. *See also* trust fund.
trust indenture [trust in.*dent*.sher]	An instrument stating the terms and conditions of a trust.
trust instrument [trust *in*.stroo.ment]	A document in which a trust is created. EXAMPLES: a deed of trust; a will.
trust inter vivos [trust *in*.ter *vy*.vose]	A trust that is effective during the lifetime of the creator of the trust. • *n.* living trust
trust officer [trust *off*.i.ser]	An officer of a financial institution who manages trust funds.
trust property [trust *prop*.er.tee]	Property that is the subject of a trust. It is also referred to as the trust res, the res of the trust, or the corpus of the trust.
trustee [trust.*ee*]	1. The person who holds the legal title to trust property for the benefit of the beneficiary of the trust, with such powers and subject to such duties as are imposed by the terms of the trust and the law. 2. In some jurisdictions, the title of certain public officials, for EXAMPLE, the members of the board of directors of a public college or university. • *n.* guardian, fiduciary, custodian
trustee ad litem [trust.*ee* ad *ly*.tem]	A trustee appointed by the court, as opposed to a trustee appointed in a trust instrument.
will [will]	An instrument by which a person (the testator) makes a disposition of her property, to take effect after her death. • *n.* bequest, bestowal, declaration, disposition, estate, legacy ("last will and testament") • *v.* bequest, confer, devise, legate, probate ("to will an estate to someone")

Missing Words

Fill in the blanks below.

1. A(n) _____ is an addition or supplement to a will.

2. _____ wills are entirely written and signed by the testators in their own handwriting.

3. _____ are gifts of personal property by will.

4. One who _____ to a will swears and bears witness that the instrument is true and genuine.

5. Failure to _____ a will means the testator did not sign the document.

6. _____ are gifts of real property by a will.

7. _____ is a person who makes a gift of property in a will.

8. A(n) _____ is an instrument by which a person makes a disposition of property to take effect at death.

9. A(n) _____ is a declaration of faith, belief, or principle.

10. A(n) _____ is a trust that is in effect during the lifetime of the trust's creator.

11. A(n) _____ is a person who is appointed by the court to manage the estate of a person who died without a will.

12. The total property that a decedent owns at death is called _____.

Matching

Match the letter of the definition to the term below.

_____ 13. Attesting witness

A. Person who observes the signing of a will

_____ 14. Attestation clause

B. A gift of personal property by will

_____ 15. Decedent

C. Pre-death arrangement of a person's property and estate

_____ 16. Devise

D. Usually at the end of a will, it provides evidence that execution of a will was observed by witnesses

____ **17.** Estate

E. Property left by a decedent

____ **18.** Estate planning

F. A gift of real property by will

____ **19.** Execute

G. The status of an estate of a person who dies without a valid will

____ **20.** Legacy

H. To sign a document, i.e., a will

____ **21.** Intestacy

I. Person who has died

____ **22.** Testator

J. One who makes a devise

____ **23.** Devisee

K. A will written by hand and signed by testator

____ **24.** Codicil

L. Beneficiary of a devise

____ **25.** Devisor

M. The judicial act where a will is adjudicated to be valid

____ **26.** Holographic will

N. One who dies leaving a valid will

____ **27.** Probate

O. Supplement to a will

Multiple Choice

Select the best choice.

____ **28.** All persons who receive bequests in a will are:
- a. beneficiaries
- b. testators
- c. trustees
- d. next of kin

____ **29.** A living trust is also called:
- a. A-B trust
- b. inter vivos trust
- c. Totten trust
- d. pay-on-death trust

____ **30.** All that one owns at death is considered:
- a. personal property
- b. real property
- c. decedent's estate
- d. community property

____ **31.** The personal representative of a decedent's estate could be the:
- a. fiduciary
- b. executor/executrix
- c. public administrator
- d. all of the above

____ **32.** The person who holds the legal title to trust property is a:
- a. trustee
- b. guardian
- c. fiduciary
- d. all of the above

____ **33.** A trustee appointed by the court is a:
- a. trust officer
- b. trustee ad litem
- c. testator
- d. legator

True/False

Mark the following T or F.

_____ 34. Testamentary capacity is a term referring to the mind of a person who is sane and competent to understand her acts.

_____ 35. Nuncupative will could be a will declared orally by a Roman Catholic nun during her last rites of the church in the presence of priests as long as her wishes are later reduced to writing by those present.

_____ 36. Attestation clause always begins a will.

_____ 37. Attestation clause is a provision in a life insurance policy that after a specified period of time the insurer shall be unable to challenge the policy's validity on the basis of untruths in the application.

_____ 38. The publication clause of a will always announces the obituary information (funeral, place of burial, etc.) that the testator wishes printed in the newspaper.

_____ 39. A trust is a fiduciary relationship involving a trustee who holds trust property for the benefit of a beneficiary.

Synonyms

Select the correct synonym in parentheses for each numbered item.

40. PERSONAL REPRESENTATIVE
(executor, beneficiary, testator)

41. TESTAMENTARY GIFT
(will clause, bequest, trust instrument)

42. FIDUCIARY
(trustee, legacy, bequest)

43. LEGATEE
(beneficiary, optional, void)

44. ESTATE OF INHERITANCE
(fee, codicil, beneficiary)

45. DEVISE
    (gift, receiver, thief)

46. BENEFICIARY
    (equitable, tangible, heir)

47. ATTEST
    (lie, beg, swear)

48. ESTATE TAX
    (use tax, transfer tax, receipt tax)

49. EXECUTOR
    (testimonium, declaration, administrator)

50. PROBATE
    (will adjudication, indemnification, ratification)

51. INTER VIVOS TRUST
    (direct, living, implied)

52. TRUSTEE
    (creator, custodian, decedent)

53. TRUST RES
    (property, principle, interest)

54. PROBATE
    (silent, written, validate)

55. INTESTATE
    (mandatory, spendthrift, no will at death)

56. DEVISOR
    (improvident, testator, miserly)

57. DECEDENT
    (trustee, beneficiary, testator)

Self-Test

Place the number of the correct term in the appropriate space.

58. Trust officer

59. Devises

60. Devisees

61. Estate planning

62. Bequests

63. Wills

64. Attest

65. Trust instrument

66. Trustee

67. Holographic

68. Estates

69. Intestate

70. Codicil

71. Intestacy

72. Administrator

Without the benefit of _____ or witnesses to _____ to their wishes, Heather and her spouse Harold each executed testamentary instruments called _____ that made _____ or _____ to specific friends, called _____. Since Heather and Harold each wrote their wills in their own handwriting, the wills are both _____ (which is not allowed in their state). If they continue to rely on the testamentary instruments they wrote until they die, both _____ will fall into _____. Could they each execute an addition, or _____, to their wills with the assistance of an attorney and make the originals valid? No, both will die _____ or without a valid will, unless they start again and prepare proper wills in the manner prescribed by their state. If the couple dies without a proper will, the court might need to appoint a(n) _____ to manage their estates.

If only Heather and Harold had consulted an attorney to review their estate plans. The attorney could have discussed the benefits of drafting a(n) _____ in addition to a will, so that their children won't inherit all their money in one lump sum. Then, the couple could have selected a close family friend as the _____, or a(n) _____ of their bank, to administer the trust.

Defining Words

Complete the definition.

73. Administrator CTA _____

_____

74. Administrator DBN _____

_____

75. Estate of inheritance _____

_____

76. Estate per autre vie _____

_____

77. Estate _____

_____

78. Intestate succession _____

_____

79. Testamentary capacity _____

_____

80. Pretermitted heir _____

_____

81. Trustee ad litem _____

_____

82. Trust estate _____

_____

83. Legatee _____

_____

84. Will _____

_____

85. Nuncupative will _____

_____

Punctuation/Capitalization

Punctuation using the colon.

The colon is used as a pointing out expression; that is, it is used to say something is coming up. That might be one thing, one sentence, or it might be a list.

Rule 1: The colon is used to point out that something is to follow. Often words like *the following* and *as follows* and *this/these* are a clue that the colon is needed.

These are the ones that are to be added: pitchers, catchers, and infielders.
I will send this to you tomorrow: Tax Summary Report, January to June.
The following should be deleted from your system: Carter files, Saenz files, and McCrae files.

Rule 2: The word after a colon is capitalized when it starts a grammatically complete sentence or is a proper noun.

Send these to me immediately: one, the list of names and, two, the dates they were deleted.
These are the ones that he reported on last week: He sent in reports on the Lakers, the Suns, and the Spurs.
I want to look at these factors: stress, family circumstances, and education level.

Rule 3: At all times, the colon must be preceded by a grammatically complete sentence. If there is not a complete sentence, the colon is not used.

The lists included the National Archives, Smithsonian, and the Capitol.
I sent a copy to the Los Angeles Times, Indianapolis Star, and Long Beach Press Telegram.
We looked at houses, condos, and apartments.

Directions: Correct punctuation in these sentences.

1. He did the inspection with: gloves, goggles, and a protective suit.

2. I want to ask you this question: Did you see anything at all that looked suspicious?

3. The package we sent included: Candy, magazines, and a novel.

4. Please turn in the following forms, Birth certificate, driver's license, and social security card.

5. He called to ask: when to leave, where to report, and what to bring.

Word Pairs

air/err/heir

air = atmosphere, sky, appearance, manner.

She took on the air of innocence on the stand.
With a Ph.D. he is up there in the rarefied air.
The pollution in the air is perceptible.

err = make a mistake. This word is often mispronounced as AIR. It should be pronounced ER. The noun form is *error.*

The court erred when it ruled in favor of the plaintiff.
The Shakespearian quote is "To err is human; to forgive is divine."
He erred in spelling her name.

heir = one who inherits. A woman who inherits is an *heiress.*

He was an heir in his own right.
She died and left no heirs to her estate.
The eldest heir is a ne'er-do-well.

deceased/diseased

deceased = person who has died.

The deceased was found in a field in the country.
I assume you mean you were acquainted with the deceased.
He has five brothers, one deceased.

diseased = ill, contaminated.

His mind is diseased from so much alcohol.
The diseased cattle were put down.
I believe it came from the diseased chickens.

device/devise

device = invention, emblem, apparatus. This is the noun form of the word.

The device was left lying on the table.
It was an electronic device to enable him to hear the conversation.
I recommended a different device.

devise = create, plan, think up. These definitions are for the verb form. In law, it is "a gift of real property by will."

He has devised a plan that he thinks will get them out of debt.
Her grandfather devised his entire fortune to her.
Did you devise a way to circumvent her control?

interstate/intestate/intrastate

interstate = between states. The prefix *inter* means "between."

It affects interstate commerce on every level.
We traveled on an interstate all the way from California to Indiana.
Extradition is an interstate issue.

intestate = pertaining to a person who dies without leaving a will.

He died intestate because of his unwillingness to even talk about death.
She is intestate, which fact is causing family strife.
Because Mr. George is an intestate, his fortune will end up in the hands of the government.

intrastate = within a state. The prefix *intra* means "within."

It is an intrastate problem between the north and the south.
Intrastate laws will be affected by the congressional act.
The travel must be intrastate because he is not licensed by any other state.

passed/past

passed = gone by, approved, moved along, did not fail. This form is always part of a verb.

She passed each level with flying colors.
The new law was passed unanimously.
He was passed over for promotion again and again.

past = time before now, former, later, beyond.

I drove right past the church without seeing it.
It seems as if that was a past lifetime.
He is grieving over things long in the past.

trussed/trust

trussed = bound, tied. The verb is *to truss*.

The boxes were trussed to the sides of the truck.
The turkey was trussed for baking.
The man was trussed after his hernia surgery.

trust = rely on, believe in. In law, it is "a fiduciary relationship involving a trustee."

I trust he will deliver the goods as promised.
They have their wishes laid out in the form of a trust.
It bears the words "In God We Trust."

trustee/trusty

trustee = person who holds legal title to trust property. The plural is *trustees*.

He is the trustee of my estate.
The trustee absconded with the funds.
We decided on joint trustees of our estate.

trusty = reliable, constant, loyal. As a noun, it is "a prisoner who has earned special privileges and is often in charge of other prisoners." It is pronounced TRUS/TEE. The plural is *trusties*.

The trusties were watching the prisoners on the road gang.

She is a trusty friend.

His goal is to become a trusty at the prison.

Directions: Choose the correct form of the word.

1. I drove passed/past the house several times that night.

2. His mother feared he had not passed/past the exam.

3. It was passed/past midnight when I got home.

4. It is left over from a passed/past relationship.

5. She passed/past the police car at about 80 miles per hour.

6. The law was passed/past by a majority of the legislature.

7. I have told her over and again that that is in the passed/past.

8. He pushed it passed/past the sign.

9. The trussed/trust area was his lower abdomen.

10. He aired/erred out his differences with her rather publicly.

11. The trustee/trusty was in cahoots with one of the guards at the facility.

12. The court aired/erred in granting that motion.

13. The design of the device/devise was faulty.

14. The device/devise to his oldest daughter included his entire fortune.

15. He stated that he was not acquainted with the deceased/diseased.

16. Within Nevada, the interstate/intrastate gaming laws prevent that.

17. She put on airs/errs/heirs with us, but we were not impressed.

18. The deceased/diseased was thought to have died interstate/intestate/intrastate.

19. The trustees/trusties met with the warden to discuss the problem.

20. I trussed/trusted her word.

Is It One Word or Two? An Apostrophe? A Hyphen?

in/into/in to

in = positioned within. This form is an adverb or preposition.

The car was sitting in the intersection.
The wallet was in my purse.
He was in a very difficult situation.

into = movement from one place or position or situation to another. This word always implies movement, whether it is physical or nonphysical. This form is a preposition.

He went into the bank via the side door.
She got into a bad relationship.
He got into trouble over his accounting methods.

in to = each word is grammatically a part of different elements, e.g., *to* is often part of an infinitive.

I went in to cash my check.
She came in to talk about the problem.
He dropped in to discuss the new provision.

There is a special idiomatic expression with the combination *turn into*.

turn into = become.

turn in to = move to the location.

He turned into a decent human being later in life.
He turned in to the driveway.
She turned into a monster when she drank.

on/onto/on to

on = positioned upon. This form is an adverb or a preposition.

He was leaning on the front of the car.
They were sitting on the bench.
We went on from there.

onto = movement toward, up, and over. This word always implies movement, whether it is physical or nonphysical. This form is a preposition.

I pulled onto the shoulder of the road.
He stepped onto the edge of the patio.
He drove onto the median strip in the center.

on to = each word is grammatically a part of different elements, e.g., *to* is often part of an infinitive or a prepositional phrase

He went on to graduate from college.
She moved on to bigger and better things.
She will go on to a better position.

Directions: Choose the correct form of the word.

1. She inadvertently turned onto/on to a private road.

2. When he drank, he turned into/in to a monster.

3. He went onto/on to become a banker.

4. I pulled into/in to the driveway.

5. They decided to go into/in to talk about it.

Proofreading

Directions: Make necessary corrections, based on the material presented in the unit. If the sentence has no errors, write the word *correct* after the sentence.

1. There were three groups represented at the meeting. Trustees, guards, and the warden. _____

2. The list of airs includes: his son, his daughter, and his grandchildren. _____

3. The trucks must have licenses under the intrastate commerce laws of: Ohio, Indiana, and Illinois. _____

4. He got in to an argument with the trustee about his share of the estate. _____

5. I drove passed the house and turned in to the driveway. _____

6. She went onto the topic of the devise of her father and would not let it go. _____

7. We past the post office and pulled on to the shoulder of the road. _____

8. Water from the north to the south of the state is an interstate issue. _____

9. We wanted to preserve the past relationship between us. Therefore, we entered into a new agreement. _____

10. Call me about the following: the trustee, the will, and the heirs. _____

An Adaptation from a Wills, Trusts, and Estates Case

Facts:

This case involves a dispute between two families over the estate of a deceased couple. On April 3, Ralph Campbell shot and killed his wife Rory and then shot himself to death. Both were survived by parents and siblings. Prior to their death the couple had executed joint wills. On the death of the surviving spouse, the property was to be distributed into three equal shares: one third each to Ralph's parents, Rory's parents, and to both their siblings. The will designated Andrea Anderson, of Rory's family, as the executrix. On May 21 the will was admitted into probate.

Procedural History:

Ms. Anderson asked the Court's assistance for direction in distributing the estate. The Surrogate Court ruled that the Campbell family should forfeit any interest in Rory's property, including her insurance and the couple's joint property. The Court allowed the Campbells to receive a share of some of Ralph's individually held property. The Appellate Division modified the order, treating Ralph as if he predeceased Rory and then had the property pass through Rory's estate and be distributed in equal thirds. Ralph's life insurance policies and retirement funds went to the contingent beneficiaries.

Issue:

Does the doctrine that disallows a wrongdoer from profiting from his or her crime at the expense of the victim's estate require that the wrongdoer's heirs and distributees be disinherited even if they are left express testamentary bequests?

Rationale:

Testamentary instruments are strictly construed to give full effect to the testator's clear intent. However, the equitable principle that one should not profit from one's wrongdoing is also applicable. Absent any evidence to the contrary, the Campbells are innocent of any wrongdoing. While any gift to Ralph might be voided, there is no reason the Campbells' gift should be voided. However, the fiction of the Appellate Division need not be applied. There is a valid will. There is a presumption against intestacy. There is no need for intestate distribution to apply here.

Ruling:

Order affirmed.

Directions for CD-ROM Transcription Exercises

In audio format are:

1. Terms for the unit with pronunciations from the thesaurus/dictionary feature.

2. Self-Test that appears in the book at mid-unit.*

3. Case that appears at the unit end.*

*speeds are 80 wpm/120 wpm for differing skill levels

CD-ROM icons appear where the three above are located within each unit.

Readers may practice transcription by listening to the CD-ROM where prompted by the icons in the book. However, for high success in testing your transcription skills, mastering all the terms and English skills in the unit is recommended before attempting the CD-ROM.

For Keyboard Transcriptionists: Listen to the CD-ROM audio file for this unit at 80 wpm or 120 wpm and transcribe from the dictation on your computer. Edit and proofread your work against the printed copy in the book.

For Reporting Writers: Listen to the CD-ROM audio file at 80 wpm or 120 wpm and take down the dictation on your writer. Either transcribe from your notes and proofread your work or edit and proofread your CAT (computer-aided transcription) transcript. Always check your work against the printed copy in the book.

Student CD-ROM
For additional materials,
please go to the CD in this book.

Online Companion™
For additional resources, please go to
http://www.paralegal.delmar.cengage.com

Index

B

M

T